Henry Prinsep's Empire:
Framing a distant colony

Henry Prinsep's Empire:
Framing a distant colony

Malcolm Allbrook

PRESS

Published by ANU Press
The Australian National University
Canberra ACT 0200, Australia
Email: anupress@anu.edu.au
This title is also available online at http://press.anu.edu.au

---

National Library of Australia Cataloguing-in-Publication entry

Author: Allbrook, Malcolm, author.

Title: Henry Prinsep's empire : framing a distant
                colony / Malcolm Allbrook.

ISBN: 9781925021608 (paperback) 9781925021615 (ebook)

Subjects: Prinsep, Henry Charles 1844-1922.
                East India Company.
                Artists--Western Australia--Biography.
                Civil service--Officials and employees--Biography.
                Western Australia--Social life and customs--19th century.
                India--Social life and customs--19th century.

Dewey Number: 759.994

All rights reserved. No part of this publication may be reproduced, stored in a retrieval system or transmitted in any form or by any means, electronic, mechanical, photocopying or otherwise, without the prior permission of the publisher.

Cover design by Nic Welbourn and layout by ANU Press

This edition © 2014 ANU Press

Contents

Dedication vii
Acknowledgments. ix
Biographical Sketches of the Family of Henry Charles Prinsep
   (1844-1922). xi
1. Introduction—An Imperial Man and His Archive. 1
   Henry Prinsep's colonial life 1
   Histories across space, place and time. 8
   Accessing the Prinsep archive. 13
2. Images of an Imperial Family. 27
   A novelised and memorialised India 27
   Governing the others 35
   Scholarliness and saintliness. 42
   A place to make a fortune 48
   Military might: The limits of violence 54
   A period of imperial transformation 57
3. An Anglo-Indian Community in Britain 81
   Influence and patronage: Indian government
      in the metropole 85
   Family narratives on mid-century India 89
   Popular narratives of Indian difference 92
   Departure for a colonial outpost 96
   Encounters with the others: 'Sights most curious' 99
4. Indian Ocean Connections 117
   Outposts of a subimperial empire. 119
   'Fate has been against you' 125
5. Meeting Aboriginal people 145
   'Fatigue, fear and anxiety' 148
   'This strange young Englishman'. 154
   George Coobul and Henry Prinsep 159
   Fanny Balbuk and Ngilgie 162
   Almost one of the family 164
6. 'Stationed but not sedentary' 183
   Letters from around the world. 188

7. 'Received into the very best society' 199
    Politics laid bare 206
    John Gribble and the Church of England
        Mission Committee 209
    A colonial bull market 214
8. Chief Protector of Aborigines 237
    'Complete separation from their savage life' 242
    'Like tribes of Arabs' 248
    A 'firm course of action' 251
9. 'Move slowly in a difficult matter' 271
    Calling 'Aboriginal expertise' 274
    'The dire necessity of a suffering race' 277
    'Neck-chaining has not a pleasant sound' 283
10. A 'southern home' 287
    'A Christian gentleman of the old school' 290
Bibliography 299
Index 339

Dedication

Dedicated to the memory of my mother, Mary Allbrook (née Wilsdon), 1921-1998, whose love and belief were unwavering and unconditional, and whose passion for music, song and story infused my life-long interest in history.

Acknowledgments

This book began life as a doctoral thesis completed at Griffith University in 2008 and developed through progressive drafts over the intervening years until publication by ANU Press in 2014. After two years working at a busy history and heritage consulting business in Fremantle, a move to Canberra and employment as a Research Associate in the School of History at The Australian National University gave me the scope to complete revisions and placed me in an environment conducive to the task of publication. It was in 2011 that Melanie Nolan, General Editor of the ANU.Lives Series in Biography for what was then known as ANU E Press, first expressed interest in receiving a manuscript and encouraged me to launch into the arduous and exacting task of preparing the thesis for publication. I am grateful for Melanie's support and advice, as I am to the anonymous readers whose detailed comments on the manuscript were of great value in transforming it into a book. I also record my thanks to all those at ANU Press for their help in reaching my objective.

It has been an eight-year journey since I began researching the archives of Henry Prinsep, and many people deserve my thanks for helping the book come to fruition. Firstly, I am grateful to my supervisors at Griffith University, Bruce Buchan and Fiona Paisley. Their supervision was exceptional and both were unwavering in their support and belief in my research, the speed with which they read and commented on numerous and wordy drafts, and their generous, sensitive and inquiring advice and suggestions. So too has the support of Anna Haebich, then of Griffith University and now of Curtin University in Perth, been appreciated, particularly her penetrating and insightful comments and suggestions on chapters dealing with Aboriginal peoples. It was Anna who first suggested that I consider Griffith University as a postgraduate venue and noted that, in a digital age, my residence in Western Australia was no impediment to enrolment. I would like to record my appreciation to Griffith University, especially Dean of Arts Professor Kay Ferres, for providing me with a scholarship to pursue my studies. The University also provided me the opportunity to give papers at a number of conferences which were of value for my research and general academic experience. These included the 'Contact Zones' RHD Conference (Brisbane 2006), the 'Australian Lives' Conference (Cornwall 2006), the 'Victorian Beginnings' Conference (Perth 2007), and ANU and National Museum of Australia sponsored postgraduate workshop on biography 'Using Lives' (Canberra 2007).

Since moving to Canberra, I have benefitted from the advice and interest of my colleagues in the ANU School of History, particularly Angela Woollacott, Pat Jalland, Nicholas Brown, Samuel Furphy, Allison Cadzow, Brett Bennett and Blake Singley. I am indebted to Ann McGrath, Director of the Australian Centre for Indigenous History, who employed me as a Research Associate on her ARC

Discovery Project on the ancient and recent history of Lake Mungo. Not only was this an absorbing and fascinating area of historical research in itself, Ann's flexibility and support, along with other staff and students in the ACIH, namely Maria Nugent, Shino Konishi, Julia Torpey, Rob Paton and Jeannine Leane, provided the perfect environment to complete the book.

Those who assisted and supported me in various ways are, of course, too numerous to mention. They include library staff members and archivists in Perth, Canberra and London, and historians from around the world who have taken the time to respond thoughtfully to my email inquiries and provide suggestions and references. I am grateful for the initial support of Emeritus Professor Laksiri Jayasuriya and Professor Bob Reece who refereed my initial application to Griffith. Many members of the extended Prinsep family have been eager to help. I am appreciative of my mother-in-law, Mrs Ailsa Smith, who has shared not only her knowledge and ideas, but her library and collection of Prinsep letters, paintings and photographs. Phillip Reynolds from Dunsborough, Diana and Rory McLeod from London and Nora Naish from Bristol have also been generous in their hospitality and interest. My many friends, particularly Ranil Ratnayeke, Greg Rowse and Helen Cattalini, after overcoming their initial surprise at my unexpected change in career, have been supportive and interested in my progress, and willing to put me up when I have visited London, Brisbane, Canberra and Tasmania. I wish to record special appreciation for my friend Tim Lindholm, of Palo Alto, California, whose shared interests have been the subject of an endless chain of email correspondence. Tim has been generous in his willingness to share his considerable collection of Prinsep images and documents, many of which appear in this book. Patrick Bunbury's support and generosity has been limitless. He has always been ready to share his combination of family history and knowledge of the Prinsep archive in the Battye Library. Dr Om Prakesh Kejariwal generously provided a rare copy of Augustus Prinsep's *The Baboo*, which was of enormous value for the chapters dealing with the Prinseps in India.

My family, of course, have been my closest and dearest supporters over the past three years, particularly my children and their spouses, Charlie Jebb, Bree Lipinski, Sarah Vincent and Nick Allbrook, my father David Allbrook, my siblings Roland, Bruce and Maryon, my brother-in-law Mike Woodcock, and sisters-in-law Nicky Partridge and Kate Smith.

My greatest supporter and confidante has been my partner, Mary Anne Jebb. She has shared my delights and agonies, constantly reassured and cajoled me, listened patiently to my meandering narratives, and provided me with the benefits of her own creative and original historical imagination.

Malcolm Allbrook

June 2014

Biographical Sketches of the Family of Henry Charles Prinsep (1844–1922)

Grandparents

John Prinsep

Born Newton Regis 1746; died London 1831; married Sophia Auriol in Calcutta, January 1783; eight sons and four daughters, and at least four illegitimate children, probably to Indian women. John lived in Calcutta between 1770 and 1788, and made a fortune from diverse business interests, including indigo, chintz and copper. Back in London, he established a trading and shipping company, Prinsep and Saunders, and was involved with other imperial projects, including the Sierra Leone Company. Prinsep was elected member for Queensborough in the House of Commons for one term in 1802. He bought properties in Leadenhall St, London, adjacent to the headquarters of the British East India Company, Thoby Priory in Essex, and in Bristol, but lost his fortune and found paid employment as Sheriff of Southwark. He was the author of a number of pamphlets on the trading activities of the East India Company, slavery and the sugar trade.

Sophia Prinsep (née Auriol)

Born Lisbon 1760; died London 1850; married John Prinsep in Calcutta, January 1783; eight sons, four daughters.

Major-General Sir Henry White

Born Scotland; died Bath 1822. White had a distinguished military career with the East India Company army, from recruitment as a Bengal cadet in 1772 until retirement in 1817. He served in numerous campaigns, including the Mahratta and Rohillas wars, the campaign against Tippu Sultan, and the siege of Bangalore.

Parents

Charles Robert Prinsep

Born London 1789; died London 1864; married Louisa Anne White in Calcutta, 1837; three sons, three daughters. Charles graduated in law from Cambridge, entered the London Bar in 1817 and moved to Calcutta in 1824, where he became a member of the Calcutta Bar and standing counsel to the East India Company. He established a lucrative legal business which allowed him to purchase property and set up agricultural enterprises in India, Singapore, Van Diemen's Land and Western Australia, and enter the passenger shipping business. He attained the position of Advocate General of the East India Company in 1852. He was appointed Royal Commissioner to inquire into the conduct of the 'white rajah', Sir James Brooke, in Singapore, 1854. He suffered a severe stroke in 1855 and retired to England, where he lived as an invalid in a succession of properties until his death.

Louisa Anne Prinsep (née White)

Born Calcutta 1819; died Calcutta 1855; married Charles Robert Prinsep in 1837 at the age of 18, three sons, three daughters. Louisa died at the age of 36 after giving birth to youngest son, Jim.

Uncles and aunts

Sophia Charlotte Haldimand (née Prinsep)

Born Calcutta 1783; died London 1861; married George Haldimand, a London merchant, in 1807; no children.

John Prinsep

Born London 1788; died Bolivia 1819. He left England for Argentina in 1807 as agent for his father's firm, Prinsep and Saunders. His life thereafter is a mystery, although it is rumoured that he was engaged in various commercial and military activities in the West Indies and South America, including service with Bolivar's army.

George Alexander Prinsep

Born London 1791; died Calcutta 1839 of cholera; married Catherine Blake in Bombay in 1822; two sons. George initially worked as his father's agent in the West Indies, before transferring to Bombay in 1822. He moved to Calcutta to work with Palmer and Company in 1825 and, after its collapse in 1830, established various enterprises, including salt manufacture in Calcutta and a newspaper in Singapore. George was author of numerous articles on the trade and commerce of the East India Company.

Henry Thoby Prinsep (Thoby)

Born Essex 1792; died Freshwater, Isle of Wight, 1878; married Sara Monkton Pattle in Calcutta in 1832; three sons, one daughter. He entered the East India Company service as a civil service recruit in 1807, initially at Haileybury College in Hertfordshire and then at Fort William in Calcutta in 1809 (at the age of 17). Thoby served in a succession of senior posts in Calcutta and on the staff of five Governors-General. He published a number of historical texts on India and commentaries on Indian affairs, and was involved in linguistic research and translation in Arabic and Persian as a member of the Bengal Asiatic Society. He retired as Chief Secretary in 1843 and returned to England. Elected to the East India Company Board of Directors in 1851, he was later appointed to the Secretary of State's Council for India in 1858, on which he served until 1874. He lived with his family at Little Holland House in Kensington from 1847 to 1871, when he retired to Freshwater. His memoirs were dictated to his son shortly before his death and form part of the unpublished volume 'Three Generations in India', held by the British Library.

Sara Prinsep (née Pattle)

Daughter of Calcutta merchant James Pattle and Adeline (née de L'Etang); born in Calcutta 1817; died Brighton 1887; married to Henry Thoby Prinsep in 1832; three sons, one daughter. Sara was known for her energetic social life, particularly her soirees at Little Holland House and her promotion of artist George Frederick Watts.

Julia Margaret Cameron (née Pattle)

Born Calcutta 1815; died Ceylon (Sri Lanka) 1879; married to Charles Hay Cameron in Calcutta in 1838; six children. Cameron was educated in France but spent most of her younger life in Calcutta before moving to England in 1848. She lived in London before moving to Freshwater on the Isle of Wight in 1860. She took up photography in 1863 (at the age of 48) and rapidly became one of Britain's best known photographers. In 1875, Julia and Charles moved to Ceylon where she continued to photograph until her death four years later. 'Aunt Jules', as she was known to the Prinsep children, was a significant figure in their early lives. Henry visited her frequently, and his sisters Annie, Lou and May lived with her for periods after their father's death.

William Prinsep

Born London 1794; died Surrey 1874; married Mary Campbell in Calcutta in 1820; six sons and two daughters. He entered the Royal Navy aged 11, but had his commission bought out by his father two years later. He went to Calcutta as an agent for his brother-in-law, George Haldimand, in 1817, and joined John Palmer's agency house, Palmer and Company, as a partner in 1819. Declared bankrupt after the collapse of the agency house in 1830, he re-entered business as a partner in Carr Tagore and Company in 1835, and was involved in diverse commercial enterprises, including opium, tea and tug boats. A prolific watercolourist and drawer, William left many images of Indian family and social life, street scenes and landscapes. He retired to a country house in Surrey in 1841. His detailed and extensive memoirs are held in the British Library.

Caroline Macaire (née Prinsep)

Born London 1796; died Switzerland 1827; married to Isaac Macaire, an academic, in Geneva in 1824.

Amelia Rebecca Prinsep (Emily)

Born London 1798; died Reading 1860. A productive artist, Emily drew images of her father and brother, and painted watercolours of family life in their London landscape. She lived with her ageing parents in London until her mother's death in 1850 and corresponded regularly with her brothers in India, particularly James Prinsep. Emily was well-known to the Prinseps of Henry's generation, who often used to spend holidays at the house she shared with her parents in Great Cumberland Street, London.

James Prinsep

Born Chelsea 1799; died London 1840; married to Harriet Aubert in Calcutta, 1822; one daughter, Ella. James is one of the great characters and humourists of the Prinsep family, as his warm and expressive letters to family, friends and scientific networks show. He went to Calcutta in 1819 to join the Calcutta Mint, and subsequently to Benares as Assay Master, where he stayed until his return to Calcutta in 1833. He was editor of the Asiatic Society of Bengal journal 1832–

1838, and in this role promoted oriental research and undertook his own projects in archaeology, numismatics and the ancient scripts of India. He was engaged in engineering projects in Benares and Calcutta, and was elected a Fellow of the Royal Society in 1828. He published *Views of Benares* in 1836, and was a prolific artist, illustrator and letter writer. His *Essays on Indian Antiquities* was published after his death, in 1858. He left India in poor health in 1840 and died soon afterwards. A ghat was erected on the Hooghly River at Calcutta in his memory.

Thomas Prinsep

Born London 1800; died Calcutta 1830 after falling from his horse; married Lucy Campbell in Calcutta in 1827; one daughter, Sophia. He went to Calcutta in 1822 after joining the East India Company Engineers, and was engaged in various engineering works in Burma and Assam, and on water diversion works on the Sunderbands near Calcutta. Thomas was a talented landscape artist.

Augustus Prinsep

Born London 1803; died at sea, Indian Ocean, 1830 of tuberculosis; married Elisabeth Ommaney in Calcutta in 1826; two daughters, Georgiana, born in Batavia, Java, died there a few days later, and Augusta, born October 1830 in Calcutta. He entered Haileybury College as a civil service recruit in 1819 and excelled in his studies. In Bengal, he occupied a succession of magistrate posts at Tirhut, Agra, Ramghur and Shergati, where he contracted tuberculosis. He was forced to turn to a 'sea cure' on a long voyage to Tasmania. Returning to Calcutta, he fell ill again and sought another sea cure and furlough in England, but died off the coast of South Africa. Augustus's short stories, journals and a novel were published by his widow after his death and include *Journal of a Voyage from Calcutta to Van Diemen's Land, The Baboo, Theodore, or Coelebs the Younger,* and *A Man of Sentiment in the Mofussil*.

Brothers and sisters

Charles John Prinsep (Charlie)

Born Calcutta 1843; died Melbourne 1898; married to Mrs Fuller. Charlie left Calcutta aged five with Henry Prinsep and was educated at Rugby. He was recruited to the East India Company army in 1857 and served in the 19th Hussars in Tirhut until he resigned his commission in 1867 to take over management of his late father's Tasmanian estate. Living off the rent of these properties, Charlie moved between Australia and England, but had little to do with his brothers and sisters, apart from one visit to Western Australia in 1870.

Anne Mary Prinsep (Annie)

Born Calcutta 1848; died Ryde, Isle of Wight 1932. Annie cared for her Uncle Thoby and Aunt Sara until their deaths, living at their home in Freshwater, and then with her sisters Louisa and May before establishing her own home at Ryde. Annie was close friends with Julia Margaret Cameron, Alfred Tennyson and George Frederick Watts, and was a regular correspondent with Henry in Western Australia.

Louisa Sophia Bowden-Smith (née Prinsep) (Lou)

Born Calcutta 1850; died London 1922; married William Bowden-Smith, a wealthy Colombo merchant, in 1872; two sons and one daughter. Louisa lived in Ceylon for 20 years before returning to England, where William died. Louisa corresponded with her brother, Henry, regularly over a period of 50 years, a correspondence of immense value for its record of colonial family life.

Mary Emily Tennyson (first married name Hichens, née Prinsep) (May)

Born Calcutta 1853; died London 1936; married first to London stockbroker Andrew Hichens in 1874 and, after his death in 1906, to Hallam Tennyson in 1918. May features in many portraits by Julia Margaret Cameron, Val Prinsep and Frederick Leighton. After the death of her parents, May lived with her Uncle Thoby and Aunt Sara at Little Holland House and Freshwater, before moving to London after her marriage to Andrew. After Andrew's death, she lived in Compton in Surrey before her marriage to Hallam Tennyson, when she moved to the Tennyson home Farringford at Freshwater. She wrote regularly to her brother Henry in Western Australia, though not as regularly as her sisters Annie and Lou.

James Charles Prinsep (Jim)

Born Calcutta 1855; died Bath 1942; married Cecily Molesworth in 1893; two daughters. Jim's mother Louisa died shortly after giving birth to him, followed by the death of his father when he was nine. Educated at boarding schols at Brighton and Bristol, Uncle Thoby and Aunt Sara Prinsep also cared for him at Little Holland House as he was growing up. He moved to Ceylon in 1875 to work on coffee estates and then to Western Australia in 1881, where he spent a year with his brother Henry. He returned to England for a career in mining administration and worked for a succession of companies until his retirement to Yarmouth and then to Bath. Jim was a regular correspondent with Henry Prinsep over the course of his life, from childhood to old age.

Daughters

Carlotta Louisa Brockman (née Prinsep)

Born Belvidere 1869; died Northam 1960; married Peter Brockman in 1900; three sons (Frank, Harry and Martin) and three daughters (Caroline, Emily and Carlotta, who died at the age of 11 in 1921). Oldest daughter of Henry and Josephine Prinsep, Carlotta features prominently in Henry Prinsep's papers, including many photographs and letters, and detailed descriptions of her childhood and youth in her father's diaries. Later in life, Carlotta wrote her reminiscences, which cover her childhood at Belvidere and Perth, as well as her married life, and is a vivid portrayal of family life in the colony during the later 19th Century. She was a talented singer and artist, as well as a skilled embroiderer.

Emily Prinsep

Born Perth 1875; died Busselton 1960. Emily lived with her parents until their deaths, and continued to live at Little Holland House in Busselton until her death. She travelled with her father to Ceylon in 1898 and then accompanied her parents on their trip to England and the Continent in 1907–08.

Virginia Reynolds (née Prinsep)

Born Perth 1876; died Busselton 1958; married to Thomas Reynolds at Busselton in 1907; three sons (Henry, Charles and Alfred) and two daughters, Virginia and Edith.

Significant cousins and in-laws

Sir Henry Thoby Auriol Prinsep

Born Calcutta 1836; died Wales 1914. Brought up and educated in London after the retirement of his father Thoby in 1843, Henry returned to Calcutta in 1855 as magistrate in the Supreme Court and eventually rose to become Chief Justice. He retired to England in 1904. He is author of 'Three Generations in India', which he compiled to show how British India had changed during the careers of his grandfather John, father Thoby, and his own 27-year career in Calcutta.

Valentine Cameron Prinsep (Val)

Born Calcutta 1838; died London 1904; married Florence Leyland in 1884. Second son of Thoby and Sara Prinsep, Val entered Haileybury College as an Indian Civil Service recruit but decided instead on a career as an artist in London. He was closely associated with the Pre-Raphaelite school of painters, particularly Millais and Burne Jones, as well as G.F. Watts. He exhibited his own work widely, including at the Royal Academy. In 1877 he was commissioned to illustrate the Delhi durbar, and later wrote about his year in India in his book *Imperial India: An artist's journal*.

Augusta Becher (née Prinsep)

Born at sea in 1830, ten days after the death of her father; died in London 1909; married Septimus Becher, an Indian Army officer. Daughter of Augustus Prinsep and Elisabeth (née Ommaney), Augusta lived for some years in India and witnessed events in the Indian Rebellion in 1857, which she later wrote about in her posthumously published *Personal Reminiscences in India and Europe, 1830–1888*. She returned to England soon after these events and lived for a short time as housekeeper with the family of Charles Robert Prinsep. Her memoirs provide a rich portrait of family and social life in India and England.

John Garrett Bussell

Born in Hampshire in 1803; died in Busselton in 1875; Henry Prinsep married his youngest daughter Josephine in 1868. After an education at Winchester College and Trinity College, Oxford, John emigrated to the Swan River Colony with most of his siblings in 1829, where the family first attempted to establish holdings at Augusta on the colony's south coast. They later moved to take up land on the Vasse River, rapidly establishing farms and homesteads. Bussell was active in the political, commercial and religious life of the colony, and became a successful farmer at his home, 'Cattle Chosen'. He was elected as MLA for the Vasse in 1870. Bussell had four daughters, Capel, Emily, Caroline and Josephine after marrying Charlotte Cookworthy while on a trip to England in 1837.

Charlotte Bussell (first married name Cookworthy, née Spicer)

Born in England in 1808; died in Paris in 1899. Charlotte was a widow when she married John Garrett Bussell at Plymouth in 1837, and accompanied him to Busselton with her three children, including daughter Frances Cookworthy. She had four daughters with Bussell: Capel, Emily, Caroline, and Josephine. After John's death in 1875, she returned to Europe, accompanied by Caroline, where she lived first in London, before moving to Paris. A regular correspondent with Henry and Josephine Prinsep, Charlotte continued to oversee the financial affairs of the family and received many visitors from Western Australia. Her grand-daughter, Carlotta Prinsep, lived with her for two years as a young woman, and another grand-daughter, Flora Brockman, lived with her for many years.

Caroline Bussell

Born Busselton 1846; died Busselton 1913. Caroline accompanied her mother on her return to Europe after the death of John Garrett Bussell and lived in London and Paris until her mother's death in 1899. She then returned to Western Australia, where she lived the remainder of her life at 'Cattle Chosen' in Busselton. She was a tireless correspondent and her letters to Henry and Josephine Prinsep over her 20-year stay in Europe provide a vivid commentary on social and family life in Paris as well as detailing her perceptions of the progress of the faraway Western Australian colony.

Capel Carter Brockman (née Bussell)

Born Busselton 1839; died Busselton 1924. Capel married Edward Reveley Brockman in 1863 and went to live at the isolated farm 'The Warren', near the south-western town of Pemberton. She and Edward had 10 children, one of whom, Peter Spicer Brockman, married Carlotta Prinsep (her sister Josephine's daughter with Henry Prinsep) in 1900. Capel was a regular correspondent with her sister, Josephine. Capel's letters provide a detailed account of life on an isolated property far from Perth and Busselton, including her perceptions of Aboriginal people in the region.

Peter Spicer Brockman

Born at 'The Warren' in 1874; died Dalwallinu, Western Australia in 1944; married Carlotta Prinsep, oldest daughter of his aunt Josephine and uncle Henry Prinsep, in 1900. After spending his childhood and youth at 'The Warren', Brockman moved to a farm near Busselton and, after marrying, to the isolated wheat-belt hamlet, Buntine, where many of his children were born.

1. Introduction—An Imperial Man and His Archive

This book is a biography of Henry Charles Prinsep (1844–1922), colonial civil servant, artist, photographer, member of Western Australia's social and cultural elite, and family man. More cogently, it is about a remarkable archive, the orderly mind that put it together, and the drive to record, in words and pictures, life in the Western Australian colony and connections throughout the wider imperial world. It is a collection that spans generations and geographic spaces, incorporating a family heritage going back to the Hastings era of the East India Company in Calcutta, to positions of influence in London business networks and society, and continuing involvement in other colonies throughout the British imperial world, the Indian army and civil service, and the Royal Navy.

From his home in the young colony of Western Australian, separated from the rest of the colonial world by vast distances and irregular communications, Prinsep energetically cultivated his networks, constantly writing letters, sending postcards, photographs and drawings, and attracting information to himself as his correspondents responded. The result is an archive created by Prinsep and his extensive network of family and friends as they moved around the world. Through this correspondence, individuals become an imperial community of family and friends, incorporating disparate life histories, perceptions of life in Britain or the colonies, imaginings of empire and their place within it. The private life of a family emerges as intimately connected through vast and complex networks which transcend oceanic and national boundaries and survive long periods of separation. It becomes possible to explore transnational as well as domestic connections and the intersections between the public and private worlds of family members, and to better understand the way family, social life and cultural formation buttressed the formal institutions of empire. Prinsep's growing Australian identity was framed within his conception of a global network of British men, women and children who lived in widely dispersed places but remained connected by a common sense of Britishness, a belief in the superiority and beneficence of British civilisation and Empire, and thus the legitimacy of the world-wide colonial project.

Henry Prinsep's colonial life

Despite the richness of the archive, Prinsep is an obscure, even contradictory figure in the narrative of Western Australian history. His entry in the Australian Dictionary of Biography describes him as 'estate manager, horse trader, artist and civil servant', and records that he was born in Calcutta in September

1844, second son of prominent, wealthy lawyer and East India Company Advocate-General, Charles Robert Prinsep (1789–1864), and Louisa (née White, 1819-1855), daughter of East India Company Major General, Sir Henry White KCB, a distinguished officer in the East India Company army.[1] At the age of four, he was sent to England with older brother, Charlie Prinsep (1843–1898), into the care of boarding schools and holidays with an extensive network of uncles and aunts in Britain, while his parents and younger siblings remained in Calcutta. The death of his mother in 1855 and his father ten years later forced the young Prinsep into a position of responsibility, both for the welfare of his four younger siblings, Annie (1848–1932), Louisa (1850–1922), May (1853–1936) and Jim (1855–1942), and the affairs of the family estate, under the supervision of three old uncles, executors Thoby Prinsep (1792–1878), William Prinsep (1794–1874) and Henry White (1798–1872).[2]

In a series of articles published in 1955 and 1977, Western Australian historian A.C. Staples described the life of Henry Prinsep, his family 'dynasty' and his activities in the colony after he had arrived from England in May 1866.[3] It was his late father Charles's business interests that led him to Western Australia to take over the 23,000 acre family estates on the Leschenault Inlet and at Dardanup. Located near the small coastal town of Bunbury, 140 kilometres south of Perth, the estates were purchased by his Calcutta-based father nearly 30 years before. Charles Prinsep invested heavily in his Western Australian venture and, in 1838, under the management of associate Thomas Little together with an Indian labour force of over 30 men and women, a stud farm was established to breed and export horses for the Indian market. By the time Henry Prinsep arrived, however, the venture was already in severe financial trouble. His father suffered a severe stroke and returned to England in 1855, and could no longer finance the operation from his lucrative legal practice in Calcutta, while the Indian labour force had left the colony under the terms of their indenture. After eight years of increasingly futile efforts to develop a trans-Indian Ocean trade in horses and timber, in January 1874, Prinsep was forced to dispose of the properties after a declaration of bankruptcy. Thus Prinsep's efforts to forge a colonial career in Western Australia as an estate manager and horse trader failed, a victim of the depressed and cash-strapped economic environment of the colony in the 1870s and ill-equipped

---

1 Staples, A.C. 1988, 'Prinsep, Henry Charles (Harry) (1844–1922)', in *Australian Dictionary of Biography*, Volume 11, Melbourne University Press, Melbourne; Prinsep Papers, State Library of Western Australia (SLWA), Acc 1972A/3.
2 I refer to Henry Prinsep's siblings and other close family members by the common names that Henry himself used in letters and correspondence, which helps distinguish them from other family members with the same names.
3 Staples, A.C. 1955, 'Henry Charles Prinsep', in *Journal and Proceedings of the Western Australian Historical Society*, Volume 5, Part 1, pp.31–53; Staples, A.C. 1955, 'The Prinsep Estate in Western Australia', in *Early Days*, Volume 5, Part 1, pp.16–30; Staples, A.C. 1977, 'The Prinsep Dynasty', in *Early Days*, Volume 8, Part 1, pp.21–33.

to succeed in the unregulated 'law of the jungle' of colonial commerce.[4] The business structure that Prinsep inherited from his Calcutta-based father, with its reliance on Indian finance and contract Indian labour, had worked while his father was alive and could supply the finances to prop up the venture. But on Charles Prinsep's death and the collapse of his Indian Ocean financial empire, the Western Australian estate was no longer able to compete, either in the domestic sphere or in the trans-oceanic horse trade with India. Without a ready source of finance and cheap labour, there was little that Henry Prinsep could do to succeed, regardless of his level of experience in business and commerce.[5]

The Prinsep family of Henry, Josephine (née Bussell) and daughter Carlotta (born in 1869) moved from the rural property to Perth, where Henry joined the colonial civil service as a clerk and draftsman in the Department of Lands and Surveys. Thus began a public career that lasted 33 years and eventually led to senior positions in the government of Sir John Forrest during the boom years of the 1890s, the period immediately following the discovery of large deposits of gold in Coolgardie and Kalgoorlie and the start of responsible government for the colony. For four turbulent years, between 1894 and 1898, Prinsep was in charge of the Mines Department, where he struggled to keep up with the rush of gold mining activity and was responsible for the initial development of an administrative structure to manage and regulate the rapid expansion of the mining industry.[6]

In 1898, Forrest offered Prinsep the new job of Chief Protector of Aborigines, and it is this role for which he is best known in the narrative of Western Australian history. He presided over a nascent government bureaucracy during a controversial period in emerging relationships between colonists and Aboriginal people. Doubts about the colonial government's ability to guarantee the protection and welfare of Aboriginal populations led the British Colonial Office to retain responsibility for Aboriginal people on the grant of responsible government in 1890. After eight years of control from London, Premier Forrest succeeded in having what was widely seen as a blight on the reputation of the colonial government removed, and turned to his old friend Prinsep, whose recent administrative experience as Secretary of Mines would allow him to establish a new Aborigines Department, primarily to distribute rations to unemployed and indigent Aboriginal people around the colony.[7] Forrest, a self-proclaimed

---

4   Staples, A.C. 1955, 'Henry Charles Prinsep', p.52.
5   Allbrook, Malcolm 2012, 'A Triple Empire … United Under One Dominion: Charles Prinsep's schemes for exporting Indian labour to Australia', in *South Asia: Journal of South Asian Studies*, Volume 35, Issue 3, DOI: 10.1080/00856401.2011.649676.
6   Spillman, Ken 1993, *A Rich Endowment: Government and mining in Western Australia, 1829–1994*, University of Western Australia Press, Nedlands, p.93.
7   The two men had been friends since Prinsep's arrival in Western Australia in 1866 and had worked together in the Department of Lands. They also had close family connections through their wives, Josephine (née Bussell) and Margaret (née Hamersley), who, like Forrest, were 'native born' into families who had arrived in the colony during its very early period in 1829 or soon after.

'expert' on Aboriginal affairs, initially retained ministerial responsibility, but had little time for the portfolio and wanted it nullified as a political problem. He directed Prinsep to establish a system based on labour contracts and the distribution of limited rations to Aboriginal people who could not be absorbed into the pastoral industry. To Forrest, government had a minimal role in the management of Aboriginal affairs. The system should be designed to facilitate the absorption of Aboriginal people into employment in the pastoral industry, private domestic work and general labour, leaving the government responsible only for those who, for various reasons, could not be employed. Prinsep however, disagreed with his boss and the two men argued. He wanted much greater powers as Chief Protector and believed that Western Australia should follow the example of Queensland's 1897 *Aboriginal Protection and Restriction of the Sale of Opium Act* and tighten government controls on Aboriginal people. In 1904, well after Forrest's departure for a career in the first Australian Federal Parliament, the State government bowed to widespread public criticism of its management of Aboriginal affairs and pressure from the Colonial Office, and established a Royal Commission under Queensland Chief Protector Walter Roth. The resultant *Aborigines Act 1905* represented the culmination of Prinsep's public career. He left the civil service in 1908 for a long retirement in Busselton, content to leave his legacy to successors, men such as Charles Frederick Gale, who succeeded Prinsep as Chief Protector until 1915, and Auber Octavius Neville, who controlled government administration of Aboriginal affairs from 1915 until 1940. In Neville's hands, the laws Prinsep had introduced became a grindingly oppressive system which affected almost every Aboriginal family in Western Australia for the next 70 years, until the Government started to dismantle the legal apparatus in the early 1970s.

The long term effects of the *Aborigines Act 1905* on Western Australian Aboriginal people, particularly its powers to forcibly remove children from their families, became increasingly controversial as the stories and testimonies of those who been affected became better known. Court cases brought by members of the Stolen Generation, as they came to be known, a national inquiry by the Australian Human Rights Commission, and sustained pressure from a range of community groups, culminated in a Government apology in February 2008, just over a century after Prinsep had retired as Western Australia's Chief Protector.[8] Prime Minister Kevin Rudd told Parliament that policies instigated by Australian governments and the actions of those who had designed and implemented them had been profoundly wrong, had brought 'indignity and

---

8   For example, Kruger v the Commonwealth 1997, in which a group of Northern Territory Aboriginal people unsuccessfully argued the legality of the *Aborigines Ordinance Act (Northern Territory) 1918*, which authorised the removal of Aboriginal children; Australian Human Rights Commission 1997, *Bringing them Home: Report of the National Inquiry into the separation of Aboriginal and Torres Strait Islander children from their families*, Human Rights and Equal Opportunity Commission, Canberra.

degradation' onto a 'proud people and a proud culture', and that the pain of forced separation on individuals and families had been 'searing', 'a deep assault on our senses and on our most elemental humanity'. In the States and Territories of Australia, 'up to 50,000 children were forcibly taken from their families … the result of deliberate, calculated policies of the state as reflected in the explicit powers given to them under statute'.[9]

Historians have played a crucial role in bringing the stories of the Stolen Generations before the Australian public, and a number of detailed studies and oral histories have documented the development, implementation and impact of the policies as they operated in various parts of Australia.[10] In Western Australia, Henry Prinsep does not fare well in the history of Aboriginal affairs administration. To Leslie Marchant, he was an 'untrained layman' dominated by a powerful boss, but who 'overcame his natural timidity', became increasingly assertive in his management of the portfolio, and developed the administration into a 'true example of Twentieth Century bureaucratic control'.[11] Peter Biskup described Prinsep as lacking 'not only drive but also imagination', and his tenure as Chief Protector as 'singularly devoid of concrete achievements'.[12] Anna Haebich regards Prinsep as unsuited to the role of Chief Protector, apart from a 'guarantee that he would pose no challenge to powerful elites'.[13] Driven by 'Victorian morality', a sense of 'charity' and 'responsibility' to the underprivileged and a 'nodding acquaintance with colonial policy and practice in British India', Prinsep earned neither popularity nor respect for the way he went about his job. Haebich says that Prinsep, increasingly frustrated in his efforts to deal with the issues he believed important, focussed on the internal management of his small department, stretching the manifestly inadequate welfare budget by introducing niggardly economies. Marchant, Biskup and Haebich all refer to Prinsep's Indian background, and hint that this might have influenced the way he saw his job. In a well-known image from the late 1890s, Prinsep is flanked by his two Aborigines Department officers, clerk E. Pechell and travelling inspector G.S. Olivey, the three of them dressed in tropical whites,

---

9 Rudd, The Hon. Kevin, Prime Minister, 13 February 2008, 'Apology to Australia's Indigenous Peoples', viewed online at http://www.aph.gov.au/house/Rudd_Speech.pdf.
10 Haebich, Anna 1988, *For Their Own Good: Aborigines and government in the Southwest of Western Australia, 1900–1940*, University of Western Australia Press, Nedlands; Haebich, Anna 2000, *Broken Circles: Fragmenting Indigenous families, 1800–2000*, Fremantle Arts Centre Press, Fremantle; Read, Peter 1998, *The Stolen Generations: The removal of Aboriginal children in New South Wales, 1883–1969*, NSW Department of Aboriginal Affairs, Sydney; Read, Peter 1999, *A Rape of the Soul So Profound: The return of the Stolen Generations*, Allen & Unwin, St Leonards, NSW.
11 Marchant, Leslie R. 1981, *Aboriginal Administration in Western Australia, 1886–1905*, Australian Institute of Aboriginal Studies, Canberra, pp.24–25.
12 Biskup, Peter 1973, *Not Slaves, Not Citizens: The Aboriginal problem in Western Australia, 1898–1954*, University of Queensland Press, St. Lucia, pp.53–54.
13 Haebich 2000, *Broken Circles*, p.213.

Prinsep with fly-whisk and solar topi, the inspector leaning on his bicycle.[14] The photograph is redolent of a bygone era; Prinsep more the stereotypical officer of the Indian Raj of his ancestors than an Australian colonial official, a relic of another time and place, haughty, detached and unburdened by anxiety over the protection of his Aboriginal wards.

The judgement of history has been much kinder to Prinsep for his contribution to the visual culture of Western Australia as an artist and leader of the small colonial art community. Art historian Janda Gooding describes him as the first professionally-trained artist in Western Australia and one of the few proficient in a range of artistic media, including drawing, watercolour and oils, portrait and landscape painting. His productivity as an artist was significant, while around him developed an art community which shared the ideals of collegiality and companionship, similar to the Pre-Raphaelite artists Prinsep had encountered as a youth in London.[15] In her catalogue of the National Gallery of Australia exhibition *Out of the West,* Anne Gray notes Prinsep's significance in the art world of colonial Perth. Not only was he a productive artist, he also thrived on company and collegiality, and used his organisational skills to set up the Wilgie Sketching Club in 1889. With fellow artists such as Herbert Gibbs, Bernard Woodward and George Pitt Morison and Daisy Rossi, the Society mounted painting expeditions into the bush near Perth, arranged exhibitions and competitions, and later evolved into the Western Australian Society of the Arts.

Prinsep's watercolours, oil paintings and pen and ink drawings are held in major national, state and private collections around Australia, including the National Gallery of Australia, the National Library of Australia, the Western Australian Art Gallery and the State Library of Western Australia. They show the landscapes of Western Australia as Prinsep encountered them: Rottnest Island, Perth and the southwest, the country around Geraldton 400 kilometres north of Perth and the goldfields. They depict the people of the colony at work and at play, excursions into the country and social events, many featuring members of his own family and social network. A series of commissioned pen, ink and watercolour images illustrate some of the great expeditions of discovery in the narrative of Western Australian history, the journeys of Ernest Giles (1875) and John Forrest (1876) into the central regions of the colony, and Alexander Forrest's 1879 visit to the Kimberley.[16]

---

14 Haebich 1988, *For Their Own Good*, p.52. The photograph comes from an album of Henry Prinsep images, SLWA, MN 773, BA 1423/347.
15 Gooding, Janda 1987, *Western Australian Art and Artists, 1900–1950,* Art Gallery of Western Australia, Perth.
16 The Art Gallery of Western Australia holds a collection of pen and ink drawings of various episodes from John Forrest's expedition across the Victoria desert in 1875, including an image showing Forrest and his party fighting off a group of Aboriginal people at Pierre Springs, and another of the Giles expedition under attack in a watercolour image 'Ullaring attacked.' A series of lithographs in the SLWA depicts Alexander Forrest's expedition crossing the Fitzroy River in the Kimberley and attempting to cross the Leopold Ranges, SLWA 85B, Volume 39.

1. Introduction—An Imperial Man and His Archive

As an artist, Prinsep had a significant role in representing Western Australia visually, as it grew from a small outpost of Empire in the south-west corner of the continent to a colony that penetrated the entire land mass within its extensive borders. In Prinsep's eyes, the country is both harsh and benevolent, and the colonists determined and resourceful as they take on and conquer all that this strange and vast country can throw at them. It is a land of great beauty and interest, with an endless number of fine landscapes to record in watercolour and pen and ink drawings. The explorers face enormous challenges in their efforts to cross the deserts and arid lands of the interior, north-west and Kimberley, as they confront Aboriginal people who occupy the lands they pass through and suffer from heat, lack of water and illness. But in the benevolent south-west, Prinsep saw a country subdued, as the colonists turn the wilderness into productive farms, towns and ports. The city of Perth grows and, in a series of paintings showing the Prinsep house and the streets of the city, becomes a place of order and development, where families can live in comfort and in harmony with their community. Some of the images Prinsep produced, particularly his exploration drawings, were published widely in the accounts of the explorers and included in national exhibitions, including the Western Australia display in the 1880 Melbourne International Exhibition.[17]

Yet only a portion of the images were intended for public display. Many were created for private purposes, sent to family members overseas or in the country regions of Western Australia and placed into albums or hung as mementoes of family life and history. Prinsep returned to his youthful enjoyment of photography after he had been in Western Australia for five years, cleaned the 'hornets nests and cobwebs' from the camera he had brought with him from England in 1866, and began recording family and social life on film.[18] As a young man in England, Prinsep's photographic interests had been encouraged by portrait photographer, Julia Margaret Cameron, who was part of the extended family. Prinsep's Western Australian albums of black and white photographs in private family collections, the State Library of Western Australia and the Busselton Museum provide vivid portraits of family life in Perth and the south-west during the late-Nineteenth and early-Twentieth centuries. Henry Prinsep and his family are pictured going about all kinds of activities as they age and mature over the years, enjoy picnics, outings and fancy dress parties. Also pictured are the private moments of affection between family members: a father reading to his daughter, family pets, the quotidian activities of reading the newspaper, feeding the chickens, and drawing water from the well. The photographs bring to life a family in its social context as it interacts with wider networks and encounters others in the small world of colonial Western Australia: the servants and working people, as well as the

---

17 Prinsep describes his efforts to produce drawings and paintings for the exhibition in his diaries, 3 June 1880, SLWA Acc. 2882A.
18 Prinsep, Henry C. 'Diaries', 19 April 1871, SLWA Acc. BA 142/201, 1423/904.

Aboriginal people Prinsep was particularly keen to record throughout his years as pastoral manager, civil servant and retired gentleman on his country property. Some were made into postcards, cabinet cards and cartes de visite, and were sent to family and friends in Western Australia, England and the colonies as part of the drive to stay in touch. In return, many were received and carefully placed into family albums. They illustrate a world of connection and interconnection, in which there were multiple ways of exchanging information and maintaining contact with a widely dispersed network of family, friends and associates.

Histories across space, place and time

By bringing individuals and their networks into the historical frame, the Prinsep archives open up a history that is far broader than narratives of state and colonial development. This is a history that extends beyond national borders and geographic boundaries, which focuses on personal networks and connections rather than on histories of national development. Historians of the British imperial and colonial world have increasingly been prepared to consider the transnational, these 'connections across space', although they have used the term cautiously.[19] 'Colonial histories', Durba Ghosh and Dane Kennedy remark in their edited volume *Decentring Empire,* 'have in recent times moved beyond the old confines of national, imperial and area studies to explore how global webs of connection and influence shaped the historical experiences of both colonisers and colonised'.[20] Tony Ballantyne has proposed 'new analytical models, that recover the movement of people, ideas, ideologies, commodities and information across the borders of the nation states'.[21] Ballantyne insists that, alongside histories of 'aggressive empire-building', there must be attention to the 'unprecedented movement of peoples over long distances' that fuelled national development.[22] Histories of 'diaspora, imperialism, exile and conflict', of 'journeys as well as moments of departure and arrival, crossings and exchanges, movements, flows, and circulation', extend narratives of bounded national development by exploring empire as an integrative system, and the 'analytical space' of historical investigation 'to the oceans and the wild spaces and borders

---

19 Armitage, David 2012, 'What's the Big Idea?: Intellectual history and the longue durée', in *History of European Ideas*, Volume 38, Issue 4, DOI:10.1080/01916599.2012.714635.
20 Ghosh, Durba and Dane Kennedy 2006, *Decentring Empire: Britain, India and the transcolonial world*, Orient Longman, Hyderabad, p.8.
21 Ballantyne, Tony 2012, *Webs of Empire: Locating New Zealand's colonial past*, Bridget Williams Books, Wellington, p.26.
22 Ballantyne 2012, *Webs of Empire*, pp.99–100.

that divide them'.²³ In the words of Atlantic historian, Matthew Guterl, they have thus served to replace 'isolationist, cartoonish' images of colonial settlement with visions of 'a densely networked, globally interconnected' world.²⁴

The ability of the transnational to transform the way historians approach imperial and colonial history has brought a corresponding increase in the volume of published histories which extend beyond the nation state to incorporate wider systems of trade, movement and exchange. Some have done this by conceiving of place itself as the protagonist in the historical narrative, considering the *longue durée*, and by adopting flexible notions of geographic boundaries and temporal periodisation.²⁵ In their histories of the Indian and Pacific oceans, Michael Pearson and Matt Matsuda are interested in oceans as places of connection and interaction which bring different people into contact rather than divide them. Theirs are histories in the broad sweep, with the oceans traversed over the *longue durée* by many different people, some leaving but traces of their presence, and others, such, as the British in the Nineteenth Century becoming dominant and making their presence felt over many years.²⁶

Other historians have examined the way 'people, paper and things' moved around the empire, and integrated the colonies into a system of movement and exchange. Kirsten McKenzie is interested in 'empires as assemblages of information', and the way that information, including news of scandals and controversies, moved around the networks of empire.²⁷ Thomas Metcalf, in his 2007 book *Imperial Connections*, explores the means by which Indian colonial experience, in the form of legal and administrative regimes, British management practices and Indian labour was transmitted throughout the Indian Ocean region, to the colonies of Mauritius, East Africa and Natal, and the networks of transport and communication which sustained them.²⁸ Others have been interested in networks and the way they functioned and were maintained. Zoe Laidlaw, for example, found networks such as the Peninsular War veterans association 'inherently interesting' for their 'role as mechanisms consciously utilised by their members' for ' the transmission of information, or patronage, or money, through the personal connections a network encompassed'.²⁹ Durba

---

23 Desley Deacon, Penny Russell, Angela Woollacott, (eds) 2010, *Transnational lives: biographies of global modernity, 1700 – present*, Palgrave Macmillan, Basingstoke and New York, p. 4.
24 Matthew Pratt Guterl 2013, 'AHR Forum, Comment: The Futures of Transnational History', in *American Historical Review*, February 2013, p. 131.
25 Braudel, Fernand 1980, *On History*, translated by Sarah Matthews, University of Chicago Press, Chicago.
26 Pearson, Michael 2003, *The Indian Ocean*, Routledge, London; Matsuda, Matt K. 2012, *Pacific Worlds: A history of seas, peoples and cultures*, Cambridge University Press, Cambridge and New York.
27 McKenzie, Kirsten 2004, *Scandal in the Colonies: Sydney and Cape Town, 1820–1850*, Melbourne University Press, Melbourne, p.7.
28 Metcalf, Thomas R. 2007, *Imperial Connections: India in the Indian Ocean arena, 1860–1920*, University of California Press, Berkeley.
29 Laidlaw, Zoë 2005, *Colonial Connections 1815–45: Patronage, the information revolution and colonial government*, Manchester University Press, Manchester and New York, p.13.

Ghosh and Dane Kennedy, in their edited volume *Decentring Empire*, emphasise the multiple networks that 'connected colonies to one another as well as to Britain and stretched across the geographical and political boundaries', and that 'colonies as well as metropoles, spun webs of empire from themselves'.[30]

Transnational perspectives on global, imperial and colonial histories have importantly brought new ways of thinking about biography and of using life stories. A life may become 'a stand-in for something else: for the nation, for the world, for the trans-nation … not offered up in the sense of your typical biography, where the goal is to unearth the minutiae of the everyday, to plot a single human being's circumstance in all of its cradle-to-the-grave detail, and in doing so to explain his or her consequence'.[31] A number of recent histories, including Desley Deacon's, Penny Russell's and Angela Woollacott's *Australian Lives in the World*, Ann Curthoys' and Marilyn Lake's *Connected Worlds*, and David Lambert's and Alan Lester's *Colonial Lives across the British Empire*, have used the life paths of imperial men and women to explore the densely networked, globally connected world of the British empire.[32] Catherine Hall and Julie Evans have used the life of explorer, colonial official and governor, Edward Eyre, in Australia, New Zealand and Jamaica, to explore questions of identity, as 'imperial men' such as Eyre encountered different sites of the empire, each articulating 'different relations of power, different subject positions, different cultural identities'.[33] While England always represented home, Eyre spent almost all his adult life overseas, and his own identity came to reflect a life spent moving in and between different sites of empire and the metropole, an identity ruptured, changed and differently articulated by place and imperial expectations.[34] Eyre's life path, as Julie Evans suggests, enables 'us to see not just a brave explorer at the beginning of his career or a brutally racist governor at its end, but an individual whose personal preoccupation tended to expose, rather than conceal, the coercive essence of colonial rule'.[35]

As well as the transnational, the Prinsep archive also exhibits what David Armitage has termed a 'transtemporal' dimension, concerned with linkages and comparisons across time that are resistant to bounded notions periodisation,

---

30 Ghosh and Kennedy 2006, *Decentring Empire*, pp.2, 8.
31 Guterl 2013, 'AHR Forum, Comment: The futures of transnational history', p.130.
32 Curthoys, Ann and Marilyn Lake (eds) 2005, *Connected Worlds: History in transnational perspective*, ANU E Press, Canberra; Deacon, Desley, Penny Russell and Angela Woollacott (eds) 2010, *Transnational Lives: Biographies of global modernity, 1700–present*, Palgrave Macmillan, Basingstoke and New York; Lambert, David and Alan Lester (eds) 2006, *Colonial Lives Across the British Empire: Imperial careering in the long Nineteenth Century*, Cambridge University Press, Cambridge.
33 Lambert and Lester 2006 *Colonial Lives Across the British Empire*, p.65.
34 Hall, Catherine 2002, *Civilising Subjects: Metropole and colony in the English imagination, 1830–1867*, Polity, Cambridge.
35 Evans, Julie 2005, *Edward Eyre: Race and colonial governance*, University of Otago Press, Dunedin, p.10.

'much as transnational history deals with such connections across space'.[36] Tom Stannage, in his 1979 book *The People of Perth*, wrote about the inadequacy of histories which gain coherence only from 'the dominance of a set of experiences or events' which come to symbolise the national story.[37] Periodisation, the practice of dividing history into short chronological periods, disguises 'underlying or fundamental patterns of social experience, and it tends to set on one side the private time scales and the rhythms of individual lives'. Regardless of the period, people of all ages and social groups went about the business of trying to lead a contented life, finding shelter and employment, bringing up families and coping with the difficulties they encountered along the way. 'In all periods', Stannage writes,

> People grew old and worried themselves about ailments, Poor Houses, their children, their estates, and the afterlife. In all ages men founded institutions and clubs, bashed their womenfolk and each other and were tender to both. In all periods women coped with the recurrent experience of childbirth, raised families and ran a domestic economy, enjoyed neighbourly conversation and suffered grievously from *anomie*. In all periods, people drank heavily or little, acted ignobly or nobly … In a single day or a lifetime a person might experience many of these things and much else besides—with transient and long term effects.[38]

Historians have increasingly turned to the private writing of imperial men and women—their letters, diaries and journals—to explore areas largely hidden in narratives of national history, including the voices of women, indigenous people and workers, questions of imperial and colonial identity, and the domestic and global networks people were part of and how they sought to utilise them. Private writing provides an avenue to encounter voices that, until the publication of volumes of colonial women's writing by Beverley Kingston (1977), Ruth Teale (1978), Kaye Daniels and Mary Murnane (1980, 1993), rarely featured in Australian historical records.[39] In her 2008 book, *Australia Through Women's Eyes,* Ann Standish suggests that this private sphere served a broader function than that of simply 'staying in touch'; it allowed women the scope to express their imaginings of empire and their place within it, and thereby complicates

---

36 Armitage, David 2012, 'What's the Big Idea?: Intellectual history and the longue durée', in *History of European Ideas*, Volume 38, Issue 4, DOI:10.1080/01916599.2012.714635.
37 Stannage, C.T. 1979, *The People of Perth: A social history of Western Australia's capital city*, City of Perth, Perth, p.8.
38 Ibid.
39 Kingston, Beverley 1977, *The World Moves Slowly: A documentary history of Australian women*, Cassell Australia, NSW; Teale, Ruth (ed.) 1978, *Colonial Eve: Sources on women in Australia, 1788–1914*, Oxford University Press, Melbourne; Daniels, Kay and Mary Murnane (eds) 1980, *Uphill all the Way: A documentary history of women in Australia*, University of Queensland Press, St Lucia; Clarke, Patricia and Dale Spender 1996, *Life Lines: Australian women's letters and diaries, 1788–1840*, Allen & Unwin, NSW.

and extends discourses of British colonialism.[40] Letter-writing, as Frances Porter and Charlotte Macdonald write in their introduction to a compendium of New Zealand colonial women's writing, 'was not something done to fill in idle hours as a kind of lady-like refinement. It was a necessity, a life line, part of the social existence.'[41] They are 'histories of 'inner lives' rather than descriptions of 'the outer life' and reveal 'something of how women made sense of their lives—in telling stories, framing events, making order out of the novel, sometimes chaotic and always unpredictable circumstances around them'.[42] As well as showing women 'interrogating their own feelings, exploring their own thoughts and reactions', diaries, journals and letters, gave women the scope to create their own accounts of colonial lives, which act 'as a kind of anchor for unfamiliar, unpredictable and isolated situations'.[43]

The private writing of families reminds us that imperial and colonial life was as much about domesticity and private life as it was about career and national development. Furthermore, it is cross-generational in its capacity to illuminate family identities as they develop over the generations, as family values, traditions and identities are formed and handed down, responsive to local circumstances but exercising a powerful influence on the way family members conduct themselves and conceive their role in their colonial or metropolitan lives. Recent histories by Stephen Foster and Emma Rothschild utilise the extensive archives of two Scottish families to illustrate family life and values over a number of generations. Foster follows five generations of the Macpherson family over three centuries, as family members move around the empire to follow their diverse interests in slavery, the East India Company, the Caribbean and North America, and as agriculturalists in Australia and the West Indies, while maintaining a strong sense of family identity and connection.[44] The extensive collection of family letters, documents and diaries reveals an imperial family life at its most intimate and private, as family members confront the highs and lows of colonial life over the generations and become aware of a rich family heritage. Similarly, in *The Inner Lives of Empires*, Emma Rothschild draws on an 'amazing amount of evidence' to illustrate 'an inner life of families as well as an outer', an 'interior, private existence of the mind and an exterior universe of events and circumstances'.[45] Her biography of the Johnstone family 'includes mistresses and servants and slaves, it extends across the frontiers between different kinds

---

40 Standish, Ann 2008, *Australia Through Womens's Eyes*, Australian Scholarly Publishing, Melbourne, p.268.
41 Porter, Frances and Charlotte Macdonald (eds) 1996, *'My Hand Will Write What My Heart Dictates': The unsettled lives of women in Nineteenth Century New Zealand as revealed to family and friends*, Auckland University Press, Auckland, p.13.
42 Ibid.
43 Ibid.
44 Foster, Stephen 2010, *A Private Empire*, Murdoch Books, Miller's Point, NSW.
45 Rothschild, Emma 2011, *The Inner Life of Empires: An Eighteenth Century history*, Princeton University Press, Princeton, New Jersey, p.4.

of historical inquiry, in that it is a history of economic life, of political ideas, of slavery, and of family relationships'.[46] It presents a history of sentiment, in which family members communicate their affections, share their emotional lives, their achievements, births, deaths and marriages, as well as their inner feelings about empire, their own colonial situations and family lives. It covers long periods of time, following the generations of family members and the connections between these generations, the family history and heritage, and the way these values were transmitted and expressed by successive generations. In some instances, such as in Peter Robb's history of the diaries of architect and surveyor Richard Blechynden in Calcutta at the turn of the Eighteenth and Nineteenth centuries, the strong and frequently complex sentimental connections between coloniser and colonised are revealed. In Blechynden's case, it was his relationships with Indian women as concubines and companions, relationships which were certainly governed by inequalities, but were also subject to 'Indian agency and therefore dialogue'.[47]

Accessing the Prinsep archive

The Prinsep archive in the State Library of Western Australia (J.S. Battye Library of Western Australian History) is an historical record of unusual depth that covers a long span of time and wide geographic spaces.[48] Most of it is concentrated on Prinsep's 78-year life, but the archive reaches back to the time of his grandparents, parents and the many uncles and aunts who had lived in Calcutta (Kolkata) in the service of the British East India Company, from the time of Warren Hastings until the middle of the Nineteenth Century. It also looks forward to the life stories of Prinsep's oldest daughter, Carlotta Brockman, born in June 1869, whose journal details the period from her childhood, youth and adult life in Perth and south-west Western Australia, until shortly before her death in 1960.[49] The archive covers the full range of family life and family history, including: the diary Prinsep maintained from the first day of 1866, the year he left England as a 21-year-old to travel to Australia; boxes upon boxes of letters from family, friends and business associates in the domestic sphere of Western Australia, Britain, India, Ceylon (Sri Lanka) and other Australian colonies; postcards and cartes de visite; albums of photographs and drawings; family bibles and other information about ancestors and family members; poems

---

46 Ibid., p.6
47 Robb, Peter 2011, *Sex and Sensibility: The diaries of Richard Blechynden, 1759–1822*, Oxford University Press, New Delhi, p.213.
48 The Prinsep Papers in the J.S. Battye Library of Western Australian History, SLWA, are accessioned MN 773, and include Acc. 449A, 931A, 983A, 1972, 1274A, 1805A, 2121A, 2140, 2882A, 3150A, 3304A, 3592A, 3593A, 3594A, 3595, 3859A and 7150A. The Prinsep photographic collection is Acc. BA 1423.
49 Brockman, Carlotta, 'Reminiscences of Carlotta Louisa Brockman, née Prinsep, 1882–1956', State Library of Western Australia (SLWA) Acc. 931A.

and jottings; and invitations and attendance lists. These are interspersed with formal and business documents such as legal agreements and contracts, letter books, accounts and budgets, promissory notes and bank statements, shares and company letters, codicils and inventories.

This is an archive that illuminates the public and private worlds of a colonial family, from attitudes about the bigger questions of politics, race, religion, the affairs of the Empire to the domestic details and internal life of a colonial family, their sentiments and emotions, networks and relationships. It speaks of a world of connections maintained over long periods and vast distances. Of particular importance was the need to stay in touch with family, wherever they might be in the global world of the British Empire. Prinsep's correspondence with his brothers and sisters is remarkable for its regularity and depth. Over a period of 50 years, it follows the highs and lows of an affectionate group of siblings, separated by long distances but prepared to go to great lengths to maintain contact. His correspondence shows just how many people he was connected to and how wide his networks were as he sought to stay in touch, not only with family, but the many people he knew in Britain and the colonies of the Empire, particularly India and Ceylon (Sri Lanka). Many life stories feature in the pages of the Prinsep archive, some detailed, others but traces of the people Prinsep encountered over the course of his life: friends and social contacts, business associates, work colleagues and fellow artists, Aboriginal people, servants and workers.

The volume and depth of material in the Johnstone family archive lead Emma Rothschild to consider ways of 'connecting micro- and macrohistories by the history of the individuals' own connections … to proceed encounter by encounter, from the history of a family to the history of a larger society of empire or enlightenment or ideas'.[50] Such a venture, the detailed and time-consuming work of connecting diverse communications over long periods and diverse geographies, demands the use of methods which can tolerate large volumes of archival material, 'new ways of doing old history'.[51] Digital technologies vastly expand the capacity of historians to utilise large and detailed archives, to consider 'microhistories' of the 'uneminent or the unimportant' and connect 'individuals and families to the larger scenes of which they were a part'.[52] 'Digitisation', as David Armitage has commented, offers 'dizzying possibilities for research over the *longue duree*', by allowing historians access to expanding 'corpora of text' and the tools to analyse them.[53] In an archive such as that of Henry Prinsep, the ability to copy, machine-read and search large volumes of family material, letters, diaries and journals, online listings and albums of photographs, expands

---

50   Rothschild 2011, *The Inner Life of Empires*, p.267.
51   Ibid
52   Ibid., p.278.
53   Armitage 2012, 'What's the Big Idea?', p.15.

the utility of the archive as a historical source. Digitisation has increased the ability to examine in detail the way that Prinsep developed, maintained and exploited his complex web of connections throughout his domestic, colonial and imperial networks. It offers the potential to plot his networks to reveal their full density and complexity, and to think about the microhistorical. Yet, it does not eliminate the 'human' task of actually handling the archive, of making sense of the densely packed and frequently illegible letters, journals and diaries, of starting to understand the networks and connections. Nor can digitisation recover the simple tactile element of handling volumes of paper and the occasional surprises they may conceal, the locks of hair from loved ones, the pressed flowers, or little watercolours and drawings.

In researching the life of Henry Prinsep, the use of digital technologies expanded the capacity to locate his life within a larger network that extended over generations, as the men and women of the family pursued their colonial lives in other times and places. The ability to access the narratives of Prinsep's forebears in India and Britain through digital collections such as the Internet Archive[54] and online collections of libraries, art galleries and museums, helped uncover a detailed picture of the extended family's relationship to India and the East India Company. Previous generations of Prinseps were similarly committed recorders of their colonial lives in words and art. Most prominent was Henry's uncle, James Prinsep (1799–1840), whose remarkably productive and enthusiastic research and writings on Indian history, language and science, and his role as editor of the Bengal Asiatic Society's *Journal* between 1832 and 1838, were widely praised by his contemporaries and later memorialised by modern authors, Om Prakesh Kejariwal and Charles Allen.[55] Grandfather John Prinsep (1746–1831), and uncles, Thoby Prinsep (1792–1878) and William Prinsep (1794–1874) recorded their Calcutta years in personal memoirs composed after their return from India, while another uncle, Augustus Prinsep (1803–1830), wrote on social and family life in Calcutta and India and published a novel, *The Baboo*, a number of short stories and a detailed journal of his travels from Calcutta to Van Diemen's Land.[56] William, James and Thomas Prinsep were enthusiastic 'lovers of the brush', who joined other artists, including George Chinnery, in India to record the landscapes, streets and people of India, and to portray their social and family lives in the city. The next generation of Prinseps to travel to

---

54   http://archive.org/.
55   Allen, Charles 2002, *The Search for the Buddha: The men who discovered India's lost religion*, Carrol and Graf, New York; Kejariwal, O.P. 1988, *The Asiatic Society of Bengal and the Discovery of India's Past*, Oxford University Press, New Delhi.
56   Prinsep, Sir Henry Thoby, 'Three Generations in India 1771–1904', OIOC MSS Eur. C. 97; Prinsep, William, 'The Memoirs of William Prinsep', 3 Volumes, British Library, OIOC MSS Eur. D. 1160/1; Prinsep, Augustus 1834, *The Baboo and Other Tales Descriptive of Society in India*, 2 Volumes, Smith, Elder and Co., London; Prinsep, Augustus 1834, *A Man of Sentiment in the Mofussil*, Smith, Elder and Co., London; Prinsep, Augustus 1834, *Theodore, or Coelebs the Younger*, Smith, Elder and Co., London; Prinsep, Augustus 1833, *The Journal of a Voyage from Calcutta to Van Diemen's Land*, Smith, Elder and Co., London.

India, Henry Prinsep's cousins, followed their forebears in memorialising their Indian experiences. Augusta Becher, the only daughter of Augustus Prinsep, wrote a detailed memoir of her life in India as the wife of an Indian army officer during the Indian rebellion of 1857. Later, Sir Henry Thoby Prinsep and Val Prinsep, sons of Henry's uncle Thoby, also recorded reminiscences of their Indian experiences.[57] Added to this private collection is an extensive archive of other Prinsep family writings: public reports and letters from their official positions with the East India Company and later the Indian Civil Service, court documents, certificates of birth, marriage and death. Taken together, the records portray lives of intense activity, as family members participated in the challenges, triumphs and tragedies of the Indian colonial enterprise.

This book locates its subject, Henry Prinsep, in the intersections between the private and public worlds of a colonial family, and explores the relationships between these two spheres, accepting that an understanding of one benefits from illumination by the other. It incorporates both the domestic and trans-imperial elements of Prinsep's life, which operated in complex relationship with one another. As well as colonisers, families such as the Prinseps saw themselves as empire-makers who helped distribute and perpetuate the ideologies, imageries and assumptions of the British Empire, all of which they were well-equipped to do by virtue of their long colonial heritage. As the colonial official with responsibility for Aboriginal affairs in Western Australia and the architect of legislation with far-reaching and long-lasting impact on the State's indigenous populations, Prinsep was a central figure in the institutionalisation of the government's response to its colonised populations. His understanding of the role and the way he undertook its duties occurred in a historical and political context in which domestic concerns were complicated by the colony's membership in a global system of empire. Issues of race and colonialism continued to be central concerns of the empire and figured prominently in imperial media, including official documents, newspapers and magazines, as well as the private sphere of letters, drawings and images. These were areas of great controversy, and colonial ideas and practices were frequently and vigorously contested. Prinsep found that it was sometimes difficult to balance the two domains, to satisfy the demands of his colonial contemporaries and imperial critics, for he was himself situated both in the domestic and the transnational, certainly a coloniser but also intimately connected with a larger, more complex system of exchange, influence and patronage.

---

57 Becher, Augusta 1930, *Personal Reminiscences of Augusta Becher, 1830–1888,* edited by H.G. Rawlinson, Constable and Co., London; Prinsep, Val C. 1879, *Imperial India: An artist's journals, illustrated by numerous sketches taken at the courts of the principal chiefs in India,* Chapman and Hall, London; Prinsep, Sir Henry Thoby, 'Three Generations in India 1771–1904', OIOC MSS Eur. C. 97.

1. Introduction—An Imperial Man and His Archive

Presented in ten chapters, the book follows the chronology of Prinsep's life against the settings of a British Indian family heritage, life in Britain and Western Australia. The next chapter examines the Indian world of Prinsep's forebears as it is portrayed in various family accounts, including their orientalist thought and the way that colonial government and attitudes to race and colonialism changed and evolved over the course of the Nineteenth Century. The perspectives of various Prinsep family members provide accounts and perspectives of life in India, including Prinsep's grandfather, entrepreneur and adventurer John Prinsep, orientalist civil servant Thoby, 'scholar-saint' James, merchant and artist William, lawyer Charles, and novelist and journalist Augustus. Chapter Three examines the metropolitan world in which Prinsep grew up and his absorption into the orientalised world of his Anglo-Indian network, before considering some of the debates over empire, race and colonialism that he was exposed to through family connections, and the literature and public imagery of the empire that was emerging in Britain during the 1840s and 1850s. Chapter Four describes Henry Prinsep's initial conception of his colonising role in his new Western Australian home, a period during which he was concerned with the political economy of empire and the potential of the young colony to develop trading relationships with India and other Indian Ocean colonies. Chapter Five discusses Prinsep's interactions with Aboriginal peoples during his early life in Western Australia, relationships which helped shape an ideological framework that was subject both to the influences of domestic priorities and the colony's place in a wider imperial world.

Chapter Six examines Prinsep's life as a colonial civil servant in Perth, a period during which he operated as both colonial functionary and private citizen. Chapter Seven explores his social and cultural world as a member of the colonial elite, intimately involved with the colonial project in both the public and private arenas. The environment Prinsep inhabited replicated that of the metropole and other colonies, and the people he associated with often came from backgrounds very similar to his own. Western Australia was thus connected to its imperial context, subject to its ideologies and mediations and the exchange of ideas and assumptions about the colonised others. Chapters Eight and Nine focus on Prinsep's role as Chief Protector of Aborigines and the ideas, attitudes and assumptions that eventually brought about the *Aborigines Act* in 1905. This was a period during which Prinsep tried to reconcile and balance domestic attitudes to colonisation with perspectives that were frequently critical of the state's policies. While he was absorbed in the complex and absorbing internal problems and relationships of the colonial outpost, his writings show a parallel consciousness of the colony as part of a vast web of external relationships, around which flowed ideas, problems and issues that, in effect, provided the raw material for unifying ideologies of late-Nineteenth Century British imperial culture and heritage. Western Australia was not alone in its concerns and anxieties, nor were its responses confined within a colonial vacuum; it too was a part of a global system.

Henry Prinsep in 1898 soon after taking up the position of Chief Protector of Aborigines in Western Australia. An inveterate socialiser, entertaining conversationalist and considerate host, Prinsep enjoyed his social and cultural life much more than his work.

Source: Author's private collection.

1. Introduction—An Imperial Man and His Archive

Henry Prinsep, the letter writer, at his desk, probably at the family home, The Studio, in Howick Street, Perth.

Source: Prinsep Papers, SLWA MN 773 BA 1423/64.

The young Prinseps circa 1862 at their father's home in Cheltenham. From left to right: Annie (1848–1932), May (1853–1936), Henry (1844–1922), Jim (1855–1942) and Louisa (1850–1922). Missing is the eldest brother, Charlie (1843–1898), who was in India with the 19th Hussars.

Source: Courtesy of anonymously held private collection.

1. Introduction—An Imperial Man and His Archive

This image, taken in Calcutta about 1850, shows Prinsep's sister, Annie, with her ayah, who may well be the woman known to Carlotta Prinsep as Jinny. She had been the ayah of Prinsep and his siblings, and was employed by him in 1870 on his visit to Calcutta to care for baby Carlotta.

Source: Courtesy of anonymously held private collection.

Charles Prinsep and daughter Annie in Calcutta, circa 1852.

Source: Courtesy of anonymously held private collection.

1. Introduction—An Imperial Man and His Archive

Henry Prinsep's father, Charles Robert (1789–1864), in 1824, shortly before leaving England to join his brothers in Calcutta. The drawing, entitled 'Studying for a Doctor', was by his sister Emily Prinsep.

Source: Prinsep Papers, SLWA MN 773 Acc 3150A.

Henry Prinsep in oriental dress, photographed in Singapore in March 1866. He stayed in Singapore for two months to inspect his late father's extensive nutmeg estates, before departing for Western Australia.

Source: Courtesy Ailsa Smith, Claremont WA.

1. Introduction—An Imperial Man and His Archive

An artefact of the British Raj, Henry Prinsep poses with his Aborgines Department staff, travelling inspector G.S. Olivey and his trusty bicycle, and filing clerk Edward Pechell, circa 1899.

Source: Prinsep Papers, SLWA MN 773 BA 1423/347.

2. Images of an Imperial Family

Henry Prinsep grew up in an England far removed from India, but in an environment dominated by his famous family's Indian background, by tales of heroism and service to the Empire, of fortunes made and lost in the raucous environment of old Calcutta, the 'city of palaces', of family mysteries, early death, illness and tragedy.[1] Most of the adults in his extended family had spent the large part of their lives in India, and his childhood was nurtured by adventures from an earlier era of his grandparents John and Sophia Prinsep (née Auriol, 1760-1850), and the tales of his surviving uncles and aunts, men and women such as Thoby Prinsep and his wife Sara (née Pattle, 1817–1887), William Prinsep, and 'Aunt Jules', Sara's sister Julia Margaret Cameron (née Pattle, 1815-1879). The walls and book shelves of the homes he lived in were adorned with the works of uncles who had died young and whose memories were cherished, the novels, short stories and travel accounts of uncle Augustus, the scholarly articles and diagrams of uncle James, and the vivid and evocative watercolours of William, James and Thomas (1800–1830). In later life, Prinsep would idealise the Indian world of his forebears as a golden age of empire, a period when things were not so 'hard set' as they now seemed, when it was easier to have an impact, to make a fortune, become famous. Their world represented a standard, a reassurance of the greater progress of the British race, an inspiration for 'us young fry' to abide by the standards that had made Britain the greatest power on earth.[2]

A novelised and memorialised India

By the time Thoby and William Prinsep came to write their memoirs as old men in the 1870s, 40 years had elapsed since the demise of the orientalist system of which they had been a part.[3] Thoby and William set out to memorialise and justify a system which seemed in danger of fading into obscurity, and record, at least for their own descendants, the roles they had played. In the process, they mounted a defence of orientalist governance as amenable to Indian requirements as it utilised knowledge that British civil servants had accumulated about India

---

1 Prinsep family correspondence and diaries often refer to their 'famous' Indian background. See Prinsep, Henry C., 'Diaries 1866–1922', SLWA Acc. 499A, 12 January 1866; Prinsep, James Charles, 'De Principe, A.D. 1574–1930', 2 Volumes, SLWA Acc. 3150 A/1–2.
2 Prinsep, H.C., 'Our Britain', SLWA Acc. 3594A/4; H.C. Prinsep to Annie Prinsep, 23 April 1874, private collection.
3 Prinsep, Sir Henry Thoby, 'Three Generations in India 1771–1904', OIOC MSS Eur. C. 97; Prinsep, William, 'The Memoirs of William Prinsep', 3 Volumes, British Library, OIOC MSS Eur. D. 1160/1. Thoby's memoir is part of a three volume set prepared by his son, Sir Henry Thoby Prinsep, to illustrate the careers of three generations of his family in India: his grandfather John Prinsep, Thoby, and himself.

and Indians, and was based on British respect for Indian cultures, languages and histories. They write of a time when relationships between coloniser and colonised were more permeable, when there was greater interaction between the rulers and the ruled. They gloss over and often glorify the colonial world of their earlier years, emphasising the good times, the family victories and triumphs, explaining what it was like and downplaying the anxieties that accompanied Indian colonial rule. Such is the nature of memoir as historical record: it allows the author to tell a story, express sentiments, create an image, explain and justify, record personal perceptions and memories. It may be a legitimising exercise, but it also locates the self within the larger forces of history and, by doing so, constructs and attempts to resolve tensions between the self and history, providing a way of communicating and informing one's descendants about a past era and filling in silences in the family history.

By contrast, Augustus Prinsep's novel *The Baboo* claims only to be a tale of British life in Calcutta. Set on the same stage as the memoirs of Thoby and William Prinsep, the novel was published by Augustus's widow, Elisabeth (Ommaney), after the author's death in 1830 at the age of 28.[4] It is set in the Calcutta lived in and known by Augustus Prinsep, populated by characters and caricatures recognisable to those familiar with the environment. By claiming the mantle of fiction, Augustus was able to address the contentious subjects of interracial sex, interracial marriage and mixed race children, to contemplate risky and controversial matters such as British attitudes to Indian populations, Indian attitudes to the British and other Indians, and to portray colonial relationships as complex and ambiguous. He understood the fragilities of the British enterprise in India, as the British characters in his novel struggle to understand their role in India and their relationships with the Indians they were supposed to be ruling, but who were also active protagonists in the British colonial presence.

The Baboo is a story of the loss and recovery of British identity in early-Nineteenth Century India in which the central character Henry Forester, a vigorous and admired British warrior, 'yields a portion of his heart to the thraldom of Oriental beauty', renounces his Britishness and Christianity, and turns 'Moosulman'. He falls in love with the niece of a Persian noble, Yoosuf Ulee Khan, the beautiful Dilafroz, who bears him a son, Moobaruk. From an initial hatred of Forester, Yoosuf comes to regard Forester as a true son-in-law:

> Together we have hunted the wild beast in the surrounding ravines, and have listened to the singing of the black-eyed nautch girls, for many a happy day in the halls of my ancestors.[5]

---

4 Prinsep, Augustus 1834, *The Baboo and Other Tales Descriptive of Society in India*, 2 Volumes, Smith, Elder and Co., London, Volume 1, p.iv.
5 Ibid., Volume 1, p.146.

Forester falls ill and, believing Dilafroz to be dead, reluctantly returns to England to regain his health, where 'all the feelings of my earliest youth revived; I was an Englishman again'. He proposes to Eva Eldridge, a 'lily-faced girl of his cold country', who plans to join him in India as soon as passage can be arranged.[6] Returning to India, Forester discovers that reports of the death of Dilafroz are wrong and, wanting to maintain his honour and avoid being cast as a 'false wretch', feigns his own death. Determined to flee with his wife, son and father-in-law to the Persian Gulf and present his 'sword to the King of Eeeran', he adopts the identity of Gholam Housein, Persian prince and devoted son-in-law of Yoosuf. Enter the brooding presence of the Hindu Baboo Brijmohun Bomijee, a 'half submissive, half bustling character', who is secretly plotting to take over Yoosuf's ancestral estates. Many of the Calcutta British establishment, from the lowest soldier to senior civil servants, are in debt to the Baboo through 'small loans in time of need, to be repaid twenty-fold in time of promotion; and by having a constant supply of the best champagne, when it was not to be purchased elsewhere'.[7] By day, the Baboo is the faithful servant, but by night, fuelled by the 'sweet water of Ganga', he vents his hatred of the 'furingee' and plots their destruction. Forester unmasks the Baboo's duplicity and rapacity and not only retrieves Yoosuf's lands, but restores the reputation of the British as people of honour and justice. Yoosuf comes to understand the values of British law and government, and swears that his people 'will henceforth be true subjects because they have found a ruler worthy of their most devoted love'.[8] He grows to understand the hitherto mysterious British attitudes to marriage and love. 'Love with us', Forester explains, 'is not as it is with you, a passion, strong indeed, but short-lived; one of amusement rather than of habit … Our wives are more than this; we have but one, the sole mother of our children, the adviser in all our actions, the mistress, and the hostess of our houses, — she is indeed what has been called in jest, the half of ourselves'.[9] Dilafroz plays her part in the restoration of Forester's Britishness, coming to appreciate 'the aristocracy of race … where the white rule, black can never squeeze in', and releasing Forester from his marriage vows to allow him to marry Eva.[10]

The complexity and depth of Augustus Prinsep's depiction of Forester's dilemmas portray an intimate appreciation of the traumas a British civil servant might confront in India. T.W. Williamson's *East India Vade Mecum*, published in 1810 and an indispensable semi-official guide for a Briton travelling to India, advised readers that cross-cultural sexual relationships were common and that

---

6   Ibid., Volume 1, pp.20, 66.
7   Ibid., Volume 1, p.312.
8   Ibid., Volume 2, p.94.
9   Ibid., Volume 2, p.65.
10 Ibid., Volume 1, stanzas ms., title page.

polygamy was 'not unprecedented among Europeans' in India.[11] However, the costs 'attendant upon concubinage' were reported as being considerable, noting that a British gentleman should be prepared for the high costs of establishing his zenanah, including clothing, jewellery and scented oils. In Williamson's view, once in India, British men could not be expected to 'act in exact conformity with those excellent doctrines, which teach us to avoid 'fornication', and all other deadly sins'. But while it was acceptable to have an Indian concubine, the Company disapproved the 'transmission of native orphans (those born of native mothers)' and forbade 'any native of India to be taken as a passenger on board any vessel proceeding to England … lest they become a burthen to the Company'.[12] An Indian wife guaranteed social isolation, and 'no lady, native of India, whatever her rank, is ever invited to those assemblies given by the governor'.[13] Nonetheless, many children were born of cross-cultural relationships and were recognised by their British fathers. William Dalrymple's history *White Mughals* provides evidence of the high proportions of bequests during the late-Eighteenth and early-Nineteenth centuries that made provision for Indian wives and children.[14] In her 2006 book, *Sex and Family in Colonial India*, Durba Ghosh draws attention to the anxieties of British fathers of mixed-race children 'about the moral upbringing, education, and social status of their children'.[15] Interracial liaisons were 'constitutive parts' of cross-cultural interactions but were 'almost always problematic': 'sexual discipline and moral superiority were as central to maintaining empire as colonial bureaucracies'.[16]

Of the illegitimate children fathered by John Prinsep during his 17-year Indian adventure (1770–1788) only one appears in the family record and none of the mothers are identified, a strong indication that they were Indian, their namelessness a code for their racial status and that of their children.[17] Half-sister Charlotte Griffiths, according to William Prinsep, was married to an East India Company army colonel and returned with him to England. Nothing is known of

---

11   Williamson, Thomas 1810, *The East India Vade Mecum: Or, complete guide to gentlemen intending for the civil, military, or naval service of the Hon. East India Company*, 2 Volumes, Black, Parry, and Kingsbury, London, p.412. Williamson claimed to have known an 'elderly military character who solaced himself with no less than sixteen, of all sorts and sizes! Being interrogated by a friend as to what he did with such a number, "Oh!" replied he, "I give them a little rice, and let them run about!"'
12   Ibid., p.457.
13   Ibid., p.458.
14   Dalrymple, William 2002, *White Mughals: Love and betrayal in Eighteenth-Century India*, Flamingo, London, p.52. Dalrymple found that during the 1780s, about one in three British wills in India made provision for an Indian wife. Between 1805 and 1810 the proportion had decreased to one in four, by 1830 to one in six, and by mid-century the practice had virtually ceased.
15   Ghosh, Durba 2006, *Sex and the Family in Colonial India: The making of empire*, Cambridge University Press, Cambridge, p.9. Richard Blechynden, an architect whose stay in Calcutta corresponded with the Prinseps, wrote openly about European relationships with Indian women in his extensive diaries, which have been recently published. Robb, Peter 2011, *Sex and Sensibility: The diaries of Richard Blechynden, 1759–1822*, Oxford University Press, New Delhi.
16   Ibid., p.25.
17   Ibid., p.19.

the other children, although all were baptised with the family name in Calcutta between 1778 and 1784.[18] While some of John Prinsep's contemporaries, such as Richard Blechynden, made provision for their Indian born children, others became enmeshed in the system of orphanages established by the East India Company to cater for the children of cross-cultural relationships.[19] According to contemporary Indologist and linguist, John Borthwick Gilchrist, these institutions were 'intimately blended with the military establishments throughout India' and all servicemen were compelled to contribute a portion of their earnings to their upkeep.[20] The children were usually removed from their parents and placed in institutions at the age of three, the parents understanding 'that every justice will be done to their offspring', although Gilchrist acknowledged that 'to part from a child, whatever may be its complexion, is a most painful struggle between duty and nature'.[21]

The vulnerability of a young British recruit to the charms and dangers of India was well understood by the East India Company, which over the last decade of the Eighteenth and early-Nineteenth Century, introduced training for 15- and 16-year-old civil service recruits, partly to equip them to withstand the pitfalls of an Indian career, but also to allow them time to mature. Governor-General Wellesley advocated an education that would influence their 'early habits' and 'effectively guard them against those temptations and corruptions with which the nature of the climate and the peculiar depravity of the people of India, will surround and assail them in every station, especially on their first arrival in India'.[22] High standards of conduct by East India Company civil servants, Wellesley believed, were not only a guarantee of more effective government, but protected the reputation of the company. By the 1800s, the Company's civil servants were no longer simply 'agents of a commercial concern; they are in fact the ministers and officers of a powerful sovereign'. Inexperienced and poorly trained officers would inevitably lead to appointments in which 'their incapacity or misconduct becomes conspicuous to the natives, disgraceful to themselves, and injurious to the state'.[23]

---

18 The Biographical Indexes of the India Office Records in the British Library list the following illegitimate children of John Prinsep but do not identify the mothers: Elizabeth Scott Prinsep, born 1778 (N/1/50/f.238r), Henrietta Prinsep, born 12/7/1778 (N/1/2/f.150), John Henry Prinsep, born 1778 (N/1/2/f. 289), John Lloyd Prinsep, born 7/12/1784 (N/1/4/f.9).
19 Robb (ed.) 2011, *Sex and Sensibility*, p.213.
20 Gilchrist, John 1825, *The General East India Guide and Vade Mecum: For the public functionary, government officer, private agent, trader or foreign sojourner, in British India, and the adjacent parts of Asia immediately connected with the honourable East India Company*, Kingsbury, Parbury & Allen, London, p.209. This guide was a 'corrected' version of the earlier Williamson *Vade Mecum*, and dispensed with the 1810 version's recommendations regarding relationships with Indian women.
21 Ibid., p.209.
22 Wellesley, Richard 1812, *Letter from the Marquis Wellesley, Governor General of India, to the Court of Directors of the East India Company, On the Trade of India: Dated Fort William, 30 September, 1800*, Richardson and Budd, London, p.15.
23 Ibid., pp.14 , 21.

Over the first half of the Nineteenth Century, appointments to the East India Company civil service increasingly came to reflect the interconnected Anglo-Indian community in India and the metropole. Until 1833, nomination by a member of the East India Company Court of Directors as a civil servant, enlistment with the Company army, or employment with a firm contracted to the Company were the only means of entering India; 'not even an Englishman was to reside who was not in the service of the company'.[24] The system of patronage allowed a director a certain number of appointments, the Chairman, Deputy Chairman and President of the Parliamentary Board of Control receiving double allocations. Directors were compelled to provide reasons for giving an appointment, including their connections to the nominee, and swear that no payment had been received from or on behalf of the applicant. Of 426 appointments by the Board of Directors between 1809 and 1850, 23 per cent were relatives of a director, and over half were on the basis of 'friendships' likely to have been formed while working in India.[25] The East India Company establishment in India steadily became the domain of a relatively defined group, most of whom had a family or kin background in the India colonies. Both Thoby and Augustus Prinsep began their Indian careers through this system of patronage, recommended by their father John and subsequently sponsored by a director.[26] The system remained intact throughout the life of the East India Company and during the 1840s and 1850s was to facilitate entry of the next generation of Prinseps to the Company ranks.

After 1806, on acceptance of their nominations by the Board of Directors, recruits were sent to a three-year program at Haileybury Training College in Hertfordshire before transfer to India at around the age of 18.[27] A Haileybury education was the first step in a middle-class boy's progression to a 'position of command over the majority'.[28] Yet, according to anthropologist Bernard Cohn, it often failed to produce civil servants equipped for a career in India: 'All we knew is that it was "beastly hot" and that there were "niggers" there, and that it would be time enough to bother about it when you got there.'[29] Some students

---

24 'The Memoirs of William Prinsep', Volume 1, p.201.
25 Cohn, Bernard S. 1987, *An Anthropologist Among the Historians and Other Essays*, Oxford University Press, Delhi, pp.520–1.
26 Laurie, Colonel W.F.B. 1887, *Sketches of Some Distinguished Anglo-Indians: With an account of Anglo-Indian periodical literature*, W.H. Allen & Co., London, pp.169, 174; Danvers, Frederick Charles et. al. 1819, *Memorials of Old Haileybury College*, Archibald Constable & Co., Westminster. Once sponsored by a director, an applicant was required to pass an entrance examination before entering Haileybury. Thoby entered the College in 1807, aged 15, and Augustus in 1819, aged 16. Thoby completed one year at Haileybury and finished his training at Fort William College near Calcutta. By the time Augustus joined the Company, training of recruits had been centralised at Haileybury.
27 Thoby Prinsep was one of the first students at Haileybury, and was transferred to Fort William after one year. He was amongst the last group of recruits to attend Fort William.
28 Ambirajan, S. 1978, *Classical Political Economy and British Policy in India*, Cambridge University Press, Cambridge, p.16.
29 Quoted by Cohn 1987, *An Anthropologist Among the Historians*, p.540.

achieved high academic standards, but many graduated knowing little more about India than when they had entered, or more about Benthamite politics from one of the long-term lecturers, utilitarian William Empson, than about the style of government developed by Hastings, Cornwallis and Wellesley.[30] The enduring value of a Haileybury education was not so much the 'training in any direct sense for the job they had to carry out in India', but the formation of 'peer relations with a group with whom they were to spend their lives working' and 'a set of values relating them to their fellow students rather than to India'.[31] The close ties with fellow civil servants and the resultant group identity were aspects of Haileybury and Fort William College that Thoby Prinsep remembered fondly as 'the bright spot in my life and a source of happiness that made me almost cease to regret the exile from country and family in which I was compelled to pass my days'.[32] He was well-established in Calcutta amongst a coterie of similar background and education by the time William Prinsep arrived as a silk merchant in 1817, and Thoby's contacts immediately gave him entrance into 'the very best society'. 'Of course I was taken around to be introduced to all the merchants', William wrote in his memoirs, 'dining at most of their houses and finding here as well as among the Company's servants the same admiration of my brother's character, all which became an additional spur to my own exertions to win an equal regard'.[33] William set up house with Thoby, whose 'chums' from the East India Company, Henry Sargent, Charles Malony, William Fane and Holt Mackenzie, formed a most 'amusing and instructive' network of friends, and helped him establish his business interests in Calcutta.[34]

By 1825, seven Prinsep brothers were employed in the Bengal Presidency: Charles, Thoby, George, William and Thomas in Calcutta, James in Benares, and Augustus 'up the country'. As well as constituting a network of influence based on family, each of the brothers married into other East India Company families, and thus the interconnectedness of their kin networks widened. Thoby married Sara Pattle in 1832, joining a family associated with both British and French colonialism in India since 1765.[35] His father-in-law, James Pattle, was an East India Company judge with wide mercantile interests built up over two periods of residence in Calcutta, and his mother-in-law, Adeline de l'Etang, had been born in the French colony Pondicherry in 1793. The Pattles had eight daughters, most of whom also married men associated with India. Through marriage, Thoby gained a kin group that included men such as Colin McKenzie, a general in the East India Company army, Charles Hay Cameron, a lawyer who worked

---

30 Stokes, Eric 1959, *The English Utilitarians and India*, Oxford University Press, London, p.52.
31 Cohn 1987, *An Anthropologist Among the Historians*, p.544.
32 Prinsep, 'Three Generations', Part 2, pp.62–3.
33 'The Memoirs of William Prinsep', Volume 1, p.232.
34 Ibid., p.308.
35 Orange, Hugh 2002, 'The Chevalier de l'Etang and his Descendants the Pattles', edited by John Beaumont, Julia Margaret Cameron Research Group, Freshwater, Isle of Wight, pp.1–16.

with Thomas Macaulay as a member of the Governor-General's Law Commission during the 1830s and '40s, Dr John Jackson, a surgeon with the Bengal Medical Service, and Henry Bayley and John Dalrymple, senior Company civil servants.[36] In 1837, Charles Prinsep married Louisa White, whose father was a Major General in the East India Company army and whose brother, Henry, was a senior civil servant.[37] James Prinsep's wife, Harriet Aubert, also came from an East India Company military family, William and Thomas married two sisters, Mary and Lucy Campbell, and Augustus Elisabeth Ommaney, all of whom had East India Company connections.

William Prinsep's memoirs portray early-Nineteenth Century Calcutta as a British enclave, where a young Briton no longer need be separated from his identity. Family networks such as the Prinseps provided opportunities to work together, and to socialise widely, pursuing cultural activities from painting and amateur drama, to boating and lavish dinner parties. While they were in daily contact with Indians at work and in the home, they related principally with these family networks and other Britons within their clique. In this tight-knit enclave of Britishness, Indians were the governed 'others', with increasingly impermeable institutional and informal barriers against too great a level of familiarity with the rulers. Not only were Indians denied access to even the lowest levels of the civil service, British officers were discouraged from forming personal relationships with Indians. According to James Prinsep, this had the effect of preventing 'the natives from abusing or presuming upon their intimacy, which is in some degree necessary with those who administer the country, but keeps them in ignorance of those they govern'.[38] To William Prinsep, Calcutta was a British domain, peopled by civil servants, military officers, and merchants such as himself and his narrow cohort of colleagues. Indians are incidental in the colonising project, always present but background to what is a British story.

The Baboo suggests a more complex array of relationships than those simply between the commanders and the commanded, in which the Indian characters exercise considerable control over their interactions with the British, inhabiting a world little known or understood by the rulers. The Baboo, Brijmohun Bomijee, wields power through financial influence, one that has the potential to destroy the careers of influential members of the colonial establishment. He knows and understands the complexity of the markets and streets, which are beyond the reach of the British rulers. Every day he feigns submission, yet he possesses the power to dominate his British masters and, if he wishes, to destroy them.[39]

---

36   Ibid., p.22.
37   Prinsep, 'De Principe', Volume 1, pp.53–5.
38   Prinsep, Amelia Rebecca (Emily), 'Chapter One: John Prinsep and James Prinsep', SLWA Acc. 1972, undated letter, James Prinsep to his sister Emily, SLWA MN 773 Acc. 1972 p.48.
39   Prinsep, *The Baboo*, Volume 1, p.120.

Governing the others

Thoby, William and Augustus Prinsep believed that the colonising venture was bound to an imperative for the British to create an enclave of their own in India, a place predominantly British, bound by familiar social and governmental institutions, whose boundaries were known and understood. Rarely did they question the British right to rule. Its rationale as a vehicle by which Indians might be rescued from the despotism of the Mughals, the rule of law restored to protect Indian masses from the demands of degenerate priests and princes, was justification enough for the British presence. In the words of historian Eric Stokes, they were 'inheritors rather than innovators … the revivers of a decayed system and not the vanguard of a new'.[40] The 1774 *India Act* and subsequent reforms of East India Company government during the administrations of Warren Hastings (1773–1784), Charles Cornwallis (1786–1793) and Richard Wellesley (1797–1805) focussed on regularising and formalising governmental systems in India, the creation of a professional civil service, modelled on a 'Whig-style' separation of executive, legislative and judicial functions, and the imposition of the 'rule of law' to sanctify private ownership of property and guide the functions of government in India.[41]

By the 1820s, the image of the 'plundering nabob' appeared well in the past. No longer were East India Company operatives assumed to be avaricious and immoral, 'rich as Croesus and hungry for power', a popular imagery associated with the Eighteenth-Century Governors, Robert Clive and Warren Hastings, which reached its zenith during the long trial of the latter after 1788.[42] As Wellesley had told the Court of Directors in 1812, the East India Company was compelled to dispense 'wise and well regulated government … to every class and description of our subjects, the permanent benefits of secure property, protected life, undisturbed order, and inviolate religion'.[43] Orientalist notions of government valued the capacity to communicate with Indians and learn about Indian culture, religions, governance and history in order to win over opinion to the benefits of British colonial rule. But within the broad consensus of this orientalist framework, there were contentious issues of policy, particularly around relationships with the elites of the pre-British era. Issues of land tenure and revenue collection had proved intractable since the period of Warren Hastings. The 1793 'permanent settlement' agreement between the Company and Bengali landowners (zamindars) overturned the system of land taxation adopted after the Battle of Plassey in 1757, under which the powers of

---

40 Stokes 1959, *The English Utilitarians and India*, p.1.
41 Metcalf, Thomas R. 1994, *Ideologies of the Raj*, Cambridge University Press, Cambridge, p.18.
42 Nechtman, Tillman 2010, *Nabobs: Empire and identity in Eighteenth Century Britain*, Cambridge University Press, Cambridge, p.11.
43 Wellesley 1812, *Letter from the Marquis Wellesley*, p.28.

zamindars to collect revenue from the peasantry (ryots) had been abandoned in favour of a system of direct land taxation. This system had contributed to the allegedly corrupt extraction of wealth by Company officials and their agents ('rent-farmers'), which had caused much controversy in Britain during Clive's administration. Furthermore, the burden of taxation had led ryots to abandon their lands, which had contributed to severe famines throughout Bengal in 1769 and 1770. Cornwallis's permanent settlement in some ways represented a return to the Mughal system of land ownership by reinstating zamindars as the point of revenue collection, but departed from the older system by instituting a fixed rate of taxation to be collected at pre-determined intervals, from which no remissions were permitted for reasons of drought or flood.[44]

Permanent settlement was a matter which particularly inflamed the passions of John Prinsep. Returning from India in 1788 with a fortune of 40,000 pounds, he sought to promote his political aspirations by publishing a series of pamphlets, one of which attacked Cornwallis's land policies under the pseudonym 'Gurreeb Doss', Hindustani for 'servant of the poor'.[45] He argued that the Company should restore the 'mocurrery' system of traditional land tenure that he believed had provided protection for the ryots. It was incumbent on the government to find ways of 'meliorating the condition, and establishing the rights of that useful and blameless race of men, the native cultivators of land in India', 'occupiers of the soil from time immemorial'.[46] By allowing zamindars a 'permanent tenure over the whole country … a great and formidable barrier will be established between the government and the people; a brazen shield to cover oppression'.[47] Such views echoed the sentiments of the English Romantic movement by seeking to 'take the peasant in all his simplicity, to secure him in the possession of his land, to rule him with a paternal and simple government, and so avoid all the artificialities of a sophisticated European form of rule'.[48]

The parameters of the debate had changed little in the Calcutta of *The Baboo* 30 years or so after John Prinsep left India. Augustus Prinsep has his British characters debate the respective merits of government through the pre-existing elites of princes, brahmans and zamindars backed by British military might, or by winning the hearts and minds of the people to the liberalism and tolerance of the new regime and abandoning the prior rulers. Lackington, 'a gentleman holding a high station in the government', argues that, 'though the Englishman's policy is cold, his heart [must be] warm'. To him, the British must restore the

---

44   Islam, Sirajul 1979, *The Permanent Settlement in Bengal: A study of its operation, 1790–1819*, Bangla Academy, Dacca, pp.18–22.
45   Prinsep, John 1792, *Strictures and Observations on the Mocurrery System of Landed Property in Bengal Originally Written for the Morning Chronicle, Under the Signature of Gurreeb Doss, With Replies*, J. Debrett, London.
46   Ibid., pp.vii, 7.
47   Ibid., p.76.
48   Stokes 1959, *The English Utilitarians and India*, p.13.

autonomy of the toiling ryots, the 'original population ... whose very existence seems connected to the soil, from which their race has never been separated'. 'We must of our edifice', he asserts, 'make a place of shelter and acknowledged benefit to the multitude; we must make it their interest to support it; we must bring them not only to admire, but to value it.'[49] The prospect of accommodating the elites, as Cornwallis and his successors had sought through permanent settlement, was doomed to failure. Already resentful at their loss of power and prestige, it was inevitable that they would grasp any opportunity to overthrow British rule:

> They are members, sons, or descendants of the old families who carried arms against us in our wars; who have lost all their glory, and importance, by our triumphs, and whose recollections of the splendours of their former career, will never suffer their passion to be interested in a Furingee dominion. I believe that we cannot make ourselves popular with the shadows of Mohummedan or Hindoo aristocracy, and rather than nurse such serpents in the bosom of our empire, I would bruise their heads.[50]

A few years after Augustus Prinsep's death, the tolerance for 'party opinions' portrayed in the novel descended into open hostility as, to use Thoby Prinsep's words, 'younger men were appointed to fill vacancies who had little pretensions to oriental scholarship'.[51] A product of the Wellesley era reforms to the civil service, Thoby's education and career cast him as an archetypal orientalist Indian civil servant of the early-Nineteenth Century. Emerging from Fort William College fluent in Persian and Arabic, he steadily ascended the senior ranks in Bengal. His first appointment as Assistant Secretary to the Governor-General the Marquess of Hastings allowed him to travel throughout the Presidency, to Nepal, Oudh, the North West Province and Mahratta. By 1820, he was head of the Persian Department, and by 1826 head of the Territorial Department. In 1834 he was appointed by seniority to the post of Chief Secretary. This position placed him in the role of supervising the political and diplomatic operations of the Bengal Government, which extended throughout north-east India and included the principalities of allied Indian states and the neighbouring kingdom of Burma. In his memoirs, he reports good relationships with most of the Governors-General he served. He particularly admired Francis Rawdon-Hastings, with whom he worked closely during his first years of service.[52] In Thoby's view, the Marquess had presided over

---

49 Prinsep 1834, *The Baboo,* Volume 1, pp.73, 121.
50 Ibid., Volume 1, p.74.
51 Prinsep, 'Three Generations', Part 2, p.176.
52 Prinsep, Henry T. 1825 (1972) *History of the Political and Military Transactions in India during the Administration of the Marquess of Hastings 1813–1823,* Volume 1, Irish University Press, Shannon, Ireland.

a glorious administration that had nearly doubled the Revenue and the territories of the East India Company ... Everywhere British Residents controlled the local Administration in order to secure a government having for its object the peoples' good.[53]

When William Bentinck arrived to take up the role of Governor-General in 1828, however, Thoby was ill-prepared for service under one with an entirely different approach from that of his predecessors. Never before had he been required to work with 'a character so deeply imbued with the love of change for change's sake', one who 'showed a desire to go everywhere and see everything with his own eyes ... who had such a love of work, and such an incessant desire to meddle with everything, small or great'.[54] The new Governor-General began to make long-term civil servants such as Thoby uneasy. 'We acted then on the true conservative principle of providing a remedy for every evil or defect that was shown to exist, but were careful that our remedy should not go beyond the disease', he reflected in his memoirs. With Bentinck, the 'principle now adopted ... was to consider every defect established to be reason for abandoning the entire system and trying a new one'.[55]

The appointment of Thomas Macaulay, one of the foremost voices of 'trenchant, generous empirical liberalism', as Law Member of the Governor-General's Supreme Council in 1834 compounded Thoby's misery and was to bring the 'most trying' period of his Indian career.[56] As a member of the House of Commons before coming to India, Macaulay had argued, in debates over the renewal of the East India Company's charter in 1833, that the British goal should not only be to train Indians to fill administrative positions, but to 'educate [them] into a capacity for better government, that having become instructed in European knowledge, they may, in some future age, demand European institutions'.[57] The subsequent *Charter Act* of 1833 owed much to Macaulay, who, in Catherine Hall's words, 'explained why Europeans were suited to representative government, while Indians, effeminate and fit only for conquest, must be subject to benevolent despotism'.[58] The Act reformed the Governor-General's Supreme Council, allowing the appointment of a Crown nominee to serve in an advisory capacity, and this position was offered to Macaulay at a substantial salary. Arriving in India in 1834, Macaulay was appointed to chair the General Committee on Public Instruction, on which Thoby and James Prinsep also

---

53 Prinsep, 'Three Generations', Part 2, p.99.
54 Ibid., pp.131–3.
55 Ibid., p.131.
56 Stokes 1959, *The English Utilitarians and India*, p.xiv; Prinsep, 'Three Generations', Part 2, p.189.
57 Macaulay, quoted by Zastoupil, Lynn and Martin Moir (eds) 1999, *The Great Indian Education Debate: Documents relating to the orientalist–Anglicist controversy, 1781–1843*, Curzon Press, Richmond, Surrey, p.25.
58 Hall, Catherine 2005, 'Writing Histories of Difference: New histories of nation and empire', The Allan Martin Lecture, Research School of Social Sciences, The Australian National University, Canberra, p.21.

served, and thus the forum was set for a controversy which manifested the differences between the orientalists and the Anglicists and marked the start of a fundamental reorientation in Indian government.

The Committee's support of the Madrassa in Calcutta and the Sanskrit College in Benares was, Thoby argued, 'designed to promote the knowledge of the law, literature and religion of the Mahommedans and Hindoos'.[59] The principles governing their operation had long been an article of faith between the East India Company government, dominated by 'men distinguished for their attainments in oriental literature ... [who] naturally maintained the system of education which they found established by the Government', and important Indian elites. But as membership of the Committee changed over time, there arose

> acute differences of opinion on the degree of support that should be given to existing Oriental colleges ... One party, known as orientalists, was for retaining the system ... The other party, the Anglicists, held that much of the money so expended would be better applied towards promoting English education.[60]

Macaulay sought to overturn years of orientalist policy on education, contending that public funds, rather than being applied to Indian languages, should instead support the introduction of the English language and a British education system. 'We have to educate a people who cannot at present be educated by means of their mother tongue', he wrote:

> We must teach them some foreign language. The claims of our own language it is hardly necessary to recapitulate ... In India, English is the language spoken by the ruling class. It is spoken by the higher class of natives at the seats of Government ... Whether we look at the intrinsic value of our literature or at the particular situation of this country we shall see ... that of all foreign tongues the English tongue is that which would be the most useful to our native subjects.[61]

Thoby Prinsep was infuriated, complaining that Macaulay had 'expressed contempt for all oriental literature and scornful intolerance of the religions professed by one hundred millions of our subjects in language that apparently defied contradiction or even criticism'.[62] There was 'a very hot argument between myself and Mr Macaulay', and a number of the Committee's orientalist members, including James Prinsep, resigned in protest at Bentinck's and Macaulay's determination to bypass its expertise and authority. Bentinck was

---

59 Prinsep, 'Three Generations', Part 2, p.173.
60 Ibid., pp.175–76.
61 Macaulay, Thomas Babington, 'Minute on Indian Education (1835)', in Barbara Harlow and Mia Carter (eds) 1999, *Imperialism and Orientalism: A documentary sourcebook*, Blackwell Publishers, Oxford, p.58.
62 Prinsep, 'Three Generations', Part 2, p.189.

unmoved and directed the cessation of government subsidies for the publication of orientalist literature and stipends for Indian students at the Madrassa and the Sanskrit College, that vacant teaching posts and secretarial posts at the two colleges not be filled, and that English language schools be established in the major towns of Bengal.

The proposals provoked controversy in Calcutta and Benares. Over the next three years, a series of petitions attracted support amongst Indian elites alleging betrayal by British authorities which had depended heavily on the literate classes since the time of Hastings.[63] Many Indians suspected that the British harboured a secret aim to undermine Indian religions and promote Christianity in order to achieve religious domination, a sensitive issue that had been exacerbated by the relaxation of residence requirements by evangelical missionaries in the 1833 charter renewal.[64] The reforms would also devalue Indian languages, as one of the petitions put it:

> Although independent in our natural wants we have become in many respects subservient to the English, and to the productions of their Country, and should we be made to depend on them with regard to our reading and writing also, we shall be rendered still more miserable.[65]

Thoby wrote a minute for Bentinck in which he rebutted each of Macaulay's arguments, but this was rejected by the Governor-General, who forwarded it to Macaulay for comment. It failed to sway him, although he admitted he 'may have committed a slight mistake or two as to details, and I may have occasionally used an epithet which might with advantage have been softened down'.[66] Thoby argued that funds allocated under the 1813 *Charter Act* were 'permanently and irrevocably appropriated' to 'native languages' and that the Government of India had no legal power to change the education provisions established by Parliament.[67] He warned of the risks of alienating Muslim opinion if funds were withdrawn from the Madrassa, claiming that the Anglicists had exaggerated the demand for English education and that the government was ill-equipped to implement its promise of providing English language schools throughout Bengal. He contended that the petitions demonstrated majority Indian support for orientalist policies, while Anglicist views were held only by a small number of British officials and very few Indians.[68] In his arguments, he found support in the metropole from Horace Hayman Wilson, by then back in England in the

---

63   Zastoupil and Moir 1999, *The Great Indian Education Debate*, p.42.
64   Ibid., p.31.
65   1838 Petition, quoted by Zastoupil and Moir 1999, *The Great Indian Education Debate*, p.42.
66   H.T. Prinsep, 'Note dated 15 February 1835, with comment by Thomas B. Macaulay', in Marriott, John and Bhaskar Mukhopadhyay (eds) 2006, *Britain in India, 1765–1905*, Volume 3: Education and Colonial Knowledge, Pickering and Chatto, London, p.10.
67   Marriot and Mukhopadhyay 2006, *Britain in India*, p.4.
68   Ibid.

position of Boden Professor of Sanskrit at Oxford. Wilson was associated with John Stuart Mill who, by 1836 had taken over the role of his ill father James with the East India Company.[69] Mill prepared an unsuccessful dispatch to the Board of Directors supporting the orientalist position, which he defended as 'the product of a long and on-going series of intellectual exchanges and cultural negotiations between Indians and British officials'.[70]

Macaulay's reforms stood, despite opposition in India and England. In 1839, Bentinck's successor, Lord Auckland, exasperated by Prinsep's and Macaulay's enmity and complaining that they 'butted at each other like bulls, blind to everything but their own joust of brains', engineered a compromise that restored the system of stipends to the Madrassa and the Sanskrit College.[71] While Thoby Prinsep saw this as a vindication of the orientalist position, the episode exposed the steady changes in Indian aspirations under the British and in British conceptions of their governmental role in India. Both the orientalists and the Anglicists claimed that their views on education reflected Indian aspirations. The former argued that support for Indian languages derived from South Asian traditions, under which governments were expected to make endowments to support social priorities. Continuation of this support was part of a compact between Indian elites and the British government to provide 'special measures to protect intellectual elites, the guardians of the national culture, from the ravages of the market place'.[72] Macaulay too drew on 'Indian opinion', in the person of influential intellectual Rammohan Roy, whose letters suggested to him that 'Indian public opinion was increasingly receptive to western ideas'.[73]

The desire by both Anglicists and orientalists to conciliate Indian public opinion shows that the arguments, for all their passions, differed little in their substance. Both sought to reconcile Indians to British domination, the former through manipulation of 'opinion', the latter through more heavy-handed approaches. The episode demonstrates the overriding power of the British in government, that 'while Indians participated in the making of imperial ideas and practices, it was the British who held the very important power of interpretation'.[74] Auckland's compromise was only the start of the diminution of Macaulay's ideals of English-language education in India. By the 1850s, a form of consensus about the utility of education in vernacular Indian languages, rather than English, had been reached. While the impact of the old orientalist-style notions declined with the retirement from service of officers such as Thoby

---

69 Zastoupil and Moir 1999, *The Great Indian Education Debate*, pp.45–6.
70 Ibid., p.47.
71 Broughton Papers, 'Letters from Lord Auckland to the President, 9 April 1837', India Office Records, British Library, F213/6, ff. 52 – 53; Prinsep, 'Three Generations', Part 2, p.245.
72 Zastoupil and Moir 1999, *The Great Indian Education Debate*, p.49.
73 Ibid., p.35.
74 Ibid., p.55.

Prinsep, echoes remained in the 'old orientalist dream of a rebirth of India through the merger of the European and Indian heritages ... that west and east might converge in ways beneficial to the people of India'.[75]

Such were the ideological elements of the debate. At another level, the conflict between Thoby Prinsep and Macaulay illustrates the changing complexion of British imperialism consistent both with generational changes in the civil service and in metropolitan attitudes to India and how it should be ruled. While the Indian experiences of new imperialists such as Macaulay confirmed a sense of overwhelming British superiority, men such as Thoby Prinsep claimed to love India, Indian culture and the Indian people, his regard for 'all things Indian' cultivated through his education and years in India driving his sense of the British mission in India.[76] But he too longed for England and looked forward to 'the time to arrive when I might return and take a permanent place in that society'.[77] Despite his long experience working and living in close proximity to Indians, by the time he left India in 1843 he was more certain than ever that British 'superiority of intelligence, and ... high-minded, disinterested, and earnest action for the public good' had marked out his country for imperial pre-eminence, just as he believed that innate differences would forever keep them apart.[78]

Scholarliness and saintliness

To his brothers, James Prinsep was a figure of admiration and pride. His brief but shining life was an inspiration to them all. William recalled that James 'carried everything he did to ... perfection, whether in writing, drawing, music or invention of any kind. In fact throughout life he excelled in everything he undertook', and was always more interested in science than the pursuit of money and riches.[79] His sister, Emily Prinsep, believed that James was unusual in that 'nothing imparted to him had been forgotten, nor had any opportunity of learning been thrown away'.[80] More recently, he has been placed alongside doyens of orientalist thought, men such as William Jones, H.H. Wilson and H.T. Colebrooke, as one who helped rescue India from 'amnesia' about its past, and who, rather than acting as an agent of British power and domination, was motivated by a love of India and a pure commitment to orientalist research.[81]

---

75 Ibid., p.64.
76 Hall 2005, 'Writing Histories of Difference', p.23.
77 Prinsep, 'Three Generations', Part 2, p.116.
78 Prinsep, Henry T. 1853, *The India Question in 1853*, W.H. Allen & Co., London, p.73.
79 'The Memoirs of William Prinsep', Volume 1, p.126.
80 Prinsep, 'Chapter One', p.20.
81 O.P. Kejariwal (1988, *The Asiatic Society of Bengal and the Discovery of India's Past*, Oxford University Press, New Delhi) and Charles Allen (2002, *The Search for the Buddha: The men who discovered India's lost religion*, Carrol and Graf, New York) have been prominent in seeking to resurrect the reputations of the British Indian orientalists from the generally critical analyses of orientalist discourse.

To Bernard Cohn, James Prinsep was one of a very small number of British men in India prepared to 'break out of the typical mould' who, while living in Benares, was prepared to 'wander daily through the town or mix ex-officially in its affairs'.[82]

Arriving in India in 1819 as Assistant Assay Master at the Company mint, James's first few months in Calcutta reunited him with brothers Thoby and William, both already well-established in the city. To William, the presence of his younger brother was delightful:

> I had the full enjoyment of his sweet fellowship in flute duets, singing, drawing &c &c. He used to give us charming chemical lectures in Thoby's house of an evening to the delight of an admiring audience and to the wild astonishment of the native servants whom he used occasionally to electrify in a string hand to hand, when each man who felt the shock would abuse his neighbour for striking him.[83]

Transferred to Benares, James Prinsep was introduced to the city by his superior, Horace Hayman Wilson, who was to have a deep influence on his Indian career. Wilson introduced him to 'quite a different set of men, the Pundits, Moonshees, and Baboos of the city, with whom he, being a Sanskrit scholar, had continual intercourse'.[84] 'I had mazurs (presents) of sugar, country almonds, and fruits, presented ten times a day', he wrote to Emily in England, 'and the Pundits put chaplets of flowers around my neck by dozens':

> Aye! And congratulatory odes were rehearsed in Sanskrit in honour of my arrival, calling me a rising son, a blushing rose, and my face broad full moon (insulting this, was it not?) These natives I am glad to find are not kept away by my knowing so little of the language; each man has already paid me half a dozen visits, and they have shamed me into studying the languages forthwith, for which purpose a Moonshee has already been put upon my establishment, and I begin to read the Devanagri fluently.[85]

James became involved in an extraordinary range of activities in addition to his employment. As a member of the Committee on Local Improvement, an affiliation of leading Indian and British citizens of Benares, he organised a census which included a detailed map of every building and dwelling in the city, engaged in massive engineering works such as the draining of the pools and swamps behind the city, built a bazaar for the citizens and a stone bridge over the

---

82 Cohn 1987, *An Anthropologist Among the Historians*, p.444.
83 'The Memoirs of William Prinsep', Volume 1, p.313.
84 Prinsep, 'Chapter One', p.47.
85 Ibid.

River Karamnasa, and dismantled and rebuilt the mosque of Aurangzeb.[86] His energy and creativity earned him the respect of the city's population, as William Prinsep recalled:

> I heard the native gentlemen of the city speak of him with almost adoration for all he had done and was doing for them, and to their great astonishment (for I dare say it was the only instance known to them of any European gentleman devoting his time and talents for their benefit) all for love! He took no reward, and made not a rupee of profit from any of the large sums they gave him to lay out upon important works.[87]

Transferred to Calcutta in 1830, James again took on major engineering works, and finished the project started by his recently deceased brother Thomas, to construct canals and a series of locks to divert the rivers of the Ganges delta around Calcutta. In 1835, as part of his official duties, he introduced a uniform coinage known as the Company Rupee, designing the die from which the coinage was cast. In 1832, he was elected secretary of the Bengal Asiatick Society (which he reformed into the 'Asiatic Society of Bengal'), and in 1833 he succeeded Wilson as editor of its monthly periodical *Gleanings,* which he later renamed the *Journal of the Asiatic Society of Bengal*. In his position as Secretary of the Society, he focussed his energies on philological and numismatic studies, aimed chiefly at interpreting the ancient Sanskrit and Delhi No. 1 scripts, which eventually unveiled evidence of the existence of the Buddhist emperor, Asoka (a figure previously considered to be semi-mythical).[88]

James Prinsep's tenure as editor of the journal brought a golden period of research activity and international repute to the Society, attested to by the number and range of contributions over the period, all of which he edited and prepared for publication.[89] His first edition, in January 1832, recorded the Society's intellectual debt to Sir William Jones:

> It will flourish if naturalists, chemists, antiquaries, philologers, and men of science, in different parts of Asia, will commit their observations to writing, and send them to the Asiatic Society at Calcutta; it will languish if such communications shall be long intermitted; and it will die away, if they shall entirely cease.[90]

---

86   Cohn 1987, *An Anthropologist Among the Historians*, p.444.
87   'The Memoirs of William Prinsep', Volume 2, pp. 83–4.
88   Two volumes of his works were published by Edward Thomas (ed.) 1858, *Essays on Indian Antiquities, Historic, Numismatic, and Palaeographic, of the late James Prinsep, FRS, to Which are Added his Useful Tables*, 2 Volumes, John Murray, London.
89   *Journal of the Asiatic Society of Bengal*, Volume 7, 1838, Part 2, Baptist Mission Press, Circular Road, Calcutta, p.916.
90   Ibid., Volume 1, January 1832, frontispiece.

James Prinsep appealed to members to submit articles on any subject, again invoking Jones' aspirations for the Society: 'the bounds of its investigation will be the geographical limits of Asia; and within these limits its inquiries will be extended to whatever is performed by men or produced by nature'.[91] He paid tribute to British men throughout India whose interests motivated their desire to explore and investigate, reminding them that they were following the examples of those such as Jones, Wilson and Nepal-based Hungarian linguist, Alexander Csoma de Körös: 'All may ... feel sensible of the devotion, zeal, and perseverance which are necessary to lead a man, alone and unpaid, into a distant and wild country, to learn its language and study its people at the fountain head.'[92] At the same time, he was conscious of the political implications of the Society's role, and recognised that contributions on minerals and mining practices 'must possess value in the eyes of a government'.[93] He suggested that governmental support for the work of the Society was justified, not only for the translation and publication of 'oriental' texts, but to help with the costs of preparing and distributing the journal.

Between 1832 and 1838, James Prinsep produced monthly editions of the journal and, as Secretary of the Society, published special editions of the *Asiatick Researches* on Indian geography, geology, zoology and anthropology. An array of topics attracted his attention: translations of classical and vernacular religious tracts, literature and poetry, numismatics, epigraphy, geology, botany, astronomy, climatology, geography, mathematics and trigonometry, ethnography and archaeology.[94] Contributions came from British men throughout India, including Wilson and amateur ethnographers B.H. Hodgson and J.S. Lushington, his brothers George and Thoby Prinsep, and travel accounts from men such as Lieutenant Alexander Burnes, who, in 1833, entered the city of Bokhára in disguise and later published a serialised account in the journal.[95]

Throughout 1835, James Prinsep corresponded with other societies in Europe to continue the task of translation and, by the beginning of 1836, was confident that alliances with the Society of Paris and the Royal Asiatic Society of London would speed the completion of an unfinished 'Bibliotheca Asiatica' of oriental literature. The status of the journal was enhanced by the excitement surrounding the research Prinsep and his circle was involved in, including his successful efforts to unravel the Brahmi script and interpret the Asokan Edicts, which he reported in a series of articles between 1835 and 1838. Historian Om Prakesh Kejariwal

---

91 Ibid., p.x.
92 Ibid., p.xi.
93 Ibid., Volume 2, January 1833, p.ix.
94 Ibid., Volume 1, January to December 1834.
95 Ibid., Volume 2, May 1833, p.224. Burnes published his account in 1834 as *Travels into Bokhara: Being an account of a journey from India to Cabool, Tartary and Persia; Also, narrative of a voyage on the Indus from the sea to Lahore*, 3 Volumes, John Murray, London.

has emphasised James Prinsep's achievement in deciphering the Brahmi script, a task demanding 'lightening intuition' and the capacity, as Charles Allen puts it, for 'absorbing, analysing, comparing and matching multiple inputs in the form of groups and symbols—the essential qualifications of a code breaker—as well as an exceptional capacity for sustained concentration'.[96] These abilities allowed the interpretation of 'one inscription after another', and revealed the wealth of historical material on the previously semi-mythical Asoka.[97]

Unfortunately for James Prinsep, the physical demands of this exacting work exhausted him and, in 1838, he was forced to relinquish his role as Secretary and Editor of the journal. 'It is with great reluctance and regret', he wrote in his resignation letter, 'that I thus separate myself from a body, with whom I have been associated in labours of much interest and utility, whose favour has encouraged my zeal, and through whose credit and reputation in the world, I have obtained the means of making generally known my own humble efforts in the cause of science, and my not unsuccessful endeavours to explore the antiquities of the country, to whose service we are devoted'.[98] Returning to England, he was diagnosed with 'a bilious affection, but the symptoms increased rapidly and the disease was traced to an affection of the brain'.[99] At least he was to die 'at home' and not left to lie unforgotten in an Indian graveyard, as he had imagined in a verse to his sister Emily in 1823:

> Civil and military feuds here slumber
>
> Doctors and patients, children without number
>
> Here death indulging with no triumphant warning
>
> Kills overnight, for burial next morning!
>
> While memory outlasts grief one hour or half
>
> To fill the fat appointments on the staff
>
> The tomb none knows, the pithless verse none sees
>
> But Chunar Stonecutters and joint trustees![100]

James Prinsep was a talented and capable man with an unusual capacity for work and scholarship. His many writings attest to an enjoyment of research

---

96 Kejariwal 1988, *The Asiatic Society of Bengal and the Discovery of India's Past*, p.209; Allen 2002, *The Search for the Buddha*, p.150.
97 Kejariwal 1988, *The Asiatic Society of Bengal and the Discovery of India's Past*, p.215.
98 *Journal of the Asiatic Society of Bengal*, Volume 7, Part 2, July 1838, p.916.
99 H. Thoby Prinsep, 'Memoir of the Author' in *Essays on Indian Antiquities*, Volume 1, p.xiv.
100 James Prinsep to Emily Prinsep, Benares, 21 September 1823, Caroline Simpson Library and Research Collection, Historic Homes Trust of New South Wales.

as his principle motivation, of one not overly interested in politics and more engaged in the pursuit of 'a body of scientific discoveries about Indian reality, a set of "factualised" statements detached epistemologically from colonial politics'.[101] Throughout his works, there is a recognition that scientific research would contribute to a consolidation of British interests in India, and that it was due to British knowledge, science and motivation that Indians were to be provided the opportunity to 'reclaim their heritage'. The producers of this heritage were British men who, by the 1830s, were located and travelled throughout the country and who often had the time and interest to pursue studies into areas of interest.

James Prinsep's other major pastime as artist and illustrator gave him scope to represent India visually and through various mediums. His *Views of Benares*, published in 1833, comprises an extraordinarily detailed visual map of the city, together with census information on the citizens, while his watercolours present another perspective on the life of the city, as the people go about their religious and family lives and the business of making a living. He was interested particularly in the facial details of his subjects. As he explained in a letter to his sister Emily in 1823, he pursued the desire to 'make use of real persons and scenes' and 'acquire the knack of hitting off a face from memory': 'my morning loungers insist on assigning a name to every face I draw; and I lose credit if they don't guess them right'.[102] This letter records his determination to draw and paint the scenes of life in India with the assistance of his brothers William and Thomas, to record even the trivial details, the embarrassing moments and the ridiculous. James gives Emily a detailed and humorous commentary on each of the images in the now missing album of paintings and drawings he had assembled to illustrate his experiences in India. Without the accompanying images, we can only imagine the scenes he describes, such as the meeting of the Benares Local Improvement Committee, showing all the British and Indian characters 'so actively zealous in the midst of the hot winds':

> We incorporated ourselves without a charter, I dubbed myself secretary without an election, Presidents and vice Presidents we esteem useless, publicity we do not court, funds we have none, meetings seldom. Yet in Chemistry, Mineralogy, Astronomy, Botany, Sanskrit and Gastronomy, we will yield to no society in India either as to our instruments, collections and exertions.[103]

James Prinsep's positions with the Benares and Calcutta mints placed him in a different position from the writers, magistrates and collectors in the mainstream

---

101 Breckenridge, Carol A. and Peter van de Veer (eds) 1993, *Orientalism and the Postcolonial Predicament: Perspectives on South Asia*, University of Philadelphia Press, Philadelphia, p.8.
102 James Prinsep to Sophia Prinsep, Benares, 21 September 1823.
103 Ibid.

civil service administration. He recognised that his official position in the mint permitted relationships with Indians, free from the hauteur he believed kept the civil servant 'in ignorance of those they govern'.[104] Advancement in his career as an assayer was not dependent on proficiency in Indian languages, orientalist studies or political economy, and thus his scholarly interests and community involvement seem to have been a matter of choice. Certainly, his family and peers believed that James Prinsep was unusual amongst the British in his closeness to Indians. For Henry Prinsep, James Prinsep—the uncle he had never known—provided an example of 'selfless' British service to colonised peoples, one of those he believed he should emulate in his own colonial career. Henry's journey to India in 1870 brought him face to face with James Prinsep's legacy: the ghat erected in his honour on the banks of the Hooghly, the bust in the Asiatic Society headquarters, the reverence with which his name was mentioned by those who had known him in Calcutta, his paintings illustrating the vibrancy and colour of Indian street life.[105] To the Prinsep family, James represented a pinnacle of colonial achievement, the epitome of British altruism and imageries of the modernising and civilising imperial mission.

A place to make a fortune

The British characters in *The Baboo* inhabit a world of opulence, their houses the size of palaces, furnished with 'ottomans and couches of light blue satin, heavy chandeliers and girandoles, musical instruments and elegant fancy tables', and attended by armies of servants who look after their employers' every need.[106] William Prinsep's paintings show the luxuries of Prinsep family life in Calcutta. His watercolour of his brother Charles's Calcutta house, Belvedere, depicts a mansion of massive proportions that, in the words of Augustus' daughter Augusta Becher, 'he never ceased adding to'. Another depicts a family gathering at Belvedere and the entertainment of Indian musicians in a cavernous, pillared hall.[107] A drawing, 'Our House, Garden Reach, Looking West', shows a man, probably William, in the act of leaving for work, farewelling his wife as he boards the ferry for his office in Calcutta. In *The Baboo,* Augustus Prinsep's interests do not extend to the entrepreneurial activities of the colonisers. His characters, while living well, are burdened by disastrous levels of debt at the hands of the unscrupulous Baboo and, moreover, are mostly portrayed as engaged in the project of delivering fair and consistent British government to the colonised Indians. Absent in the story are the nabobs of his father's era,

---

104   Prinsep, 'Chapter One', p.48.
105   Prinsep, 'Diaries', 4–28 May 1870.
106   Prinsep 1834, *The Baboo,* Volume 1, p.19.
107   Becher, Augusta 1930, *Personal Reminiscences of Augusta Becher, 1830–1888,* edited by H.G. Rawlinson, Constable and Co., London , p.112.

the merchants and entrepreneurs such as his brothers William and Charles, but the money-making activities of his contemporaries were familiar to Augustus. Political economy was the heart of the Empire, the colonies 'not coveted just for the love of possession, nor ... desired as an outlet for the surplus population. Their functions were to supply certain goods and receive certain other goods ... [as] subordinate spheres of development for the mother country.'[108] Implicit in the training of civil servants was a struggle between the demands of rampant capitalism and the requirements of a rule of law designed partly to protect native interests 'wherever they seemed to conflict'.[109]

Nonetheless, for Eighteenth-Century Britons, a career in India was often characterised as a sure way to a fortune.[110] John Prinsep certainly went to India with the firm intention of making as much money as he could. Immediately after his arrival in Calcutta as a cadet in April 1770, he left the army to go into private business as an indigo planter, copper miner and chintz manufacturer. The Company attempted to deport him in 1773 but, by that time, as his daughter Emily recalled, he had accumulated 'sufficient interest with the Council to procure that his Memorial petitioning for leave to remain in India' should be granted and the deportation order 'sent home instead'. He became a 'resident by sufferance' and was able to amass his fortune in the relatively short period of 17 years.[111] The potential of India for such a man, born into a lowly Midlands family but with considerable energy, imagination and enthusiasm, appealed immensely: 'I thought myself suddenly metamorphosed into a great man', he wrote in his journal, fragments of which are preserved in the memoirs of his grandson, Sir Henry Thoby Prinsep.[112] In a short family biography, Om Prakesh Kejariwal found John Prinsep, although possessed of a 'very fertile and innovative mind', an 'unscrupulous businessman who exploited every means to make big money'. His practice was to enter lucrative supply contracts through his networks with influential officers in the government of Warren Hastings, negotiate substantial upfront payments, and then declare his inability to fulfil his commitments, surrender or cancel the contract 'with still more handsome compensation'.[113]

John Prinsep's stay in India enabled him to return to England well set up to pursue a metropolitan career in business and with enough capital to seek political office. His return coincided with the start of the Parliamentary trial of Warren Hastings in February 1788, after Hastings' impeachment on charges of poor military judgement, undue patronage and maladministration during his 13

---

108   Porter, Bernard 1983, *Britain, Empire and the World, 1850–1982: Delusions of grandeur*, George Allen & Unwin, London, p.26.
109   Ibid., p.46.
110   Cohn 1987, *An Anthropologist Among the Historians*, pp.425–34.
111   Prinsep, 'Chapter One', pp.5–9.
112   Prinsep, 'Three Generations', Part 1, p.4.
113   Kejariwal, O.P. 1993, 'The Prinseps of India: A personal quest', in *The Indian Archives*, Volume 42, No. 1–2, January–December, p.12.

years as Governor-General of India, a time when the image of the Indian 'nabob' had never been so tarnished in metropolitan England. In his book *Nabobs*, Tillman Nechtman describes the pervasive trope of the nabob as 'rapacious and power-hungry', men 'who had extorted a criminal fortune from South Asia and hoped to translate it into power and prestige in the metropolitan world'.[114] John Prinsep pursued the task of exploiting his wealth and network of contacts in London with his customary energy. His involvement with the East India Company and marriage into another large Calcutta family, the Auriols, provided him the means to continue and expand his involvement with Indian trade and to establish trading ventures in other spheres of empire, such as South Africa, Mauritius and Australia. Through his company, Prinsep, Saunders and Co., he acted as an agent for a variety of commercial concerns with interests throughout the Empire, and maintained an extensive fleet of transport vessels. He invested in other metropolitan and imperial ventures, including the Battersea Bridge, a profitable ship insurance company, the British Fire Office, and, from 1795, as a 'director and contributor' of the Sierra Leone Company with William Wilberforce and Zachary Macaulay.[115] His election to the House of Commons as an independent Member for Queensborough in 1802 provided a forum for Prinsep to speak against the East India Company monopoly over Indian and Chinese trade, arguing that 'the interests of trade and government in one body were inconsistent and conflicting and must result in distracting the development of the resources and prosperity of that country'.[116] As such, he continued a tradition of opposition to the monopoly that had begun with Edmund Burke in the 1780s, and which eventually brought about the diminution of the Company charter in 1813, well after he had lost his seat in parliament.

John Prinsep took up other issues in a series of pamphlets published in London between 1792 and 1823, mostly related to his contention that government should provide greater support for the development of industry in India. The Jamaican sugar trade, he argued, was entirely underwritten by the 'detestable traffick' in slave labour, whereas the Indian sugar trade could provide a more economical industry if the British were to adopt 'mild and liberal principles of government over the natives, who require only to be left unmolested in their customs and religious prejudices, and at liberty to pursue their hereditary employment, after the manner of their forefathers'.[117] Elsewhere he wrote that East India Company ships should be built in India and that company trade should be undertaken

---

114 Nechtman 2010, *Nabobs*, pp.14, 77.
115 Prinsep, 'Three Generations', Part 1, p.22; Thorne, R.G. 1986, *The House of Commons, 1790–1820*, Secker and Warburg, London, p.892; Prinsep, 'Chapter One', p.9.
116 Thorne 1986, *The House of Commons*, p.892; Prinsep, 'Three Generations', Part 1, p.20.
117 'The right of the West India merchants to a double monopoly of the sugar market of Great Britain, and the expedience of all monopolies examined', published in Prinsep, John 1800, *Tracts on Various Subjects, Chiefly Relating to East India Affairs*, Volume 1, J. Debrett, London, p.76.

through these Indian-built vessels.[118] However, apart from these fragments of his own writings and some memoirs of his children, little is known about his political activities. His business links with the anti-slavery lobby through the Sierra Leone Company hint at a complexity of political alliances and networks, but these are unfathomable from the extant historical portrait of his life. It is unclear, for example, whether he supported Wilberforce's parliamentary campaign to abolish the slave trade. He had in any case lost his seat in the Commons before it passed the Slave Trade Act in 1807. John Prinsep did not appear to have been associated with the church. His son William commented that religious instruction as a boy in the Prinsep household was 'of the most careless description, confined solely to morning prayers and weekly catechism', and thus a lasting association with Clapham sect members appears unlikely.[119] While he argued against the slavery-dependent sugar-economies of the West Indies, his principle concern was the economic advantage a slave economy gave West Indian sugar over the Indian product. Similarly, his support for the land rights of Indian peasantry suggests a mistrust of Indian elites and a suspicion that too great a reliance on their intermediary role would erect a 'great and formidable barrier' between the rulers and the peasantry. From the perspective of a merchant, the economic appeal of such simplicity would be obvious, for it opened the possibility of direct negotiations with the labouring colonised without the need for the additional costs and problems associated with the 'middle-men' zamindars.

John Prinsep's interests in commerce, mercantile activity and the opportunities presented by empire to exploit new markets appear to have been his principle motivation for a parliamentary career and his public advocacy. There were sound reasons to argue for a diminution of the East India Company charter from the perspective of governance and accountability, but for a businessman like John Prinsep, the removal of the company monopoly on Indian trade had clear commercial appeal. Similarly, his writing on the slave trade and Indian land tenure suggest a commercial imperative, and suggest that he was happy to utilise moral arguments to strengthen his case. What is clear about John Prinsep is the extent to which he influenced his sons and daughters in their perspectives on the British colonial venture. His was an energetic, assertive colonialism based on commerce and markets, and on direct engagement of the colonised others in the colonial venture. To his sons, their father steered them towards careers in India and imparted his energy and enthusiasm to an education that would equip them for the lucrative world of imperial business and trade.[120]

---

118   Prinsep, John 1823, *Suggestions on Freedom of Commerce and Navigation More Especially in Reference to the East India Trade*, James Ridgway, London.
119   'The Memoirs of William Prinsep', Volume 1, p.12.
120   Prinsep, 'Three Generations', Part 1, p.43; 'The Memoirs of William Prinsep', Volume 1, pp.111, 256.

William Prinsep went to India in 1817 to work with his brother-in-law George Haldimand's family silk company, carrying instructions to deal directly with 'native merchants' and thus circumvent the East India Company monopoly.[121] Within two years, at the invitation of the 'Prince of Merchants', John Palmer, he became a partner in the agency house Palmer and Company, the main business of which was to provide services normally undertaken by banks, including managing the funds of civil and military services, investing in Bengal markets, and remitting credits to London on behalf of its clients.[122] Throughout the 1820s, his income expanded rapidly along with his business interests. Although William thought himself a man of modest lifestyle, the size and expense of his household estate also increased. Soon after his arrival, he established his own 'small house', but was 'compelled to have no less than 12 servants, less than which was impossible to a respectable position in life'.[123] By 1837, he was able to afford a Garden Reach home, 'adjoining Kyd's dock which … I had converted into a most pleasant residence with a painting studio commanding the best views up and down the river'.[124]

For an independent merchant such as William Prinsep, the 'fat gains of Mammon' were accompanied by significant hazards. Palmer and Company was the first of the Calcutta agency houses to collapse in January 1830, causing him 'terrible distress' and 'shame' at the 'unwarrantable use we had made of other peoples' deposits with us'.[125] After a period of bankruptcy, however, his partnership with Dwarkanath Tagore in Carr Tagore and Co. helped him recover his business reputation and much of his wealth. By 1836, he and Tagore were planning new ventures: opium trading with China, tea cultivation in Assam and export to Britain, steam tugs, salt, and steam ferries. Describing William's business ideas as 'bold, grandiose and ingenious', economic historian Blair Kling suggests they sometimes failed because of unforeseen technical problems, and that his particular skills lay in his ability to initiate projects, secure government contracts, and negotiate 'the shoals of official red tape' through his family contacts in the East India Company.[126] Tagore was a member of 'the most open-minded, free-spirited, and venturesome of the great Calcutta families', a political philosopher who 'envisioned a future India that was westernized and industrialized and whose inhabitants enjoyed without discrimination the rights and liberties of Englishmen' but may have had cause to regret his association with the 'ingenious

---

121 'The Memoirs of William Prinsep', Volume 1, p.191.
122 Webster, Anthony 2007, *The Richest East India Merchant: The life and business of John Palmer of Calcutta 1767–1836*, The Boydell Press, Woodbridge, pp.44–64; Staples, A. C. 1989, 'Memoirs of William Prinsep: Calcutta years, 1817–1842', in *Indian Economic and Social History Review*, Volume 26, No. 2, p. 66.
123 'The Memoirs of William Prinsep', Volume 1, p.327.
124 Ibid., Volume 2, p.260.
125 Ibid., Volume 2, pp.95–96. See also Webster 2007, *The Richest East India Merchant*, p.111.
126 Kling, Blair B. 1976, *Partner in Empire: Dwarkanath Tagore and the age of enterprise in Eastern India*, University of California Press, London, p.148.

but reckless' William Prinsep.[127] For his part, William, while admiring Tagore's 'noble' example to 'other wealthy natives', never fully trusted his judgement.[128] He believed him 'rather a spoilt child in finance, largely supported by rich native friends who had great faith in his judgement and good luck. He was inclined to be free in the support of new adventures … and I had many serious forebodings'.[129] At the same time, Tagore's networks in the Bengal business community were of enormous commercial value, enabling the company's ships such as the opium clipper Water Witch to be quickly loaded and unloaded by 'his many friends in the Bazar'.[130]

It is through Henry's father, Charles Robert Prinsep, the last of the brothers to arrive in India (in 1824) and the last to leave (in 1855), that images of the Empire as a place to make a fortune find particular prominence in the Prinsep narrative. His commercial aspirations stretched well beyond India. He sought to exploit a web of imperial connections in his endeavours to invest in the economic potential of the Indian Ocean region, with the goal of establishing what he conceived as an Indian sphere of economic power and influence. His successful legal career made him a great deal of money, and he was constantly on the lookout for property investments and commercial ventures.

A barrister in India, according to Charles Prinsep's colleague at the Calcutta Bar, William Ritchie, was able to earn a 'handsome income … the fees are nearly three times as high as at home'.[131] This was to the detriment of both Briton and Indian according to contemporary commentator J.H. Stocqueler, who believed that British law, the 'dearest and worst of all law', had brought 'great loss and sorrow on the natives': 'No wonder lawyers return from this country rolling in wealth; their fees are enormous: if you ask a single question on any affair, you may lay down your gold mohr … and if he writes a letter of only three lines, 28 rupees'.[132] Charles Prinsep's wealth allowed him to develop trade schemes between India and the emerging Indian Ocean and Australian colonies of Singapore, Western Australia and Tasmania. The loss of the East India Company's monopoly in 1833 persuaded investors to diversify their holdings and business interests.[133]

In Singapore, Charles Prinsep established a nutmeg plantation and planned a harbour and dockyard, and in Western Australia and Tasmania studs to service the demands of the Bengal and Madras Presidencies for horses. In 1837, he

---

127 Ibid., pp. 5, 16, 82.
128 'The Memoirs of William Prinsep', Volume 2, p.269.
129 Ibid., pp.248–9.
130 Ibid., p.214.
131 Ritchie, Gerald 1920, *The Ritchies in India: Extracts from the correspondence of William Ritchie, 1817–1862; And personal reminiscences of Gerald Ritchie*, John Murray, London, pp.92–3.
132 Stocqueler, J.H. 1983, 'Social Life in Calcutta during the first half of the Nineteenth Century', in Nair, D. Thankappan (ed.), *British Social Life in Ancient Calcutta (1750–1850)*, Sanskrit Pustak Bhandar, Calcutta, p.86.
133 Staples, A.C. 1955, 'The Prinsep Estate in Western Australia', in *Early Days*, Volume 5, Part 1, p.17.

and other British and Indian investors such as Dwarkanath Tagore, shipping magnate and later East India Company chairman Ross Donnelly Mangles, Edward Stirling (brother of the first West Australian Governor Sir James Stirling) and William Prinsep established an 'Australian Association of Bengal' as a vehicle for transferring investments from India to Australia and to 'create local investment in colonial enterprises making use of new technology such as steam power'.[134] Another of his proposals was to transport poor white and mixed race children from Calcutta to Tasmania as a supply of labour, which he submitted to Governor-General Bentinck in 1828.[135] The scheme, he argued, would benefit not only the children, but the colonising project in both countries, and the overall strength of the Empire. Removal from India would relieve the children of 'a languid existence commencing in dependence and ending in mendicity' and, at the same time, enhance British prestige in India by removing a population 'destitute alike of intelligence, of energy and of attachment to the land of their forefathers' which weakened 'the power of opinion without a proportionate gain of physical force'. The resultant boost to the labouring population of Australian colonies would furthermore benefit India by creating 'a source of future stability, a new market for its produce, and a bulwark of Military and Political strength', while a 'triple Indian Ocean empire' of India, Australia and South Africa 'would present to the world such a combination of means upon an extended surface as the world has not yet beheld united under one dominion'.[136]

Military might: The limits of violence

Although the family was connected, by marriage and friendship, to those whose role was to enforce the British hold on territory in India and the Indian Ocean region, the Prinseps were not military men. Their writings express the ambiguities of a colonising force which they wanted to believe was brave in war and generous in peace, the protector of the weak, loved and valued by the colonised for the benefits it could bestow, but which all too often seemed to resort to violence in order to enforce British power and prestige.

The Prinseps of early-Nineteenth Century Calcutta were engaged primarily in British cultural formation in India: administration, orientalist research and commercial activity. It was the military that did the fighting to expand British territorial interests and protect British communities in Bengal. Although the

---

134   Staples, A.C. 1979, *They Made Their Destiny: History of settlement of the Shire of Harvey, 1829–1929*, Shire of Harvey, Bunbury , p.49.
135   India Office Records, 'East India Company Board's Collections, Proposal by C.R. Prinsep for Transferring Children from India to New South Wales and Van Dieman's Land', 1830–1831, Volume 1240, 40599–40767, British Library.
136   Ibid., 11 October 1828.

world the Prinseps sought to construct in Calcutta depended on the security of an armed military presence, their writings hint at ambiguities in their attitudes to the army. Thoby, Charles and Thomas were closely connected to the military through their official positions, as well as by marriage. In his senior posts with the East India Company, Thoby Prinsep worked closely with the army, and he was involved in diplomacy and the logistics of military campaigns in Burma and Afghanistan. His personal papers reveal a person of considerable skill and knowledge of Indian political and military affairs. In his communications with Mr. Benson, the government resident in Rangoon, in the uneasy aftermath of the Burmese War of 1824–6, he dealt with matters as diverse as military logistics for a hypothetical expeditionary force to occupy Rangoon, equipment requirements and livestock needs.[137] Many of his communications contained diplomatic intelligence, including coded messages in classical Greek and Latin. Others concerned the security of the mail system, instructions that letters be put into the hands of helmsmen for direct delivery to the officer in question. He was suspicious of the King of Burma's supposed duplicity in dealings with the British, advising the resident to be on his guard: 'His Majesty would probably tolerate a lackey like kind of Resident, who would reside at Rangoon and come occasionally on a visit to the Capital, that is if he could tolerate anything English in the shape of a Government functionary.'[138]

Thoby and Augustus Prinsep's knowledge of the army and their appreciation of its functions were mediated through their familiarity with the fighting elite. The army had the role of preserving the security of the colonial venture, of securing new territories, and providing the force behind the diplomatic endeavours of government and the civil service. But while they dealt primarily with officers, and even married into their families, the rank and file were viewed as different, as objects of suspicion that, without the management of officers, might break the rules of British bravery and generosity to become like the barbarians they were supposed to control.[139] In his account of the suppression of a 'sepoy mutiny' in 1826, William Prinsep lamented that the soldiers, particularly those of Irish background, were little different from the Indian 'others' of the streets and bazaars, their equal as a mystifying, unruly and unpredictable force. Expressing horror at the violence wrought by British soldiers on the Indian population of Calcutta following a refusal by Indian

---

137 Prinsep, Henry Thoby, 'Private Papers', Oriental and India Office Collection at the British Library (OIOC) MSS Eur. D. 662.
138 Ibid.
139 This is one of the few occasions in the Prinsep narratives in which we are reminded that the British populations of Calcutta included many who were not welcome in the narrow social world inhabited by the family and their social and kin network. Clare Anderson discusses the complexity of the British population, including the presence of escaped convicts from Australia, who lived in Calcutta amongst a community of artisans, tradespeople and itinerant workers. Anderson, Clare 2001, 'Multiple Border Crossings: "Convicts and Other Persons Escaped from Botany Bay and residing in Calcutta"', in *Journal of Australian Colonial History*, Volume 3, No. 2, pp.1–22.

troops to march to Burma without a guarantee of supplies, William reported that 'many women and children were found dead as well as all the men within reach ... A most indescribable gloom seemed to descend upon the whole community of Calcutta, as if a doom of suffering must fall on the place for such an act of cold blooded cruelty.'[140] This was not how the army should behave. It transgressed the ideal of military restraint and fairness that Augustus Prinsep ascribed to the hero of *The Baboo*, Henry Forester, a heroic, almost mythical figure, 'bravest in war, most generous in peace', who leads a British force 'generous and true', who 'do not despoil the conquered'. He is the defender of women, rescuing Dilafroz from 'the unmanly grasp of his own men,' defending 'timid maidens from the approach of further barbarians'.[141]

The use of British military power was an issue that also occupied Charles Prinsep during the last two years of his long stay in India. In 1854, at the age of 65, Charles Prinsep 'extremely grudgingly' became involved in a controversy over the extent to which the British in South East Asia could legitimately exercise military force to preserve the interests of colonisers and their allies. As Advocate-General, Charles Prinsep was appointed by Lord Clarendon to head a Royal Commission to inquire into allegations against the 'white rajah' of Sarawak Sir James Brooke. Nine years earlier, in 1849, Brooke was alleged to have unilaterally used extreme force to crush the activities of Skrang and Saribas Dyak 'pirates', which resulted in a large number of deaths and the widespread destruction of villages. After a prolonged outcry in London, the Imperial Office established the Royal Commission to decide 'whether the conduct pursued by Sir James Brooke ... and the relations which he holds with the native chiefs, have been such as are becoming a servant of the British Crown'.[142] Arriving in Singapore with his wife Louisa and two daughters in August 1854, Charles Prinsep, and to a lesser extent his fellow Commissioner, East India Company counsel, Humphrey Devereux, attracted criticism over the way they managed proceedings against Brooke. Both seemed uncertain as to the precise matters before them or of the admissibility of the evidence. The *Straits Times* alleged that 'the enquiry has not been conducted in a manner calculated to ascertain or develop the proper objects of investigation ... nothing short of accusatory matter will satisfy the Commissioners, leaving all matters of complaint and enquiry to adjust themselves'.[143] 'Few Commissions can have been more haphazard and ineffectual', wrote historian Steven Runciman:

> Prinsep was highly neurotic, and was, indeed, certified insane a few weeks after his return to India. Devereux was clear-headed but somewhat

---

140 'The Memoirs of William Prinsep', Volume 2, p.44.
141 Prinsep, *The Baboo*, Volume 1, pp.123, 132, 142.
142 Barley, Nigel 2002, *White Rajah: A biography of Sir James Brooke*, Little, Brown, London, p.82.
143 *Straits Times and Singapore Journal of Commerce*, 19 September 1854.

cynical and impatient of the whole affair. The Rajah was hurt and angry and determined to be truculent; he refused to respond to any friendly gesture on the part of the Singapore authorities and forbade his staff to accept any social invitations.[144]

Prinsep's behaviour became 'more and more eccentric', and it seemed to observers that he was 'not quite right in the head'. Brooke referred to him as 'a gobbling old donkey without judgement and without dignity', alleging that the inquiry had 'secret instructions' from London, and that its real purpose was to remove him from office.[145] 'Never was there such a farce of an inquiry', he wrote, 'humiliation to me, disgrace to the Government, injury to the natives, ruin to our policy, from a Commission conducted without dignity or propriety, and all about nothing!'[146] The Commissioners could not agree on their findings and submitted separate reports, but both exonerated Brooke on charges of undue violence, and accepted that the Dayaks were engaged in piracy. Qualifying his finding, Prinsep thought it 'unfortunate' that Brooke had associated with savage allies and asked whether it had been necessary to pursue the pirates so fiercely. He held that this association was 'a strong ground against the investing of an individual, holding authority under a half-savage chieftain, with any such official character under the Crown of Great Britain, as that then held by Sir James Brooke'. In his opinion, Brooke had no powers to determine which tribes were piratical or to call for the aid of the Royal Navy. His position was none other than that of a vassal of the Sultan of Brunei, 'though his tenure was admittedly very lax and easy to discard'.[147] Fellow Commissioner Devereux was unsympathetic with what he called 'a race of indiscriminate murderers', while Prinsep was critical of the violence perpetrated by Brooke and wrote that he had exceeded an authority which was, in any case, ill-defined. The Commission therefore failed to reach a verdict on Brooke's actions or to help define the limits or legitimate exercise of British power in the region. Brooke, who had temporarily resigned his position as Governor of Sarawak during the eight years between the episode and the hearing, resumed his duties and remained in the post until his death in 1868.

A period of imperial transformation

This period of transformation in British understandings of India from 'epistemological space' of the late-Eighteenth Century to colonial territory, with

---
144 Runciman, Steven 1960, *The White Rajahs*, Cambridge University Press, Cambridge, pp.113–14.
145 Barley 2002, *White Rajah*, p.145.
146 Sir James Brooke, 6 October 1854, quoted by Jacob, Gertrude L. 1876, *The Rajah of Sarawak*, Volume 2, MacMillan and Co., London, pp.159–60.
147 Runciman 1960, *The White Rajahs*, p.116.

its accompanying demands for operational governmental systems, provides a useful context for examining the role of families such as the Prinseps. It provides an opportunity to envisage the Empire as a complex system of information and connection, to explore continuities and engage with the flow of ideas across colonies. Imperial ideas of India, such as orientalism, did not simply stay there, nor were they tried, discarded and forgotten as new generations brought different notions of Britain's colonising role. The Empire took on and consolidated the cumulative experience of places such as India, which in new colonial spaces were transformed and adapted according to their geographic and temporal contexts. The nabobs of John Prinsep's era might appear to have been superseded by the civil service reforms of Cornwallis and Wellesley, but the Empire remained a place where a Briton could make a fortune throughout the Nineteenth Century. Indeed, this was one of Henry Prinsep's prime motivations in his decision to move to Australia in the 1860s. John Prinsep's sympathy with romantic ideals of Indian society, together with his humanitarian advocacy for property rights of the Indian peasantry, found expression much later in the Australian colonial context, when colonisers such as Henry Prinsep sympathised with ideas that envisaged Aboriginal peoples being trained to become an indigenous peasantry, happy to labour on the land in the service of the colonial project. Similarly, echoes of the professionalism of East India Company civil servants such as Thoby and Augustus Prinsep, with their commitment to a rule of law, their belief that British prestige and power was best served by winning the hearts and minds of the populace, and their articulation of 'high-minded, disinterested, and earnest action for the public good', resonated throughout the world of the Empire, constituting to Henry Prinsep an ideal of colonial service which he aspired to emulate.[148]

The demise of orientalist policies in the 1830s marked a disjuncture in the development, not only of Indian government, but of metropolitan thinking on the Empire. Social and political changes in Britain, notably the *Reform Act of 1832* and the abolition of slavery in British colonies in 1833, together with the increased allure of a colonial career for young men during this troubled decade, were bringing new influences, new ways of visualising the 'others' of the Empire to the colonising venture. As colonial careers became increasingly professionalised, 'respectable English middle-class men' who went to the colonies crossed the philanthropic humanitarianism of the liberal movement with 'the sterner tone of the colonial official'. Thus, when assumptions of British superiority came under threat, 'the seeds of other ways of perceiving these 'natives' were already contained in the interstices of the philanthropic mind'.[149] The next chapter focuses on debates about the Empire in the metropole of the mid-Nineteenth Century and the changing conceptions of Britain's imperial role,

---

148   Prinsep, 'Three Generations', Volume 2, p.263.
149   Hall 2002, *Civilising Subjects*, p.42.

which were to have a significant impact on the subsequent colonising activities of a new generation, as young men such as Henry Prinsep began to contemplate their own colonial careers.

Henry's grandfather, John Prinsep (1746–1831), after his return from Calcutta in 1788.

Source: Copy of a painting by John Downman, courtesy of Ailsa Smith, Claremont, Western Australia.

Sophia Prinsep (née Auriol) (1760–1850), copy of a lost portrait by John Downman.

Source: Courtesy of Ailsa Smith, Claremont, Western Australia.

2. Images of an Imperial Family

Maintaining Britishness in an oriental setting. John Prinsep, hookah in hand, with his extended family group of Dashwoods and Auriols. Sophia Prinsep (née Auriol) is two places from his left.

Source: Detail from a copy of painting by Johan Zoffany, circa 1780, courtesy of Ailsa Smith, Claremont, Western Australia.

Henry's father, Charles Prinsep (1789–1864), at the height of his extremely lucrative legal career in Calcutta in the position of Advocate-General.

Source: Courtesy of Ailsa Smith, Claremont, Western Australia.

Henry Prinsep's mother, Louisa Prinsep (née White)(1818–1855), daughter of an East India Company officer. Louisa died while Henry was, at the age of 11, at school in England.

Source: Courtesy of Ailsa Smith, Claremont, Western Australia.

John Prinsep, drawn by his daughter, Emily Prinsep, in London in 1822, after the collapse of Prinsep and Saunders and his career as a politician, before taking up the salaried post of Sherriff of Southwark.

Source: Courtesy of anonymously held private collection.

2. Images of an Imperial Family

Henry Prinsep's father, Charles Prinsep, as a young man preparing to enter the Bar in London, drawn by his sister, Emily Prinsep.

Source: Prinsep Papers, SLWA MN 773 Acc. 3150A.

James Prinsep (1799–1840), orientalist scholar, drawn by his sister, Emily Prinsep.

Source: Prinsep Papers, SLWA MN 773 Acc. 1423/171-5.

2. Images of an Imperial Family

Augustus Prinsep (1803–1830), drawn by his sister, Emily Prinsep.

Source: Prinsep Papers, SLWA MN 773 Acc. 1423/171-5.

The only known image of Amelia (Emily) Prinsep (1798–1860), who drew images of her father and brothers, and was an enthusiastic painter of English landscapes and scenes of domestic life.

Source: Prinsep Papers, SLWA MN 773 Acc. 3150A.

2. Images of an Imperial Family

Henry Thoby Prinsep (1792–1878), East India Company civil servant, linguist and orientalist scholar, who after his return to England, served first as a Director of the East India Company and then as a member of the Council for India.

Source: Prinsep Papers, SLWA MN 773 Acc. 3150A.

William Prinsep (1794–1874) as an old man following his retirement from a 37-year career in Calcutta.

Source: Prinsep Papers, SLWA MN 773 Acc. 3150A.

2. Images of an Imperial Family

'Europeans being entertained by Indian musicians during Durga puja', by William Prinsep, an enthusiastic 'lover of the brush', who painted and drew prolifically over his long stay in India. The setting may be Belvedere, the home of Charles Prinsep, and could refer to the 'society dinner party' recorded by William in his journal in which he described the music as 'rather plaintive and sad—never brilliant and only fit for their mawkish love songs, but ravishing to Indian ears'.

Source: British Library Collections, W4035.

James Prinsep's oil painting of the mosque on Chowringee Road, Calcutta, 1830–1835.

Source: British Library Collections, G 70069-76.

2. Images of an Imperial Family

Thomas Prinsep's watercolour of the new mint on the Strand, Calcutta, circa 1829.

Source: British Library Collections, C 13771-96.

Augustus and Elisabeth Prinsep (née Ommaney) relaxing at home at Shergati in the Mofussil in November 1828, shortly after Augustus became ill with tuberculosis. The drawing is by James Prinsep and was sent home to his mother, Sophia, as shown by the inscription on the rear of the card, 'For Mama, from J.P.'

Soure: Courtesy of anonymously held private collection.

2. Images of an Imperial Family

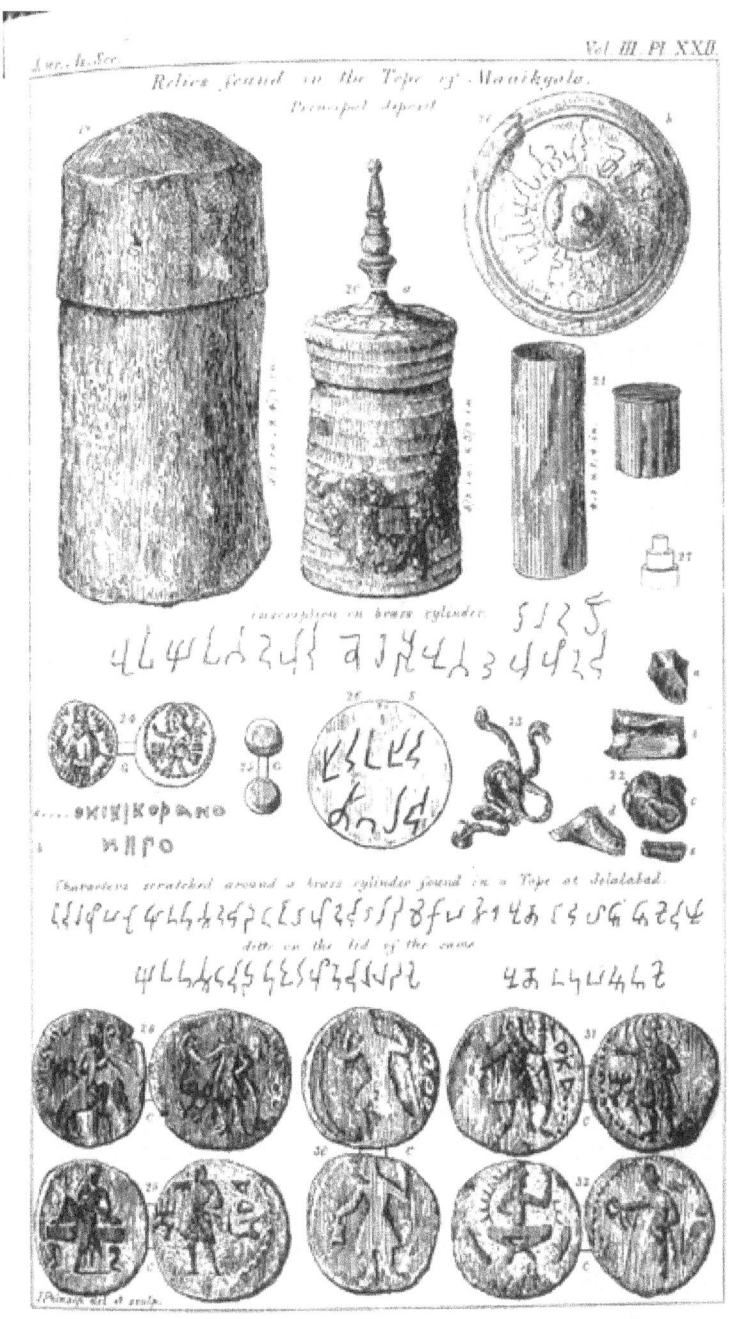

Numismatic diagrams by James Prinsep, from the pages of the Journal of the Asiatic Society of Bengal.

Source: Journal of the Asiatic Society of Bengal, Baptist Mission Press, Circular Road, Calcutta.

'Where is he? Where is he?' We can only wonder at the incident this scene by James Prinsep depicts. From a reading of Isabella Fane's account of her stay in Calcutta, it is almost certain that it is set on a 'budgerow', a native boat used for river transport before the age of steam tugs.

Source: Courtesy of anonymously held private collection.

2. Images of an Imperial Family

James Prinsep shortly before his retirement due to ill health as Secretary of the Bengal Asiatic Society in 1838, drawn by artist Coleworthy Grant.

Source: Grant, Coleworthy 1849, Lithographic Sketches of the Public Characters of Calcutta, 1838–1850, W. Thacker and Co., Calcutta.

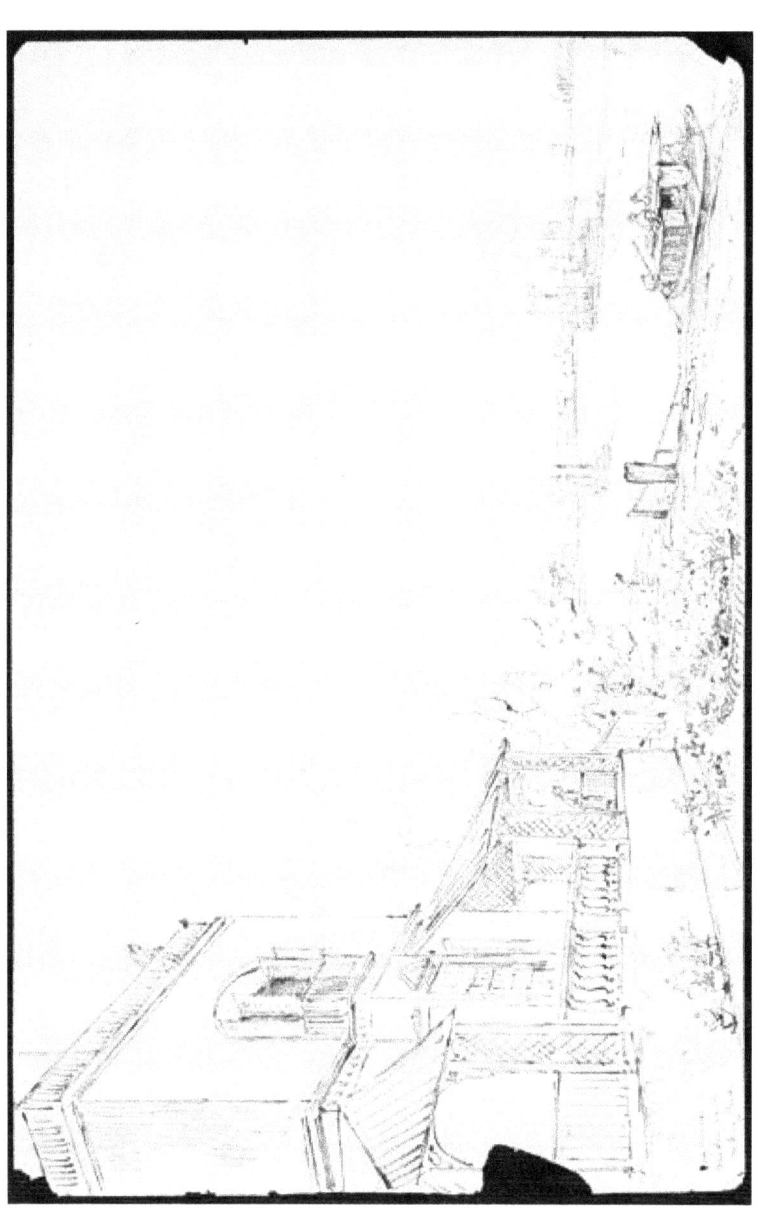

'Our home Garden Reach, looking west', William Prinsep's drawing of a man, probably himself, leaving for work, waved off by his wife Mary.

Source: Caroline Simpson Library, Historic Houses Trust of NSW, Sydney.

2. Images of an Imperial Family

'Repairing for Dinner, Bengal 1840', pen drawing by William Prinsep.

Source: Caroline Simpson Library, Historic Houses Trust of NSW, Sydney.

Tomb of Raja Rammohan Roy at Arnos Vale Cemetery near Bristol, designed and paid for by William Prinsep.

Source: Author's private collection.

3. An Anglo-Indian Community in Britain

By the time of his departure for the colonies in January 1866, Henry Prinsep had spent most of his life in Britain, but had grown up with the knowledge that his adulthood was likely to take him overseas, to India or another colony, such as Western Australia or Tasmania, where his father owned substantial estates. At the age of 21, he assumed that his departure would be temporary, and that he would soon return to London to take up his chosen career as an artist after securing his financial future and that of his younger siblings, Annie, Louisa, May and Jim. The trip to the colonies was an adventure, but one which would force him to learn as he went. He was confident that his family background, his education and understanding of colonial life would equip him for whatever challenges lay ahead. His outlook was very much that of a young Briton in mid-Nineteenth Century Britain, confident in the supremacy of his civilisation and his position within it, secure in his belief that colonisation was in the best interests of all and that the colonised had the capacity and the desire to benefit from British rule. He was well-bred, well-educated and well-connected, seemingly equipped to be a successful coloniser, and confident that the networks his background had given him would serve him well in the far-flung reaches of empire.

Britain's empire had changed much since the days Prinsep's father and uncles had lived and worked in Calcutta during the 1820s and 1830s, while, at home, Britons were increasingly conscious of the nation's pre-eminence as an imperial power. The narratives of the principal literary and cultural figures of the day, oracles such as Thomas Macaulay, John Ruskin, Alfred Tennyson and William Thackeray, accustomed Britons to notions that they belonged to the race that had acquired the greatest empire the world had seen, and that this affirmed their superiority amongst the peoples of the world. Yet, an increasing assertiveness as an imperial power also brought controversies and anxieties. In 1857, British society was shocked by reports of the atrocities perpetrated by Indian 'sepoys' against British people in India. Victorian society was incensed by the brutality and ruthlessness of an 'ungrateful' and 'unpredictable' Indian population against what was believed to be a benevolent overlordship.[1] The violence of the British response was widely seen as a fitting response to the actions of those who, employed and trusted by the British, had proven themselves treacherous. This and other revolts against British imperial authority throughout the colonial world—including the Morant Bay rebellion in Jamaica in 1856 and the

---

1   Hawkins, Angus 1984, 'British Parliamentary Alignment and the Indian Issue, 1857–1858', in *The Journal of British Studies*, Volume 23, No. 2, p.79. See also Chaudhuri, Sashi Bhusan, 1979, *English Historical Writings on the Indian Mutiny, 1857–1859*, World Press, Calcutta.

long-running 'Maori Wars' in New Zealand between 1845 and 1872—brought the affairs of the Empire into the popular British domain, unleashing public debates about how Britain was to govern its distant realm, how it should relate to the millions of people now living under British rule, the nature of race and difference, British identity and superiority.

Growing up in a self-consciously Anglo-Indian community in England, the young men and women of Prinsep's generation were subject to all the ambiguities of the British colonial mission.[2] Henry Prinsep was an avid consumer of popular literature about Britain's empire, but at the same time was closely connected through family and kin to India and the colonies. The older Prinsep generation was living testimony to a recent Indian past in which they had prospered, but which had also been cruel, as many of their family and kin lay buried in Indian soil or had, like Henry's father Charles and uncle James, returned to England with their health broken. If they survived India, they could look forward to a comfortable retirement and the opportunity to continue their involvement in Indian government and colonial commerce. Uncle William Prinsep, who had left India in 1841 and bought a country house in Surrey, still had enough capital to continue his involvement with Assam tea and the Calcutta tug boat industry, as well as dabble in gold mining in South Africa and Australia. Thoby, able to live well off his pension from over 30 years civil service in Bengal civil service, continued his role in Indian government by successfully seeking election as a director of the East India Company and then, after the assumption of direct Crown rule of India in 1858, as a permanent member of the Secretary of State's Council for India.

The Anglo-Indian community of which Henry was a part permeated almost every aspect of the life he experienced as a child and young adult. At school, he was among other children whose parents were also in India. At home, his invalid father, Charles, was surrounded by the relics and books of his Indian past in his Cheltenham house and was often visited by neighbours he knew from his Indian days. His brother, Charlie, was in India with the 19th Hussars, and his cousin, Henry Thoby, was a magistrate in Calcutta and later a judge of the Supreme Court. Five other cousins subsequently joined the civil service or army, while another cousin, Augusta Becher, the only daughter of Uncle Augustus, spent many years in India with her officer husband, Septimus. On holiday, Henry and his siblings stayed in hotels that were owned and patronised by 'Indian people'.[3]

---

2   The term 'Anglo-Indian' is used in this chapter to refer to Britons born in India of British parents or Britons who spent long periods in India, many of whom self-identified as 'Anglo-Indian'. See, for example, Grant, Coleworthy 1849, *An Anglo-Indian Domestic Sketch: A letter from an artist in India to his mother in England*, W. Thacker and Co., Calcutta, and Laurie, Colonel W.F.B. 1887, *Sketches of Some Distinguished Anglo-Indians: With an account of Anglo-Indian periodical literature*, W.H. Allen & Co., London. By contrast, in his memoirs, William Prinsep refers to 'old Indians', just as Henry Prinsep's cousin, Augusta Becher, does in her memoirs. The term 'Anglo-Indian' later came to refer specifically to those of mixed Indian and British parentage.
3   Prinsep, James Charles, 'Autobiography', SLWA Acc. 3859A, 1–2.

When they visited their uncles and aunts, William and Mary Prinsep in Surrey and Henry and Alexa White in Inverness, they continued to be surrounded by matters Indian, by cousins and kin about to go to India or on furlough, Indian visitors, Indian cuisine and Indian artefacts in the houses. India thus formed a constant background in the world in which he grew up. It was 'a second home', as Augusta Becher later put it, the land to which 'so many of the family were destined to devote their lives'.[4]

After the death of Charles Prinsep in 1864, Henry Prinsep and his younger siblings moved into the home of Uncle Thoby and Aunt Sara Prinsep, who occupied a large farm house in semi-rural land at Holland Park in Kensington. Thoby and Sara had left Calcutta in 1843, having accumulated a fortune of 50,000 pounds sterling and an annuity of 1,000 pounds a year. From 1858, their home, Little Holland House, became the focus of an active social life energetically promoted by Sara and her sisters, all of them born and brought up in Calcutta by their parents, James Pattle (1775–1845) and Adeline (née de L'Etang) (1793–1845) who had been born and died in India. James Pattle had been a prominent but notorious Calcutta merchant, later described by his great-granddaughter, Virginia Woolf, as 'of marked, but doubtful reputation who, after living a riotous life and earning the title of 'the greatest liar in India', finally drank himself to death'.[5] Woolf gives a lurid account of the deaths of James and Adeline in 1845, and the subsequent departure of their daughters, including her grandmother, Mia Jackson, from Calcutta to England. The arrival from Calcutta of four of Sara's sisters, Julia Margaret (Cameron), Maria (Jackson), Virginia (Somers) and Sophia (Dalrymple), over the next few years brought the formation of a network that was unashamedly and assertively Anglo-Indian, and willing to exhibit their Indianness in a way that appealed to London society.[6]

Little Holland House and its extensive gardens were used by Sara Prinsep and her sisters for Sunday afternoon cultural salons, with the main attraction being their permanent house guest, artist and sculptor George Frederick Watts.[7] Memoirs of

---

4 Becher, Augusta 1930, *Personal Reminiscences of Augusta Becher, 1830–1888*, edited by H.G. Rawlinson, Constable and Co., London, p.viii.
5 Bell, Quentin 1974, *Virginia Woolf: A biography*, Harvest Books, New York, p.14.
6 Olsen, V.C. 2003, *From Life: Julia Margaret Cameron and Victorian photography*, Palgrave MacMillan, New York, p.47.
7 As well as the two manuscripts by Jim Prinsep, ('Autobiography', and 'De Principe, A.D. 1574–1930', 2 Volumes, SLWA Acc. 3150 A/1–2) many of the letters received by Henry Prinsep from his siblings mention Little Holland House, Aunt Sara and Uncle Thoby, G.F.K. Watts (whom they refer to as 'Signor'), and many of the visitors. These letters are found throughout the State Library of Western Australia (SLWA) collection at MN 773, particularly in the folios comprising Acc. 3592A. Memoirs of the activities at Little Holland House are to be found in a number of secondary sources. For example Blunt, Wilfred 1975, *'England's Michelangelo': A biography of George Frederic Watts OM, RA*, Hamish Hamilton, London; Dakers, Caroline 1999, *The Holland Park Circle: Artists and Victorian society*, Yale University Press, London; Gould, Veronica Franklin 2004, *G.F. Watts: The last great Victorian*, Yale University Press, New Haven and London; and Olsen, V.C. 2003, *From Life: Julia Margaret Cameron and Victorian photography*, Palgrave MacMillan, New York.

the social life at Little Holland House glorify the artistic and intellectual activity of the visitors, drawn to the salon not only by the presence of Watts, but by the 'oriental exoticism' of the Pattle sisters and an informality that bespoke their unusual and un-English background. Pre-Raphaelite artist, Edward Burne Jones, viewed Sara's salons as 'a gallant experiment of a kind made all too rarely in England: the world at large might buckle to the forces of philistinism, but here at least the claims of talent and beauty would receive full recognition'.[8] Visitors were certain to meet interesting people and celebrated Londoners. Alfred Tennyson was one of a procession of regular guests, along with the leading lights of London's political, intellectual and cultural world, William Makepeace Thackeray, Robert Browning, George Eliot, William Gladstone, Benjamin Disraeli, John Ruskin, Dante Gabriel Rossetti, F.D. Maurice, Holman Hunt, Charles Hallé and Joseph Joachim, all of whom were made to feel at home by the Prinseps. Sara Prinsep and her sisters, 'at once homely and extravagantly artistic', promoted Little Holland House as a haven from which everything but high living and the pursuit of beauty was rigorously excluded.'[9] In *Moments of Being*, Virginia Woolf imagined Little Holland House as 'an old white country house, standing in a large garden':

> The date is around 1860. It is a hot summer day. Tea tables with great bowls of strawberries and cream are scattered about the lawn. They are 'presided over' by some of the six lovely sisters; who do not wear crinolines, but are robed in splendid Venetian draperies; they sit enthroned, and talk with foreign emphatic gestures … to the eminent men … rulers of India, statesmen, poets, painters … The sound of music also comes from those long low rooms where the great Watts pictures hang; Joachim playing the violin; also the sound of a voice reading poetry—Uncle Thoby would read his translations from the Persian poets. How easy it is to fill in the picture with set pieces that I have gathered from the memoirs—to bring in Tennyson in his wide-awake; Watts in his smock frock; Ellen Terry dressed as a boy; Garibaldi in his red shirt.[10]

The Anglo-Indian exoticism of the Little Holland House salons provided a forum in which Indian colonialism and knowledge could be exhibited to the social elites of London. Thoby Prinsep, amongst 'a great many old Indians', represented British expertise on India, reciting his Anglicised renditions of Persian epic poetry and speaking with the authority of an old orientalist on

---

8   Burne Jones, Edward 1981, *The Little Holland House Album*, The Dalrymple Press, North Brunswick, p.7.
9   Tennyson, Charles 1950, *Alfred Tennyson*, Macmillan & Co., London, p.294.
10   Woolf, Virginia 1978, *Moments of Being*, Triad, St. Albans, Herts, pp.100–1.

aspects of Indian language, ethnography and politics. 'You might turn to him as to an encyclopaedia', recalled his son Val, 'with the certainty of receiving … information on any Indian subject.'[11]

Meanwhile, the women of the family exhibited the exotic and idealised aspects of Anglo-Indian culture, dressing in oriental costumes, speaking Hindustani amongst themselves, serving Indian cuisine, and adopting relatively less formal and more personable social mores. Adding to their allure, the salons were occasionally graced by visiting 'native grandees', as Jim Prinsep recalled, former business and political colleagues from India who participated in debates about Indian government and religions, and who helped construct metropolitan images of 'what an Indian gentleman should look like and how he should behave in the imperial metropole'.[12]

Influence and patronage: Indian government in the metropole

Prinsep family social life in mid-Nineteenth Century metropolitan Britain illustrates Cohn's image of a 'self-perpetuating oligarchy', in which Anglo-Indian identity was manifest through social, business and familial networks.[13] Such identities included appropriation of aspects of Indian literature, architecture, art and design, and Indian religious ceremony, often adapted to forms suitable for metropolitan cultural consumption, which served both to glorify an idealised India and to reinforce a sense of identity distinct from other British people. The older members of the Anglo-Indian community, such as Thoby Prinsep, were products of Indian government styled on the principles of Warren Hastings, in which India was viewed as a 'fitting object for European benevolence', their role as civil servants engaged in the governmental objective of integrating Indians into an 'empire of uniformity', a colonial social body adapted to Indian 'principles and maxims and preserving Indian laws and institutions'.[14] Their later years in India in the 1830s had seen important shifts in governmental policies in the face of liberal ideas of British superiority, Indian backwardness and incapacity, and the obligation of Britain to become a 'benevolent civilizing empire' in which

---

11 Prinsep, Val C. 1879, *Imperial India: An artist's journals, illustrated by numerous sketches taken at the courts of the principal chiefs in India*, Chapman and Hall, London, p.46.
12 Burton, Antoinette 1998, *At the Heart of the Empire: Indians and the colonial encounter in late-Victorian Britain*, University of California Press, London, p.42. Henry's younger brother Jim mentions the 'Indian grandees' in his 'Autobiography', Volume 1.
13 Cohn, Bernard S. 1987, *An Anthropologist Among the Historians and Other Essays*, Oxford University Press, Delhi, p.510.
14 Buchan, Bruce 2007, 'Europe's Asia': Empire, difference and the moral Geography of European political thought, c 1500 – 1800', paper presented at 'Australasian Political Studies Association Conference', Monash University, 24–26 September, p.16.

Indians would emerge as 'brown Englishmen', as Thomas Macaulay wrote, 'a class of persons, Indian in blood and colour, but British in taste, in opinions, in morals and in intellect'.[15] The events of the Indian revolt in 1857, widely reported, novelised and serialised in the metropole, reinforced British images of Indians as barbarous and ungrateful, and the civilising mission as fraught with anxieties about the distance of coloniser from a colonised increasingly defined by difference and a perceived incapacity to progress to standards of European civility. In such an environment, the form of British relationships with the others of empire became a subject of intense debate in the metropole, from liberal expressions of the essential likeness of different humans and the capacity of the others to become like 'us' under the benevolence of a civilising empire, to contrasting views that envisaged a hierarchically ordered system in which a superior 'we' must always dominate and control the inferior, reluctant and unruly others.[16]

Families such as the Prinseps contributed to these debates from a position of familiarity with India, which they expressed through past experience, continuing family connections and oriental knowledge. As colonials, they asserted their knowledge of India and sought to influence metropolitan images of an Indian colonial project that they understood had undergone significant changes during the Nineteenth Century. Patrick Brantlinger refers to the burgeoning of a popular literature on India after the turmoil of the 1857 revolt, 'at least fifty' novels before 1900, 'at least thirty more' before World War II, and 'a deluge of eyewitness accounts, journal articles, histories, poems and plays'.[17] This popular literature helped nurture perceptions of an empire of difference, its peoples not only 'primitive and backward in contrast to European standards of progress, development or civilisation', but, since the revolt, now also potentially treacherous and unreliable.[18] A key feature of this hardening of British attitudes to Indians lay in concepts of race and racial hierarchy based on doctrines of human types in which differences were permanent, and were believed to determine the nature of social relationships between races. British superiority was assumed to be based on Anglo-Saxon heritage and membership of an Aryan race, in which the British could be represented as 'the most progressive branch of the most progressive race', which had the power and right to dominate others because of its position at the pinnacle of the hierarchy of civilisation.[19]

---

15 Macaulay, Thomas Babington, 'Minute on Indian Education (1835)', in Barbara Harlow and Mia Carter (eds) 1999, *Imperialism and Orientalism: A documentary sourcebook,* Blackwell Publishers, Oxford, p.61.
16 Curtin, Philip C. 1971, *Imperialism,* The Macmillan Press, London and Basingstoke, p.xx.
17 Brantlinger, Patrick 1998, *Rule of Darkness: British literature and imperialism, 1830–1914,* Cornell University Press, New York, p.199.
18 Buchan 2007, 'Europe's Asia', p.6; Mackenzie, John W. 1999, 'Empire and Metropolitan Cultures', in Andrew Porter (ed.), *The Oxford History of the British Empire,* Volume 3: The Nineteenth Century, Oxford University Press, Oxford, p.281.
19 Banton, Michael 1977, *The Idea of Race,* Tavistock Publications, London, p.61; Lorimer, Douglas A. 1978, *Colour, Class and the Victorians: English attitudes to the negro in the Mid-Nineteenth Century,* Leicester University Press, Leicester, p.23.

The range of opinion within such racial subjectivities was significant, Lorimer reducing it to rival visions that extended between the humanitarian goals of empire of uniformity, which saw all humans as bound by common origins and shared humanity, and the 'extreme racialists' who saw all races as distinct, with separate origins and different characteristics, and thus subject to separate and unequal development.[20]

On his return to England in 1843, Thoby Prinsep was keen to continue his involvement in Indian colonial government and British imperial affairs. He joined the exclusive Carlton and Athenaeum clubs in London and, in 1851, was elected a director of the East India Company.[21] This directorship provided Thoby Prinsep with an avenue to participate in the defence of the East India Company charter in what was to be the final renewal by the British Parliament in 1853. That year, he published a lengthy monograph which summarised his views on Indian government, derived from nearly 40 years' direct experience and almost ten years' retirement in the metropole.[22] The document betrays little of the conviction that British rule would uplift Indians and transform Indian society, which existed in his earlier works. Tinges of his days as an old orientalist surfaced in his suggestion that the abandonment of the 'grand principles' of non-interference in native religions and limits on the immigration of Europeans in the 1833 *Charter Act* constituted a betrayal of the Indian elites, whose support was essential for the success of the colonising project.

In the absence of concerted strategies to win over the 'lettered classes', which he took to have been abandoned by the Bentinck/Macaulay reforms of the 1830s, Thoby held little hope that the Indian masses could adapt to the benefits of British rule. The 'innate' differences between British rulers and Indian subjects, he argued, must continue to be reflected in systems of colonial government. The system of indirect rule should not only be maintained, but extended, both to maintain alliances with Indian elites and to recognise the knowledge and authority of British administrators in India. The integrity and training of these 'men on the spot', 'bound by the tie of interests as well as by covenant to devote the best part of their lives to India', guaranteed that 'Government is certain to be conducted in due subservience to England, and with efforts to prevent alienation on the part of the governed'.[23] The Governor-General and the East India Company administration should thus be free to govern 'with no restraints of reference to England for previous sanction', in recognition of the high-mindedness and Indian knowledge of the Company civil service. 'An

---

20 Lorimer 1978, *Colour, Class and the Victorians*, p.23.
21 Philips, C.H. and D. Philips 1841, 'Directors of the East India Company', in *Journal of the Royal Asiatic Society*, October; Prinsep, Sir Henry Thoby, 'Three Generations in India 1771–1904', OIOC MSS Eur. C. 97, Part 2, p.266.
22 Prinsep, Henry T. 1853, *The India Question in 1853*, W.H. Allen & Co., London.
23 Ibid., p.58.

acknowledgement of superior general intelligence in the members of the civil service', he wrote, should take account of the 'qualities in which the natives of India know themselves to be deficient'.[24] A powerful and knowledgeable civil service held a paternalist responsibility for guiding Indians in the correct application of European knowledge, as well as the introduction of British technology. Furthermore, without a firm guiding hand, agitation against British rule risked becoming unstoppable through the 'vain and presumptuous élèves of the Government colleges', who failed to 'appreciate the blessings of peace and order'. 'Why should the seeds of disaffection and disloyalty be sown by our own hand', he asked, 'in a soil well prepared to receive lessons of order, and impressions favourable to the permanence of British rule?'[25]

Although the charter of the Company was eventually renewed in 1853, five years later the *Government of India Act 1858* marked the end of the active involvement of the Company in India. The Act instituted direct Crown rule, and proclaimed Victoria the sovereign of India, her authority to be exercised by a Secretary of State through a Viceroy and Governor-General. In many ways it attempted to preserve continuity in Indian government, with senior Company employees confirmed in their positions, East India Company treaties with Indian principalities maintained, and other policies on equality before the law, freedom of religion and respect for indigenous customs recognised.[26] Membership of the Council of India was also designed to provide continuity, and seven of the 15 council places were initially reserved for nominees of the East India Company, particularly those experienced in Indian colonial government. The Council was constituted to entrench an independent, non-Parliamentary voice on Indian government. Members could only be removed through petition to both Houses of Parliament, the Secretary was obliged to consult the Council before issuing orders, and each member was entitled to register his opinion on any matter put before them. In 1858, Thoby Prinsep was elected to serve on the Council's Political Committee along with a 'formidable array of old Indians' to advise Secretary of State, Sir Charles Wood, who had no background in India. 'Can I, or any other Secretary of State who has not been in India, pretend to set his opinion in detail against such men?', he asked. 'Would it conduce to the transaction of business, if I was overriding them on expressions of opinion on details?'[27] Thus, although the Secretary had the power to overrule the Council, aspects of the principle of 'double government' remained. Since 1784, the Company had exercised administrative powers and the government Parliamentary Board of

---

24 Ibid., pp.70–2.
25 Ibid., p.69.
26 Moore, Robin J. 1999, 'Imperial India, 1858–1914', in Andrew Porter (ed.), *The Oxford History of the British Empire*, Volume 3: The Nineteenth Century, Oxford University Press, Oxford, p.424.
27 Williams, Donovan 1966, 'The Council of India and the Relationship Between the Home and Supreme Governments, 1858–1870', in *The English Historical Review*, Volume 81, No. 318, p.65.

Control functioned to oversee and monitor their governmental performance, but the new arrangements established the Crown 'as the initiator of policy and the Council now the check on Imperial self-interest'.[28]

Thoby Prinsep does not record his opinion about the transfer of Indian government to Crown rule, but it is likely he shared the views of his fellow Company directors and John Stuart Mill, in 1853 a relatively junior Assistant Examiner in the East India Company, but widely considered to be an authority on Indian government.[29] Like Thoby Prinsep, Mill had opposed the Bentinck/Macaulay education reforms in the 1830s, believing that they would alienate the Indian elites upon whom the government in India depended. In a draft dispatch on the Bentinck proposals, he had warned of the 'sudden change of course' which would 'destroy all confidence on the part of the people in the wisdom of their rulers'.[30] In 1853, he argued against direct Crown rule and for the continuation of the Company government, and asserted that the Company was well on the way to achieving good government in India. Its civil servants provided the 'professional knowledge' and the Company 'had done much to develop the empire … it had never interfered with Indian religions, and … as a private enterprise, it cost the British taxpayer nothing'.[31] The 'benevolent despotism' of Company government was the system best suited to India, in Mill's view, 'a legitimate mode of government in dealing with barbarians provided the end is their improvement and the means justified by achieving that end'.[32] This was what differentiated the despotism of the British from the despotism of the previous Mughal rulers: in seeking to implant British ideas of political freedom and self-government, they 'were deliberately creating the conditions for the withering away of their rule'.[33] It was of the utmost importance, according to Mill, 'to make provision … for compelling those who have a governing power, to listen to and take into consideration the opinions of persons who, from their position and their previous life, have made a study of Indian subjects and acquired experience in them'.[34]

Family narratives on mid-century India

Thoby's oldest son, Sir Henry Thoby Prinsep, born in Calcutta in 1836 and returning as a magistrate in 1855, later compiled his unpublished 'Three

---

28   Moore 1999, 'Imperial India, 1858–1914', p.425.
29   Harris, Abram L. 1964, 'John Stuart Mill: Servant of the East India Company', in *The Canadian Journal of Economics and Political Science/ Revue Canadienne d'Economique et de Science Politique,* Volume 30, No. 2, p.200.
30   Ibid., p.198.
31   Turner, Michael J. 2005, '"Raising up Dark Englishmen": Thomas Perronet Thompson, colonies, race, and the Indian mutiny', in *Journal of Colonialism and Colonial History,* Volume 6, No. 1.
32   Mill, quoted by Harris 1964, 'John Stuart Mill', p.191.
33   Harris 1964, 'John Stuart Mill', p.201.
34   Ibid., p.192.

Generations in India' to illustrate how British India had changed over the century since his grandfather John had arrived in Calcutta in 1770.[35] Drawing on the journals of John Prinsep and his father's dictated memoirs of his Indian career, Sir Henry Thoby's account of his own career focussed principally on British social life in Calcutta, and to a lesser extent on some of the highlights of his judicial life, largely ignoring Indian people, indigenous cultural and historical issues. His younger brother, artist Val Prinsep, who had spent two years at Haileybury as a teenager but decided against an Indian career, travelled to India in 1877 to illustrate the Viceroy Lord Lytton's durbar commemorating Queen Victoria's declaration as Empress of India.[36] His observations, combined with the 'vast knowledge of everything connected with the East' imparted to him by his father, gave him he felt ample authority to promote 'kindly feeling between the natives and their rulers'.[37] In his view, the British in India should 'unbend somewhat towards the native … make more allowance for his prejudices … not expect a native to be an Englishman'.[38] Acceptance of the 'innate' differences between Indian and British would improve not only the standing of the British amongst Indians, but the quality of government. The British were successful in empire because of the 'contrast we present in our characters': 'Our thoroughness inspires his respect, he believes in our honesty—he has every reason to trust our courage. We give him peace such as he has never enjoyed before, and insure his having justice, even against the great.'[39]

Indian difference and unknowability were also themes for Augusta Becher, whose memoirs of Anglo-Indian life were published posthumously in 1930.[40] Becher went to India in 1849 with her army officer husband, Septimus, and remained until she was repatriated, along with her children, to Britain during the revolt of 1857. Her reminiscences are of a familiar and introspective world of connections and inter-connections, in which Calcutta is a 'second home' for the 'famous stock' of Prinseps and their extensive networks of family and kin. Most of the men and women populating her memoirs consider themselves both British and Indian. Their links to India are expressed through family history and tradition, high levels of mobility between Britain and India, and extensive interconnections through family and social life. Becher's marriage into another 'Indian family' and relocation to India followed a well-trodden path. Even their wedding ceremony incorporated Anglo Indian traditions: 'Uncle William [Prinsep], as usual, the centre of all fun, gave out our health while I was changing dress. "How nice the Missus sounds" was Sep's only comment, after thanks, and the two embraced Hindoo fashion with "Ram Ram" at parting.'[41]

---

35 Prinsep, 'Three Generations', Part 2, p.45.
36 Prinsep, 1879, *Imperial India*.
37 Ibid., p.4.
38 Ibid., p.347.
39 Ibid., p.342.
40 Becher 1930, *Personal Reminiscences*, p.viii.
41 Ibid., p.55. A footnote explains 'Ram Ram' as 'The usual Hindu salutation – an invocation of the God Rama'.

The social life awaiting Becher in Calcutta featured many of the families she had grown up with in Britain. She lodged initially with Henry's father, Charles Prinsep, at his mansion 'Belvedere', and rapidly made contact with a wide circle of cousins, old family and school friends and connections, and it is with these British men and women that her account of her years in India is principally concerned. By contrast, the Indians that inhabit her world constitute an ever present, usually nameless, and potentially threatening presence. The house servants move 'noiselessly', and try to exploit their British employers. Charles Prinsep, reported Becher, 'spoke hardly any Hindustani, and his head bearer, Hurree, did just what he pleased in and out', but the arrival of a bilingual family member 'hustled all the servants to the right about', and they were soon suitably clothed in 'white and turbans'.[42] Soon after her arrival, she visited the household of an 'old Indian', and was surprised by the informality she found, commenting that, while 'no doubt natives preferred and understood those households better than the more civilised style of ours now coming into vogue', it was important to be 'more careful with the manners both of masters and servants'.[43] Becher's relationships with ayahs constituted her principal contact with Indians, but are tinged with suspicion that the British children will be mistreated or taught undesirable habits: 'my old ayah had washed and dressed him—quite close beside me lest she should pull his ears or nose, as I had heard natives were in the habit of doing'.[44] The period leading up to the 1857 revolt was particularly unnerving for women such as Becher, dependent as they were not only on their husbands, but on their household servants. 'There were many rumours afloat … before the Mutiny broke out', she wrote, 'it was "in the air" as the natives said, and they all knew it.'[45]

> We seemed hemmed in by a wall, without a chance of knowing if help was coming from outside. Cawnpore with its awful story magnified if possible. Shahjihanpore, every soul swept away—at first the one word 'gone!' expressed all from one place to another, Lucknow, Gwalior, Bareilly—all seemed going … our suspense and anxiety were what none can understand but those who *know*.[46]

The uprisings were suppressed with a brutality that, to Becher, was harsh but justified: 'his was the awful duty', she wrote of a 'distant cousin', 'of carrying out the dreadful sentence of blowing away from guns the mutineers, or those who attempted to break away from the regiments. It was a paramount necessity to prevent them joining the mutineers.'[47] Women and children attached to

---

42   Ibid., p.62–4.
43   Ibid., p.66.
44   Ibid., p.69.
45   Ibid., p.127.
46   Ibid., pp.138–9.
47   Ibid., pp. 142–3.

the British regiments were ordered to leave India, but their flight to Bombay increased their dependence on people now under suspicion, and brought the risk of ambush on the roads and in the towns. 'When we entered the crowded narrow streets of the city', Becher relates,

> we are each alone practically; I have only an attendant, the faithful Ganesh, beside me ... We get by on the greatest difficulty at foot pace, and feeling more than commonly nervous, for every native seemed to look bold and independent that year, and most of them peer curiously into the doolies as they pass.[48]

The Indians encountered by Becher are usually without identity, described as 'faithless', 'vociferating', 'clamouring', unwilling to act without 'buksheesh', and 'the wildest-looking men I have ever seen'. Throughout the dangerous journey to the safety of Bombay, some of Becher's Indian companions remained 'faithful' and provided 'first-rate service'. At other times she outwitted her tormentors through pluck and courage. At one point she was able to recover her supply of stolen 'buksheesh':

> I really believe I should not have dared if I had reflected, and only the quickness with which I turned on him surprised the man into showing he had the money. The others laughed all round, and shook their dirty wigs at me. I jumped into my cage and we were off.[49]

Popular narratives of Indian difference

Becher's story is but one of many contemporary British eyewitness accounts of escape from the traumas of 1857 India. Shortly after her return to Britain, in June 1858, she went to live with Henry Prinsep's family in Walton-on-Thames, and briefly took on the role of the family's governess-housekeeper. Her traumatic experiences in India would have been well known to the family of Henry Prinsep, images of the duplicity of Indians towards British rule providing a counterpoint to the orientalist sentiments of the older Prinseps who had worked in India during the first half of the Nineteenth Century. Middle-class families such as the Prinseps were inevitably subject to popular narratives on imperialism and colonialism as reflected in the literature of the day. Social contact with some of Britain's leading literary figures, novelists and social commentators, such as William Thackeray, Alfred Tennyson, Charles Dickens, John Ruskin, John Stuart Mill and Thomas Carlyle, adds to the image of family members on the periphery of, if not closely involved in changing attitudes to the imperial mission.

---

48   Ibid., p 147.
49   Ibid., p.150.

The family of William Thackeray (1811–1863) shared a similar East India Company background with the Prinseps and the families were associated both in Calcutta and after their return to England. The novelist was much older than Henry Prinsep, but both had been born in Calcutta and left as young children, never to return, and India constituted a continuing and important part of their family heritage. As a young man, Prinsep frequently met Thackeray and his two daughters Annie and Harriet, through Thoby and Sara, and became a keen reader of the novelist's popular works. Thackeray's Indian novels, *The Tremendous Adventures of Major Gahagan* (1841), *Vanity Fair* (first serialised between 1847 and 1848), and *The Newcomes* (1853–1855), portrayed a world with which Henry was familiar from his own experience of family and business life in old Calcutta, including the collapse of the Calcutta agency houses in 1830–31, which had brought financial disaster to many British families who were connected to India, including Britons at home.[50] The India of Thackeray's novels occupies a distant, peripheral space in the lives of his British characters and rarely do Indians feature as principal actors.[51] The novels are set at home, with India and other parts of the Empire 'distinctly "away," distant places of exile at the margins of Thackeray's vision of social reality'.[52] The British characters are far removed from the reality of politics, political economy and warfare in India, and instead are 'lovingly if somewhat cynically' constructed as comic parodies, to whom India represents a past, a place they have left but which exercises an abiding influence on their lives. Like the British characters in Augustus Prinsep's *The Baboo,* Thackeray's Newcomes fall prey to the duplicity and deceit of a wily Baboo, Rummun Loll, the only Bengali character and the one ultimately responsible for the final ruin of the Newcomes.[53] Rummun has succeeded in gaining the trust of British society in India, but reverts to the British stereotype of the Bengali Baboo. As Brantlinger points out, Thackeray's stereotypes of 'white hero' contrasted with 'mahogany-coloured villain' reinforced the image of India as 'a field for potential *British* achievement, conquest, and fortune making and a background of changeless oriental deceit, lasciviousness, and obsequious bowing and scraping to the master race'.[54]

The revolt of 1857 reinforced this image of Bengali deceit, duplicity and mendacity in Britain, and brought a growing conviction that it constituted a violent rejection, as well as demonstrating ingratitude and unwillingness to accept the benefits of British colonialism.[55] Popular literature represented the

---

50 Thackeray, William Makepeace 1945–46, *The Letters and Private Papers of William Makepeace Thackeray*, 4 Volumes, collected and edited by Gordon N. Ray, Harvard University Press, Cambridge, Massachusetts.
51 Brantlinger 1998, *Rule of Darkness*, p.75.
52 Ibid., pp.93–4.
53 'The Memoirs of William Prinsep', Volume 2, p.249; Prinsep, Augustus 1834, *The Baboo and Other Tales Descriptive of Society in India,* 2 Volumes, Smith, Elder and Co., London, p.312.
54 Brantlinger 1998, *Rule of Darkness*, p. 107.
55 Mackenzie 1999, 'Empire and Metropolitan Cultures', p.281.

India of 1857 to 1859 and its people in terms similar to Becher, using polarised and racially determined depictions of 'good', 'innocent', 'just', 'moral' and 'civilised' British, against 'evil', 'guilty', 'lawless', 'depraved' and 'barbaric' Indians. British literature on India underwent a fundamental change after 1857, assuming the flavour of 'self-conscious, drum-beating jingoism' popularly associated with British militarism and superiority in the Victorian period.[56] No longer was it possible in such accounts for Indians 'to progress in the scale of civilisation' as had been a common liberal view of the British colonial mission in India during the first half of the Nineteenth Century.[57] Popular accounts of the mutiny often depicted it as 'nothing more than an irrational panic on the subject of caste among credulous and superstitious sepoys', which 'evoked a cleansing sense of heroism and self-assertion' in attitudes to empire in the metropole.[58] Such accounts were not uncontested in Britain, Benjamin Disraeli for one arguing that the causes of the revolt lay in 'general discontent', brought about by 'destruction of Native authority', the 'disturbance' of property rights, and the 'tampering with religion' of a government bent on the reform of Indian society'.[59] Yet, the very volume and popular appeal of published eyewitness accounts served to reinforce a discourse of innate difference between Britain and its imperial subject peoples: 'Indians ... were not like Englishmen, and it was fatal to treat them as if they were.'[60]

The controversy over Jamaican Governor Edward Eyre's suppression of the uprising at Morant Bay in 1865 both reinforced and reflected popular views on the innate differences of the British from their colonial subjects, of the rebellious nature of native populations, and the need for strong colonial government. The depth and intensity of support in Britain for the actions of Eyre signalled 'a shift in the conception of what empire meant, and how colonised people were to be governed'.[61] Debate on the morality of Eyre's actions as governor split the British populace. His opponents included John Stuart Mill and 'the doyens of the liberal intelligentsia', while his supporters were led by Thomas Carlyle, 'the prophetic voice of mid-Nineteenth-Century England', who argued that Eyre's 'actions had been heroic, that he had saved the white people from massacre, and that black people were born to be mastered'.[62] As Hall suggests, also at stake were 'questions about Englishness itself', the debate over Eyre marking a moment when 'two different conceptions of 'us', constructed through two different notions of 'them', were publicly contested'.[63]

---

56 Brantlinger 1998, *Rule of Darkness*, p. 3.
57 Ibid., p.200.
58 Metcalf, Thomas R. 1994, *Ideologies of the Raj*, Cambridge University Press, Cambridge, pp.44–5.
59 Ibid., p.45.
60 Ibid., p.45.
61 Hall, Catherine 2002, *Civilising Subjects: Metropole and colony in the English imagination, 1830–1867*, Polity, Cambridge, p.52.
62 Ibid., p.25.
63 Ibid.

3. An Anglo-Indian Community in Britain

The perspectives on empire of a family such as the Prinseps suggests an ambiguity about a past in which the older members expressed broad sympathy with principles of English liberalism, that colonial ventures could only be fully justified if British beneficence to its subjects was protected by the rule of law. At the same time, Thoby Prinsep and other members of his generation differed from the liberalism enunciated by James Mill, Jeremy Bentham and Thomas Macaulay and their expectations that colonial policies should aim to 'form a class of persons, Indian in blood and colour, but English in taste, in opinions, in morals, and in intellect'.[64] Thoby Prinsep's understanding of Indian societies, derived from his long residence in India, his support for colonial policies designed to co-opt Indian elites into the British colonial project put him into substantial agreement with those such as Benjamin Disraeli, who believed that the aetiology of Indian opposition to British rule lay in the East India Company's abandonment of the 'grand principles' of religious non-interference, support for Indian language and culture and nurturing of elites.[65]

Yet, even old Anglo-Indians such as Thoby Prinsep were subject to popular accounts and explanations of the 'mutiny', particularly in light of the continuing family presence in India and reports of the brutalities committed by Indians against the British. The social life of the Prinseps in Britain revolved around men such as Alfred Tennyson, whose patriotic statements as Poet Laureate on the obligations of Britain to preserve its empire were well known. Thoby Prinsep was a member of Tennyson's social circle after the Prinseps left Little Holland House and established themselves at Freshwater on the Isle of Wight, near the Tennyson family home, Farringford, in 1874. To Tennyson, Britain was obliged to preserve empire in the face of rebellion and insurgency, and the outbreak of the Indian revolt served 'as a warning to all but madmen against want of vigour and swift decisiveness'.[66] Tennyson strongly supported Edward Eyre's actions at Morant Bay and in 1868 invited the former governor to visit him at Freshwater, where he was photographed by Thoby's sister-in-law, Julia Margaret Cameron, who also lived at Freshwater. Tennyson contributed to the Eyre Defence Fund 'as a tribute to the nobleness of the man, and as a protest against the spirit in which a servant of the State, who has saved to us one of the islands of the Empire and many English lives, seems to be hunted down'.[67] Charles Tennyson recorded a conversation between Tennyson and William Gladstone on Eyre:

> Gladstone was strongly against Eyre, and stated his case in an orator's tone, pity mingling with his indignation, and gesture and expression instinct with moral earnestness. Tennyson, who took the view that Eyre

---

64 Macaulay, 'Minute on Indian Education', p.61.
65 Metcalf 1994, *Ideologies of the Raj*, pp.44–5.
66 Tennyson, Charles 1950, *Alfred Tennyson*, Macmillan & Co., London, p.366.
67 Ibid.

had been justified in the steps he had taken to save European lives did not argue, but kept on asserting prejudices and convictions: 'We are too tender to our savages—we are more tender to blacks than to ourselves … Niggers are tigers, tigers are niggers [in *obligato—sotto voce*].'[68]

Departure for a colonial outpost

Henry Prinsep's youth and inexperience kept him on the fringes of the debates over empire and colonialism that took place at Little Holland House during the 1860s. Later in life, he recalled a time when, uncertain what he would do with his life, he lived the life of a 'wandering Bohemian sort of wight', training under G.F. Watts to fulfil his aspirations as an artist, working as Thoby's secretary at the India Office, and looking after his younger siblings.[69] While a career in India as an army officer had earlier seemed possible, he instead chose to immerse himself in art and photography. He enjoyed the social life of Little Holland House and Freshwater, and later recalled the people he met during this period of his life, as well as his indebtedness to Thoby and Sara Prinsep for providing him with a home. He was close to the Tennyson family, and established an abiding friendship with the poet's younger son, Hallam, which continued throughout the period in which Hallam Tennyson was Governor of South Australia (1899–1903), Governor-General of Australia (1903–1904), and when youngest sister, May, married Tennyson in 1918. He admired Tennyson deeply, as he recalled in a letter to his brother Jim in 1916:

> The old poet, dear old fellow, was particularly kind to me, I thought. He got me to help him plant a small oak tree and then he took me up to the top of his house to a sort of flat and made me admire the beautiful view there from, and then after tea in the fading sunlight, Annie Thackeray, who was seated on the sill of the French windows suddenly turned and said 'Now Alfred, you promised to read to me. Read something now.' He shook his head in a deprecatory manner, apparently rather shy, but no doubt all put on and said 'Well, what shall I read?' Annie said 'I would like to hear Maud.'[70]

It was this charmed and sociable life in England that Prinsep left when he finally bent to the demands of his father's executors to do his colonial service in Western Australia. It was 'much against my will that I left London', he later recalled, 'where I decided to take up the career of an artist, with very good prospects. I was told that I need not be more than a year away, but it was my duty to

---

68 Ibid., p.359.
69 Prinsep, Henry C., 'Diaries 1866–1922', SLWA Acc. 499A, 22 April 1871.
70 H.C. Prinsep to Jim Prinsep, 2 April 2nd, 1916 (Private collection).

come and view the land which I might probably inherit, so I consented.'[71] He knew little about the place, indeed he knew no-one who had been to Western Australia and could offer contemporary advice on the state of the young colony, the potential of the family estates and the indigenous people. The executors were instead dependent on the brief and business-like letters of the estate managers in Western Australia, such as W.B. Mitchell, who they had never met, but whose reports on the affairs of the estate were consistently gloomy.[72]

It had been nearly 40 years since Henry Prinsep's uncle, Augustus, had visited Van Diemen's Land in 1829–30 and recorded his vivid account in a posthumously published book, *The Journal of a Voyage from Calcutta to Van Diemen's Land*. Ailing from the effects of tuberculosis, Augustus was in search of a change and liked what he saw of Tasmania, which appealed to him as a place for his family to settle away from the rigours of India, to own land and participate in the development of the colony. 'The power of again ranging about the fields', he wrote, 'and conversing with nature thus easily … without fear of a burning tropical sun and the lassitude its presence produces, is to me a never-failing source of delight.'[73] He saw little to excite him in the Aboriginal people of the island colony, although he rarely encountered them during his travels around the island. They were 'luckless mortals', 'dark, short in stature, with disproportionately thin limbs and shapeless bodies, entirely naked … and a most hideous expression of countenance'. He describes their colonisation as initially harmonious, until Aboriginal people 'ran back into the woods', where they lay in wait for the white man, eager to attack with their 'formidable spears'. Because they were 'undoubtedly in the lowest possible scale of human nature, both in form and in intellect', there was no hope of reconciliation. To Augustus, it was either destroy or be destroyed.[74] There was no prospect of Tasmanians adapting to work for the Europeans, and settlers were obliged to depend for their servants either on their own 'darkies' (as he called the three Indian servants who travelled with him), or locally recruited people, which brought its own problems: 'Even in our own small ménage, our cook has committed murder, our footman burglary, and the housemaid bigamy!'[75]

In his quest to find out about Western Australia, Prinsep could also turn to the pages of Nathanial Ogle's 1838 manual for emigrants to Western Australia. Uncle Thoby gave him the copy he had acquired when he visited Tasmania in 1832, and the well-worn book accompanied him as he set off on his travels in

---

71 Prinsep, H.C. 1918m 'Memoirs of an old settler', in *The Magistrate*, 27 June 27 1918, p.86.
72 W.B. Mitchell to Thoby Prinsep, 22 June 1863, 'Letterbooks on Prinsep Estate', SLWA MN 773 Acc. 3304A/1.
73 Prinsep, Augustus 1833, *The Journal of a Voyage from Calcutta to Van Diemen's Land*, Smith, Elder and Co., London, p.64–5
74 Ibid., pp.78–80.
75 Ibid., p.52.

1866.⁷⁶ Ogle had never visited Western Australia, but gave practical advice to prospective colonists, including information on the Aboriginal people of the colony. He was optimistic that, with the right treatment, they could become useful members of the new community on the Swan River, but emphasised that colonists had an obligation to ensure that they benefitted from British occupation. 'The aborigines of Australia', he wrote, 'have been represented so degraded as to scarce deserve to be classed among the human species; and that has been given as a reason for their indiscriminate extermination.'

> The charge is false: they are not known to be cannibals; they neither scalp, nor roast or torture their captives ... Many among them are highly intelligent, and with very acute perceptions ... [and] will soon become useful allies to the settlement ... as labourers, herdsmen and messengers, every month diminishes the lingering apprehension of their becoming troublesome. As we take from them their hunting grounds and means of subsistence, it is our duty to supply them in return with sustenance; always indicating the propriety of some return in labour; thus gradually accustoming them to the exchange of food for work performed.⁷⁷

Another text available to Prinsep was his father's copy of George Grey's 1841 account of two expeditions in northern Western Australia, in which he extensively described his observations of Aboriginal people.⁷⁸ Although Grey's assumption of British superiority dominated his account, he recorded his relationships and attitudes to the Aboriginal people he encountered with authority and in unusual detail, which ensured that his observations on government and indigenous people were taken seriously both in the metropole and in colonial Australia. On his arrival at the mouth of the Prince Regent River in the Kimberley, he wondered at the responses of the Aboriginal people to his landfall, as they 'sat spectators and overlookers of every action of such incomprehensible beings as we must have appeared'.⁷⁹ Their language he found 'clear, distinct and agreeable to the ear', and the men 'a fine race, tall and athletic'.⁸⁰ When Grey later shot and killed a man in self-defence, he found it a 'horrible dream'. The wounded Australian tried to move and lift himself up and others came from the rocks 'crowding round him with the greatest tenderness and solicitude; two passed their arms round him ... and the whole party wound their way through the forest'.⁸¹ Though he was 'never fortunate to obtain a friendly interview with the natives of these parts', he did observe people at close quarters, was drawn

---

76 Ogle, Nathaniel 1839, *The Colony of Western Australia: A manual for emigrants to that settlement or its dependencies*, James Fraser, London. Henry Prinsep's copy is now in a private collection in Perth.
77 Ibid., pp.49–53.
78 Grey, George 1841, *Journal of Two Expeditions of Discovery in North-West and Western Australia, During the Years 1837, '38, and '39, Under the Authority of Her Majesty's Government*, T. and W. Boone, London.
79 Ibid., Volume 1, pp.93–104.
80 Ibid., pp.143–4.
81 Ibid., pp.151–2.

into deadly combat, and twice forced into dispute.[82] But although he was able to report their 'haunts', weapons and implements, paintings and drawing, the people had no names, nor was there any exchange of words, language or song. Nevertheless, he expressed his optimism that 'under proper treatment they might easily be raised very considerably in the scale of civilization'.[83]

Such was the imperfect and contradictory knowledge about Australian Aboriginal peoples available to a young coloniser such as Prinsep. Observers like Augustus Prinsep held out no hope that Tasmanian Aboriginal populations had the capacity to benefit from colonial benevolence. Indeed, he appears disdainful of liberal and evangelical aspirations to uplift and convert. His is an account of Caliban-like dimensions, in which Aboriginal people appear on first contact to be welcoming and willing to share their lands and resources, but as coloniser and colonised become more familiar, so does their hatred of each other grow, until it becomes a battle of survival. By contrast, Ogle and Grey acknowledge the deficiencies of Aboriginal peoples in the scale of civilisation but argue that they have the potential to benefit from British benevolence, implying that they are fitting subjects for colonial beneficence and evangelical endeavour.

Encounters with the others: 'Sights most curious'

Henry Prinsep left Britain with little direct experience of colonising, but confident that the imperial networks garnered through his family's lengthy involvement in India would serve him well. He was armed with written introductions from his well-connected uncles, and the advice of a circle that included people with past and present interests in Western Australia, men such as Thoby Prinsep's long-time colleague in the East India Company and Council of India, Ross Donnelly Mangles, an early investor in the colony and brother-in-law of its first governor, James Stirling. Prinsep assumed that such contacts would smooth his way into colonial life, and that his venture would be successful. He was nonetheless nervous about his ability to do what was necessary, as his upbringing barely equipped him for the tasks he was undertaking. His first stop was to be Singapore, to assess the financial status of his father's nutmeg plantation and make decisions on its viability on behalf of the family estate. Then he was to go to Western Australia, where the family properties were close to insolvency. His task was to either turn these enterprises around and fulfil his father's dreams of Indian Ocean trade, or dispose of them for a price that would help secure the economic future of himself and his siblings.

---

82 Ibid., p.251.
83 Ibid., p.252.

Prinsep had no notion that it would be 40 years before he returned to Britain, or that Western Australia, a peripheral and isolated Indian Ocean colony that none of his family had ever visited, would become his permanent home. The long days at sea gave him a chance to reflect on the marvels of British colonisation and his own colonial ambitions. 'How safe we feel', he marvelled from his 'perfect bit of civilised England, floating on a sea, within three miles of the pathless jungle, filled with tigers and every variety of savage beast, and men more savage still. What will civilisation not do? Aided of course by science.'[84] 'The sights that met our eyes', he wrote on arriving at Gibraltar, 'were most curious'.

> Thorough sunburnt Spaniards, with guitar and matador hats, Moorish and Barbary Jews, Mohemmedans with grave countenances and large red and white turbans according as they had seen Mecca or not—all mixed with our own neat English soldiers, in red coats or white smocks.[85]

In Alexandria, the ship was surrounded by 'crowds of Arabs from light brown to dense black, [who] swarmed to the ship and began howling and gesticulating during the unloading of the mail boxes'.[86] Arriving in Singapore, he met and socialised with Chinese merchants, 'Wat Seng the Chinaman' and 'Seng Po, the rich opium farmer', enjoying a raucous evening of exotic entertainment and cuisine, a novel experience for a young man brought up in polite London society:

> We began with the famous birds nest soup, and this was followed by stewed sea slugs, and all sorts of abominations embracing dogs, various parts of … chickens and I fancy worms of some sort, crabs and tea, all pleasantly stirred up with a tumbler of champagne or more between each, so that by the time we were at the 14th dish of nastiness we were in 7th heaven of delight. After many dishes we arrived at sweetmeats of a curious and gummy nature, still drinking, toasts & songs, the hosts making very eloquent Malay orations and among others we had a Hindu song from Alagapa Chitty, a handsome young naked gentleman who came in to look on … Wildness came on then and we even galloped about the road in the moonlight and I rode on Seng Poo after Baker.[87]

There was no doubt in Prinsep's mind that Britishness equated with superiority, civilisation and science, and that this was what set his people apart from the others of empire, qualified by right of their place at the pinnacle of civilisation to rule over them. He viewed the Empire and colonisation through the prism of an Anglo-Indian identity that had dominated his upbringing, family and social

---

84 Prinsep, 'Diaries', 12 February 1866.
85 Ibid., 10 January 1866.
86 Ibid., 19 January 1866.
87 Ibid., 27 February, 1866.

life. This was a heritage that carried its own long history, stretching back to an earlier, apparently less complex period of empire, one in which his family had played a significant role that was kept alive by his old and revered surviving uncles. But it also meant a complex, sometimes conflicting and steadily evolving intellectual and ideological legacy for a young colonialist in the 1860s.

16-year-old Henry Charles Prinsep, known to his family as 'Harry'. This image is from a photograph album held by the State Library of Western Australia and shows the young Prinsep during his final years at Cheltenham College.

Source: Prinsep Papers, SLWA MN 773 BA 1423/734.

3. An Anglo-Indian Community in Britain

Watercolour painting by Emily Prinsep, 1814, which may represent her mother Sophia and an aunt. Augusta Becher recalls her grandmother Sophia as always indoors, guarding against the sun with a white bonnet and curtains drawn, a legacy of her time in India.

Source: Courtesy of anonymously held private collection.

The oldest of Henry Prinsep's three sisters, Annie, as a young person, probably at home in Cheltenham or at Thoby and Sara Prinsep's Little Holland House in then semi-rural Kensington.

Source: Prinsep Papers, SLWA MN 773 BA 1423/429.

3. An Anglo-Indian Community in Britain

Prinsep, right, with his sister Louisa in a performance of 'Cox and Box' at the home of Charles Prinsep in Cheltenham, about 1862, when Henry was 18. The other character is E.T. Candy, 'afterwards a judge in Bombay'. Henry and his siblings were enthusiastic amateur actors, an interest he continued in Perth.

Source: Prinsep Papers, SLWA MN 773 BA 1423/464.

'Aunt Jules', Julia Margaret Cameron, Sara Prinsep's older sister, photographed by Herschel Hay Cameron. Prinsep shared Cameron's love of photography and spent much time with her family after she moved to Freshwater on the Isle of Wight in 1863.

Source: http://commons.wikimedia.org/wiki/Julia_Margaret_Cameron#mediaviewer/File:Julia_Margaret_Cameron,_by_Henry_Herschel_Hay_Cameron.jpg.

Edward Eyre (1815–1901), photographed by Julia Margaret Cameron in 1868. The controversy over Eyre's actions as Governor of Jamaica in suppressing the Morant Bay uprising in 1865 split Britain's intellectual community. It is not known whether the Prinseps shared their friend Alfred Tennyson's support for Eyre's actions or sympathised with John Stuart Mill's attempts to have him prosecuted.

Source: National Portrait Gallery, Canberra Access No. 2006.16.

Thoby Prinsep remained influential in Indian government after his return to England, first as a Director of the East India Company and later as a member of the Secretary of State's Council of India. This portrait is by G.F. Watts (1817–1904), the Prinseps' long-term house guest at Little Holland House, and is reproduced in the family scrap book/family bible, 'De Principe 1574–1930', compiled principally by Henry Prinsep's younger brother, Jim, in England.

Source: Prinsep Papers, SLWA MN 773 Acc. 3150A.

3. An Anglo-Indian Community in Britain

Henry Prinsep's younger sister May (1853–1936), portrait by her cousin, Val Prinsep. May was frequently photographed by Julia Margaret Cameron and painted by Watts and Fredrick Leighton. She married London stockbroker Andrew Hichens and, after his death, Hallam Tennyson.

Source: Courtesy of anonymously held private collection.

Another 'aunt' of the Prinsep children and one of the much admired Pattle sisters, Sophia Dalrymple (1829–1911), was sister of Sara Prinsep and Julia Margaret Cameron.

Source: Prinsep Papers, SLWA MN 773 BA 1423/704.

May Prinsep often sat for aunt Julia Margaret Cameron, including her Study of Beatrice Cenci in 1866, the same year older brother Harry left for Western Australia.

Source: http://commons.wikimedia.org/wiki/File:Study_of_Beatrice_Cenci,_by_Julia_Margaret_Cameron.jpg.

The chapel at Freshwater on the Isle of Wight, where the Prinseps, Camerons and Tennysons regularly attended service and where many are buried, including Thoby, Sara and Annie Prinsep.

Source: Author's private collection.

Henry Prinsep's cousin Val Prinsep (1838–1904), son of Thoby and Sara Prinsep. While Henry left for Western Australia, Val stayed in London, married into the powerful Leyland family, and became a prominent member of the Pre-Raphaelite circle of painters, a productive artist and member of the Royal Society.

Source: Courtesy of anonymously held private collection.

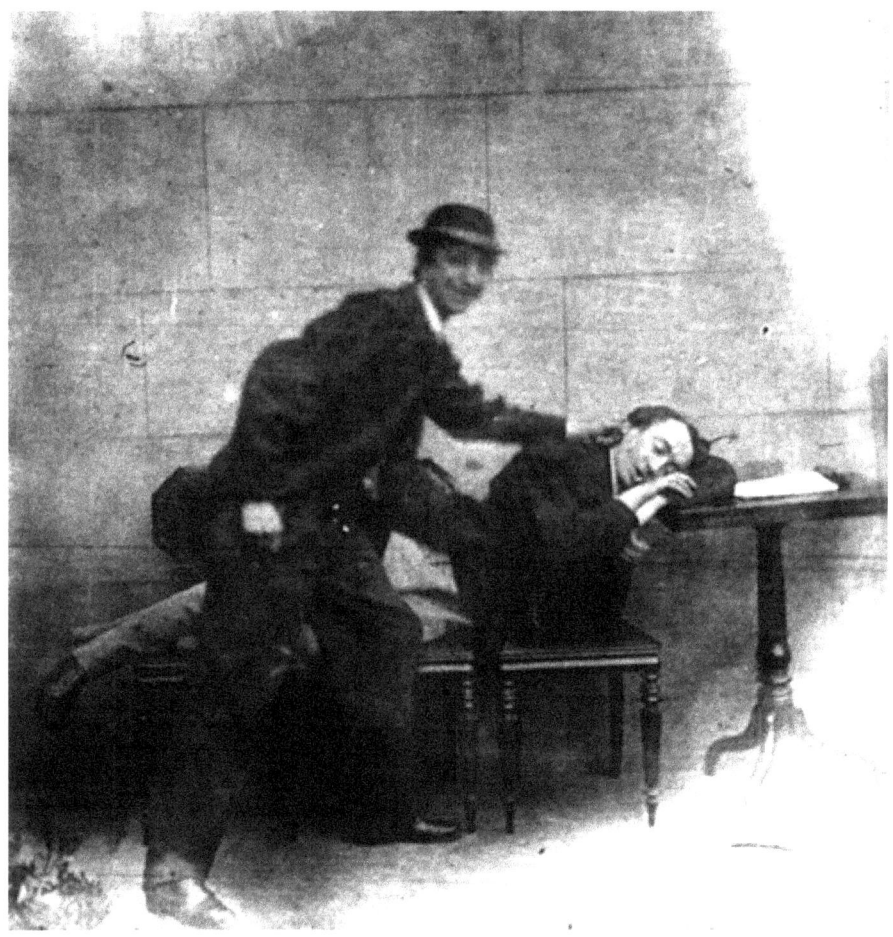

One of Henry's early photographic efforts from a microfilm reel of his photographic notebooks from 1862–1864, the original of which is missing. The photo shows Henry's cousin, Monty White, with false nose, waking up a sleeping Prinsep.

Source: Prinsep Papers, SLWA 'Phots', microfilm.

3. An Anglo-Indian Community in Britain

'The power of again ranging about the fields'. Henry's uncle, Augustus Prinsep, visited Van Diemen's Land in 1829 in an ultimately vain attempt to recover from the tuberculosis he had contracted while on service in India. Augustus found that Tasmania could indeed offer an alternative from the climatic rigours of India, which had ruined his health. He left Tasmania in 1830, perhaps intending to return, but died before the end of the year at sea, en route from Calcutta to England.

Source: Copy of a lithograph by E.A. Ommaney in Augustus Prinsep's Journal of a voyage from Calcutta to Van Diemen's Land, Smith, Elder and Co., London.

Prinsep (seated at table) at his father's nutmeg estate in Singapore in April 1866. The other British men are not identified, nor is the Malay or Chinese servant in the background.

Source: Prinsep Papers, SLWA MN 773 BA 1423/744.

4. Indian Ocean Connections

The last part of Henry Prinsep's voyage to Fremantle, Western Australia, which was devoid of port facilities to cope with modern steamships, was bound to be dull and possibly dangerous. 'I had the spirit of adventure upon me', he recalled, so rather than take a more comfortable voyage via Mauritius to the deep-water harbor at King George's Sound, he embarked on the 141 ton sailing ship, 'David & Jessie', with 'an immense box of tasty food, and much wine to comfort me on this hazardous trip'.[1] The next month was a time of almost exquisite boredom, 'an idle, slow and uncomfortable life', as the little ship rolled its way south from Singapore, encountering endlessly rough seas as it skirted the coast of Western Australia. On his first night out, Henry moved his swag from an airless cabin onto deck, and there he 'slept rolled up in my rug, on the seat over the hencoop—the captain on the same seat with his feet just beyond my pillow and during the night I got a reminder of this as my pillow was nearly kicked from under my head. Odd dreams I had of England and the people there, with most improbable renderings of the facts which happened before I left, jumbled up in a wild manner with the customs of these countries.'[2]

On the morning of 22 May, he awoke to find himself off Fremantle. As the 'David & Jessie' sailed slowly between the island of Rottnest and the mainland, he gazed at the flat, almost featureless and colourless coast of the place that was to be his new home. In this place, so different from the lustrous green of his native England and the colour and vitality of his uncles' India, he wondered whether the best thing to do would be to sell up immediately and return to England, to build a career as an artist, or make a belated attempt to enter the India Office.[3] Like many immigrants before and since, he wondered at the sun-bleached drabness of the port town of Fremantle, a place where roads and buildings alike were constructed of limestone and sand, a blinding vista after long weeks at sea. 'The only noticeable building to be seen', he recalled many years later, was Fremantle Prison, 'and from that distance I had imagined that it was a nice terrace where one could get good lodgings; no doubt if one had tried to do so it would have been possible, but it would not have been so easy to leave.'[4] He had arrived, but did not know then that it would be over 40 years before he would once again set foot in England, to be reunited with his sisters and brothers. Western Australia was to become his permanent home, the place

---

1 Henry Prinsep in *The Magistrate*, 27 June 1918.
2 Prinsep, Henry C., 'Diaries 1866–1922', SLWA Acc. 499A, 21 April 1866.
3 Ibid., 16 May 1866.
4 Henry Prinsep in *The Magistrate*, 27 June 1918.

where he would try and follow family tradition and create his own colonial dream; the little port on the edge of the Indian Ocean was where he would work to secure an elusive and ultimately unattainable fortune.

Henry Prinsep may have been excited about his voyage to Western Australia and intrigued at exotic sights in the ports along the way, but the principle purpose of his adventure was inescapable. To him had fallen the forbidding task of rescuing his father's Indian Ocean commercial vision, a venture that he hoped would be accomplished quickly, leaving him free to return to his family environment in London and resume his interrupted career as an artist. Soon after his arrival, it became obvious that the farms were close to bankruptcy and that his presence would be required for some years. Furthermore, he met and fell in love with the youngest daughter of a scion of Western Australian landowning families, John Garrett Bussell. Marrying 19-year-old Josephine in 1868, he became closely involved in the affairs of the colony and, after some hesitation, decided to stay. In Western Australia he found a network which included 'old Indians', some of whom had known and worked with his father and uncles, and others born and brought up in other colonial spheres, including the West Indies and Africa. He understood and anticipated that his colonial associations would open doors in the new colony and provide him with opportunities not available to others. He had no need to prove his abilities or *bona fides*. The letters of introduction and the fact that his family name was known and respected guaranteed him a place in the colony's elite society, an audience with the governor or senior colonial officials any time he desired it, and appointment to prestigious posts and the prospect of a civil service post if his entrepreneurial endeavours failed.

His immediate task was the pursuit of his father's ideas of an interconnected Indian Ocean world, one in which trade, goods and labour might flow freely around a series of ports radiating from India. Charles Prinsep had conceived of this web of Indian Ocean commerce as an Indian 'triple empire' with 'such a combination of means upon an extended surface as the world has not yet beheld united under one dominion'.[5] Henry Prinsep's efforts to fulfil his father's vision of developing the Western Australian colony as part of an Indian Ocean profit region, by supplying Indian markets in horses and timber using Indian money, labour and shipping, preoccupied him during his first eight years in the colony. He anticipated that his colonial networks would bring his aspirations to fruition and, although he was bereft of the commercial and managerial experience that may have given him a chance of succeeding, worked tirelessly to fulfill his father's vision, albeit with an increasing sense of exasperation. His reserves of youthful energy and enthusiasm were no antidote for the problems confronting him.

---

5   India Office Records, 'East India Company Board's Collections, Proposal by C.R. Prinsep for Transferring Children from India to New South Wales and Van Dieman's Land', 1830–1831, Volume 1240, 40599–40767, British Library, 11 October 1828.

There was little money in the colony and low domestic demand for the goods he was able to produce, while the dream of an Indian Ocean trading venture was destroyed by his inability to respond to demand from Indian markets. After eight years, Prinsep was forced to dispose of the properties to meet the substantial debts accumulated by the venture. Despite his commercial failure, he decided to stay in Western Australian, a place where he could own land and utilise his colonial connections and status as a member of the colonial elite.

Outposts of a subimperial empire

Charles Prinsep's land and business interests in Singapore, Western Australia and Tasmania were formed from a perspective of Calcutta as an imperial hub, a source of administrative and military expertise, Indian labour and goods, and a destination for the produce of these nascent colonies. As historian Thomas Metcalf shows in his 2007 book, *Imperial Connections*, there were many in India who advocated the idea of an Indian 'subimperial center', 'a nodal point from which peoples, ideas, good and institutions … radiated outwards' to other British colonies in the Indian Ocean region.[6] Both Indians and Britons 'hastened to take advantage of the opportunities provided by the growth of the colonial empire' through investment of capital, particularly those 'technically trained personnel and military officers', who 'saw in colonial service a way to carve out for themselves positions of greater responsibility' than were available in India.[7] To Charles Prinsep, Singapore offered considerable potential for the investment of Indian expertise, money and labour in agriculture and transport infrastructure. It was an administrative outpost of the Bengal Presidency and a strategically located depot close to Chinese ports. As Augustus Prinsep wrote in 1829, it was an 'infant Hercules of commerce, which has already strangled the two snakes, Penang and Malacca, that thought to eat him up in his cradle'.[8] It was also a place where former British Indians might settle, its climate 'more salubrious' than that of Calcutta and 'not so thickly crowded'. 'People of all nations, Oriental, European' and 'grotesque though scanty groups of Chinese, Malays, and demi-English', wrote Augustus, 'submit themselves to the smiling or astonished face of the visitor.'[9] For one accustomed to the rigours of life as a civil servant in the Mofussil, Singapore offered a much better social life, boasting 'an amazing number of merchants, and no less than nine lady-families'.[10] Charles

---

6   Metcalf, Thomas R. 2007, *Imperial Connections: India in the Indian Ocean arena, 1860–1920*, University of California Press, Berkeley, pp.1, 7.
7   Ibid., pp.4–5.
8   Prinsep, Augustus 1833, *The Journal of a Voyage from Calcutta to Van Diemen's Land*, Smith, Elder and Co., London, p.17.
9   Ibid., p. 5–6.
10 Ibid., p.27.

Prinsep invested heavily in land, the development of a nutmeg plantation and in a joint stock company to develop harbour facilities, 'an enterprise … much wanted for the trade of this important entrepot', according to William Prinsep.[11] Charles was also enthusiastic about the potential of Australia as a place to invest in land and enterprises, and as a possible destination for his extended family after their Indian service. In 1829, Augustus Prinsep reported favorably on the prospects of Tasmania as a place to live. On arrival in Hobart, he was delighted to find 'a thousand English associations … carts and cottages, ships and shops, girls in their pattens, boys playing at marbles; above all the rosy countenances, and chubby cheeks, and English voices'.[12] Here he believed members of our 'hitherto lucky family … might have a chance of happiness, and plenty'.[13]

Charles Prinsep's interest in Western Australia arose nearly a decade after he had bought land in Van Diemen's Land and was, according to Henry Prinsep's memoirs, almost accidental. His father, he wrote, was 'fond of investing his money in newly discovered lands, he was also fond of horses, and his idea … was to establish horse breeding stations from which could be drawn first-class animals for the Indian turf or the Army'.[14] Intent on purchasing land at Port Phillip, he changed his mind after meeting Swan River Colony Governor, Sir James Stirling, who 'happened to arrive in Calcutta, and my father, hearing of it, invited him to his house': 'Of course there was much talk of Australia, and Admiral Stirling by the end of the evening had persuaded my father that Swan River was far more advantageous as a theatre of operations than Port Phillip.'[15] This whimsical account of Stirling's intervention in Charles Prinsep's plans hints at the growing interest in India in the potential of Australia as a place to invest, particularly after the dilution of the East India Company's trading monopolies in the charter renewals of 1813 and 1833.

Established in 1829 and much closer to Calcutta than the eastern seaboard colonies of Sydney and Hobart, the conveniently-located new colony on the Swan River offered distinct advantages for Indian investment. Chief proponent and foundation Governor, James Stirling, marshalled his Indian connections, including Calcutta-based brother, Edward, and Ross Donnelly Mangles (Chairman of the East India Company in 1857 and a member of the Council of India after 1858), to pressure Imperial authorities to support his proposals. He based much of his argument on the strategic importance of the Swan River, which would serve to augment British trading networks in the Indian Ocean. Initial responses from the Colonial Office, however, were lukewarm. While it could

---

11 Prinsep, William, 'The Memoirs of William Prinsep', 3 Volumes, British Library, OIOC MSS Eur. D. 1160/1, Volume 2, p.46.
12 Prinsep 1833, *The Journal of Voyage from Calcutta to Van Diemen's Land*, p.51.
13 Ibid., p.107.
14 Henry Prinsep in *The Magistrate*, 27 June 1918.
15 Ibid.

appreciate the value of forestalling French claims to the west coast of Australia, it doubted that a colony would do much to expand 'commercial intercourse with India, the Malays'. Furthermore, the well-known hazards and lack of safe ports on the Western Australian coastline meant that the captains of Indiamen would continue to avoid the area.[16] The Colonial Office had 'no objection' if the East India Company wanted to establish a settlement 'for any purpose at Swan River … and would afford them every proper facility, but I am not aware of any sufficient motive to induce them to embark on such a project'.[17]

The colony eventually got underway after support from Colonial Office Under-Secretary, R.W. Hay, and New South Wales Governor, Sir Ralph Darling, and with assurances by Stirling and Thomas Peel that it would entail minimal cost to the British government, being largely based on a land grant system aimed at attracting 10,000 investors: 'All that would be required would be for the Government to annex the land, send a minimal civil establishment to administer its distribution and uphold the legal system, and a small military detachment for its protection.'[18] Large grants of land were allocated to Stirling and Peel, and other lands in Western Australia were thrown open for selection on similar terms. Potential colonists would be granted lands proportionate to their investments, including the cost of passage for immigrants, transport of stock and farm infrastructure, building materials and other materials needed to establish a house and farm.[19] Investors were initially eager to take advantage of the opportunity to join the venture and embark with James Stirling as he left Portsmouth for the Swan River in February 1829. Two more fleets arrived in August and October, and, by December, Thomas Peel's establishment of 182 men, women and children arrived in 'The Gilmour'.[20] Land selections soon covered the river frontage of the Swan River and extended along the coast and inland. In the words of colonial historian Warren Bert Kimberly, it became evident that 'numbers of the settlers were very ill suited to pioneering'. 'They huddled together on the beach', pestered Stirling with 'ignorant questions', blamed him for attracting them to the colony, and made plans to leave. Their 'doleful and exaggerated' reports helped fuel an image of a colony in trouble, where settlers were forced to contend with a hostile and inhospitable terrain, and chronic shortages of food and supplies. On his recuperative visit to Van Diemen's Land in 1829, Augustus Prinsep imagined the Swan River settlers 'floundering in the mud and sand', their expectations of

---

16 Eddy, J.J. 1969, *Britain and the Australian Colonies 1818–1831: The technique of government*, Clarendon, Oxford, p.242.
17 Statham-Drew, Pamela 2003, *James Stirling: Admiral and founding Governor of Western Australia*, University of Western Australia Press, Nedlands, p.100.
18 Ibid., p.109.
19 Kimberly, W.B. 1897, *History of Western Australia: A narrative of her past, together with biographies of her leading men*, F.W. Niven and Co., Melbourne, p.37.
20 Ibid., p.49.

a bountiful land dashed by a land 'that had no trees'.[21] Yet, by the time Stirling finished his term as governor, in December 1838, the colony had established a firm foothold on the west coast of Australia. The new governor, John Hutt, set about implementing changes to Stirling's policies on land ownership and, during nearly eight years in the colony, encouraged new settlement schemes in Britain and India. In May 1840, Governor Hutt's brother, William Hurt MP, was instrumental in establishing the Western Australia Company, along with E.G. Wakefield, Charles Mangles and a number of Western Australian businessmen, with the intention of purchasing land in the colony and establishing a settlement to be named Australind, so as to appeal to Calcutta investors.[22]

There was also substantial interest in Western Australia from British interests in India, particularly from Charles Prinsep's group of associates in Calcutta, who were looking for new Indian Ocean commercial ventures in the wake of the 1833 dilution of the East India Company monopolies. In 1837, Prinsep formed the Australian Association of Bengal, 'for the purpose of transferring investments from Calcutta to Australia', along with a number of Calcutta business associates, including his brother, William Prinsep; his business partners, Dwarkanath and Prosonacoomar Tagore; East India Company Director, Ross Donnelly Mangles; and James Stirling's brother, Edward.[23] As one of its first acts, the Association chartered the 391-ton barque, *Gaillardon*, to transport Prinsep's establishment to Fremantle, under the management of an Irishman, Thomas Little, a former East India Company soldier and an experienced manager of Indian labour, with the aim of establishing a stud to supply cavalry mounts to the Indian army and beef for domestic markets. Arriving in February 1838, the ship disembarked 13 British men, one 'Chinaman and 37 Lascars', along with building supplies, a herd of Indian buffalo, 20 bags of rice (two for Sir James Stirling), and barrels of ghee.[24] On Prinsep's behalf, Little purchased 1,000 acres on a narrow strip of land between the sea and the western bank of the Leschenault Estuary, 140 kilometres south of Perth, which he named Belvidere, after Prinsep's home in Calcutta. Further purchases at Dardanup, near Bunbury, meant that, by 1850, Charles Prinsep held 23,277 acres of 'ideally situated land ... on the fertile foothills and alluvial flat country; ideal for running horses and cattle'.[25]

---

21   Prinsep 1833, *The Journal of Voyage from Calcutta to Van Diemen's Land*, p.115.
22   Kimberly 1897, *History of Western Australia*, p.113; Staples, A.C. 1979, *They Made Their Destiny: History of settlement of the Shire of Harvey, 1829–1929*, Shire of Harvey, Bunbury, p.68.
23   Staples 1979, *They Made Their Destiny*, p.67.
24   Government of Western Australia, State Records Office, Colonial Secretary's Office Files Acc 36, 38/158, 60/137. The term 'Lascar' was commonly used in early colonial Western Australia and seems to have been applied loosely to any arrival from India. Webster's Dictionary, however, defines the term as, 'In the East Indies, a native seaman or a gunner'.
25   Staples, A.C. 1955, 'The Prinsep Estate in Western Australia', in *Early Days*, Volume 5, Part 1, p.20. Note the difference in spelling from the name of Charles's Calcutta property, Belvedere.

The properties, stocked with Indian buffaloes and horses from Prinsep's Adelphi estate in Tasmania, initially did well. By 1854 they carried a herd of 162 buffaloes and 259 English cattle, which attracted good prices on the local market.[26] The Indian workers, employed under contracts of indenture, were a relatively cheap labour force. To this was added Aboriginal and European labour to muster an expanding herd of cattle and horses. According to Western Australian historian, Charles Staples, Prinsep 'favoured his Indians as domestic and agricultural labourers' because they were so 'docile', and provided a cheap and flexible labour force to grow crops of vegetables and fruit to supply the estate's needs and sell at local markets.[27] After a promising start, however, the development of the properties faltered as domestic markets declined, and there were continual problems in exporting Australian-bred horses to India. The overall value of exports from the colony to India, Singapore and the Dutch East Indies steadily declined, after a peak of 14,035 pounds in 1858, and, after 1872, was crippled by a period of low prices for both horses and cattle.[28] Letters from W.B. Mitchell, a Yorkshireman who took over management of the estates in 1860, warned Charles Prinsep about the growing difficulties facing the properties.[29] 'It is difficult to dispose of produce for money here', he wrote in 1862, 'as a good deal of the trade is done by barter. It is quite impossible to make the concern pay without reckoning on the horse produce.'[30] Transport was a further problem. Charter arrangements were unreliable and expensive, while underdeveloped port facilities in Fremantle and Bunbury discouraged captains from seeking Western Australian cargoes and made the safe loading and care of horses risky. By 1863, domestic and Indian prices were falling, and Mitchell predicted that the properties faced inevitable losses: 'Anyone compelled to sell horses to shippers here in the present state of things must make up his mind to accept prices not at all commensurate with the expenses of breeding', he reported in 1862.[31] He nonetheless accepted that exports to India were a promising commercial option and that, despite high transport costs, profits were still to be made on good quality stock. The colonial government and media supported the potential of an Indian horse trade, and the *Perth Gazette* and *The West Australian Times* regularly reported successful sales of 'strong, weight-bearing animals … [which] will always command remunerative prices in

---

26 Staples 1979, *They Made Their Destiny*, p.67.
27 Ibid., p.24. By the time of Prinsep's arrival, most of the original workforce had left Western Australia, probably to return to India. A man named Luttah remained working on the Prinsep estates, but returned to India with Prinsep in 1870. Another man, Naseeb, came to Western Australia with Charles Prinsep's original establishment and remained. He is referred to in CSO file Acc 36, 366/171, as an 'incurably blind' indigent, living on rations in Bunbury in 1856, 'he having no one whatever to look after him'.
28 Milward, John, 'Pioneers of the Warren', unpublished manuscript, personal collection, pp.33–4.
29 Henry Prinsep in *The Magistrate,* 27 June 1918.
30 W.B. Mitchell to C.R. Prinsep, 19 April 1862, in Mitchell, W.B., 'Letter Books', SLWA Acc. 3304A.
31 Ibid.

India'.[32] According to the media, prospects for Western Australian trade with India were encouraging, charter ships were available, and completion of a new jetty at Bunbury in 1863 promised greater efficiency in transport.[33]

By the time Henry Prinsep disembarked in 1866, a small population and sluggish economy made Western Australia an unpromising place to do business, particularly engaging in an enterprise on the scale envisaged by Charles Prinsep. It was a Crown Colony, the only Australian colony ruled by a Governor and Executive Council of official members, with a predominantly advisory Legislative Council, made up of officials and four appointed non-official members.[34] It was not until 1870 that property-owning colonists were granted a limited form of representative government, under which they were empowered to elect 12 members of an expanded 18-member Legislative Council to sit alongside three appointed and three official members: the Colonial Secretary, the Surveyor-General and the Attorney-General. The Governor, however, retained an almost untrammeled level of power, including the power to call and prorogue sittings, dissolve the Council and call elections, a general power of veto, and sole responsibility to introduce money bills.[35]

Nearly 40 years after foundation, the colony continued to have trouble attracting and retaining a population of settlers. Its status as 'a private enterprise venture which would be government controlled but not government financed', in which administrative costs were to be met predominantly from the sale of land, meant a chronic under-supply of money and labour, and extremely slow rates of growth.[36] The inception of convict transportation in 1850 artificially boosted a settler population that numbered less than 7,000 and brought an influx of low cost labour and funding from the Home Office. By the final year of convict transportation in 1868, the numbers of convicts were estimated to be 9,700, a significant proportion of the still tiny population of just over 22,000, nearly two-thirds of whom were male, which was concentrated in Perth and the south-west, including the small settlements of Champion Bay (Geraldton), Bunbury, Busselton and Albany. Colonisation had barely touched the expansive regions north of Perth.[37] It was Henry Prinsep's misfortune to arrive in the colony only two years before the cessation of convict transportation brought a return to the depressed conditions that had previously characterised the colonial economy.

---

32 *Perth Gazette*, 21 June 1845; *The West Australian Times*, 11 February 1864.
33 *Perth Gazette and Independent Journal of Politics and News*, 11 October 1850.
34 De Garis, B.K. 1981, 'Political Tutelage 1829–1870', in C.T. Stannage (ed.), *A New History of Western Australia*, University of Western Australia Press, Nedlands, p.304.
35 Ibid., p.326.
36 Ibid., p.302.
37 Australian Bureau of Statistics 2006, 'Australian Historical Population Statistics', Catalogue No. 3105.0.65.001, viewed online at http://www.abs.gov.au/AUSSTATS/abs@.nsf/DetailsPage/3105.0.65.0012006?OpenDocument . Data used by the ABS for Western Australia is derived from Colonial Censuses of 1848, 1854, 1859, 1870, 1881, 1891 and 1901.

His initiation into the world of colonial business was to be dominated by a scarcity of money, high labour costs, an underdeveloped network of land and sea transport, and unstable markets, conditions that would test even the most experienced of operators.

'Fate has been against you'

Prinsep's economic fortunes steadily declined during his first eight years in the colony. This was a period in which he was acutely conscious of the transnational context in which he was endeavouring to succeed in his business aims. He communicated constantly with family and business contacts in Britain, Calcutta, Madras, Ceylon and Singapore on a variety of business and personal matters, ideas as diverse as the supply of horses and timber to India and Ceylon, and the importation to Western Australia of 'coolie' labour from India. Within three years of his arrival, it was clear that his father's dream of the properties' potential to profitably supply horses to the Indian army was close to failure, and the estate close to bankruptcy. Low prices for horses on the Indian market, the high costs and unreliability of sea transport, and problems with delivery to the Indian market meant that, for each of Prinsep's attempts at export, his losses accumulated. His uncles in England and Scotland, the executors of his father's estate, warned him not to rely on them for financial assistance. 'It is our duty to devote all we get to the payment of debts existing at the time of your father's decease', wrote Thoby Prinsep in March 1871.[38]

> You know the resources on which we depend for clearing the debts; they are the Tasmanian rent say 750 per annum. This is subject to interest claims amounting to about 400 pounds. This year I only got a little more than 500 pounds from Tasmania owing to your brother's having intercepted 225 pounds to pay the expense of his visit to the island and return. Beside this I got near 200 pounds from Singapore and shall have the same next year but your bills of 200 pounds from Calcutta took all the balance I had in hand … we can give you no present help from this source.[39]

Thoby suggested that the properties in Western Australia either be leased as small agricultural blocks, like those in Tasmania, to realise 'a fixed income however small', or sold, at a minimum of 7 shillings and sixpence an acre, a price Henry thought would be impossible to achieve in the depressed economic conditions of the colony.[40] He progressively leased each of the properties to concentrate on

---

38 Thoby Prinsep to H.C. Prinsep, 23 March 1871, private collection.
39 Thoby Prinsep to H.C. Prinsep, 23 December 1870, private collection.
40 Prinsep, 'Diaries', 3 August 1869.

the Indian horse trade and, from 1869, the export of timber sleepers to supply the expansion of the Indian rail system. In March 1870, he decided to risk most of his resources on a shipment of 40 horses and 4,460 sleepers to Calcutta, and sailed from Bunbury on the sailing ship 'Heimdahl', accompanied by Josephine and baby Carlotta. This was to be his first visit to India since his departure as an infant in 1848, and he looked forward to seeing his birthplace, optimistic that the business contacts of the Prinsep family would guarantee a commercially successful voyage. After a six-week voyage to the mouth of the Hooghly River, about 200 kilometres from Calcutta, the ship ran into trouble:

> At about 7 o'clock the pilot ordered the anchor up and we commenced to beat up, tack after tack, the tide was with us and carried us along. But as we were off Rangerfulla (?) sand, the pilot allowed the vessel to drift too much to the Eastward … and we suddenly felt the vessel lean over on its port side and the Captain and Pilot shouting loud for the anchors to be let go. All seemed confusion and more and more we leaned over till we thought the vessel would capsize … The anchors were got out but still the vessel stuck hard and fast. The tide was roaring against us making a surf under the starboard side … it was an alarming sight and the captain was much distressed. A small anchor was taken out over the stern and a warp attached to a big block at which all hands pulled with all their force, but the anchor only jumped two or three times. The boats were got out and the Captain told us he would have to send us ashore and some of the deck horses, to do the best we could.[41]

After a three-hour row to the shore, Josephine was left 'with a well-oiled black man who wore nothing but a loin cloth and turban', while Prinsep surveyed the route to the nearest settlement:[42]

> In the distance we could see hundreds of Brahmanic cattle grazing and numbers of thatched houses … It was a long rough walk occasionally through very muddy creeks, overgrown with rank vegetation, affording us I thought cover to tigers … we did indeed learn on arriving at the Semaphore that some tigers had only a week before carried off some of the cattle from the very spots we had traversed. As we approached the Semaphore the bund was in better preservation and fields were on our right or the eastward and the Dhoob grass most pleasant to our eyes as well as those of the horses. The dogs chased the cattle and I thought the

---

41 Ibid., 30 April 1870.
42 Brockman, Carlotta, 'Reminiscences of Carlotta Louisa Brockman, née Prinsep, 1882–1956', State Library of Western Australia (SLWA) Acc. 931ACarlotta Brockman, 'Reminiscences', no page numbers.

countrymen would rise in arms against us, but they seemed astonished and numbers of almost naked black men with turbans & c followed us as if we were a show.[43]

Visiting the wreck the next day, the extent of the disaster became evident, as Prinsep found a scene of 'great confusion', full of dead and trapped horses and the captain intent on declaring the ship a wreck for the purposes of insurance. Returning to shore, Prinsep watched as 'two big native boats put off for the wreck, swarming with natives … like large cockle shells' and proceeded to 'strip whatever was valuable from the ship'.[44] Later, 'we heard strange voices and saw an English boat manned by Chittagong sailors and a gentleman in pucka Anglo Indian garb, solar hat, white trousers and all, but no coat or waistcoat. He came up to the house and bowed, told us he would rescue us.'[45] Arriving in Calcutta, the extent of his financial misfortune gradually dawned on Prinsep, who found that his cargo had not been insured before departure, an oversight he blamed on his Fremantle-based agent, Walter Bickley. Furthermore, he had signed over the cargo to the captain as salvage and so was unable to claim proceeds from the eventual sale of the surviving horses. He arrived in Calcutta with very little money, exacerbated by the loss of his carrier bag with letters of introduction en route.

Despite these severe setbacks, Prinsep's diaries do not disguise his excitement and wonder at Calcutta, where he was quickly contacted by old family friends. Two days after arriving, he went to see Prinsep's Ghat and the Asiatic Society museum, where he viewed 'Uncle James' bust and also a copper one of Uncle Thoby given by Cholaum Mohamed, also a painting of Uncle T'.

> Dr. Atkinson the curator was very affable and wished us to become his correspondents and collectors in W. Australia of snakes and animals and promised to give us a collecting box to take back with us. Mr Cantor showed me the house where my mother died and took me to E.I. Reg. Offices and introduced me to Palmer the manager, who gave me little hope of doing anything in sleepers.[46]

He was entranced by Calcutta and its surroundings: 'Such a pretty place and through such a populous country, tanks & villages everywhere, palms, banyans … and tamarinds, interspersed among English houses with large compounds and natives' huts.'[47] Impressed by the social life of the 'many excellent people' he met, 'quite a walking peerage', he socialised with cousins and maternal uncles, and was introduced to a large circle of kin and people who had known his Prinsep

---

43 Prinsep, 'Diaries', 30 April 1870.
44 Ibid., 1 May 1870.
45 Ibid., 1 May 1870.
46 Ibid., 4 May 1870.
47 Ibid., 10 May 1870.

forebears.[48] A visit to Agra, to stay with Josephine's relatives the Vines, allowed him to view and paint the Taj Mahal: 'A description would give very little idea of its grandeur, situated as it is on the banks of the Jumna, asleep for ever in its large, dark shadowy gardens, lost to all utility by a home for an antiquary, an architect or contemplative philosopher.'[49] The wonders of British innovation and engineering enthralled him: responses to telegrams to England within 72 hours, a slaughterhouse where 'nearly 200 oxen can be slaughtered at once, with 260 sheep and many other beasts', and sewerage works featuring a 'huge HP engine which pumps up the watered sewerage at the rate of 1200 gallons per minute'.[50]

Prinsep was introduced to Calcutta business men, British and Indian, in an effort to secure future contracts for wooden sleepers, gun-carriages and telegraph poles, and sandalwood. Prinsep assured them that he was able to supply Western Australian hardwoods according to their requirements and subsequently entered a contract with George J. Landells, who had previously been in Australia and accompanied the 1860–61 expedition of Burke and Wills as camel master, before quarrelling with Burke and leaving.[51] The 'export' of Indian maids to the service of 'Western Australian gentlemen' appealed as another possible venture:

> It was very interesting to me to see 120 little girls from four to 15 assembled to service … They cooked their own dinners, cleaned each their own brass basin and on week days guided six sewing machines, turning out 31 suits of police clothing each day. They all seemed happy and clean and I saw a fund of maids on which I mean the W. Australian gentlemen to draw.[52]

One morning he was confronted with evidence of his past, during a visit by 'Nawab Khan, my father's consummate for 6 years … [who] brought a letter of my mother's and a piece of writing done by Charlie and me in 1848'.[53] Carlotta Brockman related the day his parents' former servants came to remind him of an old contract;

> An old man came up to him, 'salaamed' with great respect and gave him a scrap of dirty paper. To my father's great surprise he read scrawled in capital letters upon it 'I promise that when I am a man I will take back all my father's old servants. Charlie Prinsep, Harry "Baba"'. This had been given to my Grandfather's Indian butler by the two little boys when they had left India for England when my father was only five years old.

---

48   Ibid., 25 May 1870.
49   Ibid., 28 May 1870.
50   Ibid., 25–28 May 1870.
51   Ibid., 3 July 1870; Fitzpatrick, Kathleen 1969, 'Burke, Robert O'Hara (1821 – 1861)', *Australian Dictionary of Biography*, Vol. 3, Melbourne University Press, Melbourne, pp. 301 – 303.
52   Prinsep, 'Diaries', 28 May 1870.
53   Ibid., 28 May 1870.

> And the faithful old fellow had kept it all these years and when Harry 'Baba' had at last turned up again he had collected all the old servants and now they presented themselves to serve again the little boy they had loved, the son of their adored old master! But alas! The little boy was not making his home again among them and 'Jinny' his old Ayah was the only one he could employ and she became my nurse while we remained in Calcutta.[54]

Prinsep's financial situation in Calcutta forced him to borrow money from unwilling cousins and rely on old family friends for accommodation. When Landells offered to advance his passage back to Western Australia, he immediately left, apparently pleased to be doing so, disappointed that his voyage had been unsuccessful, but with renewed hope that timber would eventually be profitable. Prinsep was never again to visit India, although he travelled to Ceylon at least twice over the remainder of his life. To Prinsep, India was remarkable for its natural and built scenery, its British and classical Indian palaces full of 'grandeur', while the countryside, although 'pretty', concealed tigers, was often muddy and overgrown, and presented a contrast to the 'beautifully clean and luxurious' British structures. To Prinsep, India in 1870 was a British place, full of British people and institutions, the centre of imperial commerce in the region, and a place that could make or break his fortunes in a nascent colonial outpost.

He was pleased to return to Western Australia, to 'the flowers and grass 'of his homestead at Prinsep Park after six months away, but creditors began to call in debts almost immediately and it now appeared only a matter of time before the onset of bankruptcy proceedings. Prinsep retained his optimism that Indian prices for horses and wood would recover, particularly now that he had first-hand knowledge of the kind of products needed in India. Two charters later in February 1871, however, only increased his level of debt, and horse prices remained 'disastrous', while the next year he received the unwelcome news that his shipment of sleepers had been rejected by Indian purchasers.[55] His diaries evoke the desperation of his search for solutions: he might sell off the estate parcel by parcel, start a dairying business with his sister-in-law, Frances Cookworthy, from her estate at Busselton, sell up and work for his father-in-law, or possibly even leave Western Australia for England or another colony. His diaries betray his exasperation that things were not easier for him. But still he hopes that things will soon turn around, 'for nothing could be better for me and for all of us brothers and sisters than a sudden rise in the value of land here'.[56] In April 1873, a substantial vineyard at Prinsep Park realised '115 gallons of Constantia, 22 gallons of burgundy, 24 gallons of white wine', an enterprise

---

54   Brockman, 'Reminiscences'.
55   Prinsep, 'Diaries', 5–8 August 1871.
56   H.C. Prinsep to Annie Prinsep, 2 November 1873, private collection.

that drew the enthusiastic support of Thoby Prinsep in England: 'I long to get a dozen of your first brew and hope to drink your health in it by Christmas. Your Colony wants sadly some article of export, but it will be some years before it will produce more wine than its inhabitants can drink.'[57] Despite the difficulties of his position, Western Australia still promised better prospects than a return to England, as Prinsep wrote in April 1871:

> I remembered that this day was the anniversary of my landing ... I thought how very different things were with me but still I felt I was more certain of happiness with my darling wife and child though all things looked so depressed, than I formerly was as a wandering Bohemian sort of wight and I knew I could give happiness to them which is the most comforting of all my thoughts.[58]

His life as a colonial land-owner, even one in financial straits, allowed him the status of a gentleman and member of the colonial elite. He became involved in local politics as a member of the Bunbury Town Trust, and actively supported his father-in-law's efforts to seek election to the Legislative Council. In 1869, he was appointed a Justice of the Peace and was regularly called to hear charges and pass sentence on offenders, as well as undertaking other quasi-judicial roles around the colony.[59] In 1871, he was called on to visit the mid-western port of Geraldton to sit as a Justice in the local court. He stayed for a month in this 'dreary town ... with no trees, no flowers and no society, all sand and broken bottles & several large limestone buildings'.[60] The Geraldton hinterland was 'fearfully sandy and the remainder rocky and uneven', 'remarkable for the almost total absence of any trees but jam wattles, and for the numerous flat topped hills and small grassy peaks'. Prinsep had plenty of time off from his official duties, and took the opportunity to paint and sketch his way around the region, helped by 'an old native woman [who] held my umbrella over me'.[61]

By the middle of 1873, Prinsep was forced to concede that the affairs of the Western Australian estate were untenable. His level of debt and the uncertainties of Indian Ocean trade compelled him to settle his affairs and dispose of the family properties. Charles Staples suggests that Prinsep's inexperience and lack of commercial guile were ill-suited to the unregulated 'law of the jungle' of Western Australian colonial commerce. 'Perhaps his business methods were at fault', he speculated, but 'many more experienced men than he went to the wall during the depression of the 1870s'.[62] Sara Prinsep agreed that 'fate has

---

57 Thoby Prinsep to H.C. Prinsep, undated, SLWA Acc. 3592A/24, 15/12.
58 Prinsep, 'Diaries', 22 April 1871.
59 Ibid., 23 March 1869.
60 Ibid., 24 November 1871.
61 Ibid., 26 November–7 December 1871.
62 Staples, A.C. 1955, 'Henry Charles Prinsep', in *Journal and Proceedings of the Western Australian Historical Society*, Volume 5, Part 1, p.34.

been against you', and the estate's executors thought he had been manipulated by 'older and more experienced men … whose proceedings I can only say are unusual'.⁶³ Prinsep believed that the English executors had been 'harsh with him and would do little to help him straighten out the tangles of the Estate, expecting a very young, inexperienced man to do what was too difficult a task for themselves'.⁶⁴ Yet his relief when he finally settled his affairs was enormous. With personal assets valued at a mere 20 pounds, he called a meeting of his creditors and assigned his father's assets to meet the claims against him, 'then rode along homewards with a more relieved mind than I had felt for months … I sat up with Josephine for a long time both very happy that our great troubles were over'.⁶⁵ Colonial Secretary Frederick Barlee's offer of a temporary position in the Department of Lands and Surveys in Perth, even at a low rate of pay, was sufficient incentive for Prinsep to turn his back on life as a gentleman farmer and launch into a new life in the city. As he wrote to his sister Annie, 'I hope to give satisfaction and get permanent employment when they see what I can do. One thing does comfort me and that is that there now occurs a chance of turning to account the education my father gave me, which I have felt all along was getting very rusty in my present position.'⁶⁶

Prinsep continued to explore trade and business opportunities with India after his move to Perth, but they became one of many sidelines to supplement a salary that remained low until he became a senior civil service executive in 1894. His active involvement in Indian Ocean trade and his efforts to fulfil his father's dreams of a 'triple empire' ended at this point. The horse and timber trades with India were never to become significant agricultural exports compared with wool, the colony's main export earner until it was overtaken by gold in 1893. The timber trade partially recovered in 1874, after two years of very low exports, but remained a small export industry compared with wool and minerals.⁶⁷ The horse trade with India, after reaching a peak in 1853, declined thereafter, averaging a value of 8,120 pounds per annum.⁶⁸ To Prinsep, a salaried position in the relative comforts of Perth, close to the social and cultural life he craved, seemed a much more attractive option, and 'a delightful change from the hard life we have lately led'.⁶⁹

He retained a peripheral interest in Indian Ocean trade relationships with India throughout the 1870s and 1880s, and promoted a scheme to import Indians to

---

63 Henry White to H.C. Prinsep, 24 March 1871, private collection; Sara Prinsep to H.C. Prinsep, 23 March 1872, private collection.
64 Brockman, 'Reminiscences'.
65 Prinsep, 'Diaries', 10 September 1873.
66 H.C. Prinsep to Annie Prinsep, November 2 1873, private collection.
67 Appleyard, R.T. 1981, 'Western Australia: Economic and demographic growth, 1850–1914', in C.T. Stannage (ed.), *A New History of Western Australia*, University of Western Australia Press, Nedlands, pp.235–6.
68 These figures are estimates based on Milward, 'Pioneers of the Warren', pp.34–5.
69 Prinsep, 'Diaries', 31 January 1874.

Western Australia as a cheap source of contracted labour to work on farms and as domestic servants. In 1874, he discussed his ideas with Colonial Secretary Frederick Barlee, who promised to raise the matter with the Legislative Council.[70] Prinsep opened communication with W.S. Halsey, a potential recruiting agent in Calcutta, who offered his services enthusiastically and told Prinsep that he could 'take about a hundred coolies from here tomorrow if wanted', and within a few years 'could get five or six thousand'. He could 'lay my hands on some capital carpenters, the head man of whom has worked for me for some time and can get plenty of his country men for all sorts of work, such as masons, blacksmiths, gardeners, shoemakers': 'When I told him that in your colony he could get possibly eight shillings a day (about five rupees) he got very excited and wanted me to take him there directly saying "I can catch plenty Chinamen".'[71] Prinsep's ideas did not proceed, failing to gain the support of the Legislative Council, which in 1874 enacted restrictive legislation to control Chinese and 'Asiatic' immigration, exempting arrivals on labour contracts to Western Australian colonists and imposing fines on captains embarking unauthorised immigrants. In following New South Wales and Victoria in moving to restrict Asian immigration, Western Australia was taking its first steps towards participation in a 'white Australia', which would use discriminatory procedures as an effective instrument of exclusion for the next 70 years.

---

70 Ibid., 6 May 1874.
71 Halsey to Prinsep, 24 November, no year, SLWA Acc. 3594A/63/1.

Louisa Clifton's (1814–1880) painting of Koombana Bay, near the coastal settlement of Bunbury. Clifton arrived in 1841 with her father, Marshall Waller Clifton, who took up land on the Leschenault Inlet. Australind was established by the Western Australia Company in 1840 along the principles of settler immigration enunciated by E.G. Wakefield. The name was intended to appeal to British investors in India. The land Charles Prinsep purchased in 1839, and which Henry later occupied, was located on the sandy strip to the west of the Clifton settlement.

Source: Art Gallery of Western Australia.

Henry Prinsep travelled constantly around the south-west of Western Australia in search of harvests of jarrah and karri, which he sought (unsuccessfully) to export to India to exploit the expansion of the railway system.

Source: Prinsep Papers, SLWA MN 773 BA 1423/216.

4. Indian Ocean Connections

Prinsep stops to light his pipe in the hollow of an old jarrah.

Source: Prinsep Papers, SLWA MN 773 BA 1423/201.

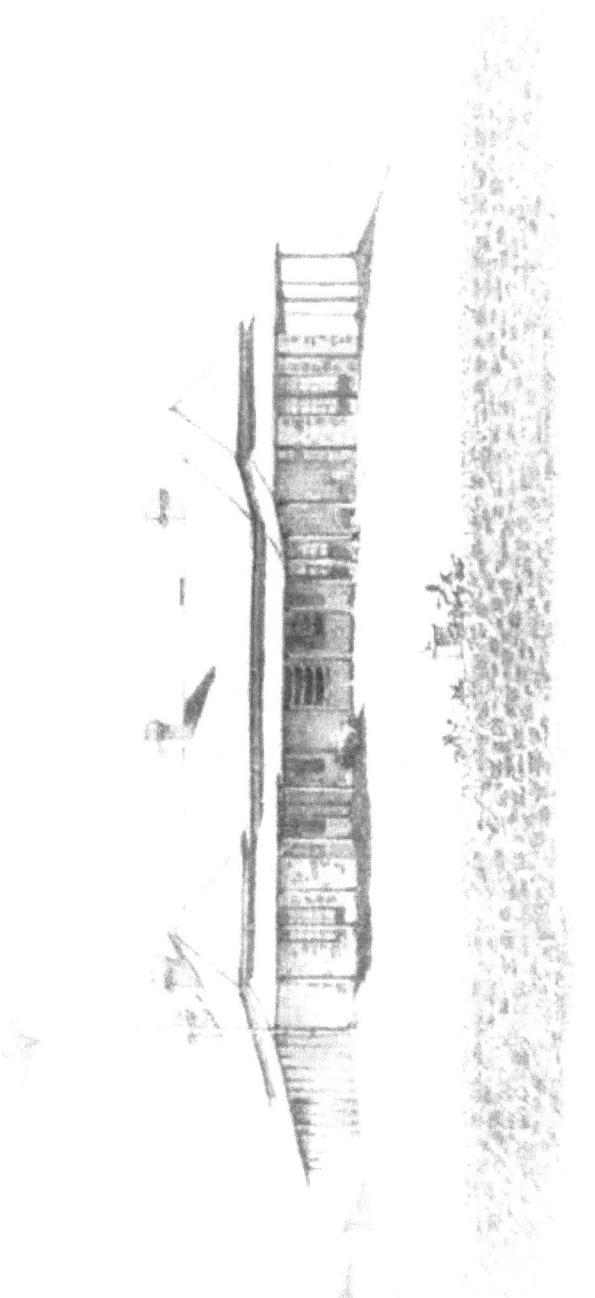

The government residence at Geraldton on Champion Bay in 1871, a place Prinsep described as 'a very dreary town, with no trees, no flowers and no society'. He spent his two weeks in the region painting and drawing the scenery, sitting as a Justice of the Peace and arranging a shipment of horses to Calcutta.

Source: Courtesy of Ailsa Smith, Claremont WA.

4. Indian Ocean Connections

While at Champion Bay, Prinsep took the opportunity to travel around the Murchison region, visiting stations such as Knockbrack with his friend, lawyer Septimus Burt.

Source: Courtesy of Ailsa Smith, Claremont WA.

Prinsep painted this large oilpainting, 'Mrs Boldt brings home the Mowberry', with the aim of exhibiting it at the Melbourne International Exhibition in 1880. Before it was sent to Melbourne, he exhibited it in Perth and Fremantle where many paid to see it, earning the artist a reasonable sum. It failed to sell in Melbourne and Prinsep had it brought back to Western Australia, where it hung on the walls of his homes in Perth and Busselton until about 1960.

Source: Courtesy of anonymously held private collection.

'Map showing Explorations in Western Australia by Miss Hocking, without government authority, 1876, by H.C. Prinsep, Geographer to Her Excellency'.

Source: Scenes of Travel and Adventure in Western Australia, National Library of Australia, Bib ID 3546775.

'Kangaroo Hunting, Serpentine Plain', 1880. This is part of a series of pen and ink illustrations of a trip through the south-west in 1876 with Bessie Hocking, a 'lady of means', who visited the Prinseps in Perth and travelled with them, seeing the sights, drawing and painting the scenery. In the background, Prinsep watches a woman who is most likely Josephine, 'an excellent rider', running down a kangaroo. Prinsep was a keen botanical sketcher, as seen by the detail in this image. For many years he provided sketches and pressings for Dr Hooker at Kew Gardens.

Source: Scenes of Travel and Adventure in Western Australia, National Library of Australia, Bib ID 3547143.

'Bonchop thinks he sees a sea breeze', 1880. Prinsep signed his series of 'Travel and Adventure in Western Australia' 'Bonchop', a nickname of uncertain origin, by which he was known to his friends Bessie Hocking and colonial attorney general Henry Hocking. The party travelled through the Perth hills in a four-wheel trap, camping, visiting scenic places, picnicking and painting.

Source: Scenes of Travel and Adventure in Western Australia, National Library of Australia, Bib ID 3547575.

'An awkward corner of the Woongong Brook', 1880. Two men, probably Prinsep and Henry Hocking, help a woman, either Josephine Prinsep or Bessie Hocking, negotiate a tricky climb on the Woongong Brook in the Darling hills south-east of Perth.

Source: Scenes of Travel and Adventure in Western Australia, National Library of Australia, Bib ID 3547580.

4. Indian Ocean Connections

'Our costume skating soiree, Town Hall, Perth WA 1878'. Contemporary accounts, including the memoirs of Prinsep's daughter, Carlotta, provide a rich context for this otherwise mysterious scene. The Prinseps, including Henry, spent days preparing for the Governor's costume ball. In the centre is Captain Harris, with the complicated structure Henry designed to represent Cleopatra's Needle, in the act of bowing before the Governor Robinson and his wife. Henry as harlequin, Josephine as Contadina, Carlotta and her friend Maude Stone, occupy the foreground, all wearing roller skates.

Source: Scenes of Travel and Adventure in Western Australia, National Library of Australia, Bib ID 3547598.

Henry Prinsep's watercolour of Serpentine Pool in the Darling Range shows a place that is still popular as a swimming and picnicking spot for Western Australians.

Source: Scenes of Travel and Adventure in Western Australia, National Library of Australia, Bib ID 3547608.

5. Meeting Aboriginal people

By marrying into the Bussell family, Henry Prinsep became part of a nascent colonial elite with substantial land holdings throughout the south-west of the new colony. In March 1830, soon after the establishment of the Swan River Colony, four Bussell brothers had arrived on *The Warrior*, accompanied by Captain John and Georgiana Molloy, expecting to be granted land in the vicinity of Perth and Fremantle. With most of the good land allocated, they soon left for the outpost of Augusta on the south-western tip of the continent, where they were granted land in the heavily forested Blackwood River region. In 1834, the Bussells and Molloys relocated their holdings to a more fertile 3,500-acre grant at the Vasse, where they established Cattle Chosen and a number of other farms, and a new settlement, which they named Busselton. The leader and family patriarch was oldest brother, John Garrett (1803–1875), who, before emigrating, had studied theology at Oxford with the aspiration of following his father William into the clergy. The younger members of the family, some of them born in the colony after John had brought back a new wife from a return visit to England in 1837, widow Charlotte Cookworthy (née Spicer), grew up in the rural south west and married into other colonising families, such as the Brockmans, who had similarly extensive agricultural interests on the Swan River and at the Warren, about 90 kilometres south-east of Busselton.[1] By the time Henry Prinsep arrived, there was already the beginnings of a colonial gentry in the new colony, a small group of families who held much of the good land and whose influence in the colony continued through the activities of their children.

John Garrett Bussell was an avowed humanitarian who largely supported the colonial government's policies of non-violence and benevolence towards the region's Aboriginal people. Yet his primary purpose as a coloniser was clear. His family sought to own land and carve out an estate exclusively for its own benefit. His humanitarianism might allow the giving of food, and sometimes shelter, to the region's prior owners, and might extend to good relations, even friendships, but not the sharing of land and its resources.[2] Family biographer, E.O.G. Shann, believed that Bussell 'recognised the white man's duty to provide for the black, out of the surplus his better use of the land would provide'.[3] On the one hand, the Noongar traditional owners were troublesome, untrustworthy and of limited value to the colonial project, but Bussell also respected and often

---

1 Carmody, Freda Vines 1966, 'John Garrett Bussell', in *Australian Dictionary of Biography'*, Volume 1, Melbourne University Press, Melbourne.
2 Shann, E.O.G. 1926, *Cattle Chosen: The story of the first group settlement in Western Australia, 1829–1841*, Oxford University Press, London, p.99.
3 Ibid., p.92.

depended on them for their knowledge of the country.⁴ Bussell wrote of his fear of encountering Aboriginal people in the bush: 'there is something that makes one shudder when he crosses unawares in his path the naked "lord of the forest"', but at the same time, he eulogised their willingness to guide him to water.⁵ Despite what he believed to be their innate deficiencies, Bussell believed they were capable of eventually benefiting from British civilisation and, in the process, growing to be useful labourers for the mission of colonisation. Once their initial opposition to colonisation had been overcome, the process of civilisation could proceed through the agency of local relationships based on patronage, loyalty and labour.

Like his father-in-law, Prinsep believed the status of coloniser carried a duty to dispense Christian teaching, benevolence and patronage, and to assist Aboriginal families by distributing blankets, clothes and food, and by raising funds for orphanages and schools. Colonisation had devastated Aboriginal societies, and compensation was due, but this was to be solely on the terms of the coloniser, in the form of missionary activity and rations.⁶ Since 1835, there had been pressure within the colony for official support of missionaries. An early colonial official, Frederick Chidley Irwin, believed that 'a formal treaty' should be negotiated 'as a measure of healing and pacification'. Calling for the Church Missionary Society in England to send a missionary to Western Australia, he lamented Australia's poor treatment of Aboriginal peoples: 'Not only has Australia ... experienced none of those compensatory results ... but, on the contrary, evils which are of rare occurrence in colonisation—evils the most inflicting and appalling have been—thoughtlessly it is hoped, inflicted.'⁷ In 1882, Church of England Bishop, Mathew Blagden Hale, a friend of the Prinseps, declared the 'solemn obligation' of the coloniser to impart to Aboriginal people 'the blessings of Christianity':

> These aborigines have suffered grievous wrong at our hands. If they were poor and destitute before we came amongst them, their destitution and misery have been enormously increased by our intrusion ... We have in short, in a variety of ways, increased their suffering, and made

---

4 Contemporary south-western Aboriginal peoples identify and refer to themselves collectively as Noongars, which is pronounced and spelled in various ways according to particular regions. This convention is followed throughout this book. Within the culturally contiguous south-western Noongar block, a number of interrelated groups are recognised, although terminologies vary considerably. The language group of the south-western coastal area from Augusta to Bunbury is widely known as Wardandi, the coast and hinterland from Bunbury north to Mandurah and Pinjarra is Binjarub, and the Perth region Wajuk. Thieberger, Nicholas 1993, *Handbook of Aboriginal Languages South of the Kimberley Region*, Department of Linguistics, Research School of Pacific Studies, The Australian National University, Canberra.
5 Shann 1926, *Cattle Chosen*, p.56.
6 Haebich, Anna 2000, *Broken Circles: Fragmenting Indigenous families, 1800–2000*, Fremantle Arts Centre Press, Fremantle, pp.166–7; Attwood, Bain 1989, *The Making of the Aborigines*, Allen & Unwin, Sydney, p.82.
7 Irwin, F.C. 1835, 'The State and Position of Western Australia: commonly called the Swan River Settlement', cited in Bruce Kaye (ed.), *Anglicanism in Australia: A history*, Melbourne University Press, Melbourne, pp.227, 340.

their lot in life more miserable than it was before ... it must be our duty to impart this blessing to those who are here at our very doors, and to whom we owe a heavy debt of reparation.[8]

This obligation, however, did not undermine the basis of colonisation, nor the means necessary to secure the land required for the colonial project. Even a mild-mannered and polite young man such as Henry Prinsep acknowledged that force might be necessary to induce Aboriginal people to accept that colonisation would be to their ultimate benefit, that initial conflict and violence might be an inevitable phase on the path to eventual pacification and civilisation. Like children, Aboriginal people were in need of guidance and firmness before they would understand that colonisation was in their best interests. If, because of their 'innate deficiencies', they eventually proved incapable of benefitting from British civilisation, then this was part of the 'inexorable laws of natural selection', their extinction sad but inevitable.[9]

Although the Colonial Office and early Australian governors in Western Australia, including Stirling, warned settlers to avoid violence against Aboriginal peoples, populations throughout Australia declined drastically in the aftermath of colonisation. In the face of widespread evidence of the failure of policies of non-violence, humanitarians deplored aggression against Aboriginal people, but were 'unwilling to cease or radically amend the colonisation project', instead accepting population decline as an inevitable part of colonisation.[10] The 'silent condoning, sometimes agonised acceptance' of the 'rhetoric of Indigenous decline' drowned out other options, such as negotiating the use and ownership of land. These were 'choices they were not prepared to entertain because they fundamentally approved of the civilising process in which they were engaged'.[11] The 'primary logic' of settler colonialism rested on the elimination of the Aboriginal presence, an imperative that undercut the 'redemptive hope' of humanitarians and liberals that indigenous peoples would eventually assimilate to the structures and imperatives of the coloniser. Liberal and humanitarian concerns over the decline of Aboriginal populations in the Australian settler colonisation process were 'much less altruistic than much current white Australian historiography has tended to assume', as they operated within a context that sought to better manage colonisation, to 'make it more godly, liberal, profitable and populous, hopefully the sexual division of labour and avoiding prodigious waste of "native" life'.[12] The decimation of indigenous populations at the hands of colonisation

---

8   Hale, Mathew Blagden, 1882, 'The Responsibility of the Church of England as Regards the Aborigines of Australia, the Chinese, and the Polynesians', in *Supplement to the Church of England Messenger and Ecclesiastical Gazette for the Dioceses of Melbourne and Ballarat*, 23 December 1883, pp.20–1.
9   Attwood, Bain 1989, *The Making of the Aborigines*, Allen & Unwin, Sydney, pp.87–8, p.6.
10 Ibid., p.29.
11 Ibid.
12 Kociumbas, Jan 2004, 'Genocide and Modernity in Colonial Australia, 1788–1850', in A. Dirk Moses (ed.), *Genocide and Settler Society: Frontier violence and stolen indigenous children in Australian history*, Berghahn Books, New York and Oxford, p.90.

thus came to be seen, not as a consequence of colonisation and dispossession, but of the immorality of the lower classes of white and the assumed moral debasement of Aboriginal peoples.

Contradictory as they were, such views found expression later in Prinsep's life when he assumed official responsibility for the colony's Aboriginal policy in 1898. He never questioned the morality of the colonising project, his humanitarian principles dictating that dispossession was necessary in order to bring the benefits of civilisation and modernisation to Aboriginal peoples. His concerns were not the destruction of Aboriginal societies, but the incapacity of Aboriginal peoples to benefit because of their own deficiencies and the debasing influence of white lower classes. Colonisation was the province of gentleman and ladies with the necessary codes of morality and chivalry to bring Aboriginal people to a state of enlightenment. Colonisation could and probably would result in their extinction, but the responsibility of colonisers was to mollify its worst excesses and look after those indigenous peoples who, because of their deficiencies, were its unintended and helpless victims.

'Fatigue, fear and anxiety'

After the establishment of the Swan River Colony in June 1829, government policies sought to simultaneously guarantee Aboriginal rights of protection under British rule of law and the proprietary rights of the colonisers. What Biskup termed the 'twin design' of colonial policy was intended to promote imperial commercial interests while 'imparting the blessings of civilisation' to the indigenous people through the propagation of Christianity.[13] In his proclamation speech, founding Governor James Stirling stressed that colonists behaving in a 'fraudulent, cruel, or felonious manner towards the aboriginal inhabitants of this country … will be liable to be prosecuted and tried for the offence as if the same had been committed against any others of His Majesty's subjects'. At the same time, anticipating 'attacks of hostile native tribes', he ordered all male colonists between the ages of 15 and 50 to enrol in a militia 'to assist His Majesty's regular troops in the defence of the lives and property of the inhabitants of the territory'.[14] During the early years of the colony, there was considerable conflict between Aboriginal populations and colonisers, often backed up by members of the small military force, the 63rd Regiment.[15] Colonists

---

13 Biskup, Peter 1973, *Not Slaves, Not Citizens: The Aboriginal problem in Western Australia, 1898–1954*, University of Queensland Press, St. Lucia, p.11.
14 Kimberly, W.B. 1897, *History of Western Australia: A narrative of her past, together with biographies of her leading men*, F.W. Niven and Co., Melbourne, p.41.
15 Carter, Bevan 2005, *Nyungah Land: Records of the invasion and theft of Aboriginal land on the Swan River, 1829–1850*, Black History Series, Swan Valley Nyungah Community, Perth.

were, in effect, encouraged to defend themselves and their property, and, by early 1833, Government Resident in Perth John Morgan made it known that firearms were available from his office to inflict 'prompt and heavy punishment on the natives, should their conduct at any time be considered to deserve it.'[16]

The first half of 1833, while Stirling was absent in England, pleading the colony's case for greater support from the Colonial Office, was a particularly traumatic time for the new colony, as the Wajuk Noongar traditional owners resisted their dispossession ever more fiercely. In May, Midgegooroo, Munday and Yagan, three of the leading Wajuk men, were declared outlaws by Lieutenant Governor Irwin, who offered a reward for their capture, 'dead or alive'.[17] Within a few weeks, Midgegooroo was captured and executed without trial by a military firing squad. Soon after, his son Yagan was shot by a 16-year-old boy. The killing of Yagan was celebrated by the colonists, who believed that his death marked the end of resistance and harassment by the traditional owners. He had been one of the most notable of the Perth Noongars during the first three years of the colony, 'tall, slender and well fashioned ... of pleasing countenance', and was apparently prepared to accept the new colonial regime and act as a broker between the colonial government and his people. 'No meeting was complete without him', according to an anonymous correspondent to the *Western Mail* in 1915, 'and no dinner party could take place without a song and a dance from Yagan'.[18] His seemingly inexplicable transformation from 'friend' of the colonisers to an implacable and brutal enemy confirmed what many Swan River colonists had long assumed: Yagan's abandonment of his 'thin veneer of civilisation' showed there was no prospect of coexistence with a people so incapable of benefiting from British colonisation.[19] One year later, the colonial government confirmed its stance of official intolerance to Noongar resistance when it ruthlessly attacked the Binjareb Noongar people, the so-called 'Murray tribes', whose traditional lands lay 90 kilometres south of Perth. James Stirling joined a combined military and civilian posse to attack a riverside camp of about 70 people near the small outpost of Pinjarra, killing between 25 and 30 men, women and children in a dawn raid.[20]

---

16   Stannage, C.T. 1979, *The People of Perth: A social history of Western Australia's capital city*, City of Perth, Perth, p.41.
17   *Perth Gazette*, 4 May 4 1833.
18   *Western Mail*, 16 July 1915.
19   Ibid.
20   *Perth Gazette*, 1 Nov 1834. A website created by contemporary Binjareb Noongar people lists the names of 21 people killed at Pinjarra, and includes detailed archival information on the massacre: http://www.pinjarramassacresite.com/. See also, Biskup 1973, *Not Slaves, Not Citizens*, p.8; Green, Neville 1984, *Broken Spears: Aborigines and Europeans in the southwest of Australia*, Focus Education Services, Perth, pp.71–8; Fletcher, Christine 1984, 'The Battle for Pinjarra: A revisionist view', in Bob Reece and Tom Stannage (eds.), *Studies in Western Australian History*, Issue 8: European–Aboriginal Relations in Western Australian History, University of Western Australia Press, Nedlands, pp.1–6.

To landholding families such as the Bussells, who were 200 kilometres from the seat of colonial government, the killing of the Perth Aboriginal leaders and the massacre at Pinjarra were evidence that their views and concerns were finally being heeded. To Charles Bussell, violent retribution was the only way to counter Aboriginal harassment. Like many colonisers, he was critical of the benevolent policies of the colonial government, which allowed 'offenders to escape … exciting a wild and savage population to further acts of revenge and bloodshed'. In 1837, he wrote approvingly that the change in tactics at Pinjarra had guaranteed the security of the colonists. 'The natives', he argued, had only got what they deserved. They had 'kissed the rod by which they have been scourged, and the white is permitted to walk unarmed and unharmed through scenes which have witnessed repeated murders of his unfortunate countrymen'.[21] The government's previous refusal to allow colonisers to punish local Wardandi people for attacks on property, he argued, imposed unbearable hardships and anxieties on the family enterprise. 'How will all these wars and rumours end?', Bessie Bussell wondered in an 1835 letter to an aunt in England. 'The natives completely beset us':

> They nearly drive me out of my mind. I am obliged to stand around and watch them, and when I am able to return to my lawful labours I find myself thoroughly tired … To me now it seems sacrilege to breathe the name of native in an hour of rest, it is so fraught with fatigue, fear and anxiety.[22]

The conflict between the Bussells and Wardandi traditional owners escalated over the next four years, as the family increasingly adopted harsh tactics to stop Wardandi from visiting their farms and imposed their own punishments for the theft of flour, potatoes and attacks on livestock and property. As well as firing on intruders, the brothers increasingly resorted to taking hostages, on one occasion holding a 'little girl', on another, four women and a child.[23] In June 1837, they were involved in a massacre in which at least nine Wardandi men and women were killed in retaliation for the spearing of a servant. Bessie Bussell wrote that she feared 'more women were killed than men'. Her brothers, Vernon and Alfred, later 'went down to the estuary, and saw that the natives had been afraid to return and bury their dead. So they left their cows and came home for spades to perform this last office for them. They threw in the dirt and laid the sods carefully like an English grave.'[24] In a letter to John Bussell in England, Charles reported that 'the war with the natives had been properly conducted', and expressed satisfaction that so far no European had died, although the

---

21   Shann 1926, *Cattle Chosen*, p.102.
22   Ibid., p.104.
23   Ibid., pp.98, 106.
24   Ibid., p.107.

family had been admonished by the government for taking the law into their own hands. After his return from England with his new wife, Charlotte, John used his powers as a Justice of the Peace to arrest Nungandung, a Noongar he suspected of trying to spear his servant Dawson, near Bunbury, but was ordered by Bunbury Government Resident, G.F. Eliot, to release him. In February 1841, after the killing of George Layman, a settler at Wonnerup near Busselton, John put aside his humanitarian leanings to join a posse. At least seven Wardandi were killed 'in the confusion', and a number of others were wounded.[25] In his monumental 1897 volume, *History of Western Australia*, American freelance-historian Warren Bert Kimberly called this 'one of the most bloodthirsty deeds ever committed by Englishmen':

> The soldiers and settlers ... surrounded the black men on the sand patch. There was now no escape for the fugitives, and their vacuous cries of terror mingled with the reports of the white men's guns. Native after native was shot, and the survivors, knowing that orders had been given not to shoot the women, crouched on their knees, covered their bodies with their bokas, and cried, 'Me yokah' (woman). The white men had no mercy. The black men were killed by dozens, and their corpses lined the route of march of the avengers. Then the latter went back satisfied.[26]

Bussell letters to family and friends in England portray their venture as a noble battle against intractable odds in a new country, a place where not only the country itself, but its occupants conspired to frustrate the family enterprise. John is the patriarch and philosopher, the 'mainspring of the whole machinery', who deals with the colonial government and restrains the impetuosity of his brothers, Charles, Vernon, Alfred and Lenox, who labour unceasingly to establish the farms, build the houses and protect the family. The sisters, Bessie, Fannie and Mary, deprived of the comforts of civilised life, become 'practical and active', face their challenges with stoicism and determination in the domestic sphere in an attempt to bring their 'savage brothers into some kind of order'.[27] Almost absent are the perspectives of the Wardandi people trying to maintain their way of life, although Shann mentions that the family farm, Cattle Chosen, lay on a prime hunting ground and that 'like all humans', the Wardandi were 'tenacious of the land that gave them birth and being'.[28] The colonisers shut them out of their traditional lands and hunted out the kangaroos 'with their dogs and guns, making the game scarcer every year, and then objected with

---

25 Ibid., p.119.
26 Kimberly 1897, *History of Western Australia*, p.116.
27 Shann 1926, *Cattle Chosen*, p.47.
28 Ibid., p.92.

violence when the blacks speared in the open forest their horses and cattle'.[29] 'No doubt the blacks had been wronged', Shann concludes, but 'how else could colonisation proceed?'[30]

The absence of Aboriginal voices in the Bussell colonising venture is also characteristic of the records of the Swan River Colony. Some colonisers understood what lay behind the resistance and were surprised at the 'moderation and even kindness' shown in the face of the loss of the best Wajuk lands and access to game, fish and bush foods.[31] Others understood that violence was often a response to 'improper treatment … rather than from a natural disposition to ferocity on their part'.[32] Using the pseudonym Philaleth, Attorney General and landowner George Fletcher Moore reminded colonists that they were facing the consequences of a venture that had barely considered the 'rights of the owners of the soil, of the probable consequences of that violation, or our justification for such an act'.[33] In his memoirs, Moore paraphrased a conversation with Yagan, a man he admired for his bearing and manliness, but mistrusted as 'the very spirit of Evil, as he is often considered in that light'.[34] Although he understood little of the language, Moore knew that Yagan was furious that the colonisers were taking their assets and refusing to share their food, asking him why, when 'we walk in our own country, we are fired on by white man?'[35] Yagan suspected that his father, Midgegooroo, had been killed by the colonial government, but Moore, outnumbered and plainly sympathetic to his arguments, denied this was so. Yagan terminated their heated argument by walking away, on his face a look of 'ineffable disdain' only to return to part 'the best of friends'.[36] Soon after Yagan's death, the 'Perth Gazette' reported that two of the remaining senior Wajuk men, Munday and Migo, met Lieutenant Governor Irwin in Perth, and spoke 'with a degree of fluency we could scarcely have anticipated', with the aid of an interpreter, 20-year-old colonist Francis Armstrong. They wanted to know 'whether the white people would shoot any more of their black people', and gave the names of the Aboriginal people in the Perth area who had been shot and those who had shot them. They recognised that their people might be shot for stealing white men's property. Although they were adamant that this was a 'punishment too severe for the offence', they promised that the 'quippling' would cease. They also undertook to stop spearing white men, but explained to Irwin that this had only been done to

---

29 Ibid., p.120.
30 Ibid., p.111.
31 Berryman, Ian (ed.) 2002, *Swan River Letters*, Swan River Press, Glengarry WA, p.206.
32 *Colonial Times*, 29 June 1831.
33 *Perth Gazette*, 27 July 1833.
34 Moore, George Fletcher 2006, *The Millendon Memoirs: George Fletcher Moore's Journal and Letters, 1830–1841*, edited by J.M.R. Cameron, Hesperian Press, Victoria Park WA, p.235.
35 Moore, George Fletcher 1884, *Diary of Ten Years Eventful Life of an Early Settler in Western Australia: And also a descriptive vocabulary of the language of the Aborigines*, M. Walbrook, London, pp.159–60.
36 Moore 2006, *The Millendon Memoirs*, p.236.

avenge killings of their people or to punish those 'who had behaved ill towards them'.[37] Munday and Migo told Irwin that their people were starving because of the disruption of their traditional economy and the loss of their sources of food. Because the white man had taken their country, they explained, he was obliged to give them a fair share of its food. Soon after, the Governor established a ration station, under Armstrong's control, just outside the town at Mt Eliza, a move that earned the ire of some Perth colonists who wanted to see Aboriginal people excluded from the town boundaries altogether.[38]

The massacres at Pinjarra in 1834 and Busselton in 1841 largely succeeded in intimidating the Noongar populations, making them wary of taking on the power of the colonisers. When John Wollaston arrived to establish his Picton parish near Bunbury in 1841, at first he thought the local Wardandi people 'a singular and intelligent race—well-disposed towards the whites, who in general treat them with kindness: but indolent and sly, remarkably indifferent to foreign things and customs which in general excite wonder or curiosity in savages'.[39] Five months later, he recorded a series of 'distressing incidents' around Bunbury, Australind and the Vasse, but hoped that 'no serious result [would] follow' these 'accidents'. 'All this slaughtering of blacks by the whites', he wrote on 15 March 1842, was 'distressing and lamentable. And it is difficult to convince these savages that the death of any of their people is caused by accident. At present all seems to blow over with them and they are perfectly quiet.'[40] By May 1842, his opinion was 'much altered about them'. He no longer thought he should 'encourage them about the premises, unless they are employed. They are of too rude a nature to bear it.'[41] Instead, he proposed a plan to remove Aboriginal children from 'the baneful influences of heathen customs', and '(the greatest obstacle) the evil example of the white people of the common sort', and instead have them educated at the cost of settler families, who would then be able to employ them as domestic servants.[42]

Such were the limited options available to Aboriginal people in the minds of many of the colonists. Thereafter, relationships between the steadily growing settler population of the south-west and the largely subjugated and dispossessed traditional landowners came to be based on the harsh benevolence of what historian Mary Anne Jebb, writing on Aboriginal people and the pastoral industry in the Kimberley during the early-Twentieth Century, called 'pastoral paternalism'. Noongar families who had survived the initial onslaught of colonisation and

---

37 *Perth Gazette,* 7 September 1833.
38 Stannage 1979, *The People of Perth,* p.43.
39 Wollaston, Rev. John Ramsden, n.d., *Wollaston's Picton Journal (1841–1844), being Volume I of the Journals and Diaries (1841–1856),* Paterson Brokensha Pty. Ltd., Perth, p.9.
40 Ibid., pp.59–60.
41 Ibid., p.82.
42 Ibid., pp.82–3.

remained in their country were forced to learn 'the rules of occupation' and find 'a place that assured their survival'.⁴³ While the loss of land at the hands of the British devastated traditional society and severely disrupted traditional economies, Noongar families sought to manage and ameliorate the threat to their way of life as best they could. Within an ever-increasing domination of their world by the colonisers, it was still possible to move around their traditional country and escape, if only for a short time, the growing constraints on their freedoms of movement.⁴⁴ Henry Prinsep's rendition of encounters with his Noongar workforce hint at a parallel life, largely unrecognised by the writer, and at the strategies for survival adopted by Noongars in the face of colonial domination. Often this meant making oneself invisible to the gaze of an alien and intrusive colonial presence, as many people continued to live in the bush away from white people, while some took up jobs with white colonisers, continuing to live as they could within a new regime, doing their best to maintain their own freedoms and family lives. Resistance took many forms. As Noongar authors Kim Scott and Hazel Brown put it, it 'was trying to avoid conquest ... adapting different strategies to maintain certain values as others fell away. Resistance was merely surviving, and in such circumstances there must have been a lot of slippage, a lot of compromise and shifting ground.'⁴⁵

'This strange young Englishman'

By the time Henry Prinsep arrived in Fremantle in May 1866, relieved to once again 'get among people all speaking English', the traumatic events of the first few years of the colony seemed well in the past.⁴⁶ After presenting his letters of introduction to Governor John Hampton, Bishop Hale, Colonial Secretary Frederick Barlee, and other notable citizens of the colony, Prinsep had every reason to expect that his colonial adventure would get off to a smooth start. Barlee offered him a room in his riverside home and made sure he got to meet all the right people. Prinsep encountered Aboriginal people for the first time on the day he arrived in Perth. As his daughter Carlotta recalled, 'old "Billy Barlee", a very black old native with white beard and hair, poked his head in at the bedroom window and said "hullo" to him with a very broad smile on his funny old face. The old fellow was so inquisitive to see this strange young

---

43 Jebb, Mary Anne 2002, *Blood, Sweat and Welfare: A history of white bosses and Aboriginal pastoral workers*, University of Western Australia Press, Nedlands, p.121.
44 Haebich, Anna 1988, *For Their Own Good: Aborigines and government in the Southwest of Western Australia, 1900–1940*, University of Western Australia Press, Nedlands, pp.1–6, records the findings of travelling inspector G.S. Olivey in 1902 that many south-western Noongars continued to lead a 'vigorous life of hunting in the bush' throughout the late-Nineteenth and early-Twentieth centuries, interspersed with periods of employment on farms and stations.
45 Scott, Kim and Hazel Brown 2005, *Kayang and Me*, Fremantle Arts Centre Press, Fremantle, p.85.
46 Prinsep, Henry C., 'Diaries 1866–1922', SLWA Acc. 499A, 23 May 1866.

5. Meeting Aboriginal people

Englishman!'[47] On his first Sunday in the colony, Prinsep attended a Church of England service in a bush school house, observing that 'half the little room was filled with convicts': 'For the first time I heard the penal prayer, which asks for the punishment of all sinful men and wicked doers and that the sword entrusted to the care of the governor may be wielded with justice & c. I did not like the idea somehow.'[48]

One week later, Prinsep departed on horseback on the three-day, 140 kilometre journey south to take up management of the three family estates: Belvidere on the Leschenault Inlet, and Prinsep Park and Paradise stations near Dardanup. On his first night out, he was awoken by the alien sounds of 'a native corrobarry … a strange and curious sight to hear the cries and uncouth singing of the blacks round their fires, keeping time by slapping a lump of wood with their hands'.[49] After a tiring journey through 'wild country, all the same', he was comforted to arrive finally at the Paradise homestead, located in country which reminded him 'more than anything I had lately seen of England'.[50] The next morning, he met some of his station workers, including 'five English, one Hindu and two native Australians, Coolbool (George) and an object called Nooky', as well as Timbal, Kitty, a young women employed in the house, and Tommy Cattle, who later became the main informant for colonist Jesse Hammond's book on Aboriginal people, *Winjan's People*.[51] Their responses to the new boss confused Prinsep, who thought them 'funny fellows' after showing little of the deference he expected of his employees. They would 'always burst their boilers as it were with two big shouts of laughter for the first 3 days or so that I knew them', this being 'their way', he decided, 'of showing bashfulness to a stranger'.[52]

Despite this hesitant beginning, George Coolbul and Charlie Neeribun ('Nooky') became not only important workers in Prinsep's initial management of the station, but a source of company, entertainment and sustenance. Through them, he met Aboriginal people who were independent of the colonial economy, living nearby in the hills to the east of the properties, who he could sometimes hear 'howling and screaming a mile and a half away through bush'.[53] The homestead was visited by families coming to hold ceremonies nearby, and Prinsep took a keen interest in their music and dancing, learning from Coolbul how to throw a 'kyle or boomerang'.[54] The hunting skills of Coolbul and Neeribun provided the

---

47 Brockman, Carlotta, 'Reminiscences of Carlotta Louisa Brockman, née Prinsep, 1882–1956', State Library of Western Australia (SLWA) Acc. 931A.
48 Prinsep, 'Diaries', 27 May 1866.
49 Ibid., 30 May 1866.
50 Ibid., 31 May–2 June 1866.
51 Hammond, J.E. 1933, *Winjan's People: The story of the South West Australian Aborigines*, Imperial Printing Company Limited, Perth.
52 Prinsep, 'Diaries', 3 June 1866.
53 Ibid., 22 September 1866.
54 Ibid., 8 June 1866.

station with a supply of fresh meat, as they regularly returned to the homestead carrying wild game, such as swan or kangaroo. He attempted to learn the Noongar language, and wrote up a 'short list of aboriginal words' for clothing, livestock, water and food, language useful for managing an Aboriginal workforce.[55] Soon after his arrival, he ordered them to stop wearing their 'dirty kangaroo skins' and bought them new shirts, boots and trousers.[56] The transformation from savagery to worker for the white man appeared complete when a cricket match was organised between a team of Noongars and local colonists, who won easily.[57]

Coolbul, Neeribun and the other Noongar workers were excellent horsemen and stockmen, and Prinsep's carefully prepared budgets made allowance for their work, but at a rate much lower than for his European labourers. In 1870, Prinsep allocated 60 pounds for each European stockman, 36 for a 'native st. man', and 25 for a 'native helper'.[58] Labour became a chronic problem for Prinsep, and he had difficulty retaining his European workers, whose poor attitudes and 'surliness' towards their boss, along with their capacity to trade their labour for higher wages, meant that the stations experienced a high turnover of staff. Coolbul and Neeribun often caused him problems, being absent without his permission for long periods and frequently in trouble for drunkenness and fighting. Prinsep tried to assert his authority over his Noongar workforce by using his fists, tying them up and, on occasion, using a stock whip. The task of controlling workers who accorded him limited respect as a boss justified the sudden and unexpected resort to aggression and violence. This was a pattern of behaviour that recurs throughout narratives of British colonisation, in which are found conceptions of indigenous people being like children, who require short, sharp punishments to keep them under control, contradicting humanitarian principles of non-violence and equality before the law.[59] Men such as John Bussell and Henry Prinsep, who professed to abhor violence, were able to rationalise its use to control unruly workers and servants. They record what seems to be unnecessary aggression against Aboriginal people with almost a sense of relish and mirth, certainly without recognisable expressions of guilt or remorse. A man like Prinsep might appear, as his sister-in-law, Capel Brockman, remarked, a 'clever well educated, gentlemanlike young man', and 'not so strong and robust looking as our colonial youths', but he too was prepared to use force on his Noongar workers in order to assert his command.[60] This sort of violence coming from a man who

---

55 Prinsep, Henry C., 'List of Aboriginal Native Words', SLWA Acc. 3592A/73.
56 'Diaries', 15 June 1866.
57 Ibid., 26 June 1869.
58 Ibid., 28 October 1869.
59 One is reminded of John Borthwick Gilchrist's advice to East India Company recruits in 1809, on how they should maintain control of a domestic Indian workforce by the language of command and use of threats such as, 'I shall turn you off, as a good-for-nothing fellow; take care! Or the House of Corrections will be your lot.' Cohn, Bernard S. 1996, *Colonialism and its Forms of Knowledge: The British in India*, Princeton University Press, Princeton, N.J., p.40.
60 Milward, John, 'Pioneers of the Warren', unpublished manuscript, personal collection, p.26.

otherwise seems gentle and mild in temperament might have seemed shocking to his friends and family, back in the metropole, but Uncle Thoby and other old Indians would probably have understood, for no-one knew better how to control an unruly workforce than the 'man on the spot'.[61] Absences from duty, the use of alcohol, or a failure to obey the orders of the boss might be punishable by violence, or threats to call the police and have the offender jailed. One day, Prinsep recorded that 'Neeribun appeared at sundown inebriated and got more troublesome, until I had to eject him forcibly'.[62] Another time, 'Neeribun gave immense trouble half killing his wife & c. I pummelled him, whipped him and at last had to tie him up, when he set a wail which he kept up for a long time most dolefully'.[63] On another occasion:

> Coolbool was troublesome in the evening and I was hiding for him and chasing him with a stockwhip all about the fields. He called out for his spears but the other blackfellows knew too well not to give them to him. It was fine fun in the moonlight but he was too wary and swift tho' I very nearly had him once or twice.[64]

Prinsep's diaries hint at the complexity of relationships on the stations, but are framed by a focus on Coolbul and Neeribun as workers, and on their kin as exotic and mystifying but potentially troublesome presences in the landscape. There is little obvious curiosity in Prinsep's account about the Noongar people around him. The words or views of Coolbul and his kin are rarely recorded. They are simply 'funny fellows', valuable but erratic and troublesome workers. Prinsep was familiar with some of the Noongar kin networks, and identifies many individuals in his diary, but for him, their presence was incidental; they were simply 'there', a people without a history and devoid of family and cultural context, in Mary Louise Pratt's words, a 'speechless, denuded, biologised body'.[65]

After Prinsep's initial excitement about farming life, its complexities, difficulties and isolation started to weigh him down. Gradually he became burdened by debt, lack of income and the difficulties of doing business in the colony. 'I wish I had an adviser here', he wrote in October 1866, 'but I am lonely both in mind and body and have to think a good deal about what is the good … I am looking for some great piece of luck to turn up under my very nose amd keep my eyes

---

61 The superior knowledge of the colonial man on the spot over the metropolitan population constitutes something of a trope in colonial literature, as noted in Chapter Three. Thoby Prinsep remarked on it in his *The India Question in 1853*, as did J.S. Mill, the East India Company Board of Directors, and John Gilchrist in his *Vade Mecum*. Prinsep, Henry T. 1853, *The India Question in 1853*, W.H. Allen & Co., London; Gilchrist, John 1825, *The General East India Guide and Vade Mecum: For the public functionary, government officer, private agent, trader or foreign sojourner, in British India, and the adjacent parts of Asia immediately connected with the honourable East India Company*, Kingsbury, Parbury & Allen, London.
62 Prinsep, 'Diaries', 30 May 1869.
63 Ibid., 22 August 1869.
64 Ibid., 21 July 1869.
65 Pratt, Mary Louise 1992, *Imperial Eyes: Travel writing and transculturation*, Routledge, New York, p.53.

wide open on each side of that nose, for other advantages besides luck'.⁶⁶ The 'great piece of luck' arrived in his association with the Bussell family, who were delighted when he married Josephine. His mother-in-law, Charlotte, was charmed by his 'energy and activity', as well as his 'command of means to carry out all his undertakings, with an agent in Calcutta to consign them to'.⁶⁷ By the time Prinsep entered the scene, the Bussells were well on the way to elevating themselves to the status of colonial gentry, acutely conscious of their role as pioneering legends and colonial history-makers. 'Josephine told me such lots about various antique Vasse heroes and heroines', wrote Henry, 'that we have determined on the formation of a book of gossip in manuscript to immortalise the doings in older days, which book will be of great value 50 years hence and may be the Doomesday Bk of W. Australia as regards the pedigree of future WA families.'⁶⁸ This was a history which sanitised the relationship between the Noongars and colonists. Noongars no longer constituted a threat to the colonising enterprise and instead became the onlookers, 'funny fellows', sometimes useful, but more often a 'nuisance', their periodic appearances in the family records portrayed with cynical amusement and a sense that they were destined to disappear from the landscape. Writing her memoirs in the 1950s, Prinsep's oldest daughter, Carlotta, characterised the early days of colonisation as a time of 'very little trouble … except when my grandfather [John Bussell] was away for a time, when there was some trouble from the blacks learning how good the white mans' food was, would often steal it'.

> It must have been a great temptation to them after the life they had been accustomed to, a sort of 'hand to mouth' existence. There was trouble at Wonnerup when Mr. Layman was killed, but that was his own fault, because he pulled a blackfellow's beard, a terrible insult.⁶⁹

Carlotta Prinsep's account conceals the reality of colonial relationships in a contact zone such as the south-west of Western Australia. A closer reading of historical narratives such as Prinsep's diary suggests that these relationships were infinitely more complex than their authors portray. Behind the imagery of Noongars as a people doomed to disappear in the face of a rampant colonising force, there are glimpses of a people seeking to maintain culture and family, and to develop ways of minimising the intrusion of an unwanted colonising presence into their way of life.

---

66 Prinsep, 'Diaries', 22 October 1866.
67 Charlotte Bussell to her sister-in-law, Fanny Bussell, March 1868, in Heppingstone, Ian D. and H. Margaret Wilson 1973, 'Mrs. John: the Letters of Charlotte Bussell of Cattle Chosen', in *Early Days*, Part 1, Volume 3, Part 4, pp.7–28; Part 2, Volume 7, Part 5, p.59.
68 Prinsep, 'Diaries', 24 January 1869.
69 Brockman, 'Reminiscences'.

George Coolbul and Henry Prinsep

That George Coolbul's name survives the historical records of the south-west is largely due to the records kept by Henry Prinsep. His name appears nowhere else, not in a dictionary of Aboriginal people of the south-west between 1829 and 1840, nor in genealogies recorded by Daisy Bates at the turn of the Twentieth Century.[70] He remains a misty figure, the reality of his life as a worker for the white man and how he was able to maintain his connections and responsibilities as a Noongar man being marginal to the matters occupying the attention of Prinsep the diarist. A closer reading of the interactions between Coolbul and Prinsep, together with an appreciation of the cultural and historical context in which they were functioning, suggests a relationship full of complexity, with Coolbul a liminal figure, fully engaged with his people's efforts to deal with the colonial onslaught. He did his best to work for Prinsep, but was unable to fully meet the demands of his employer and would be absent for days at a time, attending to family and cultural obligations. Prinsep tried to control his movements, threatening to have him imprisoned, using his fists and the stock whip to break up fights at the camp. After six years of a relationship full of complexities and misunderstandings, Prinsep reported Coolbul's death in a fight in 1872:

> I found poor George very bad, the spear had gone right through him to the left of the navel. The women were lamenting and nursing him … I sent Bejine with a letter to P. Clifton asking him to send Lovegrove and a policeman. When I returned I found Mr. Charlie [Neeribun] had decamped. I was glad of this because he had served us for many years formerly and I should not like to have been instrumental to his conviction which would only have been founded on native assertions. Poor George I think will not recover tho' James Maguire says he has known similar cases before with sorcery. [Doctor] Lovegrove and [P.C.] Slack came out at about 1.30 and we went to examine George, who was in great pain. Decided to send him into Bunbury. Lovegrove bandaged and washed him and gave him some Dovers powders to ease his pain and then we returned to dinner … Mack went up to put George in the cart … and returned saying George was dead. Lovegrove and I rode down to see the body and met a large number of about 20 natives armed with spears and painted going in search of Charlie. I told them not to spear him but to bring him bound to Bunbury or tell the police. We found

---

70   Hallam, Sylvia and Lois Tilbrook 1987, *Aborigines of the South West Region, 1829–1840*, Volume 8: Bicentennial Dictionary of Western Australians, 1829–1888, University of Western Australia Press, Nedlands; Bates, Daisy, 'Papers of Daisy Bates, Detailed List', National Library of Australia, MS 365, Acc. 6193/A, Folios 97/473–465, 88/322.

poor Kitty, George's pretty wife in a great agony of grief and about four other women singing their dirges over his body. We told them not to bury him until Mr Pearce Clifton has seen him tomorrow morning.[71]

Prinsep, a Justice of the Peace, attended an inquest the next day and was keen to protect his other Noongar worker, Charlie Neeribun, his value as a worker outweighing the gravity of what appeared to the inquest as simply a 'tribal fight' over Coolbul's wife, Kitty, the passion of the protagonists fueled by alcohol and jealousy. The evidence of witnesses was that Neeribun speared Coolbul, but this was dismissed as only 'founded on native assertions'. The inquest exonerated Neeribun, finding that Coolbul 'met with death from spear wound inflicted by person or persons unknown'. There was no material evidence to show Charlie had done it, Prinsep recorded, 'tho' we all thought so'.[72] Two days later, a violent storm brought down a tree at the back of Prinsep Park homestead, and it landed 'where George and Kitty generally lay'. Later, Prinsep came across 'a lot of natives, strange tribe, on the road in the moonlight and expected to hear something about Charlie'. Finally, in April:

> We were disturbed by Burman and Gippy, two native relatives of Coolbul, who was killed. They were in great agitation from mingled grief and wine, and swore Charlie's death which I strenuously warned them against. Burman ... mentioned having noticed some words flying along the telegraph wire about George's death, to Fremantle where he was, and when he went to the office, sure, the words were written down exactly the same.[73]

Prinsep does not mention that Coolbul was a keen artist, nor that he had supplied him with pastels and paper to encourage his interest. A sample of Coolbul's drawings was selectively assembled into an album by Prinsep after Coolbul's death, one of few extant examples of art by a Nineteenth-Century Western Australian Noongar. In a short foreword to the album, Prinsep records that he had employed Coolbul, who came from the Vasse, on his cattle station, provided him crayons and paper, and that the drawings were a selection from the 'very many' from their six years contact on the stations. From the limited range, there are only hints of what Coolbul was seeking to express in his art and what might have motivated him to put the images on paper. There are none of the notations or explanatory words that accompany works of other Aboriginal artists of the Nineteenth and early-Twentieth centuries, or of the native American 'ledger-book' artists.[74] Coolbul's drawings depict activities on

---

71 Prinsep, 'Diaries', 7 March 1872.
72 Ibid., 8 March 1872.
73 Ibid., 7 March 1872.
74 Callaway, Anita 2002, 'Balancing the Books: Indigenous autobiography and ledger-book art', in Rosamund Dalziell (ed.), *Selves Crossing Cultures: Autobiography and globalisation*, Australian Scholarly Publishing,

a pastoral property with which the artist was familiar and which attracted his interest. They show white people and the animals and activities that caught Coolbul's imagination and with which he was involved, such as horse work, hunting and racing, and kangaroo hunting. One shows four horses and a white rider around a fenced yard, in which trees and possibly a waterhole are enclosed. The man is dressed for riding in spurs, red riding jacket, helmet and riding breeches, and carries a long stick. The horses are in silhouette, showing Coolbul's keen observation of the shape and movement of the animals. Another is a representation of horse and human at full gallop, the white rider in racing apparel, carrying a whip, the horse with a plaited mane and tail flowing. A pencil drawing shows a woman, probably Josephine, on horseback. The horse is majestic, its head upright, held firmly by the bridle. The woman is in full riding apparel, sitting side-saddle in full control of the animal. Another blue pastel drawing is a study of a horse's motion, showing Coolbul's ability to freeze the movement of the animal, while another scene, of a kangaroo pursued by dogs, shows the final moments of a hunt, the kangaroo on the point of being run down by two dogs, teeth bared and ears back, at full stretch.

Coolbul's drawings provide a glimpse into the way he expressed a British presence that, in 1866, was still new and strange, but becoming increasingly intrusive into Noongar lives. The new regime sought to control Noongar freedoms but far from being a population in the throes of 'disease and despondency', Prinsep's diary suggests that, in the late 1860s and early 1870s, Noongar families continued as best they could to maintain traditional law, culture and way of life. Ceremonies and traditional practices continued, people still 'painted up', moved around their country, and made and used spears and boomerangs. Families and travelers visited and camped with their relatives working for white men, many of them unknown to white bosses such as Prinsep. To Prinsep, Aboriginal people were primitive, of temporary but probably marginal value in the new white economy, their culture of occasional interest but little value to one whose relationship with them was based on his own values and religion and the assumed superiority of his own Britishness. The perceptions of those such as Coolbul, confronted with the challenge of survival in the face of rapid change at the hands of white men, whose ruthlessness and lack of respect for him and his people was all too evident, can only be imagined. Coolbul worked for the white man, but there is evidence that he sought to negotiate the substance of the relationship. The jobs he was assigned, mustering cattle and breaking in horses, he did well, but he, Neeribun and other Aboriginal workers had broader responsibilities to family and kin, which they were trying to combine with their new and imperfectly

---

Melbourne; Sayers, Andrew 1994, *Aboriginal Artists of the Nineteenth Century*, Oxford University Press Australia, Melbourne; Coyne, Cynthia, 2005, 'Bye and Bye When all the Natives Have Gone', in Anna Cole, Victoria Haskins and Fiona Paisley, *Uncommon Ground: White women in Aboriginal history*, Aboriginal Studies Press, Canberra, pp.199–213.

understood role as workers for the white man. The fact that Neeribun and Noongar people were working for the white man, and presumably were seen by their bush compatriots as able to intercede and negotiate with station owners on their behalf, also suggests that they played a role as cultural mediator between their people and the newcomers. Coolbul and the other Noongar workers took on the difficult role of negotiating interactions between the white boss, who now occupied their lands, and their own families and kin. Noongar men such as Bejine and Burman, who also feature in Prinsep's diaries, were not employed directly by the station, but came and went as they pleased, moving between the colonised world and that of their families, who continued to live in the bush.

Fanny Balbuk and Ngilgie

Although some of the British paid lip-service to the impoverishing consequences of the loss of lands and hunting grounds for Noongar families, there was little sympathy and only a partial sense of obligation to provide material compensation. The prevailing response was simply to allow the older people to die, at times with a sense of mild regret, and to view them as artifacts of a dying culture, the last of their people. Demonstrations of Aboriginal resentment were viewed with amusement or disdain, as amateur ethnographer Daisy Bates's description of Perth Noongar woman, Fanny Balbuk, in the early 1900s reveals:

> To the end of her life she raged and stormed at the usurping of her beloved home ground. One of her favourite annoyances was to stand at the gates of Government House, reviling all who dwelt within because the stone gates guarded by a sentry enclosed her grandmother's burial ground …Balbuk had been born on Huirison [sic.] Island at the Causeway, and from there a straight track had led to the place where once she had gathered *jilgies* and vegetable food with the women, in the swamp where Perth railway station now stands. Through fences and over them, Balbuk took the straight track to the end. When a house was built in the way, she broke its fence-palings with her digging stick and charged up the steps through the rooms. Time and again she was arrested, but her former childhood playmates, now in high positions, would pay the fine for her, and Balbuk would be free to get drunk again, and shout scandal and maledictions from the street corners.[75]

While Aboriginal adults were dying from the impact of colonisation, their children were viewed by the colonisers as worthy recipients of beneficence. The records of the Prinsep, Bussell and Brockman families tell of orphans they

---

75   Daisy Bates, 'Fanny Balbuk-Yoorel, The Last Swan River (Female) Native', in *The Western Mail*, 1 June 1907.

believed they had rescued, to be brought up as one of the family. Historian Anna Haebich has observed that being 'part of the family' generally meant 'cheap clothes, little food and no pay': 'They could train, mould and discipline the children as they wished', she observes, 'and, if there were any problems, they simply blamed the children's racial inheritance.'[76] After a childhood in the family home, these children grew up to become retainers or 'man Fridays', living nearby the family, on permanent duty as general farm and domestic labourers.[77]

Most of what we know of Ngilgie comes from Daisy Bates, who knew her as an old woman living at the Welshpool reservation near Perth, where a 'kindly understanding government had given her a plot of ground'.[78] Born in about 1845 on the Bussell property at Ellensbrook near Margaret River, Bates's almost folkloric account tells of her birth, 'just at the moment her mother was caught red-handed robbing a potato-patch, and her unexpected arrival made the potato-patch her ground thereafter, and she became an amusing protégée of the white people who owned it'.[79] Ngilgie 'became the pet of the family' and 'received the same education as the other children until she was 12, when she returned or was taken back by the tribe', as Bates put it, resuming 'the native life con amour'.[80] In 1866, Ngilgie married George Blechynden, a man described by Bates as a 'half-breed', and went to work for Charlotte Bussell at Cattle Chosen, where George also found employment as a shearer. Charlotte was ambivalent about Ngilgie as a domestic employee and was concerned about her adherence to 'native ways', even though she had been given 'every advantage and kindness' during her childhood at Ellensbrook.[81] After leaving Cattle Chosen, Bates records that she moved around the south-west between her traditional Wardandi country and Perth, 'her path ... marked with altercations and affrays, either with natives or with the white servants of successive mistresses', working as a domestic labourer, shepherd or 'relapsing into native camp life'.[82]

Daisy Bates met Ngilgie during the 'early 1900s' when she was 60 years old and living on the Aboriginal reserve established by Prinsep at Welshpool near Perth in 1901.[83] In three articles, Bates praised Ngilgie's ability to inhabit her own culture and that of the colonisers:

> She was always liked and trusted by the whites, for her early associations having been amongst gentlefolk she had unconsciously absorbed their

---

76 Haebich 2000, *Broken Circles*, pp.78–9.
77 Milward, 'Pioneers of the Warren', p.134.
78 Bates, Daisy 1923, 'The Adventures of Ngilgian', in *Australia*, November. Ngilgie was also known as Ngilgi, Nilgee, and Ngilgian.
79 Ibid.
80 Heppingstone and Wilson 1973, 'Mrs. John', p.40; Bates 1923, 'The Adventures of Ngilgian'.
81 Charlotte Bussell to Josephine Bussell, 20 October 1866, MN 771 Acc. 1972A/51.
82 *The West Australian*, 8 February 1908, article by Daisy Bates, 'An Aboriginal's Adventures: Nilgee'.
83 *The West Australian*, 23 March 1935, article by Daisy Bates, 'Ngilgi: An Aboriginal Woman's Life Story'.

ways and manners and fine principles, but the wild in her blood was ever upper-most and none of the joys of 'jang-ga' life could equal the delight in taking a dancing part in the 'ke'ning' (corroborees) of her own folk and listening to the myths and traditions of 'Demma Goomber' (great grandparents) times.[84]

Bates was dependent on Ngilgie for her cultural knowledge of the people of the Margaret River area, and utilised her Bibbulman linguistic skills to prepare a 1,400-word vocabulary, which was eventually published by Isobel White in 1985 as part of *The Native Tribes of Western Australia*.[85] She is described by Bates as 'the rich widow' of the Welshpool reserve, and 'the proud possessor of seven goats, 12 fowls and 32 dogs, incredible mongrels all'.[86] She lived out her life on the reserve, working as a domestic labourer for nearby white families, looking after her animals, and hiding from the police who wanted to destroy them. Eventually the police succeeded, and, according to Bates, 'mercifully destroyed all save the single whole specimen', whereupon 'she shook the dust of the reserve from her shapely feet and retired to the outskirts of Guildford, where she busied herself cleaning and washing for the white man'.[87]

Almost one of the family

In 1953, Henry's daughter Carlotta Brockman recalled the Aboriginal people she had known as a child at Belvidere and the family properties in the south-west. Her handwritten childhood memories touch on older traditional bush people such as Burman, whom she admired for his nobility and grandeur, 'a man 'so black with bundle of long spears, his "cooter bage" made of possum skin and his large cloak ... made of Kangaroo skins neatly sewn together with a bone needle and kangaroo tail sinews'.[88] She remembered the Aboriginal people of her youth as 'very primitive ... wandering from one hunting ground to another, making no permanent houses and wearing no clothes but their kangaroo skin Bokas ... gentle and friendly in the district, for the white settlers had treated them kindly'.[89] Others lived in 'a collection of bark huts' near the homesteads, and were often noisy, drunk and unruly:

---

84   Bates 1923, 'The Adventures of Ngilgian'.
85   Bates, Daisy 1985, *The Native Tribes of Western Australia*, edited by Isobel White, National Library of Australia, Canberra.
86   Bates 1923, 'The Adventures of Ngilgian'.
87   Bates, Daisy 1938 (1966), *The Passing of the Aborigines: A lifetime spent among the natives of Australia*, Second Edition, Heinemann, Melbourne, pp.71–2.
88   Brockman, 'Reminiscences'.
89   Ibid.

5. Meeting Aboriginal people

> Sometimes there would be a lot of shouting and screaming that used to frighten the children. I remember one day running into the kitchen where my grandmother was busy cooking ... and close to her was a half naked black woman who was sobbing and most unhappy and to my horror I saw a great spear wound in her leg, all bleeding and sore. I think the men had been fighting about her and that was what all the shouting had been about.[90]

These 'camp natives' could be called on to labour on the farms and around the homestead, but were unreliable and often a nuisance. Carlotta writes of one old Noongar man who 'kept bothering' a Bussell neighbour, who threw a pot of boiling potatoes over him: 'That settled him!'[91] Other Noongars lived in close proximity to the family but had strictly defined relationships with family members. One was Carlo Sears, 'rescued' by Charlotte Bussell, who had been 'distressed to see the pretty little half caste being brought up in the natives' camp, so asked the old black woman to let her have him, which she seems to have been quite willing to do. My grandmother always said she bought Carlo for a stick of tobacco.' Also at Cattle Chosen were Joolbert, his 'half-African' father Tim Harris, and mother Caroline, who was 'not much of a favourite with the family, nor was Joolbert either'. Janey, 'half-African' and 'very fat and black with frizzy hair', worked in the house, and 'was very fond of creeping into the drawing room and picking out tunes on the piano, while we were at meals in the dining room below'.[92]

On another family property near Pemberton on the Warren River, Edward Brockman and his wife, Josephine Prinsep's older sister, Capel (née Bussell), also lived in close proximity to the region's Noongar traditional owners.[93] After taking up the land in 1861, the Brockmans had seven children, four sons and three daughters, who spent their childhood at the station. Capel characterised the Noongar population of the bush environment as 'plentiful and friendly', trading kangaroo skins for flour and tobacco and working 'around the garden, digging potatoes, grubbing palms and gathering palm wool for their rations'.[94] Family biographer, John Milward, writes that the Brockmans had a 'good relationship with the natives, and treated them a great deal better than some of the other settlers'. They occasionally worked for the family but were 'itinerant in the main, whenever the spirit moved them they worked at odd jobs at the Warren for a few days and then moved on again ... The local Royalty, in King Bunglish and Queen Jenny honoured the Warren family with a visit on occasions, but

---

90 Ibid.
91 Ibid.
92 Ibid.
93 Milward, 'Pioneers of the Warren'.
94 Ibid., p. 47.

Capel does not mention as to whether they were received with due formality.'[95] Most of those who worked for the family stayed at the camp on the other side of the nearby Warren River, away from the main homestead, and were known by the names given to them by the settlers: Polly, Charlie, Noble, Gharley, Mingo, and old Mary. Others lived with the family, slept and ate meals at the homestead away from the camp. They included children, who were taught to read and write, with the aim of turning them into good, reliable workers. They were also companions to the Brockman children and worked with the sons, who became fluent speakers of the Noongar language and learned about the bush, hunting, and the collection of bush foods. One such person was Nathanial Leyland, universally known to the family as Nutty. Milward remembered him as 'one of the mainstays of the Warren workforce', 'a fine looking man in his youth,' who was 'more copper coloured than black'. Leyland was not a Noongar and, like many of these so-called orphans, was said to have been 'given' to the Brockmans when he was a child. He was believed to have been born in the Pilbara region on one of the Brockman stations, son of a white man and an Aboriginal woman who allegedly did not want him. Milward says that Nutty came to the Brockman family after 'he attached himself as a young boy to Harold Brockman'. 'Having no further use for Nutty when he reached Perth, and realising that Nutty would have a good home and be useful to his kinsman at the Warren, he passed him on to Edward and Capel, who brought him up almost as one of the family.' Leyland grew up with the Brockman children at The Warren and, 'like a lot of aboriginals', was a 'born horseman' with an 'inherent bushcraft'.[96] In 1894, he left The Warren and moved to Busselton, where he continued to work for the Brockmans and Bussells and lived in quarters near the family homesteads, Sandilands and Beachgrove. Here he spent his retirement doing odd jobs and driving 'the family to church every Sunday in the Phaeton.'[97]

According to Milward, many colonial families in the region had similar relationships with Aboriginal people, who had been 'adopted' as children and grew up as companions for the settler children. Some were given a rudimentary education but, as they grew older, became part of the station workforce or general labourers around the homestead. The Prinseps themselves considered taking on a child, to be brought up by Josephine and trained to provide domestic labour for the family. 'Little Chloe, Fanny the native's whitey brown child is now at Sandilands under F's [Josephine's aunt Fanny] charge, proposed for Josephine's adoption', wrote Henry Prinsep in 1872, 'a good clever little child, about 6.'[98] Sammy Isaacs lived at Alfred Bussell's coastal homestead, Walcliffe, at

---

95 Ibid.
96 Ibid., p.53.
97 Ibid., p.51.
98 Prinsep, 'Diaries', 14 September 1872.

the mouth of the Margaret River; Carlo Sears lived at Cattle Chosen; while Isabel Brockman at Beachgrove had her 'man Friday', Jimmy Isaacs, 'on appearance part Aboriginal and part Negro':

> Employed as a handyman, gardener, cowmilker or whatever, Jimmy was unrivalled as to unreliability. Jimmy lived with his De Facto, Eliza Nettup, in an iron and hessian humpy … within easy calling distance of Beachgrove. Jimmy's hearing defects caused Isabel no little perturbation when the house cows were bellowing at the yard gate waiting to be milked. The older members of the Brockman family can well remember 'Aunty Bel' standing on the back verandah at Beachgrove, vigorously ringing an old cow bell and screaming 'Jimmee' at the top of her voice, in the vain hope of attracting his attention.[99]

Milward rationalises the paternalism of these relationships, and says that the kind of long-term contacts between these Noongar families and their colonial patrons was 'very hard for the younger generation to understand'. They were not 'servile slaves' he asserts, but each was respected 'as a man, stockman and equal' and, in turn, gave respect 'without any sense of inferiority'.[100] Nonetheless, they were still treated as naughty and unreliable children, and were firmly under the authority of their patrons. Their patronage did little to protect men such as Leyland from the steady encroachment of colonial and later State laws designed to regulate Aboriginal labour and curtail freedom of movement over the course of the 1890s and 1900s. Nutty reportedly became unreliable and 'developed a taste for wine', brought on by the 'loss of his children':

> It is believed that he never really recovered … and that loss led to his loss of self respect and his periodic lapses onto the bottle. While those outbreaks caused much shaking of heads and muttering to one another by members of the family, they were regarded by them as those of a very naughty child and were soon forgiven.[101]

Over the 1890s and 1900s, when Henry Prinsep was Chief Protector of Aborigines, Leyland and many like him lost custody of their children, who were removed from their families to mission schools and government reserves. Prinsep's membership of the Bussell and Brockman families counted for little, and may even have facilitated the rapid removal of his children from Leyland's care. Prinsep seemed loathe to use his status or contacts to help in any way, and refused to intervene when Leyland was locked up for drunkenness. 'Although the likeable and cheerful Uncle Harry had been Protector of Aborigines', Milward reports, 'and would have wielded some influence, it is doubtful whether he

---

99 Milward, 'Pioneers of the Warren', pp.134–5.
100 Ibid., pp.53–4.
101 Ibid., p.54.

used that influence in Nutty's case, as it is believed that Harry frowned on the relationship that Nutty had with the Warren people.'[102] Many years later, in 1987, a grandson of Henry Prinsep, Frank Brockman, expressed his sorrow at the disappearance of Leyland's children and said he had 'always wondered' where they went. He remembered playing with them when he was a child, but one day they had vanished, never to be seen by him again.[103] Leyland's children had suffered the same fate of mission or government removal from their homes as many Aboriginal people in the south-west. In 1988, Isobel Bropho, a daughter of Leyland, wrote that she and her six siblings had been removed from her father and taken from Busselton to Perth to be placed in a mission home:

> Before we was taken to the orphanage, we used to live in a tent behind an old homestead ... we camped there and that's where my father Nathaniel ... used to ride off to work every day. ... That lasted until we was taken by the missionary, Annie Lock. One day she picked us up from Busselton. She took us away from there and put us in a home she was starting near Perth. She said she'd come to pick the children up and take them away to this home, where they can have some schooling. And that was that.[104]

Isobel Bropho's account provides a counterpoint to Milward's depiction of equality and mutual respect, and Frank Brockman's nostalgia for his childhood playmates. Leyland did not simply 'lose' his children, they were removed from him, his status as a trusted retainer to the Brockman family providing no immunity from the inexorable application of official benevolence. As Isobel Bropho's son, Robert, later described, their removal did nothing to improve their lives, as they all became fringe dwellers on the outskirts of Perth in their later years. He wrote that his mother, father and aunties lived 'in tin camps at Caversham which was buried away in the scrub of the banksia trees, the sheoak, the redgum and the jarrah and the stinkweed', and shifted from place to place in an attempt to make themselves invisible and escape the grasp of the protectors.[105]

Arthur Joolbert Harris, the son of a white man, lived at Cattle Chosen for many years with his mother, Caroline Mullane, the woman remembered by Carlotta Prinsep as 'not much of a favourite', and her 'half-African' husband, Timothy Harris. Historian Lois Tilbrook records that Harris was the son of a European sealer and whaler, and an unnamed Aboriginal woman, while Caroline Mullane's father was also a whaler of West African or American origin who, 'as they

---

102   Ibid., p.134.
103   This was from a conversation between the author, Frank Brockman, and Brockman's grand-daughter, Mary Anne Jebb in 1987, shortly before Brockman's death.
104   Carter, Jan 1981, *Nothing to Spare: Recollections of Australian pioneering women*, Penguin Books, Ringwood, Victoria , pp.20–1.
105   Bropho, Robert 1986, *Fringedweller*, Alternative Publishing Co-operative, Chippendale, NSW, p.21.

5. Meeting Aboriginal people

beached to obtain fresh water and to treat their catch … had the opportunity to form relationships with the Aborigines in the area, which they could renew the next season when they were in the area'.[106] Caroline was 'very attractive and was known locally as Caroline of the Vasse'. She had at least 12 children with a number of husbands, including Harris. Joolbert married Janie McCarthy, who also worked in the house at Cattle Chosen, and 'took a deep interest in the welfare of his half-sisters and brothers', including Leyland's children by his half-sister, Clara Harris. Isobel Bropho believed that it was Joolbert who reported them to the Aborigines Department, and that this resulted in their removal to Perth.[107] Joolbert himself suffered the same fate later in his life, after he had outlived his usefulness as a farm worker. He was also removed from Busselton to the Welshpool reserve near Perth in 1901, a place established by one of Prinsep's initiatives as Chief Protector, to provide 'a comfortable and safe home for many of the old natives who have faithfully worked for white settlers, and are cast off when of no further use'.[108] Again, his connections with the Bussell family were of no value, for, in 1905, Prinsep recorded that 'Joolbert had been annoying Ngilgie at Welshpool, so I wrote to the Victoria Park police to turn him off the reserve and if need be to arrest him as a vagrant'.[109] Joolbert later moved to Yokine, a northern suburb of Perth, where he occupied a block of land and a house, supplied leeches to hospitals and bred dogs.[110]

The extent to which these Aboriginal families were able to retain their freedom from mission and government control depended on their continuing value as workers, as well as their perceived capacity to stay away from alcohol and care for their children in a manner conforming to the standards of white families. The family of Sam Isaacs, 'an Aboriginal or an American' who worked for Alfred Bussell at Walcliffe Farm, appears to have escaped the experience of Leyland. Isaacs is believed to have been born about 1850, and arrived at Ellensbrook as 'a curly-haired little boy saying he had lost his pigs. He was taken in and so liked the Bussells that he stayed on.'[111] He grew into a 'big, strongly built man and an excellent worker', and is best known for his role with Alfred's daughter, Grace Bussell, in rescuing passengers from the 'Georgette', which ran aground near the homestead in 1876. He married Lucy Lowe, daughter of an American Lieutenant Major, who had arrived in the colony in 1886. Sam and Lucy had six sons, at least two of whom grew up to work for the Bussell or Brockman families in the area. One of these sons, also Sam, was born in 1879, and lived in the vicinity of Walcliffe as he was growing up. In 1906, he married Jennie Councillor, a

---

106   Tilbrook, Lois 1983, *Nyungar Tradition: Glimpses of Aborigines in South-Western Australia 1829–1914*, University of Western Australia Press, Nedlands, p.205.
107   Ibid., p. 207.
108   Aborigines Department, 'Report for Financial Year ending 30 June 1902,' p.9.
109   Prinsep, 'Diaries', 5 April 1905.
110   Tilbrook 1983, *Nyungar Tradition*, p.207; Haebich 1988, *For Their Own Good*, p.6.
111   Heppingstone and Wilson 1973, 'Mrs. John', p.37.

'half-caste waif', who had been brought to Ellensbrook from Northampton at the behest of Prinsep as Chief Protector in 1900, and who became another of the family favourites.[112] Later, Isaacs became one of the first Aboriginal people to achieve citizenship under the exemption provision of the *Aborigines Act*, which meant that legally he was 'deemed to be no longer a native or aboriginal'.[113] Sam and Jennie had four children, one of whom, another Sam, later settled in the northern Goldfields at Gwalia, where it is believed he worked as a miner. Jimmy Isaacs, Sam's fourth son, lived most of his adult life with his wife Eliza Nettup (née Hill) in Busselton where he lived and worked at Beachgrove as Isabel Brockman's 'man Friday'.

It was relationships such as these that later exerted an influence on the way Henry Prinsep approached his role as Chief Protector in 1898. Although his domain of responsibility as Chief Protector covered the entire colony, his experience as a primary producer within an extensive family of south-west landholders meant that the issues and priorities of the south-west assumed a prominent place in his formulation of government policy. To Prinsep, the settler bore a level of responsibility to provide relief for the destitute, the role of government being to supplement their efforts, and to dispense relief to those who, for one reason or another, were outside the ambit of the colonial economy. Those able to work were required to do so, but when their labour was not required the official preference was that they resort to traditional ways of providing for their families, by hunting and fishing, or moving elsewhere to obtain work. The children of these Noongar families, particularly those with a British parent, were believed to have the ability to learn British ways and adapt to a future as rural or domestic labourers. Removal and separation from the barbaric environments of their Aboriginal families was seen as essential, as it was believed that, if there were left to grow up as 'savages', Aboriginal people would take on the worst characteristics of both races and become a threat to colonial society. Benevolent patronage of the kind extended by his family members, Prinsep believed, established a precedent that both the government and colonists in other districts should be required to emulate. He was convinced that the decline of this sense of benevolent responsibility represented a particular threat to the well-being of the colony's Aboriginal population. This was brought about chiefly by an increasing proportion of colonists who did not appreciate the 'old ways', as he put it, and a government unwilling to act decisively.[114] As he stated in his first report to Premier Sir John Forrest, 'the settlers who held the country when the last mentioned were able to work have now left and the new generation cannot have the same regard for them as their

---

112 Prinsep, 'Diaries', 9 May,1900.
113 Collard, Len 1994, *A Nyungar Interpretation of Ellensbrook and Wonnerup Homesteads*, National Trust of Australia, Western Australia, p.82.
114 H.C. Prinsep, report to Forrest, 30 June 1898, AD File 571/98, 'First report for financial year ending 30 June 1898, and three months following'.

old masters would no doubt have preserved'. Amongst the 'old settlers' in the south-west, 'everywhere I found great sympathy with the remnants of the black race … the greater part of the charity that was due to them was afforded by the settlers themselves'.[115] Prinsep's life in Perth, away from the anxieties of direct management of a Noongar workforce, did little to alter his sympathies for the paternalistic benevolence of these old settlers. Instead, their beneficence seemed all the more important, as political and economic developments started to change the face of colonial society, bringing new settlers who did not seem to hold the same ideas about looking after the remnants remaining on their properties.

'Pastoral paternalism'. This group of dispossessed Noongar people, many of them likely to be Wardandi, whose traditional country encompassed Bunbury and Busselton, was photographed by Prinsep in 1880 at Berry Hill, adjacent to the Government Resident's home near Bunbury. The photograph is unusual in that many of the group are identified by name in Prinsep's handwriting, along with the white man.

Source: Courtesy of Ailsa Smith, Claremont, Western Australia.

---

115 Ibid.

Zillah, a Wardandi woman who died at Karridale in about 1900 and spent her life in her traditional country at the Brockman farm The Warren, near Pemberton, and the Bussell homestead Cattle Chosen near Busselton.

Source: Courtesy of the Butter Factory Museum, Busselton WA.

5. Meeting Aboriginal people

Zillah and a man known as King Billy, believed to be at The Warren, probably during the 1880s.

Source: Prinsep Papers, SLWA MN 773 BA 1423/165.

King Billy, photographed by Prinsep, probably in the early 1900s, possibly at Cattle Chosen.

Source: Prinsep Papers, SLWA MN 773 BA 1423/166.

5. Meeting Aboriginal people

Prinsep and Josephine believed in their Christian duty to dispense patronage to Noongar families in the vicinity of their farms. Here Prinsep talks to a Noongar woman and her children, circa 1870.

Source: Prinsep Papers, SLWA MN 773 BA 1423/196.

Onlookers in the colonial project, two unnamed Noongar men kneel in the foreground on either side of their boss, at this homestead near Busselton.

Source: Courtesy of the Butter Factory Museum, Busselton WA.

5. Meeting Aboriginal people

Posed and under control, a photograph by Prinsep of an unnamed Noongar man in traditional dress, circa 1880.

Source: Scenes of Travel and Adventure in Western Australia, National Library of Australia, Bib ID 3547143.

Two studies of Europeans, probably Prinsep and Josephine on horseback, by George Coolbul, 1866–1871. Coolbul worked for Prinsep on his stations at Belvidere, Prinsep Park and Paradise before being killed in a fight in 1871. Prinsep encouraged Coolbul to exercise his artistic interests and gave him pencils, pastels and paper. He later bound these in a volume he called 'Western Australian Native Art'.

Source: Native Art of Western Australia, George Coolbul, Art Gallery of Western Australia.

5. Meeting Aboriginal people

George Coolbul, kangaroo being run down by hunting dogs.

Source: Native Art of Western Australia, George Coolbul, Art Gallery of Western Australia.

George Coolbul, horse.

Source: Native Art of Western Australia, George Coolbul, Art Gallery of Western Australia.

5. Meeting Aboriginal people

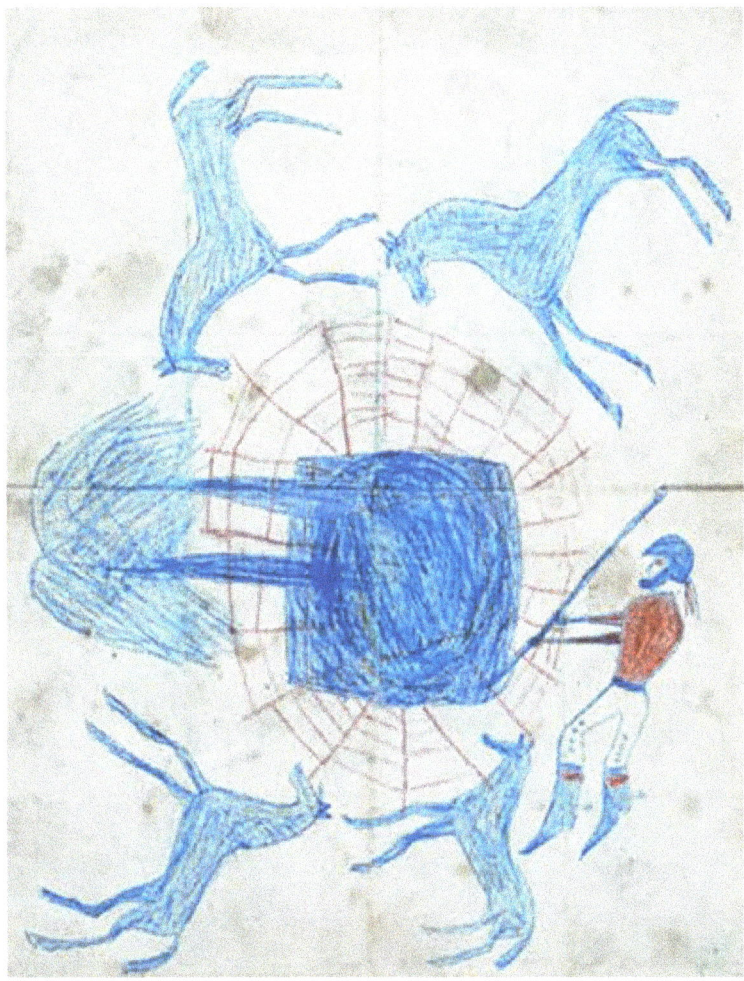

George Coolbul, who worked for Prinsep on his stations between 1866 and his death in 1872, was provided with pastels and paper by Prinsep. This drawing depicts a European man and horses around a yard, and was probably drawn with the paper on the ground, rotated as the artist added the features.

Source: Native Art of Western Australia, George Coolbul, Art Gallery of Western Australia.

6. 'Stationed but not sedentary'

In *The People of Perth*, Tom Stannage portrays 1870s Perth as an ordered, conservative and insular community, in which social life emanated from the Governor's establishment and politics was 'the prerogative of the Imperial officialdom, the landed gentry, and the leading town merchants'.[1] Prinsep's place in the colonial society, and his interest in its social institutions and attitudes to those excluded from Perth's elite social life, illuminates the manner by which, to use David Cannadine's terms, settler colonialists sought to 'replicate the layered, ordered, hierarchical society they believed they had left behind at home', establishing and patronizing the same institutions and social relationships as in the mother country.[2] Those who held power in the colony were confident in their prestige, and intent on keeping it that way. The son of Charles Prinsep's first agent in Western Australia, Sir Luke Leake, symbolised 'the decorum of colonial politics' in his behaviour as a Member of the Legislative Council. At election time he would stroll through the streets, 'personally acquainted with almost every elector, (speaking) to each as an old friend, knowing his history, knowing his views, and certain at any rate of a friendly reception'.[3] When Prinsep's younger brother, Jim, visited Perth in 1882, he found a 'very nice quiet little place, where everyone knew everyone else, and no-one had any money':

> People were most sociable and constantly had little dances and theatricals for which Harry usually painted the scenery, and often acted and so did I. Everything was done in the simplest fashion, no-one arrived late and only a few dressed even for the evening functions unless for something quite exceptional. No-one ever drove out to entertainment or kept carriages. Only a few people had horses and they lent them freely to anyone wanting a ride.[4]

Perth was still an outpost of Empire with a tiny coloniser population of little more than 6,500, marginally more than its port twin town, Fremantle, in a total colonial population of about 25,000. A census of the settler population in 1870 recorded that that the majority was born overseas, mostly in Britain, and that over two-thirds of the immigrant arrivals were male. Of the 9,500 women in the colony, well over half had been born locally over the 42 years since its establishment. Ten years later, a new census showed that the settler population

---

1 Stannage, C.T. 1979, *The People of Perth: A social history of Western Australia's capital city*, City of Perth, Perth, p.88.
2 Cannadine, David 2001, *Ornamentalism: How the British saw their empire*, Penguin Books, London, p.28.
3 Stannage 1979, *The People of Perth*, p.88.
4 Prinsep, James Charles, 'Autobiography', SLWA Acc. 3859A, Volume 1.

had increased by only 6,000, but the demographic profile had changed significantly. By then, nearly 60 per cent of a non-Aboriginal population of nearly 30,000 was born in Western Australia, although the continuing preponderance of men (nearly 60 per cent) reflects an immigrant population still heavily dominated by male arrivals.[5] The colony continued to be handicapped by a small population and had difficulty retaining settlers, some of whom were abandoning Western Australia for the more populous and economically buoyant eastern colonies, or returning to Britain. But for those who remained, there is a sense of increased belonging to the new colony, of starting to look inwards towards the potential of Western Australia as home. Families such as the Prinseps were in the process of re-adjusting their gaze, from seeing Western Australia as a subservient supplier and service centre, a small link in an Indian Ocean web of imperial influence and power, to a vision of the colony as an independent entity, its future and economic potential no longer dependent on the vagaries of Indian or other regional markets. They were becoming Western Australians, increasingly prepared to view the colony as a permanent project, with its own identity, issues and internal dynamics, a place to stake their future, own land, make a home for themselves and raise their children.

The Prinseps thus became part of a society increasingly comfortable in its Western Australian environment. Many in their family and social networks had, like Josephine Prinsep, been born in the colony and brought up in the bush, developing and tending the farms and pastoral runs acquired by their immigrant parents. The 'native born' men, such as Josephine's brother-in-law, Edward Brockman, and his five sons, and family friends, such as John and Alexander Forrest, constituted a new generation of muscular colonists, 'strong and robust looking', confident in their ability to survive in the bush and undertake all the duties of managing a farm, familiar with Aboriginal people and often fluent in indigenous languages.[6] All of Josephine's sisters were born in the colony and were proud of their self-sufficiency and capacity to tolerate hardship and deprivation, but at the same time able to manage the domestic sphere and 'act as a young lady should', by learning 'singing, pianoforte and painting in watercolours'.[7] According to Josephine's sister, Caroline, the relative absence of domestic comforts and their distance from 'society' made Australian-born women even more determined to conform to social expectations than their relations in England. 'Mamma and I often say', she wrote to her Aunt Fanny Bussell from her temporary home in London in 1878, 'that girls in Australia have much better opportunities of mixing in society and forming good manners

---

5   Australian Bureau of Statistics 2006, 'Australian Historical Population Statistics', Catalogue No. 3105.0.65.001, Table 70: 'Population, sex and country of birth, WA, Census Years 1959–1891', viewed online at http://www.abs.gov.au/AUSSTATS/abs@.nsf/DetailsPage/3105.0.65.0012006?OpenDocument.
6   Milward, John, 'Pioneers of the Warren', unpublished manuscript, personal collection, p.26.
7   Ibid., p.90.

than most girls of their station in England. None of [Aunt] Edith's children has a quarter such pleasing manners as their Australian cousins. There is always some reformation wanted in bush houses. People are apt to get careless and one coming back sees what is wanted and works to achieve it.'[8]

Alongside the men and women born in Australia, the Prinsep social circle in Perth included many, like Henry, who had been born and brought up in Britain and the colonies of the Empire. They had arrived in Western Australia as adults, either intent on owning land and raising their families in the colony, or as colonial civil servants to whom Perth represented one of a succession of imperial postings. Prinsep's diaries and letters illustrate his connections with a large circle of friends and colleagues of a broadly similar background to himself, and who had extensive family and social connections throughout the Empire. They included Colonial Secretary, Sir Frederick Palgrave Barlee, who provided introductions to the Governor and other political leaders on Prinsep's arrival in the colony, and later arranged his job in the civil service. Before coming to Western Australia in 1855, Barlee had been in the civil service in Sierra Leone and, on his departure from the colony after a 20-year stint, was appointed Lieutenant Governor of British Honduras.[9] Similarly, Chief Justice Sir Archibald Burt and his son Septimus, who became Prinsep's closest friend, had both been born in the West Indies, where the older Burt had been a member of the Legislative Council of St. Christopher and Anguilla, and held the rank of Attorney-General.[10] Malcolm Fraser, born in Scotland and with previous service in New Zealand, came to Western Australia in 1870 as Surveyor-General, and was Prinsep's first supervisor.[11] Fraser lived in Western Australia until his retirement in 1890 and went on to fill the posts of Registrar-General and Colonial Secretary. He continued to correspond with Prinsep after he left the colony, and became friends with Prinsep's sisters, Louisa, May and Annie, on his return to England. Another friend was Henry Hicks Hocking, born and educated in England, who took up the position as Attorney-General in 1873, during the governorship of Frederick Weld. He remained in the colony until 1879, when he was transferred to Jamaica to take up the role of Attorney-General.[12] Alexander Onslow was another lawyer and confidant. He came to Western Australia in 1880 as Attorney-General after a 16-year term in the equivalent post in British Honduras, staying in the colony until just before his death in England

---

8   Caroline Bussell to Fanny Bussell, 16 March 1878, SLWA Acc. 1972A/50.
9   Honniball, J.H.M. 1969, 'Sir Fredrick Palgrave Barlee, 1827–1884', in *Australian Dictionary of Biography*, Volume 3, Melbourne University Press, Melbourne.
10 McClemans, Sheila 1969, 'Burt, Sir Archibald Paull (1810–1879)', in *Australian Dictionary of Biography*, Volume 3, Melbourne University Press, Melbourne.
11 Crowley, F.K. 1972, 'Sir Malcolm Fraser, 1834–1900', in *Australian Dictionary of Biography*, Volume 4, Melbourne University Press, Melbourne.
12 Government of Western Australia 1870/71–1880, *Votes and Proceedings of the Legislative Council*, SLWA Acc. 328.941 WES.

in 1908.¹³ When Onslow was appointed to act as Administrator for a year in 1884, it was to Prinsep that he turned to act in the role of his aide-de-camp and Private Secretary.¹⁴ This cemented the relationship between the families, which revolved around a shared love of music and the arts, as well as business and politics. Music and art was the basis of a friendship with the family of Alfred Hensman, who was born in England and served with the East India Company army in Madras, before qualifying as a lawyer and coming to Western Australia as Attorney-General in 1884.¹⁵

It was people such as these who formed the Prinsep social circle, a group styling itself as a colonial elite and rigorously maintaining the boundaries between the 'shop girls and slavees', as Henry once referred to them, and the gentlemen and ladies of the colony. In such a society, people without property, those who laboured for the gentry, or were former convicts, 'were socially inhibited and legally intimidated by the Master and Servant Act; to the casual observer they seemed to reflect uncritically their "ordained" position in colonial society'.¹⁶ Occasionally, some of the powerless, non-indigenous others of colonial society appear in the Prinsep papers, illuminating the ways in which social barriers in this small community were maintained and reinforced by the British elite. In his encounters with British men and women of low status, Prinsep used terms little different from those used to describe the savagery and unknowability of other races. When, in 1880, he went to Fremantle to visit John Forrest, at that time Comptroller of Convicts, he attended Sunday service at Fremantle Prison and was intrigued and horrified by what he saw:

> The ranks of unfortunate men, some sullen, others joining in a mechanical way but all still and disciplined to the utmost. A collection of bad, very bad faces and heads as a lot, low foreheads, evasive eyes, prognathous jaws with very few exceptions. I was struck at the number of very bald heads among them, even in middle aged men, and put it down to the small caps and hot hats they use in the summer and the caps being probably worn as night caps in the winter.¹⁷

Later that day, Prinsep visited the pensioner's quarters and was shocked by the 'dirty, lazy, diseased looking men crowded in each room', each 'room apparently full and each man thinking only of himself, utterly regardless of the condition of those around him. Several blind, some palsied, some lame and all degraded.'¹⁸

---

13 Braybrooke, E.K. 1974, 'Sir Alexander Campbell Onslow, 1842–1908', in *Australian Dictionary of Biography*, Volume 5, Melbourne University Press, Melbourne.
14 Government of Western Australia 1884, *Government Gazette*, 27 November.
15 Birman, Wendy 1972, 'Hensman, Alfred Peach (1834–1902)', in *Australian Dictionary of Biography*, Volume 4, Melbourne University Press, Melbourne, pp.380–81.
16 Stannage 1979, *The People of Perth*, p.87.
17 Prinsep, Henry C., 'Diaries 1866–1922', SLWA Acc. 499A, 6 June 1880.
18 Ibid.

His observations show another side of a relaxed and harmonious community, a population existing in the background, mistrusted by the citizens of Perth and controlled as rigidly as possible. By the time Prinsep visited in 1880, the cessation of transportation in 1868 had left a remnant convict establishment of former inmates, most of them free, and ex-officials, most of them pensioners. 'Many men', wrote Stannage, 'eked out semi-pauperised existences in an inhospitable physical and social environment'. Some died as official paupers, others went insane and were locked in 'barbarous and inhuman places', but all have tended to be 'suppressed in folk memory and edited out of W.A. historical writing'.[19] Stannage suggests that it was the desire to control this 'enormous social disequilibrium' and protect the citizenry from its possible consequences that underwrote the prevailing ideologies of internal peace and harmony of a society modeled on that of the mother country. Colonisers such as Prinsep might do all they could to portray Perth as a harmonious replica of Britain, but its discords at times became very much evident to those who lived there.

As prominent members of the Church of England congregation in Perth, Henry and Josephine Prinsep responded to the needs of the underprivileged by joining and becoming active in the Bishop's relief and child protection programs, helping to raise money and food, and taking in the children of paupers. Sometimes, as in the case of Mary Anne and Louisa Currie, whose mother had died and whose 'drunken stepfather' was unable to look after them, these arrangements lasted almost for life. Mary Anne lived with the family and worked as a domestic, and Louisa went to the Bussells at Cattle Chosen.[20] The Noongar traditional landowners, meanwhile, had experienced a process of colonisation that left them with few choices of where to live, who they worked for, or how they cared for their children. By the time the Prinseps moved to Perth, Noongar traditional landowners were at the margins of the social and political structures of the colony. Those who had survived the violence of initial contact, the measles and whooping cough epidemics in the 1860s, or incarceration at Rottnest Island prison, either worked as virtual slaves to landowning colonists, or lived as dispossessed fringe dwellers in camps on the outskirts of the city.[21] In 1886, a senior Noongar man, Tommy Dower, described his people's situation as one of absolute marginalisation and dispossession:

> That white man take all blackfellows' country, and that blackfellow no place to sit down. That white man build houses, fence land, run cattle,

---

19 Stannage 1979, *The People of Perth*, pp.98–9.
20 Brockman, Carlotta, 'Reminiscences of Carlotta Louisa Brockman, née Prinsep, 1882–1956', State Library of Western Australia (SLWA) Acc. 931A.
21 Stannage 1979, *The People of Perth*, pp120–1.

sheep, horse, on blackfellows country. But poor blackfellows, no horse, no kangaroo or emu left. That plenty blackfellow die, and no notice taken of him by white man.[22]

Letters from around the world

Absences from Britain and its institutions brought a sense of alienation and longing for the company of others of the same background perhaps understood by all British colonists, regardless of their environment. Henry Prinsep's letters to family and friends in Britain constantly sought to reassure them that all was well in Western Australia, that it was a good place to live and stake his personal future. His new life in Western Australia was both different and remarkably similar to the lives of many of his network of correspondents. The images he provided to them portrayed his fascination with the exoticism of Western Australia, its landscape and topography, the indigenous population, flora and fauna. But they also reassured his family about the connectedness of the colony to the Empire, that there was much in the social values of Western Australia that his correspondents would find familiar. Responding to his sister Annie in 1874, Prinsep urged her to forget her worries about the hardships of colonial life:

> I can assure you that for a great many reasons the colonies are far preferable to the old country. A gentleman or lady here can keep up their position without that expenditure of money necessary at home. We are not ashamed of performing honourable necessities here and no one thinks the worse of me because I go to the well and draw up the water to make tea for myself. Of course when we can we get maids and few are without them, but there is not that outward show which costs so much.[23]

His life in Perth was pleasant, the excellent climate allowing for a healthy and active social and outdoor life. He was enjoying a simpler and less complex life than was possible in Britain and at the same time had the company of many who shared a similar background and identity. In the surviving outward letters to his family to be found in the Prinsep Papers, Prinsep portrays a life in which pleasure and relaxation play a large part, of engagement in political, social and cultural events, and of horseback trips to the country. He reports the arrival in the colony of new officials, such as Lord Gifford, previously with the army in India, South Africa and Cyprus, who arrived as Colonial Secretary to replace Frederick Barlee in 1880. He was delighted that the colony had gained a man

---

22 Tommy Dower, *The Inquirer*, 13 October 1886, quoted in Bolton, G.C. 1988, 'Tommy Dower and the Perth Newspapers', in *Aboriginal History*, Volume 12, Australian Institute of Aboriginal Studies, Canberra, p.81.
23 H.C. Prinsep to Annie Prinsep, 23 April 1874, private collection.

'most cordial and with such nice quiet pleasant manners', and particularly that Gifford knew his sister, Louisa, and brother-in-law, William Bowden-Smith.[24] But in letters to 'old' Western Australians, such as Charlotte Bussell and Josephine's sister, Caroline, who relocated to Paris after the death of John Garrett Bussell in 1875, Henry reveals that life in Perth still presented problems. He writes of his low salary, lack of opportunity for advancement in the civil service, and failure to gain appointment to higher status positions as local Resident Magistrates in places such as the Vasse and Derby. The health of the family is a major worry, as Josephine started to show signs of mental illness that resulted in long periods of convalescence in Bunbury and Melbourne, and a stay in the Fremantle Lunatic Asylum. Henry's friend, Alfred Hillman, related through marriage, was concerned that Josephine's 'mania was becoming permanent, as she has so many relapses', while Henry, 'at the best not a strong minded man, is at his wits end to know how to deal with her, it is very sad.'[25] Three days later, Josephine was taken to the asylum, which Hillman thought was best for her, 'although there is a natural repugnance to putting a friend or relative into such a place, but I really think it is the best for all parties. It is a great drawback to that asylum that no private apartments are furnished.'[26] Charlotte Bussell wrote quickly from Paris:

> It was a dreadful shock to me when I first read that she was in the asylum and I could quite enter into your agony when told that she must be taken there. But on reflection, I felt thankful that there was such a quiet safe retreat for her, where she would have good nursing, and a kind, judicious, moral attendant in Dr Barnett. The change to the cool sea breezes of Fremantle should also do her an immensity of good. It was far better than irritating her poor brain almost to becoming frantic by the opposition she must have met with by remaining longer at home. In a room where she could do no harm she might throw about the things as much as she liked, as a child with its toys, or open and shut the window till she was tired of the occupation, but the constant opposition to what she wanted to do was making her worse and worse. So it was a wise and beneficial thing to remove her, dear Harry, hard tho' it seemed at the time to take her to such a place, the name of which makes one shudder, but the asylum at Fremantle is very different to an asylum in England. There it is like a safe home, but in England it is like a prison. You cannot see the loved one when you wish, nor can you ask any questions. All is gloom and misery, at least so I have been told.[27]

---

24 H.C. Prinsep to Charlotte Bussell, undated, SLWA Acc. 1274A.
25 Hillman, Alfred James 1990, *The Hillman Diaries, 1877–1884*, F.J.B. Hillman, Perth, 16 and 18 January 1880.
26 Ibid., 21 January 1880.
27 Charlotte Bussell to Henry Prinsep, 10 March 1880, SLWA Acc. 1972A/61.

Amongst these difficulties, Henry enjoyed an active social life with his circle of friends and acquaintances, who moderated the absence of family in Western Australia. In this, he realised he was far better off than many of his fellow colonisers in places around the Indian Ocean. When Jim Prinsep spent five years in Ceylon between 1876 and 1881, trying out his skills at coffee-planting, he wrote to his older brother bemoaning the strangeness of his environment. 'I've got a berth now', he wrote from Pusilawa in the Ceylonese highlands, 'you may perceive its heathenish name above. This is a pretty place, lots of work and most woefully dull. I don't see a white face from Sunday to Sunday.'[28] Holidays were 'confounded dull' and often unnecessary, as 'none of the staff are Christians… These Canjanies are the curse of the place as they prevent direct communication with the coolies acting as some kind of middle man.' Henry replied, suggesting that he should consider coming to Western Australia, as a 'good sheep station here would be far happier and healthier life for you and not half the risk'.[29]

Although a place like Ceylon might be strange to a young man like Jim Prinsep, there was still plenty to evoke a sense of familiarity. His sister Louisa Bowden-Smith lived in Colombo in a 'very nice house called Darley House on the Lake and entertained a great deal', and her family are described as being 'rather the leading people in Colombo'.[30] In 1875, Aunt Jules (Julia Margaret Cameron) and her husband, Charles, moved from England to their hill station house, Dimboola, joining their son, Ewen, and other close family members. The presence of family served to reduce Jim's sense of isolation. Nor did Louisa forget her brother on the other side of the Indian Ocean. She wrote to Henry almost every week, relaying news of social life in Colombo, the affairs of family and friends in Britain, and sending him mementos and photographs of their shared childhood in England. Letters from his sisters constantly sought to reassure Henry that he remained very much a part of the family and had not been forgotten in far-away Perth.

His sisters, aunts and brother regularly wrote to tell Henry of family events and give news of their friends. Louisa, in particular, made an effort to involve Henry in the affairs of the family in her weekly correspondence, during which she gave accounts of the death of older family members, the pain of separation from her young children, who were staying in England with relations while she was in Ceylon, and forwarded letters from members of the extended family, including Julia Margaret Cameron and Aunt Sara Prinsep. The correspondence between Louisa and Henry runs almost unbroken from the time of his arrival in Western Australia until his death in 1922, just before Louisa died in the same year. It is a remarkable collection, Louisa's letters providing a vivid account of her life, a youth spent in England, marriage and children in Colombo, frequent

---

28   Jim Prinsep to H.C. Prinsep, 14 March 1876, SLWA Acc. 3592/A/30A.
29   Henry Prinsep to Jim Prinsep, August 6th 1877, SLWA Acc. 1274A.
30   Prinsep, 'Autobiography'.

trips to England to visit her children and have medical treatment, the death of her husband, her return to Britain, and her steady descent into disability from the effects of arthritis. Her early letters are a model of tidy handwriting and legibility but, as illness takes hold, they become increasingly difficult to read, the later letters virtually illegible. She is desperate to keep her widely dispersed group of siblings together, and bemoans the fact that older brother, Charlie, who had inherited the Tasmanian estates and moved between Britain and Australia, has 'drifted into anonymity' and 'does not seem to belong to the family'. Her letters are full of affectionate and vivid news about members of the extended family and social network: May is 'looking prettier than ever', Uncle Thoby 'stoops very much' but otherwise is 'just as nice as ever', Aunt Sara 'looks just like a Pompadour picture', her white hair giving her a much softer and even younger look', Signor (Fredrick Watts) is 'lively as ever' and has 'quite changed his Messiah like ways and goes about the country everywhere', while Annie Prinsep is still unmarried and has become 'quite the daughter of the house' at Thoby and Sara's home on the Isle of Wight.[31] Members of the family continue to travel to work in the colonies, many of their Prinsep and White cousins in India, while cousin Monty White in Antigua had 'gone quite bald'. Most surprising of all was the decision by Aunt Jules to leave England and her growing reputation as a photographer for Ceylon in 1875, because 'old Uncle Charles wants to die there', a move May's husband, Andrew Hichens, thought to be 'total madness'.[32] In 1874, Louisa forwarded a letter from Cameron describing the move of Thoby and Sara Prinsep from London to a new home in Freshwater, the Briary, designed and paid for by Watts:

> Aunt Sara, Uncle Thoby and Signor all got out of the Tennyson's carriage and all seemed wonderfully fresh and as my boys say 'fit'. Of course there was great excitement but we did not allow them to stand about to look at the outside of House. There is a long covered passage bricked at foundation with trellis walk on one side and wall on the other side leading up to house, then a hall and studio. Best part of the house, a delicious stove that emits great heat and not a blazing fire, that is to say, not a fire that shows. A stair case with some trellis work of small squares in centre of hall and immeasurable rooms, none very large but all very good aspect, very sunny. Great running about from room to room, Uncle Thoby alone with me in studio before dancing a fandango or some very quickstep. … he was vastly delighted. Aunt Sara does not yet understand the designed rustic simplicity wondered at their being no cornices & c. She will come to admire it well. It was a great day for Signor, he who had received at their hands for more than a score of years

---

31 Louisa Bowden-Smith to Henry Prinsep, undated (c.1875), SLWA Acc. 3592A/16A.
32 Louisa Bowden-Smith to Henry Prinsep, Andrew Hichens to Henry Prinsep, undated (c.1875), SLWA Acc. 1972A/12.

was now conferring. Very pleased he seemed and I felt very glad for him. A whole bunch of newly gathered snow drops from this, his new garden he offered gracefully to Aunt Sara. All was prosperous and Uncle Thoby declared he was more hungry than he had been for 20 years and baskets were opened and the first family meal occurred.[33]

Four years later, Louisa wrote to describe the funeral of Uncle Thoby Prinsep at Freshwater, mourning the loss of the 'dear old man', whose passing requires all of the family to close 'a page in one's life, and turn over to begin another life in which he does not figure as a grand central figure for all to turn to'. She reassured Henry that, 'whatever he may have written to you in business, I never heard him speak of you with anything but affection'.[34] Sister Annie Prinsep wrote from England to give news of Tennyson and Watts, telling Henry that they still remembered and asked after him. She wrote of taking 'long walks' with Tennyson in London, 'in which I saw more of London in a few days than in many driving', and of 'charming evening parties … where we met all the great and peculiar people, Gladstone, Knowles, Browning, Du Maurier & c.'[35] In 1878, a letter from Malta describes her holiday with Watts: 'It is certainly a splendid winter place':

> Signor is able to get out twice every day whereas he used to be shut up in his room for weeks during the winter at home. He means to come here every winter. The place is a mass of forts and is very gay. I've been to several dances already.[36]

Prinsep reserved his correspondence with Uncle Thoby Prinsep, and later his young brother, Jim, and brothers-in-law, Andrew Hichens and William Bowden-Smith, for discussions of business, including the complicated affairs surrounding the managements and settlement of his father's estate, and Henry's disposal of the properties in Western Australia in 1874. Between 1866 and his death in 1878, Thoby was a regular correspondent, his letters mostly dealing with matters of the estate and Henry's management of the Western Australian properties, with family news often added by Sara. Through his aunt and uncle, Henry learned about the trouble sister Annie was having in her final year at school and their plans to send her to Western Australia to join Henry, once he had built a 'stone and mortar' home that will 'keep out the wet and the wind better than wattle and daub'. 'I should be very glad if Annie came out', Thoby wrote in 1867. 'She is now very happy with Julia Cameron, except that she pines for a Miss Vasick, the music mistress at Miss Clarence's for whom she has conceived an unnatural attachment, writing to her every day and fretting and

---

33   Julia Margaret Cameron to Louisa Bowden-Smith, 6 February 1878, SLWA Acc. 1972A/66.
34   Louisa Bowden-Smith to Henry Prinsep, 17 February 1878, SLWA Acc. 1972A/20.
35   Annie Prinsep to Henry Prinsep, 2 May 1878, SLWA Acc. 1972A/135.
36   Ibid.

pining because she isn't allowed to go back to school to resume her relations with her whatever they may be.'[37] In 1876, Jim Prinsep wrote to Henry from Pusilawa in Ceylon to tell him that, at the age of 28, Annie was losing her hearing. Although Annie seemed disinclined to marry, May continued her efforts to find a husband for her, 'continually hunting up new candidates for the honour'.[38]

Andrew Hichens, a London stockbroker who had married May in 1874, took on the task of disentangling the family affairs after Thoby's death and reported to Henry that the situation was worse than he had imagined:

> The accounts of the estate crediting each child with his or her share of the trust income and debiting each with their expenditure has been very carefully made out and approved by Desborough and my lawyer and Charlie's lawyer. From these accounts it appears that in order to discharge the debt due to your Father's marriage settlement and the first charge to the daughters, there will be some £8000 required besides the debt to the National Bank. As there is no prospect of the W. Australian estate realising more than £5000 or £6000 at the outside, it follows that Charlie will have to raise the remainder which owing to your unfortunate proceedings will probably be increased by the cost of a law suit or full payment of the Bank claim. Now the net income of Charlie's Tasmanian property manages about £800 a year and if he has to burden it with a mortgage of some £4000 at 6 per cent he will have barely £500 left, so his position as eldest is not very brilliant at all. As to Jim he will get his share of the settlement after deducting what has been spent on his education in excess of his proportion of income and it will come to about £1800 or about £80 a year.[39]

Hichens admonished Henry for requesting 2,000 pounds to support a scheme to reinvest in property in the vicinity of Bunbury, which could 'yield no profitable result'. 'West Australia seems to be a drag in the market', he wrote. Potential investors had no interest in colonial schemes where there was an absence of managers, no agents 'whom they knew and could absolutely trust', and 'the property was valueless as an investment'.[40] He was not a rich man, he told Henry in 1876, and even if he had the 2,000 pounds Henry was requesting, he would 'resist all demands to advance it on so doubtful a matter':

> I have a good business so long as I am able to work at it and it allows me to live comfortably and to do something to help the very numerous poorer members of my family, which you may suppose to be abundant

---

37 Thoby Prinsep to Henry Prinsep, 26 August 1867, SLWA AN3592A/15.
38 Jim Prinsep to Henry Prinsep, 14 March 1876, SLWA Acc. 3592A/30A.
39 Andrew Hichens to Henry Prinsep, 23 March 1876, SLWA Acc. 1972A/80.
40 Ibid.

> when I tell you that I have 40 nephews and nieces. But I have not large means and I have very full claims as such as I have. All these are details which I would prefer not revealing but your letter compels me to do so. I can only repeat that I will gladly do my share in any feasible plan for improving your position, but certainly not in the manner you propose.[41]

William Bowden-Smith, who was in business in Colombo, was similarly reluctant to invest his finances in Henry's business proposals, although he was prepared to lend Henry 200 pounds, 'free of interest, so that you may carry on with your purchases'.[42] Similarly, in 1876, Hichens reluctantly agreed to support Henry's request to supply materials to allow him to go into business as an art teacher, warning him in the process to be 'careful not to let your artistic scheme interfere with your permanent work'. After consulting with Watts and Val Prinsep, Hichens consigned an order for '½ dozen small colour boxes for beginners, one dozen tubes of moist colour of each the 12 most important colours, some 4 ½ dozen brushes, six dozen pencils F. and six dozen B., 2 quins of Whatman paper, a gross of drawing pens, a dozen copies of Vere Foster's programme studies Landscape, 3 programme studies (Vols by Leitch), two or three dozen sheets of French drawing studies of figures and architectural designs, a pound of India Rubber'.[43] Despite the obvious unwillingness of Hichens and Bowden-Smith to invest their funds in schemes in Western Australia, Henry continued to request their financial support for his plans to invest in land, and later to import indentured Indian labour to develop the north-west of the colony. Again, Hichens refused, as Jim Prinsep wrote in 1891:

> Though I don't suppose Andrew cares one dump whether the NorWest is populated by Hindoos, Chinese or any other race, or that he is prepared to embark in any scheme for introducing Hindoos or kicking out Chinese, for his own private gain or profit, I am sure if he can do anything that might be to your private advantage he will do so gladly.[44]

Other letters deal with the important matter of patronage, connections and introductions to networks that might help Henry get ahead in his colonial environment. In 1876, Hichens wrote that he would be pleased to speak to the new Governor of Western Australia, Sir William Robinson, who he believed he might have known when he was at the Colonial Office as a clerk: 'If he … is a dark good looking man about 40 with a pretty tenor voice he ought to be an old musical pal of mine, and in that case I would write and ask him to do what he could in the way of looking after you.'[45] In 1878, after entertaining Henry's

---

41 Ibid.
42 William Bowden-Smith to Henry Prinsep, undated, SLWA Acc. 1972A/12.
43 Andrew Hichens to Henry Prinsep, 3 November 1876, SLWA Acc. 1972A/80.
44 Jim Prinsep to H.C. Prinsep, 10 December, 1891, SLWA Acc. 3592A/43.
45 Ibid.

boss, Commissioner of Crown Lands, Malcolm Fraser, Hichens advised Henry that there was little point in cultivating Colonial Office contacts, as Fraser is 'a very good friend to you and I think he will take advantage of any opportunity of getting you on, but he says you must have patience, for it is impossible to push a man, but if you do your work well and give no cause for complaint he will see that you have any thing that may be going'.[46]

More often, it was Henry who did the introductions for friends visiting Britain from Western Australia. When Colonial Secretary Frederick Barlee visited England in 1875, he spent time at Freshwater with Thoby and Sara Prinsep, meeting Annie Prinsep, Watts and Tennyson. Barlee reported that Thoby bore no ill-will towards Henry from the failure of his business ventures and would like to help him in whatever way he could. He understood it was Henry's 'inexperience and impetuosity' at the time that had made him ill-suited to the task of rescuing the enterprise, but this should not bring 'the slightest taint upon his character or fitness for future employment of any kind'.[47] Frederick Watts 'often wishes you were here with him to aid in his studies and play on the violin'. Barlee was particularly delighted to be introduced to Tennyson,

> to take a long walk with him, when he pointed out to me all the beauties of Freshwater. Such a chance does not occur to everyone. He is a man who hates to have any fuss made of him, but is pleasant, full of fun and wit, a species of very amusing dry humour, and I need hardly say, possesses an enormous fund of information. He greedily sought more information about Australia and sometimes surprised me by the obtuse nature of the questions that he asked.[48]

Later in 1875, Hichens apologised to Henry for not being in London when his 'distinguished friend' explorer John Forrest called, but 25 years later he was able to meet the man who had risen to the rank of Minister of Defense in the newly founded Commonwealth of Australia and introduce him to the Lord Mayor of London.

Letters from family and friends throughout Australia and the Empire continued to arrive throughout Henry's and Josephine's lives, and the arrival of colonial and British mail was eagerly awaited. Prinsep's Tasmanian friend, Georgia Bisdee, wrote to give 'you who have so many associations with Calcutta' news of her recent visit to India. His old friend, Harry Hocking, described his new position in Jamaica and his engagement to negotiate a 'reciprocity treaty'

---

46 Andrew Hichens to Henry Prinsep, 21 November 1878, SLWA Acc. 3592A/43.
47 Frederick Barlee to Henry Prinsep, 11 February 1875, SLWA Acc. 1972A/7.
48 Ibid.

between Jamaica and the United States in 1891.⁴⁹ Letters arrived asking Prinsep to help new arrivals in the colony. In 1907, his cousins, Fanny Daniell and Neta Sanderson, wrote asking him to look after Fanny's son, Frank, forced to leave India because of his wife's illness and wanting to 'continue colonising' in order to provide a healthy life for his children rather than return to England. 'I believe someone in India has given him a letter of introduction to Uncle Harry', wrote Sanderson: 'Mrs. Daniell thinks he will like to settle permanently in WA and wants Uncle Harry to help him get something to do. I wonder how often he has that request made of him.'⁵⁰ There are many letters about conditions in Britain, firmly in the grip of social, political and industrial change. Prinsep's old school friend, Alfred Harrison, kept him informed of Britain's political development from his position as a clerk in the House of Lords:

> The House of Commons is becoming, or rather has become, quite unmanageable. This is, of course, a result of the extension of the franchise, which has made it possible for men to get into Parliament who cannot, by any stretch of courtesy, be called gentlemen, and who would not have had a chance of getting in formerly.⁵¹

Josephine's cousin, Frances Ardagh, wrote that London's 'streets are as full as ever, crammed in some places but with a totally different population than one is accustomed to. Lots of foreigners and country folk. In the trains and buses one hears Yorkshire, Devonshire—broad South and the Eastern Countries dialects with French and German.'⁵² The events of the Empire, particularly war, are the subject of many letters. In 1918, Hallam Tennyson, soon to marry Prinsep's sister, May, who was widowed after the death of Andrew Hichens, commented on the contrast between the peace of the rural Isle of Wight and the battlefields of France:

> Lovely spring weather has begun here and all the snowdrops are coming out of the sheltered rocks among the bushes. The crocuses have also begun to send up their tiny flowers. The rooks caw very loud and are beginning to build their nests and the thrushes are shouting from the thickets. All this peace and a hundred miles away turmoil, death and destruction.⁵³

Prinsep's sister, Annie, wrote to provide her solution to the industrial unrest that followed World War I: 'This last strike of railway men is simply wicked. My

---

49 Georgia Bisdee to Josephine Prinsep, 17 December, 1911, SLWA Acc. 3593A/38; Harry Hocking to H.C. Prinsep, no date, 1880, SLWA Acc. 3594A/30/1; Bessie Hocking to H.C. Prinsep, June 11 1891, SLWA Acc. 3594A/26/28.
50 Fanny Daniell to H.C. Prinsep, 11 May, 1907, SLWA Acc. 3594A/26/3.
51 Alfred Harrison to H.C. Prinsep, 20 June 1881, SLWA Acc. 3592A/35.
52 Frances Ardagh to Josephine Prinsep, August 26 (no year), SLWA Acc. 3593A/9.
53 Hallam Tennyson to H.C. Prinsep, 24 February 1918, SLWA Acc. 3592A/67B.

verdict would be that every man who strikes should pay £5 for every idle day and have the back of his hand tattooed to mark him for life. Talking is not of the slightest use as the strikers know perfectly well the harm they are doing.'[54] But although the Britain Prinsep remembered was undoubtedly changing, imperial ideals of the superiority of its institutions and modalities continued to be held close. These ideals were expressed in a letter to Josephine, written shortly after Prinsep's death by his nephew, Bill Bowden-Smith, in retirement after a career with the Royal Navy and postings around the world:

> All the villages round are lovely. The Downs which separate Berks from Wilts four miles to the south and the Thames seven miles to the north. Oxford only ten miles away, a place full of interest as you will know. I find any amount to do in addition to looking after this place and my family. They have made me a magistrate, and I am President of every mortal thing in the village, from the Conservative Assocn downwards—British Legion, Boy Scouts, cricket club, football club, Church Council.[55]

---

54 Annie Prinsep to H.C. Prinsep, September 1918, SLWA Acc. 3592A/67B.
55 Bill Bowden-Smith to Josephine Prinsep, 15 February 1927, SLWA Acc. 3593A/11.

7. 'Received into the very best society'

After the rigours of life on the land, Henry Prinsep settled into a career in the Department of Lands and Surveys, applying his technical and drafting skills to the tasks of allocating, managing and cataloguing a steadily-expanding colonial estate. 'The work is what I like', he wrote to Annie in April 1874:

> I have a very large table for my own use, high up and fitted for plan drawing, a shaded window in front of it and colours, mathematical instruments ... here I am stationed but not sedentary. We ... are in charge of the multitudinous charts, plans, tracings, documents connected with the management of lands of the colony and every application for sale, pastoral lease, agricultural lease, reserve & c has to come through our hands first of all before going on to the Commissioner of Crown Lands and the Governor. Each of these applications & c has to be calculated and plotted on the working plans to scale and entered in a variety of books. We are constantly interrupted by all manner of extra incidental jobs, such as tracings wanted for this that the other, questions about certain places, alterations of boundaries, surveys & c, so that there is heaps of work but it is work that allows plenty of movement and chat together and is not too monotonous. My chief is very gentlemanly and always trusts to our honour, so gives us leave whenever we ask it in reason. Josephine gives me a little lunch wrapped up in paper before I start in the morning. It takes me about seven minutes to reach the office and at four I come out. Then we either go calling, shopping or amusing ourselves till dusk and then sit down to a table dinner. As yet we have no servant, but you cannot imagine how quietly and imperceptibly J seems to get through everything, even the washing. The dinners are the most recherché little affairs as far as they go. We have been received into the best society with open arms and have been considerably gay ... sufficiently tickled to prevent our lives seeming dull.[1]

Prinsep was a perfect civil service recruit for, in addition to his technical and drafting skills, he possessed 'a good education in England having passed the examination for entrance into Woolwich, is a man of culture and of general knowledge, and may be safely relied on to maintain the dignity of the post both in its official and social relations'.[2] Importantly, the job allowed him the flexibility to

---

1 Henry Prinsep to Annie Prinsep, April 1874, private collection, Claremont WA.
2 Notation in support of H.C. Prinsep by A.C. Onslow, 23 April 1885, SROWA, Colonial Secretary's Office File Acc. 527 1668/1885.

participate in the social and cultural life of the small city. He cultivated contacts with a succession of Governors and was a loyal supporter of the Governor's supreme authority over the Crown Colony until the late 1880s. His diaries refer to dinner parties at Government House, attendance at balls 'as part of the vice-regal party', 'tennis at Government House', and a social standing that allowed him to call on the Governor informally.[3] Prinsep was a popular companion whose 'multi-faceted and convivial personality … drew people of talent to his hearth'.[4] His diaries are littered with descriptions of social life, 'grand dinners' at Government House, musical soirees, 'jolly days' on the Swan River and at the riverside family holiday cottage, The Chine, of fishing, crabbing and eating oysters with friends, and gentlemanly conversations and business dealings at the exclusive Weld Club for the city's political and business elite. Contemporary diarist, Alfred Hillman, related to Prinsep by marriage, referred to the constant social activity surrounding the Prinsep household: 'After dinner walked up to Prinsep's where, as usual, we found a host of visitors but not the particular one we went to see'.[5] Prinsep was active in amateur theatre, directing, acting and painting the sets for local productions. His adaptation of 'The Colleen Bawn' in 1880 was warmly praised by the local newspaper:

> Now we were in a wild dell, now in a country house, by a lake or in a cavern. Not only had Mr. Prinsep carefully considered the requirements of the piece, but the different portions were in thorough working order, and there was not the slightest hitch or delay in the movement. The drop scene … is a masterpiece, and we feel sure that if it were exhibited at the emigration agents' in London, numbers of adventurers would speedily flock to our shores.[6]

Prinsep's positions within the Department of Lands and Surveys were relatively lowly and, until 1894, he never advanced beyond the level of a senior clerk, except for a brief period in 1884 when he served as Private Secretary and Aide-de-Camp to the Administrator, his friend and mentor, Alexander Onslow.[7] To Prinsep, paid employment seems to have been a necessary but unwelcome intrusion into the more valued aspects of life. His family now numbered five, with the birth of daughters Emily in 1875 and Virginia in 1879. Maintaining his family's social position was of supreme importance to Prinsep, his diaries betraying an abiding concern with the rigid barriers between his position in

---

3   For example, see Prinsep, Henry C., 'Diaries 1866–1922', SLWA Acc. 499A, 3 July 1871, 14 April 1874, 25 April 1882, 7 December 1885.
4   Frontispiece, *Early Days: Journal of the Royal Western Australian Historical Society*, Volume 7, 1972.
5   Hillman, Alfred James 1990, *The Hillman Diaries, 1877–1884*, F.J.B. Hillman, Perth, 11 January 1880.
6   *The West Australian*, 9 December 1879.
7   Prinsep's starting salary was 2 pounds and 2 shillings a week, as he wrote in his diary entry for the 6 January 1874. By 1876, his pay as a temporary officer, as recorded in 1876 estimates for the Department of Lands and Surveys was 10 shillings a day, or 156 pounds and 10 shillings per annum. Government of Western Australia 1870/71–1880, *Votes and Proceedings of the Legislative Council*, SLWA Acc. 328.941 WES.

Perth society and numerous others, whose family backgrounds, income and land holdings disqualified them from the social, business and cultural concerns of the elite few. Prinsep was able to offer his skills as one of the colony's few competent, trained artists who had the time and expertise to teach art and photography to the citizenry and their children, which supplemented his meager civil service income. His professional competence as an artist, together with his interest in theatre and music was one of his chief contributions as a member of the colonial elite, ensuring his active involvement in many of the city's cultural activities and nascent institutions, such as museums, art galleries and theatres. He utilised his knowledge of art and his skill as an artist to reinforce his social relationships, giving art lessons to Governor W.C.F. Robinson's wife, Frances, and providing 'designs of swans' and invitation cards for Lady Broome.[8]

His artistic activity further illustrates his place within networks encircling the British imperial world, both as a creator and distributor of colonial imagery, and as a purveyor of the methods and principles of British art in the colony. Art historian Janda Gooding described his involvement in setting up the first of the colony's artistic societies, the Wilgie Sketching Club, in 1889 as an attempt to build a 'collegiate environment among artists through a mixture of painting classes and social gatherings', based on the 'hospitality, friendship, creativity and congeniality he had absorbed in London'.[9] The club gave him the opportunity to work closely with other prominent Western Australian artists, including Herbert Gibbs and his daughter, May, George Temple Poole, Bernard Woodward, and Margaret Forrest. He was also diligent in calling on artists visiting Perth, such as botanical artists, Marianne North (a friend of Julia Margaret Cameron) and Ellis Rowan, who was described by Prinsep as 'an astonishingly clever flower painter (amateur)', whose 'perspective and hues were most excellent'.[10]

The Western Australian art market was too small to sustain a professional artist and much of his painting and drawing activity was due to his sheer enjoyment of the craft. Prinsep was nonetheless able to earn additional income through commissions and art classes, and by exhibiting and selling his work. One money-making artistic venture in 1880 was his 'grand painting' of Mrs. Boldt, the wife of a sea captain, who had earned public admiration for her feat in bringing the ship 'Mowbury' into Brisbane harbour after her husband had fallen ill. Prinsep's oil painting shows a heroic Mrs. Boldt standing alone at the wheel, the ship buffeted by massive waves. In a letter to mother-in-law Charlotte in Paris, he described an 'animated and fascinating scene, she standing bare headed

---

8 Prinsep, 'Diaries', 22 April 1882; Lady Broome to H.C. Prinsep, no date, SLWA Acc. 3594A/26/16.
9 Gooding, Janda 2005, 'Henry Prinsep, 1844–1922', in *Acquisitions and Discourse*, Friends of the WA Art Gallery, Perth.
10 Prinsep, 'Diaries' 14 January 1882. See also, Rowan, Ellis 1898, *The Flower Hunter*, Angus & Robertson, London, in which she describes her visit to Western Australia.

with her eyes fixed on the fore yardman, a scanty costume, bare arms and eager face, the main object of the picture'.[11] The canvas was exhibited over a number of days in Perth and Fremantle, and then sent to the Melbourne Exhibition where Prinsep hoped it would be sold for a good price. Tickets were available for 'sixpence to gentlemen and three pence for working men', and brought in 27 shillings and sixpence on the first day, 19 shillings on the second and 30 on the third. When it was exhibited in Fremantle, 'the crowds came in to see it,' and he was delighted to make 68 shillings and ninepence on the first day.[12] Later that year, London-based friend, Alfred Harrison, told Prinsep of a 'very flattering notice of your picture' in 'some Glasgow paper'. 'You can have no competitors worth mentioning in Australia', he wrote, 'so I see no reason why you should not really make a very good thing of it. At any rate, you have made an excellent start, and I for one heartily wish you success.'[13]

In addition to painting and drawing, Prinsep had been an enthusiastic photographer since his school days at Cheltenham in the 1860s. His prints and cabinet cards depict aspects of colonial life and scenery, many of which he sent to family and friends in Australia and overseas, while others were used to illustrate books and official documents on Western Australia. Many show the forests and trees of the colony, which were among his favourite subjects. Family life also features prominently: prints of the family at home, on holiday at The Chine or one of the family homesteads in the south-west. There are photographs of Aboriginal people from places throughout the colony, particularly the south-west and Perth, but also more distant regions, such as the Goldfields and the Gascoyne. The exchange of photographs was part of the currency of his interconnected world, and images of far-flung family members regularly arrived in the mail, including cartes de visite, cabinet cards, and richly illustrated volumes prepared by leading British photographers, including Julia Margaret Cameron.[14] Although the subjects of some of these photographs often cannot be identified, they vividly illustrate the transnational perspective of a man such as Prinsep, and the way his connections and interests extended well beyond his local colonial environment.

Prinsep took on the role of colonial image maker through his art and photography with enthusiasm. While he was part of the social elite and had a peripheral involvement in political life, he was primarily focussed on the task of portraying Perth as a good place to settle, boasting an active cultural and social life, an efficient system of government equipped to manage the development of the land, and hardy settlers engaged in the venture of making their homes and

---

11   Henry Prinsep to Charlotte Bussell, August 6 1877, SLWA MN771, Acc. 1247A.
12   Prinsep, 'Diaries', 17 August 1880.
13   Alfred Harrison to H.C. Prinsep, 29 December 1880, SLWA Acc. 3594A/30/6.
14   Louisa sent him Cameron's illustrated volume of Tennyson's 'Idylls of the King' as a birthday present in 1876.

turning a harsh environment into a productive one. His paintings, drawings and photographs portray an orderly world in which the colonisers are well in control of a sometimes unruly and rugged but beneficent land. Rustic settings and arcadian parklands feature prominently in his landscapes of Western Australia, set against an unusual and exotic natural environment, different trees, flowers and animals, wild places that would soon be tamed by the onset of orderly British development. The imagery of the new colony also required a gallery of its leading men, and Prinsep was regularly commissioned by the colonial government to prepare portraits of governors and speakers of the Legislative Council and other great men of the colony, including the explorers who risked their lives to open up the vast interior and north of the colony. These explorers encountered all that was wild and different in the interior: resistance and anger from 'savage' Aboriginal peoples, continuous hardship, thirst, and risk of death. It was the job of Prinsep and others like him to illustrate such episodes in the development of the colony and, in the process, build and perpetuate an image of the colony in its transnational world, in many aspects different, yet intimately connected with the metropole and its sister colonies.

Prinsep's paintings and drawings of John Forrest's explorations of the Western and Victoria deserts in 1874, and Alexander Forrest's exploration of the Kimberley in 1879, portray the Aboriginal people encountered by these expeditions as savage aggressors, attacking randomly, despite the reported efforts of the explorers to avoid violence. Prinsep utilised the field sketches and written descriptions of the explorers and then submitted preliminary sketches for their comment and correction: 'Very busy with two new duplicates of A. Forrest's arrival at the Fitzroy R at p[hoto] lith[ograph] office, the first one having been found defective in that the river was too narrow.'[15] The drawings for John Forrest's account of his 1874 expedition, from Champion Bay through the continental interior to Adelaide, which included nine pen, ink and watercolour plates of scenes from the expedition, were completed by the end of March, when Prinsep 'showed them to Mr Fraser who took them to the Governor who was much pleased with them and ordered them to be sent to Melbourne for reproduction'.[16] Each of the illustrations matched Forrest's account of a particular episode, including his dramatic description of a battle with Aboriginal people at Pierre Springs, in which they were portrayed by Forrest as determined to attack, despite his efforts to be friendly. 'The Skirmish with Natives at Pierre Springs' illustrates the restraint of the Forrest party, as its five members face a large group of Aboriginal people, spears poised, advancing in battle formation. Forrest stands at the head of his party, his hand held up in an attempt to forestall the attack, rifle pointed downwards:

---

15 Prinsep, 'Diaries', 4 August 1880.
16 Ibid., 22 March 1875. The illustrations are included in Forrest, 1875, *Journal of proceedings of the Western Australian exploring expedition*.

> While they were about 150 yards off I fired my rifle, and we saw one of them fall, but he got up again and was assisted away … The natives seemed determined to take our lives, and therefore I shall not hesitate to fire on them should they attack us again. I thus decide and write in all humility, considering it a necessity, as the only way of saving our lives.[17]

A similar illustration was prepared for Ernest Giles' account of his 1872–1876 expedition through the Victoria Desert. As with Forrest, Prinsep used Giles's field accounts and sketches to illustrate a violent clash between Aboriginal people and the exploration party at a place called Ullaring.[18] Giles's journal description is puzzling, for he records that his party was repeatedly warned to stay away from the place they had chosen as a camp, and that the Aboriginal traditional owners, rather than wantonly seeking violence, went to great lengths to avoid confrontation. The attack took place on the evening of 16 October 1875, and Prinsep's illustration faithfully follows Giles's account. A ground cover is laid where the exploration party had been about to enjoy their supper before being disturbed by the 'grand and imposing army', its warriors 'painted, feathered, and armed to the teeth with spears, clubs, and other weapons … ready for instant action', looking like 'what I should imagine a body of Comanche Indians would appear when ranged in battle'.[19] The 'inoffensive spies' in the ranks of Giles's party, two men and one 'pretty little girl', sought to distract the party. One of the men 'ran and jumped on me, put his arms round my neck to prevent my firing', The young girl, meanwhile,

> became almost frantic with excitement, and ran off to each man who was about to fire … clapping her small hands, squeaking out her delight, and jumping about like a crow with a shirt on. While the fight was in progress, in the forgetfulness of his excitation, my black boy Tommy began to speak apparently quite fluently in their language to the two spies, keeping up a running conversation with them nearly all the time … After the attack, Tommy said, 'I tole you black fellow coming,' though we did not recollect that he had done so.[20]

Other Prinsep images of Aboriginal people infantilise its subjects, locating them in a state of nature or portraying them as noble savages. An 1880 collection of drawings, paintings and photographs, entitled 'Scenes of Travel and Adventure

---

17 Forrest, John 1875, *Journal of Proceedings of the Western Australian Exploring Expedition Through the Centre of Australia: From Champion Bay, on the west coast, to the overland telegraph line between Adelaide and Port Darwin, commanded by John Forrest, F.R.G.S.*, Government Printer, Perth, p.189.
18 Originals of the Giles Expedition paintings are held by the Art Gallery of Western Australia. Lithographs representing episodes from all three expeditions are in the relevant Parliamentary Papers volumes in the State Library of Western Australia.
19 Giles, Ernest 1889, *Australia Twice Traversed*, viewed online at http://etext.library.adelaide.edu.au/g/giles/ernest/g47a/, University of Adelaide, Adelaide
20 Giles 1889, *Australia Twice Traversed*.

in Western Australia', the original of which was purchased in 2005 by the National Library of Australia, illustrates a series of journeys in the bush by Henry and Josephine Prinsep with an English 'lady of means', Miss Hocking, sister of Prinsep's friend, Attorney General Henry Hocking.[21] Prinsep later made lithograph copies of this album to send to his brother, sisters and extended family overseas and friends in Perth, and was commissioned to produce a number more for the colonial government. Aboriginal people appear as background in some of these drawings, such as those depicting Rottnest Island, in which they are distant figures carrying spears. In others, they are represented as caricatures of domestic servants, working while Prinsep and his companions relax over a pipe and a cup of tea. Another set of pen and ink drawings by Prinsep was included in an 1882 report by Surveyor General Malcolm Fraser on the colonial timber trade. These present a contrast between the forests in their natural state, complete with Aboriginal lords of the forest, and as a harvested economic resource. Prinsep's illustrations depict two Aboriginal people in a state of nature in the foreground, walking through the jarrah forest, carrying weapons and implements on the one page, contrasted with a similar scene, this time of two Europeans dwarfed by massive karri trees, no doubt contemplating their value as a harvestable economic resource.[22]

Prinsep's collection of photographs of Aboriginal people at times continues the portrayals of his art and drawings. Often the subjects are posed, frequently painted up in traditional costume and carrying spears and boomerangs, but nameless, suspended from their geographical and spatial context, representations of a disappearing people on the postcards and images of the Empire. Others document the grim reality of a colonised people and the various points in which their lives came up against the colonial social body. They portray the marginality of Aboriginal lives in the colony, incarcerated men on their way to jail, ragged children, and large, usually unnamed groups of people in camps and ration depots. Housing is makeshift or non-existent, clothing is poor, and the expressions on the faces of some of the subjects suggest reluctance and alienation, a hope that the unwelcome intrusions of the photographer will soon end and leave them to their own affairs. This was indeed becoming the overarching reality of their colonised lives under the new regime, hunger and dispossession, alienation from the system of power and authority, loss of control over destinies and life freedoms. Many of Prinsep's photographs portray this creeping subjugation, the white boss or missus in the background, a part of the photograph, but obviously the one in control, distanced from the subjected others by dress, bearing and authority.

---

21 Prinsep, Henry C., 1880, 'Scenes of Travel and Adventure in Western Australia', National Library of Australia, http://nla.gov.au/nla.pic-vn3542902.
22 The drawings are reproduced in Crawford, Patricia and Ian Crawford 2003, *Contested Country: A history of the Northcliffe area, Western Australia*, University of Western Australia Press, Nedlands, pp.47–8.

Alongside this imagery of a colonised and marginalised people, Prinsep's photographs also illustrate the known and the familiar, a nuanced and subtle portrait of a world where people lived alongside each other, interacted constantly, and knew each other's family lives and histories. They are products of Prinsep's photographic eye, part of a photographic diary, capturing moments of spontaneity, everyday interactions in which the subjects pose for the camera rather than act as props, and are actively engaged in the recording exercise, gazing directly at the lens, showing off their clothing, lifting a child to be included in the picture, sitting around the homestead with the white people, smoking pipes and relaxing together. Far from being disheveled, dirty or apparently intruded upon, these are people known to the photographer, who directly engage with one who is both known and understood, and whose family is part of the local community.

Politics laid bare

As a prominent citizen of Perth and member of a large landholding family, Prinsep inevitably became involved in the internal politics of the small Crown Colony. From the 1870s, constitutional development was an area of particular conflict, as powerful members of the elite social body became increasingly impatient for Western Australia to follow its eastern Australian neighbours into a system of responsible government. Imperial authorities balked at the idea, principally because of doubts that a small and sparsely-distributed population of colonisers had the capacity to govern an enormous land area, much of it still unexplored. The colony's ability to govern the large indigenous populations spread throughout the territory was a particular concern to imperial authorities, and allegations of violence, cruel treatment and conditions of virtual slavery fuelled a reluctance to cede responsibility for Aboriginal populations to colonial authorities without the mollifying involvement of the Colonial Office. For their part, the colonists resented imperial portrayals of them as incapable of protecting Aboriginal peoples from cruelty and exploitation, and worried that continued bad publicity would cast a slur on the colony's international reputation. The colony's ability to attract imperial business interests and banks to invest in the colony's economic development in the 1890s was a crucial concern to the first colonial government of John Forrest. In his ten years as Premier, he energetically pursued the rapid development of the gold industry, with massive international borrowings to allow major capital projects, including harbours, railways and water pipelines. By 1900, the public debt had reached 12.8 million pounds, while annual revenue had increased from 1.2 million pounds to 3.08 million pounds.²³ The colony was very much in debt to the banks and businesses of the metropole, a bad time to acquire such an indifferent reputation as a manager of its internal affairs. Forrest went to great efforts to restore the reputation of the colonial government. In 1894, he travelled to England to argue the case for the repeal of the Imperial Government's reservation of powers over Aboriginal affairs, and talk to banks and investors about the potential for business in the colony, particularly in the gold mining sector.²⁴

Prinsep was on the periphery of many of these developments in colonial politics, initially a loyal supporter, but later a critic of the system of Crown rule. His civil service position gave him a particular perspective on the life of the colony, involved as he was on a daily basis with a system of land management to regulate, catalogue and map lands throughout the vast land area of the colony. He was an unabashed supporter of Crown rule, socially close to a succession of governors and their families, and proud to proclaim himself a conservative.²⁵ Although he tried to maintain a relationship with Frederick Broome, governor between 1883 and 1889, he found himself caught between loyalty to the Governor and the pro-responsible government sentiments of some of his closest friends. Broome, in fact, supported the colony's movement towards responsible government and did all he could to promote a new constitution in London, but poor relationships with some of the colony's elite meant that matters became personal between the Governor and the colonial social body. The Governor was thus often portrayed as the embodiment of all that was wrong with the system of Crown rule. Broome's suspension from office of Alexander Onslow in 1885, and Alfred Hensman in 1886, and an enduring resentment about low pay and lack of promotional opportunity in the civil service, changed Prinsep's mind about representative government. He also found his family excluded from the Government House circle, as Carlotta recalled: 'The Governor and Mr. Onslow and others had a dispute over some law case and all Perth took sides and one night they had a dreadful scare burning the poor Governor in effigy on the Esplanade. Charlie Stone came up and told us all about the shocking affair.'²⁶

Thereafter, Prinsep's opposition to Broome intensified as he dispassionately recorded the growing antagonism of his friends to the Governor. A public meeting, at which Broome's effigy was burned, is described by Prinsep as a 'tremendous public meeting in Town Hall protesting against the Govr's interdiction of Onslow, the Ch Justice and proposals by the people to have the Govr recalled. HE's [His

---

23 Appleyard, R.T. 1981, 'Western Australia: Economic and demographic growth, 1850–1914', in C.T. Stannage (ed.), *A New History of Western Australia*, University of Western Australia Press, Nedlands, p.222.
24 Constitution of Western Australia, 1890, Section 70.
25 Prinsep, 'Diaries', 30 September 1874.
26 Brockman, Carlotta, 'Reminiscences of Carlotta Louisa Brockman, née Prinsep, 1882–1956', State Library of Western Australia (SLWA) Acc. 931A.

Excllency's] effigy was burnt. We heard loud cheering at our home.'[27] Next day he chided one of Broome's supporters, Sir Thomas Cockburn Campbell, when he came to visit for 'affecting knowledge which he really had not got on which to base tales of Onslow and Forrest & c at Govt House and I warned him to desist such schemes in future'.[28] In a letter to Charlotte Bussell in Paris, he wrote of the 'exceedingly bad terms' between Broome and his friend, John Forrest, that had brought a situation where 'HE does his best to upset every recommendation that Jack makes and to ride rough shod over him'. Nonetheless, he was confident that his 'upright and so clever and cautious' friend would succeed in seeing the Governor 'suffer a recall for the exceedingly unconstitutional and personally actuated way in which he is acting'.

> It is the same with Hensman and he certainly has two stout opponents in J [Forrest] and Hensman and is sure to be tripped up at the last. The great fault in his character ... is selfishness and an overbearing dictatorial manner. There is no suavity about him, or consideration for others.[29]

Prinsep's sympathy with the anti-Broome forces and support for Onslow, Hensman and the native-born John and Alexander Forrest became public as he joined the editorial team of Alexander Forrest's weekly newspaper, *The Possum*, whose chief aim was the removal of Broome, and contributed satirical poetry and graphics to its first series of productions. In the first issue, his cartoon depicted a young boy looking at the stately Queen Britannia; 'Appeal!' the caption read, 'Please let me paddle my own canoe Mammie!'[30] Also included was a poem by Prinsep, written under the pseudonym 'Dry Crust Harry', entitled 'A Leaf from the Diary of a West Australian Ninety-pounds-a-year Slave (to Society)', which expressed resentment against gubernatorial domination of the civil service. Later editions referred to Broome as 'Frederick the Little', as 'that lump, which occupies the top position of our body, and which some people have the impertinence to call a head, is now completely addled—we are lost in a maze of doubt and perplexity'.[31] The Legislative Council was accused of 'toadyism': 'A certain author once wrote, "It is human to err." If the author of that terse remark had only been acquainted with the proceedings of the West Australian Legislative Council, he would have added "and they do little else."'[32] The colonists finally got their wish when Broome left the colony in December 1889, acting as Governor of Barbados and, from 1891, of Trinidad, a position he filled until his retirement and death in England in 1896. A new constitution, which Broome himself had advocated, was ratified by the House of Commons

---

27 Prinsep, 'Diaries', 17 August 1887.
28 Ibid., 18 August 1887.
29 Henry Prinsep to Charlotte Bussell, undated, SLWA Acc. 1274A.
30 *The Possum*, Volume 1 No. 1, 30 July 1887.
31 Ibid., Volume 1 No 6, 24 September 1887.
32 Ibid., Volume 1 No. 4, 10 September 1887.

in August 1890, in which the Imperial Government reserved responsibility for Aboriginal people in Western Australia. Social life rapidly returned to normality for Henry Prinsep after the ructions of the Broome years and he and his family once again became regular visitors and enjoyed the benign patronage of Broome's successors, William Robinson (1890–1895) and Frederick Bedford (1903–1909).

John Gribble and the Church of England Mission Committee

A recurring discourse in the story of Henry Prinsep is the belief that the injury suffered by indigenous populations through colonisation was the responsibility of the coloniser, who had the duty to provide compensation by making sure the colonised were provided with the benefits of colonisation, including induction into Christianity. As described in chapter five, as early as 1834, Captain F.C. Irwin called for establishment of a Church of England mission to Swan River Noongars, while another evangelical settler, Robert Menli Lyon, strenuously advocated a treaty and conciliation between the colonisers and colonised.[33] Shortly afterwards, the Reverend Dr Louis Giustiniani arrived in Perth as a missionary and, by 1837, earned the wrath of many colonists by defending Noongars against the violence and exploitation of settlers, publicising a list of principles which he argued should guide relationships between the two populations. These included the relief of destitution, equality and justice and the suspension of punitive expeditions, together with a threat to expose the colonial social body before 'enlightened British public, and the whole civilised world'.[34] Guistiniani's subsequent departure from the colony set an unfortunate pattern. Those who spoke out in support of Aboriginal populations became liable to vilification, and were often left with no other alternative but to leave.

This was the context in which Prinsep joined a new Mission Committee on the invitation of the 'saintly, scholarly and idealistic' Bishop H.H. Parry. Like Prinsep, Parry was a man of the Empire, born in Antigua and educated in England, who had arrived in Perth to take up the role of Bishop in 1876.[35] The Prinseps had long been close to the leading figures of the colonial Church of England establishment, men such as Mathew Blagden Hale, the first Bishop of Perth, who in 1848 had married Sabina Molloy, eldest daughter of Captain John and amateur botanist Georgiana Molloy, who had been associated with the Bussell family in the south-west. Hale frequently expressed his anguish over

---

33 Reynolds, Henry 1998, *This Whispering in our Hearts*, Allen & Unwin, St. Leonards, Australia, pp.71–84.
34 Ibid., p.85.
35 Haynes, Mark 1974, 'Parry, Henry Hutton (1826–1893)', in *Australian Dictionary of Biography*, Volume 5, Melbourne University Press, Melbourne , pp.407–8.

the poor relationships between colonizers and Aboriginal people, calling for a treaty and a commitment from his church to establish missions throughout the colony. But his advocacy was muted by recognition of the realities of the conflict between colonised and coloniser, the political sensitivities that if they were infringed could damage both his own standing in the colony and the prestige of the church.

After Hale left Perth to become Bishop of Brisbane in 1875, Parry decided that a northern mission to the colony's Aboriginal population was necessary, and established a committee, with Prinsep as one of its members, to negotiate a lease with the Government and recruit a missionary. It took some years for the Bishop to overcome the hesitancy of the Government to support the venture, historian Su-Jane Hunt remarking on the opposition by elected members of the Legislative Council to 'any endeavour to civilise and christianise these northern natives'.[36] *The West Australian* foresaw tension between missionaries and pastoral station managers, and called for 'tact' in 'understanding of the relative positions of the whites and blacks in the district'.[37] In John Gribble, the mission committee thought they had found the right person for the job. He was a man with extensive mission experience in New South Wales and Victoria who was also knowledgeable and had published papers on Aboriginal issues.[38] He held strong views on the obligations of colonisation, which he enunciated in December 1885 at a public lecture in Perth, stating his opinion that mission activity was part of the compensation owed to Aboriginal people for the loss of their lands and traditional economy.[39] Arriving in the Gascoyne port of Carnarvon in September 1885, Gribble quickly alienated the local community of pastoralists and police who, within three months of his arrival, realised he was intent on confronting them about their practices on the use of Aboriginal labour. As he later described, 'at one station where I called, and where I found a large number of natives in the ownership of the manager',

> I drew attention to the neglected appearance of certain of the natives, and that if the blacks were unkindly treated they would certainly run away. I was told in reply that the treatment was quite good enough for the 'niggers', and that it was absurd to think they should have tea, sugar, etc. And mark—these same natives I found were saving this very station hundreds of pounds per annum.[40]

---

36 Hunt, Su-Jane 1984, 'The Gribble Affair: A Study in Colonial Politics', in Bob Reece and Tom Stannage (eds.), *Studies in Western Australian History,* Issue 8: European–Aboriginal Relations in Western Australian History, University of Western Australia Press, Nedlands, p.43.
37 *The West Australian*, 12 March 1880.
38 Gribble, J.B. 1884, *'Black But Comely': Or, glimpses of Aboriginal life in Australia*, Morgan and Scott, London.
39 Prinsep, 'Diaries', 9 December 1885; *The Inquirer*, 11 December 1885.
40 Gribble, J.B. 1987, *Dark Deeds in a Sunny Land: Or, blacks and whites in North-West Australia*, University of Western Australia Press, Nedlands, p.10.

He described the 'intolerable conditions' under which Aboriginal people were employed, how they were 'chained like so many dogs to each other round the neck', and the sexual exploitation of Aboriginal women by white men.[41] He quickly learned that, in the minds of the white population, the scope of the mission was extremely limited. Aboriginal people 'belonged to the owner of the runs on which they were found, and … the Mission had no right whatever to any but the old and crippled.'[42] Public meetings of the white population demanded his recall, and within a few months, his role in the Gascoyne came to an end. As Gribble put it, in his three months in the Gascoyne he had,

> Travelled 400 miles into the interior, built Mission house and native hut, commenced school house, fenced part of garden block, sunk well, small community of natives gathered by their own free will. Church services for whites organised and regularly maintained: and last, but not least, got the whole district (I will not say town of Carnarvon) against me—Why?[43]

Gribble wrote a full exposition of his experiences for publication in the colonial press, in which he not only described what he had seen, but named and criticised. This caused enormous controversy in the city and further alienated him from the pastoralist lobby, to the extent that he was attacked and physically threatened on a voyage from Carnarvon to Fremantle in January 1886. His attempt to lay charges further antagonised his critics. The charges eventually lapsed, in Gribble's opinion because of the opposition of key colonial officials. This caused him to refer his complaints to the Secretary of State for Colonies, sending copies of his letter to the Governor, the Colonial Secretary, Dean Joseph Gegg, in the absence of Bishop Parry, who was in England, and the Mission Committee. The Committee, however, condemned his actions, Prinsep recording in January that they 'sat a long time discussing Gribble's conduct as Missionary at the Gascoyne. The feeling was against his action in publishing his late journal and I was against spending too much' on the Gascoyne venture.[44] Resolutions were adopted, criticising the 'temporarily excited feeling' on the part of 'many influential settlers' as 'discourteous, so unjust in mode of procedure, and so unconstitutional', but also expressing an 'unqualified condemnation' of Gribble's actions. The Committee especially deplored the publication of his allegations 'which has already done much to alienate the public … and which must prove extremely detrimental, if not fatal, to the success of the mission among the white population'.[45] It demanded that Gribble publish a statement regretting 'that he should have taken the course which he did in publishing to the world, after so short an acquaintance with the district, the details of the domestic life and faults

---

41   Ibid., p. 11.
42   Ibid., p. 13.
43   Ibid., p. 14.
44   Prinsep, 'Diaries', 26 January 1886.
45   Church of England Mission Committee, Minutes, October 1 1887, SLWA Acc. 996A/5.

of the settlers therein committed to his pastoral care', and sought to prevent him from sending further reports to the newspapers of the colony.[46] By February, the Committee had decided to restrict Gribble's activity to the Dalgety Reserve, 400 kilometres east of Carnarvon, and, by June, at the instigation of Dean Gegg, he was refused permission to preach at the cathedral in Perth. Effectively isolated and with support from the Church heavily qualified, Gribble published his exposé, 'Dark Deeds in a Sunny Land', in the pages of local newspaper, *The Inquirer*, which had supported Gribble against what it saw as the interests of the narrow colonial elite dominating the Mission Committee. 'Of whom is this committee composed?' asked *The Inquirer*: 'Mainly of men who, however honest they may wish to be, have their interests bound up with the settlers—men some of whom would feel keenly in a pecuniary sense the defection of influential members of their church.'[47]

In Hunt's words, 'Dark Deeds' was received in Perth 'with a tone bordering on hysteria', and Gribble was accused of seeking only 'to catch the ear and tickle the fancy of Exeter Hall'.[48] By doing so, he had 'traduced and maligned the settlers of Western Australia in the eyes of the world'. The whole colony was 'held up to execration', and had been 'insulted and degraded before the whole world'.[49] *The West Australian* called Gribble a 'lying, canting humbug', which caused him to sue the proprietors of the newspaper, one of whom, Charles Harper, served with Prinsep on the Mission Committee.[50] The resultant case was heard before two judges, including Onslow. Although it was eventually decided in favour of the defendants, the case had wide ramifications. Onslow was accused by the proprietors of the newspaper of bias towards Gribble, who expressed his view that a 'conservative colonial element' was behind the attack in an attempt to preserve its proprietary interests in land and access to a cheap labour force.[51]

Prinsep found his involvement in the Mission Committee challenging, and his diary entries imply exasperation at the time he was required to spend on the matter and the level of controversy surrounding Gribble. He shared the concern of other members, such as Joseph Gegg and Charles Harper, at Gribble's willingness to go public with his allegations and the potential damage to the colony's reputation overseas, and supported resolutions to restrict his activities. At the same time, he was worried about the virulence of the attack on Gribble, which may have underlined his horror at the frontier violence Gribble was alleging. While nowhere in his diaries does he express an opinion on Gribble's

---

46   Ibid.
47   *The Inquirer*, 23 June 1886.
48   Hunt, 'The Gribble Affair', p. 46.
49   Reynolds, *This Whispering in our Hearts*, p. 153.
50   Church of England Mission Committee, Minutes, October 1st 1887.
51   Hunt 1984, 'The Gribble Affair', p.47.

allegations, there are many instances in which members of the family express their abhorrence of the kind of violence Gribble claimed to have witnessed. 'The natives should be made to understand', wrote Prinsep's sister-in-law, Caroline Bussell, from Paris, 'that a white man has no rights to flog a Black and the Whites should be punished severely for doing so. They are so much stronger and more muscular than the poor natives that they cannot judge of the deadly effect of their blows on the weaker bodies of the natives.'[52]

The Gribble affair, as it came to be known, had a lasting impact on the subsequent mission policies and the reputation of Western Australia in the eastern colonies and metropolitan Britain. Prinsep recorded in November 1888 that, in preparation for the visit of the Archbishop of Adelaide, whose jurisdiction included Western Australia, the Committee met to prepare a statement 'vindicating our actions' in the Gribble case. The previous year, it had adopted a policy to guide future mission functions, in which it adopted advice provided by Gribble. In a confusing and contradictory statement, the Committee accepted that the 'Australian aboriginal' had just as much right to humane treatment as any other indigenous subject of Britain: 'The Australian aboriginal (as compared with the North American Indians, & c) is a difficult subject to deal with owing to his lack of manhood and want of intelligence in his native state.'

> But the broad principle should stand that a Christian nation or colony should not be guilty of taking and leasing land occupied by aborigines without rendering them as compensation proper legal protection, bodily maintenance, and Christian teaching. Any forcible occupation without such compensation is theft.[53]

The statement set out future priorities for mission activity. 'Boarding schools' in each district should be established for all children aged from three to 14, 'to be under the management of clergymen, the children to be taught to read and write and do useful work, clothed and brought up religiously, and returned to their stations at the end of their schooling period. A law of compulsory education for the future education of the children would be only an apparent cruelty.' Adult Aboriginal people employed on stations would be the responsibility of 'an itinerating minister', whose responsibility would be to 'instill into their minds the simple truths of the Gospel'. Reservations would be established for 'wild natives', who would be compulsorily collected by constables ('and kind treatment would do the rest') and placed under the control of an 'experienced manager' on a property on which there would be 'a school, church, and resident minister, made self supporting'.[54]

---

52 Caroline Bussell to Josephine Prinsep, 3 June 1898, MN 773 Acc. 3593A/25.
53 Church of England Mission Committee, Minutes, October 1 1887.
54 Ibid.

The Gribble affair had the effect of unifying resistance in Western Australia to what was believed to be external interference in Aboriginal affairs in the north of the colony. It served to limit the future role of missions to frontier districts where there was little likelihood of interference in the relationships between pastoralists and Aboriginal people. Missions would, in future, complement and support colonial demand for labour by confining their activities to regions where there were no pastoral interests, by removing unproductive children from the stations and training them for a return to station work, and by restricting the activities of missionaries to the 'spiritual needs' of the Aboriginal station workforce. Missions thus accepted the primacy of the need for cheap station labour over their own interests, and sought to avoid establishing missions as local alternatives to the exploitation of labour by the pastoral industry. Future missions were to take account of the power of the colonial landholding elite, and avoid any hint of imposition on their jealously guarded rights to the labour of Aboriginal people. The next 30 years saw a small number of missions established well away from the scope of the pastoral industry, in places such as the Cambridge Gulf and Sunday Island on the Kimberley coast. While the Dalgety mission that Gribble had first sought to establish retained its status as reserved land, future mission interest moved to the Forrest River in the Kimberley, where, in the early 1900s, Gribble's son Ernest would take up his father's mantle of missionary. As such, the ramifications of the Gribble affair extended into Prinsep's tenure as Chief Protector of Aborigines, the Church of England manifesto on mission activity which Prinsep had helped to craft also coming to influence the development of government policy on Aboriginal affairs.

A colonial bull market

An unwelcome consequence of the Gribble affair was the attention from outside the colony that came to be focussed on Western Australia, which meant that its treatment of Aboriginal people would be scrutinised overseas and in the eastern colonies of Australia for the next 30 years. This attention would come to occupy much of Prinsep's time and energy when he became Chief Protector. Meanwhile, the colony was forced into a position where its reputation overseas was of crucial importance. It was vital to project the image of a well-governed and well-managed colony, a safe environment for imperial investors to put their money. Prinsep's long-awaited promotion to the senior position of Under Secretary of Mines in 1894 launched him into the world of mining and economic development, and into a civil service position in which his office was charged with regulating the rampant capitalism of transnational business by managing and facilitating development of new and lucrative industries. By the early 1890s, major discoveries of gold in the Eastern Goldfields and Murchison districts, north-east of Perth, brought an 'economic watershed for the whole community'. In a single decade it experienced a 'fourfold increase in population and an increase in capital which lifted infrastructure to a level hitherto thought impossible to achieve'.[55] For families such as the Prinseps, the rapid rise in population, from 48,502 in 1890 to 179, 967 in 1900, changed the colony forever. Perth no longer was like a village in its social and community life, the inflow of capital and population bringing a massive expansion of construction in the metropolitan area.

Prinsep took up his new position early in 1894 and was immediately launched into a maelstrom of work to establish the new department. By 1896, he was complaining to his brother, Charlie, that he had no time to do anything. 'I am beset by crowds of people who daily pour into my office', he wrote, 'I've never worked so hard or continuously in my life before.'[56]

> The revenue of our Department alone has jumped others—for the year ending June 30 1895 it was £5,000 and for the year ending 30th June next it will have been £135,000 and it increases monthly. Machinery is pouring into the fields and that is the wand which will create a miracle almost. ... The office is almost overwhelmed with work. Last week we recorded in three days 500 incoming letters and Crockett and I are slaving away till 11 or 12 every night and four or five other men come in too. Poor Fred Roe the accountant hardly knows which way to turn.[57]

As Under Secretary, Prinsep was responsible firstly to the Commissioner of Crown Lands, William Marmion, and, after December 1894, to a newly created Minister for Mines, Edward Wittenoom. His initial tasks were to establish the administrative machinery to process demand for licenses, and supervise the network of quasi-judicial mining wardens and surveyors. He was also responsible for establishing a regulatory framework, which included drafting amendments to the Mining Act to establish local mining boards with the power to regulate activities through by-laws. In 1886, he prepared the *Goldfields Bill*, which reduced the powers of mining wardens to act summarily, restricted the issue of miners' permits to 'Asiatics, Afghans and Chinamen', provided exemptions from requirements to lease land that was exclusively alluvial, and included reef gold deposits within the purview of the legislation.[58] By 1895, the new *Goldfields Act*, which repealed previous goldfields legislation and established 'liberal leasing provisions and specific reservation of the Executive's regulation-making powers', was passed.[59] The size of the Mines Department increased to meet these

---

55   Appleyard 1981, 'Western Australia', p.219.
56   H.C. Prinsep to C.J. Prinsep, 23 December 1896, SLWA Acc. 3595A/9/9.
57   H.C. Prinsep to C.J. Prinsep, 26 June 1896, SLWA Acc. 3595A/9/8.
58   Western Australian Parliamentary Debates, Volume 6, 1894.
59   Spillman, Ken 1993, *A Rich Endowment: Government and mining in Western Australia, 1829–1994*, University of Western Australia Press, Nedlands, p.93.

demands, particularly in its employment of surveyors and draftsmen who, by the end of 1894, had produced lithographs of all mining centres and adopted a system of keeping them up to date.[60]

A scan of Mines Department files from the years of Prinsep's administration suggests a competent administrator, who provided consistent and clear advice to his Minister and managed the growing staffing establishment of the department in a professional manner. Prinsep and his staff earned the praise of parliamentarians, such as Charles Moran, member for the Eastern Goldfields electorate of Yilgarn, for the manner in which they undertook their duties, 'and the courteous and obliging treatment they always extended to the public'.[61] Summing up Prinsep's performance as Under Secretary, Spillman remarked that 'his dedication to the service of government was unquestioned':

> Working long hours, he had overseen the Department's growth and played a large part in determining its future role. Administering the orderly development of a notoriously disorderly industry was an unenviable task, but Prinsep had shirked nothing. A succession of salary increases had taken his salary from £350 to £550 per annum, and recognised the quality of his service and the importance of the position he held.[62]

After four hectic years, Prinsep left the position of Under Secretary in May 1898 for what he anticipated would be a less onerous role as Chief Protector of Aborigines. He maintained his salary of 550 pounds per annum, but was relieved of the responsibility for managing a department that, by the time of his departure, had grown from five to over 50. His diaries, the relative neglect of which during his period as Under Secretary is indicative of his work-load, refer to bouts of gastritis and periods of illness that forced him to take a seven-week holiday in Ceylon in late-1897, where he was joyfully reunited with his sister, Louisa, and his extended Cameron family and other old friends.[63] On his return, at the age of 54, John Forrest's offer of the Chief Protector's role must have seemed to Prinsep to promise welcome relief from the unrelenting grind of mining administration. In such a role, he could practice his humanitarian beliefs and perhaps even see them into official government policy. Unbeknown to him, the new position was to bring probably the most politically and socially fraught period of his career.

---

60 Ibid., p.85.
61 Western Australian Parliamentary Debates, Volume 6, 29 August 1895.
62 Spillman 1993, *A Rich Endowment*, p.99.
63 *The West Australian*, 30 November 1897.

7. 'Received into the very best society'

The Chine, Prinsep's holiday home on Freshwater Bay, Swan River, about 15 kilometres downriver from Perth. Prinsep's youthful connection with Freshwater on the Isle of Wight was reflected in his choice of the name for his resort.

Source: Prinsep Papers, SLWA MN 773 BA 1423/353.

The Chine was a place of peace and relaxation for the Prinsep family, where Henry could get away from the cares of the office and the city. Walter Roth congratulated him for escaping to the Chine to avoid the 'great hubbub' greeting the release of the 1905 inquiry into Aboriginal affairs in Western Australia.

Source: Prinsep Papers, SLWA MN 773 BA 1423/354.

The Prinseps reached The Chine either by river or the recently opened Perth-Fremantle railway, when they would arrange with the driver to stop at Bullen's Siding and walk along a bush track to the river.

Source: Prinsep Papers, SLWA MN 773 BA 1423/355.

The Chine, a panorama from the low limestone cliffs behind it.

Source: Prinsep Papers, SLWA MN 773 BA 1423/351.

7. 'Received into the very best society'

The children of the expanding Prinsep family could run barefoot at The Chine, go boating, swimming and crabbing on the waters of the Swan. In this photograph, Josephine and Emily Prinsep watch Frank and Caroline Brockman as they negotiate the waters of the well.

Source: Prinsep Papers, SLWA MN 773 BA 1423/350.

Nothing remains of The Chine today apart from two carvings by Prinsep. The image above shows his invocation to 'dip your nose in', which he carved in Greek letters next to the well.

Source: Author's private collection.

7. 'Received into the very best society'

On moving to Perth, Henry Prinsep supplemented his meagre earnings as a civil servant by taking on commissions to illustrate books, paint portraits and other design projects, such as the capitals for St George's Hall in 1871, still visible as a façade to a new office block in Hay Street, Perth.

Source: Author's private collection.

Mary Anne Tichbon (née Currie) who, with her sister Louisa, was taken in by the Prinseps as live-in maid after their mother died and their father was unable to care for them. Mary Anne stayed with the family in Perth for many years, while Louisa went to live with the Bussells in Busselton.

Source: Prinsep Papers, SLWA MN 773 BA 1423/38.

7. 'Received into the very best society'

The women of the Prinsep family amongst friends, probably in the gardens of the Studio in the late 1890s. At center sits Josephine Prinsep, next to her is Carlotta, with Virginia at her feet and Emily on the far left.

Source: Prinsep Papers, SLWA MN 773 BA 1423/242.

Family group, from left to right: Emily, Carlotta, Josephine, Virginia and Henry Prinsep in their garden at 'The Studio', Howick Street, Perth.

Source: Prinsep Papers, SLWA MN 773 BA 1423/240.

7. 'Received into the very best society'

The Prinseps were enthusiastic participants in fancy dress balls. This image, taken by Henry Prinsep, records one such event. Josephine is seated centre.

Source: Prinsep Papers, SLWA MN 773 BA 1423/547.

Rottnest Island holiday. Henry Prinsep is fifth from the right, with Premier John Forrest third, Margaret Forrest first, and Prinsep's second daughter Emily next to him.

Source: Courtesy of Ailsa Smith, Claremont, WA.

7. 'Received into the very best society'

Mementoes of family in England. The family of Henry's sister Louisa Bowden-Smith (sitting at left) and William (right), including Vee (standing), Charlie (standing) and Bill (front). In the centre is Annie Prinsep. The image was taken in England, possibly at Brockenhurst, during the early 1900s.

Source: Prinsep Papers, SLWA MN 773 BA 1423/456.

'Lots of work and most woefully dull'. Prinsep's brother Jim spent a few years in Ceylon in the 1870s, trying his hand as a coffee planter. In this image, Jim lies in front, with extended family members H. Cumberbatch and F.A. Fairlie. The Sri Lankan servants are not identified.

Source: Prinsep Papers, SLWA MN 773 BA 1423/904.

7. 'Received into the very best society'

Jim Prinsep, Henry's younger brother, during his career as a mining company secretary in London.

Source: Prinsep Papers, SLWA MN 773 Acc. 1423/910.

Aunt Julia Margaret Cameron lived in Ceylon, where she continued her photographic interests and was periodically visited by friends, such as botanical artist Marianne North, from 1875 until her death in 1879. This photograph captures North at the easel, creating an image of a Ceylonese labourer on the verandah of Cameron's house, Dimboola.

Source: http://commons.wikimedia.org/wiki/File:Marianne_North_in_Mrs_Cameron%27s_house_in_Ceylon,_by_Julia_Margaret_Cameron.jpg.

7. 'Received into the very best society'

Henry Prinsep with his staff in front of the Department of Mines, which he headed from 1894–1898, presiding over a period of expansion in the Forrest Government's efforts to regulate the burgeoning Western Australian mining industry.

Source: Prinsep Papers, SLWA MN 773 BA 1423/87.

Prinsep's pen and ink illustration of a scene from John Forrest's 1874 exploration into the Central, Victoria and Western Deserts.

Source: Art Gallery of Western Australia.

7. 'Received into the very best society'

'Ularring (Attacked)', an incident from the Giles exploration of 1875, which illustrates the episode as described by Giles in his journal Australia Twice Traversed.

Source: Art Gallery of Western Australia.

Prinsep's mock-up of his illustration of an incident from the Giles exploration through the Victoria Desert in 1875.

Source: Art Gallery of Western Australia.

8. Chief Protector of Aborigines

Henry Prinsep took up the role of Western Australia's first Chief Protector of Aborigines anticipating a change from the unrelenting grind of the Mines Department, but soon realised the job would place him in the midst of fraught political battles over the colony's indigenous populations. His first parliamentary master, Premier John Forrest, had an active interest in the portfolio and wanted the job done as he determined. A self-proclaimed expert on Aboriginal matters, Forrest believed that governments should intervene only in the most extreme cases of mistreatment or poverty. It was his conviction that Aboriginal people were, in any case, disappearing and would have little future in the development of the State. He wanted his new Aborigines Department to stay small and cost little. It was the responsibility of pastoralists and farmers to look after their Aboriginal workforces, and Aboriginal people should be compelled either to work or sustain themselves in their traditional way. Prinsep's job was to remain in his Perth office and efficiently manage a meagre budget and staff, devoting his efforts to providing rations to a population of dispossessed Aboriginal people that was expanding rapidly as colonisation spread throughout Western Australia.

Prinsep's qualifications for the position of Chief Protector of Aborigines were not immediately evident, even to members of his family. Like many colonists in the country areas of Western Australia, Prinsep had encountered Aboriginal people intermittently as pastoral workers, and had been involved in the humane activities of dispensing rations, clothing and blankets, principally as a member of the church. To Julius Brockman, son of Josephine's sister, Capel, who spent his adult life running pastoral stations in the Gascoyne and Pilbara, Prinsep was too closely aligned to Forrest and 'too busy playing charades at Government House' to give his full attention to the job.[1] From her home in Paris, Caroline Bussell told her sister Josephine Prinsep that a better candidate would have been her childhood friend, Harold Hale, who, in 1896, had unsuccessfully tried to establish a Church of England mission at Forrest River in the East Kimberley.[2] To Caroline, it was Hale's background in one of the old Western Australian families that made him suitable:

> I suppose Harold was too proud to ask for work under the Government. If he had I should think he might have got something. Considering that his Grandfather [John Molloy] was one of the first settlers and magistrates, that his Grandmother [Georgiana Molloy] died from the privations she

---
1 Brockman, Joan (ed.) 1987, *He Rode Alone: Being the adventures of pioneer Julius Brockman from his diaries*, Artlook Books, Perth, p.295.
2 *The West Australian*, 6 July 1898.

underwent as wife of a pioneer, and then his father [Mathew Blagden Hale] did so much in helping procure education for the young people apart from his generosity to the Church. Many who are now members of the WA Government owe their education to the Bishop's School.[3]

But Prinsep possessed many of the attributes John Forrest was looking for. His achievement in efficiently setting up the Mines Department over the previous four years suggested he could do the same for another domain of colonial government activity. Forrest wanted a person who would not unsettle the colonial social body, as John Gribble had done in the 1880s, and would present a humane and efficient face to the policies of the government. Prinsep was well known and well connected in the colony, Britain and the imperial world, an attribute that would be handy in placating continuing criticism of the colony's treatment of Aboriginal people. Telling Prinsep he must quickly 'get a firm grip on the question and attend to it', Forrest had every reason to believe that his new Chief Protector would faithfully represent the benevolent paternalism of old settlers such as himself.[4]

As Prinsep's Minister, John Forrest held firm views on the future of Aboriginal people, derived from a life-time's contact, from his childhood in proximity to Noongar families around Bunbury, to extensive contact with Aboriginal societies during his explorations around Western Australia, and his associations with Aboriginal guides, such as Tommy Windich, Tommy Pierre, Tommy Dower, and Billy Noongale Kickett, who helped mediate his encounters with Aboriginal peoples he encountered in the bush. Biographer F.K. Crowley saw in Forrest a man of 'humane outlook', who viewed Aboriginal people as 'very intelligent', their language 'euphonious and … easily acquired', and as 'tractable and willing to work'. At the same time, they lived 'a savage and precarious life', and made 'no provision for the morrow, using no means to cultivate the land, no permanent habitations, a mere animal living in savagedom'.[5] Forrest told Legislative Councilors in 1883 that 'we owed these natives something more than repression … Anyone would imagine … that the natives were our enemies instead of our best friends. Colonisation would go on with very slow strides if we had no natives to assist us.'[6] Aboriginal people should be preserved 'from

---

3   Caroline Bussell to Josephine Prinsep, 3 June 1898, SLWA Acc. 3593A/25. Caroline was referring to the son of her friend, Sabina Molloy, who had married Bishop Mathew Hale, the founder of Bishop Hale's School, the first private school for the sons of gentlemen in the colony. Forrest attended Hale's School along with many of the Brockmans and Bussells. The grandparents of Harold Hale referred to by Caroline were Georgiana Molloy and her husband, Captain John Molloy, who had settled in the Augusta area and then the Vasse during the 1830s. Caroline is referring to Harold Hale's involvement in an ill-fated attempt by the Church of England to establish a mission at the Forrest River in the East Kimberley.
4   SROWA Series 3005, Cons. 255 AD File 1426/98.
5   Crowley, F.K. 2000, *Big John Forrest 1847–1918: A founding father of the Commonwealth of Australia*, University of Western Australia Press, Nedlands, pp.34–6, 109.
6   Ibid., pp.49–50.

extinction', yet he believed in the inevitability of their withering in the face of a more robust culture. Governments should 'do just enough to smooth their passing and to ensure that they should serve the higher civilisation before they went'.[7] As Premier, Forrest was much more concerned with the pastoral and industrial development of the colony than with the interests of Aboriginal people as traditional landholders.

Forrest acted immediately to cut the spending of the dismantled Aborigines Protection Board. Section 70 of the *Western Australia Constitution Act 1890* had specified the financial arrangements under which the Board, constituted by the *Aborigines Protection Act 1886,* was to function. An annual sum of 5,000 pounds or 1 per cent of gross revenue from the colony's consolidated revenue was to provide Aboriginal people 'with food and clothing when they would otherwise be destitute, in promoting the education of Aboriginal children (including half-castes), and in assisting generally to promote the preservation and well-being of the Aborigines'.[8] As the colony's revenues increased after 1890, so did the annual revenue of the Aborigines Protection Board, which reached 23,563 pounds in 1897/98.[9] Although he had been an early member of the Board, Premier Forrest criticised it whenever the opportunity arose and effectively froze it out of a role in the colonial government. The Secretary of State for Colonies finally relented to Forrest's pressure and, in 1897, legislation was passed to wind up the Board and establish the position of Chief Protector as head of a new Aborigines Department, responsible to the executive.[10]

Prinsep found himself heading a department with no money and no powers. Along with a single staff member and a part-time accountant, he was expected to remain in Perth, with few resources to travel to other areas to supervise compliance of the *Aborigines Act 1897*. The regional presence was, instead, to be through a network of unpaid local protectors, mostly police officers, pastoral managers, resident magistrates, missionaries and medical officers. Local protectors were given no extra resources to undertake their functions under the 1897 laws, and their capacity to undertake the role was additionally compromised by their other responsibilities, which, in the case of police, primarily involved the protection of European populations. The Chief Protector had no authority to direct local protectors and was forced to rely on good will. As Prinsep put it in 1905: 'It is very difficult for me to pat with one hand and slap with the other. If I were threatened by the refusal of the police and the squatters to help me

---

7   Goddard, Elizabeth and Tom Stannage 1984, 'John Forrest and the Aborigines', in Bob Reece, Bob and Tom Stannage (eds), *Studies in Western Australian History,* Issue 8: European–Aboriginal Relations in Western Australian History, University of Western Australia Press, Nedlands, Nedlands, p.56.
8   Western Australia, *Constitution Act 1889*, Section 70.
9   Biskup, Peter 1973, *Not Slaves, Not Citizens: The Aboriginal problem in Western Australia, 1898–1954*, University of Queensland Press, St. Lucia, p.46.
10   Western Australia, *Aborigines Act 1897*.

carry out my duties, I should be in a sorry plight.'[11] The periodic employment of Travelling Inspector G.S. Olivey, whose job was to visit stations and farms employing Aboriginal people and provide reports on their numbers, conditions and treatment, gave the department a very limited profile in the regions. It remained dependent on the good will and integrity of a network which, by virtue of distance and a non-existent level of supervision, retained considerable discretion over Aboriginal people at the local level.

Such was Forrest's approach to Aboriginal governance, a weak act and a level of funding designed to limit the department's capabilities to a function largely restricted to a niggardly obsession with relief and ration payments. This was the home grown solution to the problem, defined by the way in which local politicians and interest groups viewed Aboriginal populations as a doomed race, fated to die out in the face of modernisation and dispossession. The duty of the government was one of benign benevolence, which aimed to make the passing less painful, relieve the misery of the old and indigent, and either put the able-bodied to work, or leave them to fend for themselves, until the colonisers required their land and labour. By the time Prinsep took up his job in 1898, Western Australia was one of the few Australian colonies without intrusive legislation designed to micro-manage Aboriginal populations. Prinsep drew the attention of Western Australian legislators to laws and systems in other Australian colonies, which had established Aborigines Protection Boards with extensive powers to remove and institutionalise Aboriginal children.[12] Queensland and the Northern Territory seemed to provide precedents relevant to the colony. Like Western Australia, they were colonies with vast northern and desert areas, large Aboriginal populations, and sparse colonial settlement. The Queensland *Aborigines Protection and Restriction on the Sale of Opium Amending Act 1897* subsequently provided a precedent for laws in Western Australia, South Australia, and the Northern Territory.

Prinsep repeatedly alerted Forrest to the weaknesses of the *Aborigines Protection Act*, pointing to a budget plainly inadequate to deal with rising levels of poverty and dispossession among Aboriginal populations throughout Western Australia. He warned that pastoral landowners were increasingly seeking to defray the costs of rations on to the government, and that there were demands also from the missions for resources to establish institutions for the care and education of Aboriginal children throughout the colony. As the government had learned from the Gribble affair, the churches were not averse to making public their allegations of government inefficiencies or lack of action. Prinsep brought new

---

11 *The West Australian*, 2 February 1905.
12 Prinsep to Forrest, 10 December 1900, SROWA Series 3005 Cons 255 AD File 180/1900; Haebich, Anna 2000, *Broken Circles: Fragmenting Indigenous families, 1800–2000*, Fremantle Arts Centre Press, Fremantle, p.144.

problems to the government's attention, including the increasing population of mixed-race children, whose unregulated presence implied a threat to the harmonious future of the colony. The occurrence of venereal disease in country regions, ports and mining centres, posed a threat not only to the future of the Aboriginal population and their children, but to working men of European origin. Criticism of the colony's alleged toleration of violence and forced labour, coming from outsiders in Britain and the eastern colonies, would not go away, prompting Prinsep's clerk, Edward Pechell, to ask in 1907: 'when is it going to end—why cannot they leave us alone, as we do the natives in other states?'[13]

During its first year, the Aborigines Department's budget of 5,000 pounds represented a 75 per cent reduction from the final year budget of the disbanded Aborigines Protection Board. Fixed items in the budget included Prinsep's salary of 550 pounds, the costs of an accountant and a clerk, and annual allocations to the Swan Natives and Half Castes Mission of 750 pounds, and Bishop Salvado's New Norcia Mission of 450 pounds. The small amount left over for relief guaranteed that much of Prinsep's attention would be given to cutting expenditure and scrutinising claims from station owners and protectors. Prinsep often sought Forrest's approval for expenditure, even for small items, such as 1 pounds 10 shillings for a child's funeral in the Eastern Goldfields town of Norseman. The request was grudging approved by the Premier, 'for the sanitary benefit of the town than for the Aborigines and I think the sanitary board should pay'.[14]

Forrest was reluctant to approve extra funds, yet directed the Department 'not to be harsh or to be niggardly—each case must be dealt with on its merits'.[15] 'The natives', he wrote, 'must be fed and given water.' Prinsep informed him that the problem lay in the decline of paternalistic obligations amongst the colonial social body, along with a widespread failure to look after the 'old and indigent' and those unable to work for their living. In his mind, there was a distinction between the old colonists who understood their responsibilities, and 'a new order who do not recognise the claims on them of the Aboriginals'.[16] In letters to pastoral managers in the north, Prinsep emphasised that Aboriginal people should be required to 'fend for themselves' wherever possible, particularly when 'there is much game and many able young men in the tribes to get it and so feed their old relatives'. He warned against 'pampering' Aboriginal people 'with too rapidly afforded relief, which in some parts of the colony has been said to have pauperised them needlessly'.[17]

---

13 E. Pechell to H.C. Prinsep, 23 December 1907, SLWA Acc. 3593A/34.
14 Forrest to H.C. Prinsep, SROWA Series 3005 255 AD File 1898/78.
15 Forrest to H.C. Prinsep, SROWA Series 3005 Cons 255 AD 1898/375.
16 H.C. Prinsep to Forrest, SROWA Series 3005 Cons 255 AD File 1898/387.
17 H.C. Prinsep to Arthur Clifton, manager of Yeeda Station, West Kimberley, 25 May 1900, SROWA Series 3005 Cons 255 AD File 1900/6.

Prinsep predicted a crisis in the Aboriginal labour market, 'which sooner or later will require attention'.[18] Increasing numbers of farmers in the southern districts preferred to employ white rather than Aboriginal labour, and were refusing to provide food and relief for Aboriginal people camped on their properties. This meant that even able-bodied Aboriginal people had difficulty obtaining work which, combined with the 'extinction of their natural food', and 'their being brought up on stations and so hav[ing] lost the art of catching their food', added to the burden on the rations budget. By July 1898, Prinsep informed Forrest that expenditure on relief would have to be restricted to 180 pounds per month if it was to last the financial year.[19] Forrest refused to believe that 'there were so many absolutely indigent natives about', and feared that station owners were defraying their labour costs to the government, but grudgingly acceded to Prinsep's request for additional funds in February 1899, directing Treasury to make an extraordinary payment of 3,000 pounds. A system of subsidiary payments, to top up the meager parliamentary vote, continued for the next three years until, in 1901, an annual budget of 10,000 pounds was allocated. But these additional funds were provided reluctantly and failed to disguise the prevailing government conviction that money spent on Aboriginal people was money wasted.

'Complete separation from their savage life'

The situation confronting Aboriginal, and particularly 'half-caste' children, soon came to preoccupy Prinsep in his role as Chief Protector. In his 1901 Annual Report, he reported on the 'number and condition of the half-castes', removing details that 'allude personally to men as fathers of half-castes and other passages which it will be advisable not to publish'.[20] 'Where there are no evil influences', he advised, 'these half-castes can be made into useful workmen and women', yet most of them lived in communities 'whose influence is towards laziness and vice; and I think it is our duty not to allow these children, whose blood is half British, to grow up as vagrants and outcasts, as their mothers now are'.[21] The vagrancy provisions of the criminal laws allowed him to ask police to detain Aboriginal people but, in some areas, this would mean the arrest of whole communities, since the 'natural custom of their race is one of vagrancy'.[22] The power to compulsorily remove half-caste children would allow the government to enforce 'complete separation from their old savage life, which is a desirable end in the case of all half-castes'. Furthermore, the government should make

---

18   SROWA Series 3005 Cons 255 AD File 1898/941.
19   Ibid.
20   SROWA Series 3005 Cons 255 AD File 1901/351.
21   Government of Western Australia 1900/1, *Annual Report of the Aborigines Department*, Perth, p.4.
22   Ibid., p. 4.

these children wards until the age of 18 to reduce the probability that, on their return home, 'they may revert to a more evil, because educated, barbarism than before'. Legal guardianship of all half-caste children would see most of them 'placed under proper care, and brought up in useful knowledge'.[23]

What this proper care might entail was another question confronting Prinsep. The small number of mission institutions funded by the department in 1901 varied considerably in their methods and target populations. The major recipient of government aid was the Church of England Swan Native and Half-Caste Mission near Perth, which accommodated 14 boys and 33 girls, and received per capita payments for most of the children. Girls were taught laundry work, bread-making, cooking, sewing, gardening and 'other household occupations … with good results', but the supervisor, David Garland, expressed his 'grave concern' for their future, believing that discharge would be 'attended with the most serious dangers.' He and Prinsep agreed that, on their release, they should be placed with settler families to work as domestic servants. The boys would be transferred to the orphanage 'for white boys, where they receive the same school and practical instruction on handicrafts, gardening, and farming as the white boys', and progress to employment as labourers on farms.[24] The Pallotine Beagle Bay Mission in the Kimberley dealt both with children and their families. Twenty children were given two hours schooling a day, the remainder of their time occupied 'making bricks, others repairing fences, others doing stock work amongst the cattle etc.; and if they are inclined to be idle, the threat of not being allowed to attend school has an instant effect'. The mission aimed to 'civilise' about 70 adults, 'all well-dressed, clean and respectable', singing 'hymns in their own lingo … and made the responses very audibly and, apparently, correctly'.[25] Prinsep approved the methods of the Bishop Salvado's Benedictine New Norcia Mission, 100 kilometres north-east of Perth, whose creed he thought 'eminently practical'.

> The experience of the good Bishop Salvado … is that we must not forget they are savages, and we must first try to enable them to make their own work worth their food and clothing, and, if they gain this knowledge, reading and writing may then be taught; but, as they can never hope to have the same status as a white man, it is useless to teach them those things which a labourer does not require.[26]

Ellensbrook Farm School, about 60 kilometres from Busselton in the south-west of the colony, provided the kind of environment Prinsep particularly favoured. Under the management of Josephine's cousin, Edith Bussell, 'a lady well-known

---

23 SROWA Series 3005 Cons 255 AD File 1902/12202.
24 Government of Western Australia 1900/1, *Annual Report of the Aborigines Department*, Perth, p.9.
25 Ibid., p. 47.
26 1898/99 Annual Report, SROWA Series 3005 Cons 255, AD File 1899/782.

for her knowledge of the natives', Ellensbrook was 'a farm home for such young natives and half-castes as cannot for some reason be lodged in other recognised institutions':

> They are taught reading and writing—indoor work for girls, sums, and milking, vegetable gardening and all the small farm industries so as to become useful farm hands, both male and female, in a practical manner and such as is in vogue in our country districts. The children are encouraged to bathe frequently. They spend every Sunday on the sea beach and have plenty of milk and vegetables and meat food.[27]

Through Prinsep's influence, Ellensbrook received per capita payments of between six and nine pence a day, and government grants for extensions to the buildings, clothing and school equipment. Edith Bussell strongly believed that she 'ought to have some hold' on the children until they reached the age of 16, and resisted efforts by local settlers to recruit them as farm labourers. Many are the letters from Bussell to Prinsep in which he is urged to act promptly on behalf of the facility. 'I really must scold you', she wrote in 1903, 'for not taking a bit of notice at my requests. You have never sent my poor girls any wearing apparel for a great many months.'[28] Other letters thank him for sending shoes, clothes and building materials, to erect 'another room for my black people' after Bussell complained that 'at present the boy Tommy is sleeping in my kitchen which is so disagreeable'.[29] Many children were sent to Edith Bussell, some by mistake, such as the time in 1901 when 'the wrong child was sent to me':

> I was so sorry to part with her. I sent her back by coach last Thursday 16th. I hope she will be all right, poor wee mite, it seemed so dreadful to bundle her off again after travelling so far. She is such a nice pretty little girl but could not speak a word of English. It was so funny to hear her prattling away in her own language and none of us able to understand a word.[30]

A series of letters to Prinsep from Mr. Pius, whose son, Willie, was sent to Ellensbrook in 1903, led to the boy's return home, although with some opposition from Bussell. Pius told Prinsep repeatedly that his son had been wrongfully removed and that he and his wife were suffering:

> I have as much love for my dear wife and churldines as you have for yours and I can not afford to luse them so if you have any feeling atole pleas send the boy back as quick as you can it did not take long for him

---

27 H.C. Prinsep to Daisy Bates, 'Daisy Bates Papers', Folio 97/473–5, SLWA Acc. 6193/A.
28 Edith Bussell to H.C. Prinsep, 30 October 1903, SLWA Acc. 3594A/45/38.
29 Edith Bussell to H.C. Prinsep 15 February 1901, SROWA Series 3005 Cons 255 1901/106.
30 Edith Bussell to Josephine Prinsep, 18 August 1900, SROWA Series 3005 Cons 255 AD File 1900/61.

to go but it takes a long time for him to come back and I do not think that fare you may thing because I am black I can't look after him but I am as kind to him than I am to my own I have more love for him than I have for my own.[31]

Bussell blamed the boy's mother for the mistake:

> Little Willie is going on well and is a very jolly little fellow, a favourite all round. I suppose you have had letters from his mother as I have asking for him to be sent back to her. She must be a very silly woman. If she felt like that about him, she should not have parted with him at all.[32]

Some of the Ellensbrook children feature in Prinsep's diaries, letters and photographs over many years. Jennie Councillor first came into Prinsep's sphere in May 1900, when he took 'the little half caste girl who was so badly burnt at Champion Bay' to Ellensbrook.[33] The next year, departmental files record Prinsep sending her shoes and writing to Bussell that he had been in contact with the police in her home town of Northampton giving them news of the girl and asking them to let her mother know she was well. 'The girl is very nearly well of her wounds', he wrote, 'and quite happy. The only thing she wants is to see her mother and I have promised to offer Mrs Councillor a railway passage to the South, so that she may stay a few days with her daughter and see her.'[34] At Bussell's urging, Jennie wrote to Prinsep telling him how much she was learning at Ellensbrook:

> My dear Sir, Miss Edie wants me to write you a few lines to show you how I can write. I cannot write a very long letter but I think it will be enough for you to examine my writeing [sic]. My writing is not very good this time but I will do better next time. I have a pet kangaroo and a dear little kitten. I am well and very happy and I hope you will come down at Christmas time. I am yours respectfully Jane Councillor.[35]

As Jennie grew up, Bussell realised she would soon leave Ellensbrook and marry a local boy. 'Jennie has a lover', she informed Prinsep, 'young Sam Isaacs, he is very fond of her … but she does not quite fancy him, says he is too dark, which is quite true, he is a nice little fellow but not half good enough for Jennie'.[36] Jennie later married Isaacs, and Prinsep travelled to Ellensbrook for the wedding and presented the couple with a set of knives and forks as a wedding present. She

---

31   Mr. Pius to H.C. Prinsep, 26 September 1903, SROWA Series 3005 Cons 255 AD File, 1903/12.
32   Edith Bussell to H.C. Prinsep, 5 September 1903, SLWA Acc. 3594A/13.
33   Jennie's name is rendered in various forms in the letters. Prinsep and Bussell called her Jennie, while she signed her name as Jane.
34   SROWA Series 3005 Cons 255 AD File, 106/01.
35   J.J. Councillor to H.C. Prinsep, 31 October 1902, SROWA Series 3005 Cons 255 AD File, 1902/117.
36   Ibid.

and Isaacs formed one of the Aboriginal families that Prinsep believed he and Bussell had saved from their Aboriginality. Although her marriage to another Aboriginal person was not what they had planned, she moved to the Isaacs' property 'Ferndale' near the Bussell's Walcliffe farm and continued to live and work for the family for many years.

'Mary', however, who lived at Ellensbrook for a number of years with her two young boys, was one whose supposedly innate Aboriginal deficiencies prevented her from benefiting from the paternalism of the Bussells and Prinseps. From Roebourne in the central Pilbara, she came to Ellensbrook after being abandoned in Bunbury, but Bussell turned against her and had her removed. 'This horrible woman Mary', she wrote to Prinsep, 'has again been up to her tricks and I think that she will be laid up in July.'

> The partner of her disgusting behaviour is that useless infamous fellow Eli Lowe. Oh I do wish you could punish him for it, could it not be done? I think he ought to get a divorce from Sarah and be compelled to marry Mary. I am very glad you do not think I have been careless for indeed I have not ... I must ask you to write to someone at Busselton to arrange about some place for Mary to go. You don't say what we are to do with her afterwards. I am afraid it would be a very bad example for the other girls to have her back here, however you must decide about this.[37]

Another Ellensbrook child was Tommy Ah Hong (or Ah Hay), who lived there for about two years between 1900 and 1902. His status was different from the other residents in that his father was 'a Chinaman', resident at Williambury station near Carnarvon, a property leased by Mervyn Bunbury, another member of one of the 'old settler' families from the south-west who was closely associated with the Bussells. Tommy's father asked Prinsep to take the boy away from the property for his education and paid for him to go to Ellensbrook. This earned him Prinsep's praise as one of the 'few fathers of half-caste children doing their duty, and contributing to the support of these unfortunates; most notably among these is a Chinaman'.[38] After two years at Ellensbrook, Tommy returned to Williambury at the request of his father, where he started work for Bunbury as a cart boy and stable hand.

The 1897 legislation provided the Chief Protector limited powers to regulate Aboriginal labour, allowing him only to recommend cancellation of a permit whose holder was deemed 'unfit' to employ Aboriginal people.[39] To Prinsep, employment contracts should tie Aboriginal families to a white boss and 'missus', whose obligations extended to providing rations for old and sick members of

---

37 Ibid.
38 'Government of Western Australia 1900/1, *Annual Report of the Aborigines Department*, Perth, p.4.
39 *The Aborigines Act 1897*, Section 11.

the family, providing a rudimentary education and training for children, and acting generally to protect the families from the ravages of colonisation. These obligations were implicitly understood by old settlers such as Prinsep's extended family, but not by the 'new order who do not recognise the claims on them of the Aboriginals' and thus threatened the paternalistic relationships he favoured.[40] The family of Donald and Charlotte McLeod, another cousin of Josephine's, on their Minilya pastoral property 100 kilometres north of Carnarvon, provided a perfect illustration of the pastoral relationships Prinsep envisaged, as he told the Parliament in two Annual Reports. Like Prinsep, McLeod had married into the Bussell family and was a devout Anglican and humanitarian. Born in Victoria in 1848, he had managed a pastoral station in the Pilbara before returning to farm in Victoria, where he held the seat of Portland in the Legislative Assembly for six years and became an active member of the Society for the Protection of Aborigines.[41] The McLeods were 'very experienced and wise trainers of the native race', Prinsep wrote in his 1901/02 Annual Report, and encouraged 'a large number of natives to congregate at Minilya'.

> And no wonder, for they have found out that under the new management they receive kindness and justice, with liberality. The children are clothed, and all the natives are compelled to wash themselves and their clothes, and to keep their hair short, and to appear weekly in a clean condition. Their appreciation of this—quite a new sensation I should fancy—appears quite evident. The children are taught every day not only their letters and sums, but in everything which tends to civilise and Christianise them, and the parents seem very grateful for the kindness shown to their children. Mr. McLeod does not let his efforts be any burden to the Department, but I think it is only due to him to supply him with a certain amount of drapery stuffs to assist him in clothing neatly such a large number.[42]

McLeod wrote frequently to Prinsep, sometimes to thank him for sending blankets for the 'old women … to protect their poor old frames these cold nights', but often to scold the government and criticise the church for their failure to protect Aboriginal people from evil influences, provide relief and education for the children.

> I take a great interest in the Native question and I think neither Church nor State is doing what is due to them in this direction … It is high time and past that something was done to endeavour to rescue the perishing

---

40   H.C. Prinsep to Forrest, SROWA Series 3005 Cons 255 AD File 1898/387.
41   Lomas, L. 1986, 'McLeod, Donald Norman (1848–1914)', in *Australian Dictionary of Biography*, Volume 10, Melbourne University Press, Melbourne, pp. 333–4.
42   Government of Western Australia 1901/2, *Annual Report of the Aborigines Department*, Perth, p.8.

> … My big family of natives all doing well. Lottie takes two of her little half caste girls with her. They could serve as an object lesson of what can be done with even two years' training.[43]

'Like tribes of Arabs'

Prinsep was reluctant to openly criticise pastoralists who were not fulfilling their obligations under the Act, mindful of the powerful representation of landowners in both houses of parliament. In his 1901/02 report, he described the situation found by Olivey and 'Magistrates, Police Officers and others in various districts' as 'satisfactory'. In the Kimberley, 'the natives are generally left to their original lives or are being utilised and kindly treated by the pastoralists'. The main problem was cattle-killing, with the police seeking to 'make examples' of the few they were 'able to apprehend'. The system of pastoral paternalism generally worked, according to Prinsep, in contrast to the mining districts, particularly the gold mining towns of Kalgoorlie and Coolgardie.

> Here we have several hundreds of natives in a totally pauperised state with scarcely any actual food or water, and very little opportunity of employment. They wander about like tribes of Arabs pitching their camps for a short time at one goldfields centre, and then on to another begging from whites and reported to be earning a good deal by prostitution.[44]

Without a pastoral industry in the region, the Aboriginal people of the goldfields 'have very little idea of work' and, with no access to their traditional food and water sources, have 'nothing but grasses and insects'. They live in a state of 'complete beggary', 'considered as a nuisance, and feel themselves to be such'. Prinsep recommended that 'they be collected in reserves, the support of them would come to a good round sum—more than I can set apart out of my present votes.'[45] Forrest agreed that a system of reserves should be established in the goldfields, but refused to provide additional funds. He favoured a 'central station', where Aboriginal people 'could be free from want and demoralising influences and a good way from a town, with land fit for cultivation, where farming, fruit and vegetables … could be carried on … where they could marry and settle down … To this place young men and women would gladly come.'[46] Prinsep considered various options for a reserve in the region, including islands off the south coast in the vicinity of the small town of Esperance, or the use of

---

43 Donald McLeod to H.C. Prinsep, 16 November 1903, SLWA Acc. 3594A/7.
44 Annual Report 1902/03, SROWA Series 3005 Cons 255, AD File 1903/148.
45 Government of Western Australia 1901/2, *Annual Report of the Aborigines Department*, Perth, p. 8
46 Forrest to H.C. Prinsep, 19 November 1900, SROWA Series 3005 Cons 255 AD File 1900/830.

Rottnest Island as 'the only one in this part of the State where I thought natives could live permanently but this, of course, would not do, so long as the prison existed there'.[47]

Prinsep proposed extensive powers to control the movements of unemployed Aboriginal people, to create Aboriginal reserves and white reserves, declare prohibited areas and prohibit cohabitation of white or Asian men with Aboriginal women. These were designed to limit contact between the races and, as historian Raymond Evans has observed in the context of similar policies in Queensland, were widely supported by the colonial social body. To humanitarians, they represented an opportunity to free Aboriginal people from the pernicious influence of colonisation and thereby preserve the remnants of a ravaged population. Others viewed segregation as a way of removing Aboriginal people to a distant and largely inaccessible stage.[48] Pastoralists could readily see benefits in the potential of reserves as a labour pool which could in the process provide limited training and initial assimilation to western ways. The objective was not only to protect Aboriginal populations from pernicious contact with whites and Asians, but also from each other. As Prinsep identified in his annual reports, it was the immorality of Aboriginal people that brought about the problems of the 'half-caste' population, prostitution and venereal disease. In the coastal towns of the Kimberley, 'strong and able men' were known to live on 'the immorality of their women', but Prinsep assured the Parliament that most resident magistrates were assiduous in their efforts to deal with the perpetrators of such immorality. The Wyndham magistrate, for example, was 'determined to put a stop to this sort of thing':

> I want Wyndham to be a clean town, and I wish the people in it to be respectable and healthy-living residents. You may depend that any deserving case will have my prompt attention. Old and decrepit natives will be looked after and attended to in the usual way, but young demons who live on the prostitution of their unfortunate women shall receive no quarter at my hands, and I have instructed the police to take immediate steps to rid the town of such pests.[49]

In Prinsep's view, this was 'the right way to talk'. He nevertheless felt obliged to address immorality, even though the 'subject is a nauseous one, but the worst phase of it is the readiness with which the natives take to an immoral life, the men ... finding so many temporary advantages accruing from the degradation of their women'.[50] In the Kimberley pearling ports of Broome, Lagrange and

---

47 Government of Western Australia 1900/1, *Annual Report of the Aborigines Department*, Perth, p. 6.
48 Evans, Raymond, Kay Saunders and Kathryn Cronin 1975, *Race Relations in Colonial Queensland: A history of exclusion, exploitation and extermination*, University of Queensland Press, St. Lucia, p. 118–9.
49 Government of Western Australia 1901/2, *Annual Report of the Aborigines Department*, Perth, p.6.
50 Ibid., pp.6, 8.

Wallal, Prinsep was keen to prohibit contact between 'Asiatics' and Aboriginal women, which was believed to bring 'a great deal of sexual disease', but more seriously risked populating the north with a 'mongrel race, very inimical to their future quietude'.[51]

Prinsep periodically initiated inquiries into mistreatment or immoral behaviour by pastoralists, but was unable under his powers to lay charges or gather evidence and, in any case, was generally sympathetic to the situation of the pastoralist. In 1898, he informed the Premier about an allegation of the 'unlawful detention' by pastoralist and local Justice of the Peace Walter Nairn, manager of Byro station in the Murchison district, of two women, 'Caroline' and 'half-caste Polly':

> There seems no evidence that the Messrs Nairns are cruel, or even harsh with the natives in their employ—but there is evidence of a very low morality, which I presume we cannot interfere with, until the native woman complains ... The white ladies on the station seems to be living in the most blissful ignorance of what is going on "down in the gully and just outside the garden wall."[52]

Prinsep was equally concerned with the protection of young men from 'highly reputable families' who, 'in their youthful ardour', became 'so enamoured of some black girl as to wish to marry her, and thus blast their future lives'. 'Everything should be done', wrote Prinsep to the Colonial Secretary, 'to protect them from their own folly.'[53] In Prinsep's view, efforts to regulate interracial relationships in country regions would remain ineffectual without legislation giving the Chief Protector the power to intervene directly. The powerlessness of the department was exacerbated by the status of many of the pastoralists as members of the political and social elite in Perth, which virtually guaranteed their immunity from prosecution or even censure over ill-treatment of Aboriginal people. Much as Gribble had encountered a wall of silence about the true state of relationships between pastoralists and Aboriginal populations ten years before, so did the Aborigines Department stand little chance of prosecuting cases of mistreatment or regulating sexual liaisons, even if Prinsep and his staff had been inclined to vigorously pursue alleged offenders.

---

51   Ibid,. p.8.
52   H.C. Prinsep to Forrest, 21 December 1898, SROWA Series 3005 Cons 255 AD File 1898/373.
53   H.C. Prinsep to Colonial Secretary, 16 November 1906, SROWA Series 3005 Cons 255 AD File 1906/533.

A 'firm course of action'

Prinsep believed that Aboriginal people were vulnerable to the corrupting influences of lower class whites and Asians, and that the only means of slowing the process of moral and physical decline was to isolate black from white.[54] In 1899, he wrote to Forrest telling him that venereal disease was rife in the Aboriginal population and that, unless the government took a 'firm course of action', Aboriginal people would completely disappear from the north; he did not want to be held responsible:[55]

> The growing prevalence of venereal disease amongst the Aborigines in some places compels me to suggest that our curative efforts should be assisted by legislation with the object of preventing them, in their own interest, from loitering in towns and other places where the evil exists—affecting both the black and white population.[56]

Historian Mary Anne Jebb suggests that 'venereal disease and prostitution were tied together as a gauge of both the moral and physical degeneration of Aboriginal people'.[57] By enabling Aboriginal men to 'live well' off the earnings of women from prostitution, the pastoral labour force was destabilised and the 'social distance' between the white and Aboriginal populations reduced.[58] The reports of G.S. Olivey, along with constant complaints from pastoralists, fuelled the view that Aboriginal peoples were increasingly abandoning an 'honest living' and congregating in towns and mining camps where they lived 'off the prostitution of their women'.[59] This was a particular concern to pastoralists, who were worried that their Aboriginal workforces would 'drift away' to become victims of venereal disease and prostitution. Prinsep's proposals to control Aboriginal movement and prohibit sexual contact were thus designed to preserve a permanent pastoral workforce, and to limit the numbers of people leaving the stations and moving to the towns and camps, where they 'insultingly refuse employment and dress well, drink much, and are a general nuisance irrespective of the diseases which are disseminated in their immoralities to both black and white'.[60]

---

54 SROWA Series 3005 Cons 255, AD File 782/1899/782; Government of Western Australia 1901/2, *Annual Report of the Aborigines Department*, Perth, pp. 3–5; Government of Western Australia 1903/04, *Annual Report of the Aborigines Department*, Perth, p.5.
55 Prinsep to Forrest, 17 October 1899, private collection.
56 Ibid.
57 Jebb, Mary Anne 1987, 'Isolating the Problem: Venereal disease and Aborigines in Western Australia', Honours Thesis, Murdoch University, p.16.
58 Ibid., p. 34.
59 Letters to Prinsep from Arthur Weston, Murchison; F.T. Smith, Upper Gascoyne; E.J. Brockman, Gascoyne; Ball Bros, De Grey; and J. Isdell, Nullagine in SROWA Series 3005 Cons 255 AD File 1900/51.
60 SROWA Series 3005 Cons 255 AD File 1905/97.

Prinsep's proposals were designed to curb sexual contact between Aboriginal women and white or Asian men, but they also acted to limit 'Aboriginal women's survival opportunities outside the parameters of state ration depots or the pastoral industry'. Consequently, Aboriginal women who continued to participate in casual sexual liaisons with non-Aboriginal men reinforced their position as prostitutes, entrenching their immoral status and providing a rationale for increased state control.[61] The 1905 laws served to institutionalise the immoral status of Aboriginal women by providing the Chief Protector with powers to detain and remove half-castes or other problem populations including venereal disease and leprosy sufferers.'[62]

Prinsep's response to the problem of venereal disease in the north was to establish Lock Hospitals on Dorre and Bernier islands off the coast near Carnarvon, one for men, the other for women. The proposal, which relied principally on the legislative powers of the *Aborigines Act*, was the result of a co-operative effort by the Aborigines Department, an initially reluctant Health Department, and the police. The rising status of the medical and health professions in the early 1900s, partly through the perceived success of public health in the control of disease, contributed to perceptions that an important role of the state was to prevent disease, and that a state of health was 'the root of the nation's happiness'.[63] Perceptions of a large, venereally diseased population of Aboriginal people in the north and the threat of contagion demanded a response from the government to a population that could be treated through medical science, and at the same time segregated under the *Aborigines Act*.

Part of the role of Travelling Inspector G.S. Olivey was to dispense medical care to diseased Aboriginal people, by distributing potassium iodide, zinc-based ointments, carbolic acid, washes of epsom salts and sandalwood oil.[64] Yet reports of 'loathsome' venereal disease in the northern Aboriginal population and fears of an epidemic decimating the Aboriginal workforce increased in the period between 1900 and 1904, and medical treatment became a higher priority for the Aborigines Department. In 1906, suggestions that Aboriginal venereal disease was a treatable problem came to occupy the minds of Prinsep and the Health Department, signifying a shift in emphasis from limiting sexual contact between races to control and treatment. In a Lock Hospital, Aboriginal people could be 'treated under lock and key and not permitted to leave until cured', thereby dealing with two connected problems, enforced medical treatment and the fears in the white population about contagion. Prinsep's plan was to place the two islands under the dual control of the Aborigines and Health Departments, his

---

61   Jebb 1987, 'Isolating the Problem', p.39.
62   Ibid., p. 41.
63   Department of Health, *Annual Report*, 1914, quoted by Jebb 1987, 'Isolating the Problem', p.43.
64   Jebb 1987, 'Isolating the Problem', p.50.

department providing funding and the powers to collect and detain Aboriginal people, and the Health Department the medical expertise. In October 1907 the islands were temporarily reserved for use as Lock Hospitals and 2,000 pounds was added to the Aborigines Department vote.[65]

By the time the Lock Hospitals were established, Prinsep was on leave in Europe, prior to his retirement. Edward Pechell wrote in December 1907 with the news the government had finally decided to reserve Dorre and Bernier Islands as hospitals for 'sick natives', and had made a special allocation of 4,000 pounds.[66] Pechell foresaw 'a lot of trouble in connection with it, collecting the natives will be no easy matter'. Police officers throughout the north subsequently assumed an active role in collecting diseased Aboriginal people and arranging for their transport to the islands. The anomalous function of police thus continued, their dual role as protectors and law enforcers blurring the distinction between punishment, protection, arrest and coercion. The proclamation of the islands as reserves under the Act allowed the Minister to issue warrants for the removal and detention of any Aboriginal person suspected of carrying a venereal disease, which in practice allowed the police collectors considerable discretion. Some examined Aboriginal people themselves, while others relied on the advice or station managers and local residents.[67] E.L. Grant Watson, who visited the islands with Radcliffe-Brown and Daisy Bates in 1910, criticised collections as 'neither humane nor scientific': 'A man, unqualified except by ruthlessness and daring and helped by one or two kindred spirits, toured the countryside, raided native camps and by brute force "examined" the natives … diseased were seized upon … chained by the neck … marched through the bush in search of further syphilitics … eventually to the coast.'[68] Collections were pursued vigorously until 1911, when, with the election of a Labor government, enthusiasm began to wane. During the ten years of the hospital's operation, over 600 people were incarcerated, including 428 women and 209 men. 170 people died on the islands.[69] Daisy Bates described the Lock Hospitals as a 'ghastly experiment', with 'no ray of brightness, no gleam of hope'.[70]

> Deaths were frequent—appallingly frequent, sometimes three in a day—for most of the natives were obviously in the last stages of venereal disease and tuberculosis. Nothing could save them, and they had been transported, some of them thousands of miles, to strange and unnatural surroundings and solitude. They were afraid of the hospital,

---

65 Ibid., p.64.
66 Pechell to H.C. Prinsep, 23 December 1907, SLWA Acc. 3593A/34.
67 *The Aborigines Act 1905*, Section 12; Jebb 1987, 'Isolating the Problem', p.78.
68 Grant Watson, E.L. 1968, *Journey Under Southern Stars*, Abelard-Schuman, London and New York.
69 Jebb 1987, 'Isolating the Problem', p.101.
70 Bates, Daisy 1938 (1966), *The Passing of the Aborigines: A lifetime spent among the natives of Australia*, Second Edition, Heinemann, Melbourne, pp.101–4.

> its ceaseless probings and dressings and injections were a daily torture. They were afraid of each other, living and dead. They were afraid of the ever-moaning sea.[71]

The closure of the island hospitals in 1918 signified a loss of interest by health authorities, attention shifting to control of other tropical diseases, particularly leprosy. The labour force needs of pastoralists were also changing, and venereal disease was no longer seen to be a problem. The period of labour instability had passed, while southern and goldfields half-caste populations came to occupy the energies of Prinsep's successors, Gale and particularly A.O. Neville.[72] Nevertheless, the precedent of government intervention to limit contagions on the basis of race had been set and was, from 1936, to be applied to the collection and compulsory detention in the control of leprosy in the north. Because the provisions of the 1905 laws allowed for the compulsory detention of Aboriginal people, the problem of venereal disease could be defined on racial grounds as an Aboriginal problem. There was no need for new and contentious contagious diseases legislation to forcibly collect and treat Aboriginal people, as the *Aborigines Act* provided all the powers necessary to sanction their arrest and removal to a reserve.

---

71 Ibid., pp.98–9.
72 Jebb 1987, 'Isolating the Problem', p.154.

'Neck-chaining has not a pleasant sound, and perhaps that is the worst part of it.' Prinsep's final few months as Chief Protector were spent trying to defend Western Australia's practices in the transnational sphere, including attending a meeting with the Secretary of State for Colonies Lord Elgin in 1908 to explain the government's continued toleration of the practice. This image shows unnamed Aboriginal men probably in the Kimberley, date unknown.

Source: Prinsep Papers, SLWA MN 773 BA 1423/149.

An unnamed Aboriginal man in the vicinity of Willambury Station, 300 kilometres from Carnarvon in the Gascoyne region of Western Australia, a property owned by Prinsep's kinsman Mervyn Bunbury and his wife Millie (née Priess).

Source: Lovegrove Images, SLWA 28614P.

8. Chief Protector of Aborigines

As Chief Protector, Prinsep was appalled at what he believed was the depraved condition of Aboriginal children in the vicinity of regional towns such as Carnarvon. This group of children was photographed by Thomas Lovegrove on a visit to the region in 1908 in the river bed of the Gascoyne near Carnarvon.

Source: Lovegrove Images, SLWA 28614P.

Tommy Dower on his death bed in 1895. Dower had accompanied Alexander Forrest on one of his explorations and took the role as a spokesman for Perth Noongars from the 1870s to 1890s. Ngilgie and Joobaitch, with dogs, sit at the front, while the man standing behind Joobaitch may be Timbal, who was employed by Prinsep on his stations as a young man. The identities of the others are not known.

Source: Prinsep Papers, SLWA MN 773 BA 1423/154.

'Corunna Downs natives', 1905. The Pilbara station was owned by members of the Brockman family, who also ran stations elsewhere in the Pilbara, the Kimberley and the Gascoyne. Aboriginal children from these stations, some of them fathered by white men, were sometimes sent south to work as domestics or farm labourers for Brockman families living in Perth or on farms in the south-west. Nathanial (Nutty) Leyland was one of these children, born in the Pilbara and taken south to be brought up and work on Edward and Capel (née Bussell) Brockman's farm, The Warren.

Source: Courtesy Ailsa Smith, Claremont WA.

The meagre resources of the Aborigines Department were stretched as Prinsep sought to meet the demands for rations from the ever-increasing numbers of dispossessed Aboriginal people around the state, as their traditional lands were steadily appropriated by white pastoralists. Ration stations, such as the LaGrange bay station shown in this picture, were established throughout the State. This picture shows a group of people, probably Karajarri traditional owners, camped in the vicinity of rations.

Source: Prinsep Papers, SLWA MN 773 BA 1423/148.

8. Chief Protector of Aborigines

Prinsep's efforts to segregate Aboriginal populations on reserves received little support from Government, although he was able to establish the Welshpool (Maamba) reserve to confine Perth people. Few of the people can be identified. Joobaitch stands in the centre, his head adorned with a new boater hat. Daisy Bates, at that time employed by the government to record Aboriginal languages, is in the background on the far right.

Source: Prinsep Papers, SLWA MN 773 BA 1423/150.

Ngilgie and her animals at the Welshpool Reserve, date unknown. Daisy Bates called her 'the rich widow of the Welshpool Reserve', and 'the proud possessor of seven goats, 12 fowls and 32 dogs, incredible mongrels all'.

Source: The Western Mail, 1 June 1907.

8. Chief Protector of Aborigines

The 'half-castes' of Ellensbrook in 1902, from left to right: Ivy, Miss Griffiths, Tommy, Emil-Penny, Mary, Frank, Dora and Jennie (Jean Jane) Councillor. Rather than calling them 'inmates' as he did other institutional residents, Prinsep called the Ellensbrook residents his 'protégées'. They wrote letters to him, and he regularly visited and sent them presents of clothing and shoes.

Source: Courtesy of Ailsa Smith, Claremont, WA.

Edith Bussell, 'a lady well-known for her knowledge of the natives', and a cousin of Prinsep's wife, Josephine, ran Ellensbrook Farm Home from 1898 to 1916.

Source: Prinsep Papers, SLWA MN 773 BA 1423/166.

Tommy Ah Hong, whose father had asked Prinsep to take him to Ellensbrook from Williambury station in the Gascoyne, and met the costs for his keep. This brought Prinsep's praise as 'one of the few fathers of half-caste children doing their duty', particularly notable because he was a 'chinaman'.

Source: Prinsep Papers, SLWA MN 773 BA 1423/134.

Williambury station in the Gascoyne, showing a boy believed to be Tommy Ah Hong after he had left Ellensbrook. The image was taken by Millie Bunbury (née Priess), a family friend of the Prinseps who spent most of her time living in Busselton in between visits to her husband Mervyn Bunbury at Williambury.

Source: Courtesy of anonymously held private collection.

Ellensbrook, today a National Trust property, with interpretive panels and walk trails. Located 30 kilometres from Margaret River, the place is a well-visited spot.

Source: Author's private collection.

'My big family of natives all doing well'. Prinsep informed the government that the Aboriginal people on Donald and Charlotte McLeod's station were 'compelled to wash themselves and their clothes, and to keep their hair short, and to appear weekly in a clean condition'.

Source: Courtesy of Ailsa Smith, Claremont, WA.

8. Chief Protector of Aborigines

The Isaacs children off to school, at the Ferndale property Sam Isaacs was given in recognition of his heroism in rescuing the passengers of the stricken Georgette in 1876. Ferndale was located near Alfred Bussell's homestead, Wallcliffe, at the mouth of the Margaret River.

Source: Courtesy of the Butter Factory Museum, Busselton WA.

Native Camp, Strelley Street, Busselton, in 1901, near Henry Prinsep's home, Little Holland House, on the Vasse River.

Source: Courtesy of the Butter Factory Museum, Busselton WA.

9. 'Move slowly in a difficult matter'

After six months in the job, Prinsep presented his first annual report to Forrest. His efforts to establish a colony-wide system of ration distribution had made him conscious of matters which urgently demanded the government's attention. He described the situation of Aboriginal people throughout the colony as 'moribund', and noted that, 'though there are a good many natives working for the settlers', there were 'very few young men' working on the farms and station.[1] As colonisation spread throughout the land area of Western Australia, more and more Aboriginal people were displaced from their lands and forced into relationships with European settlers in the towns and pastoral stations. Prinsep warned about the increasing numbers of destitute Aboriginal people throughout the colony, a situation he predicted would worsen.[2] 'One of the most important questions of the immediate future' was the prostitution of Aboriginal women and the spread of venereal disease, which he argued would be the chief causes of inevitable extinction. 'From a humanitarian point', he told Forrest, 'one cannot contemplate without horror the immense amount of pain and misery which lies before the unfortunate natives'.[3] Forrest refused to allow the report to be printed, ostensibly because it covered only a portion of the financial year. He also disagreed strongly with its conclusions, and criticised Prinsep for providing little evidence to support his reports of the dire situation facing the colony's Aboriginal populations.

Early efforts to document and enumerate Aboriginal populations throughout Western Australia constituted the beginnings of a system of government knowledge which, as the Twentieth Century proceeded, eventually evolved into a detailed archive 'to inform further practices of governing' and 'test the rationer's understandings of Indigenous people'.[4] In his second annual report, Prinsep assured Forrest he had 'taken much care in its preparation, and have authority for every statement'.[5] Evidence had been gathered by his traveling inspector Mr. G.S. Olivey, 'a good bushman, a man of … independent character and … knowledge of medicine and surgery', who travelled throughout the northern and central reaches of the colony on his departmental bicycle, visiting stations and towns along the way. Prinsep estimated that 12,307 Aboriginal people were in contact with the colonial regime, 6,690 of whom were 'self supporting'. There were, however, 'what may be called wild natives' in the East

---

1 First report for Financial year ending June 30th 1898, and three months following', SROWA Series 3005 Cons 255 AD File 1898/571.
2 Ibid.
3 Ibid.
4 Rowse, Tim 1998, *White Flour, White Power: From rations to citizenship in Central Australia*, Cambridge University Press, Cambridge, p.5.
5 '1899/1900 Annual Report', SROWA Series 3005 Cons 255 AD File 1899/782.

Kimberley, whose population was 'stated to be very large ... their physique much superior to those further south, owing probably to the fertility of the country and abundance of game'. These populations would soon be affected by colonial expansion, and many would become destitute and diseased in the face of the 'pernicious influences' of contact with Europeans.[6] He argued for a system of pastoral paternalism which could both protect displaced Aboriginal people from the worst impacts of colonialism, and tie them to pastoral stations under compulsory employment contracts. In his experience, pastoralists might, on occasions, 'find it necessary to be strict', but they were rarely 'cruel' and provided conditions that seemed 'quite as comfortable and less full of hardship than it originally was'.[7]

No other system was practicable in Western Australia, Prinsep argued, as 'the primeval habit of the several tribes to remain on its own patch of country' meant that 'settlers round up the natives at signing season' when they required seasonal labour. The absence of contracts would bring 'much inconvenience, litigation and possibly the discontinuance of their employment', while 'the native, with his natural acuteness, would soon be found hawking his services to the highest bidder, possibly turning swagman'. Prinsep recognised that such a system might bring continued criticism from humanitarians in Britain and the eastern colonies, but this must be dismissed as 'written by those who have not much experience of native life and customs'.

> To those who are accustomed to the luxuries of civilised life, the animal existence, habits and rough surroundings of a native camp always seem deplorable; but we must remember that this has been their condition since time immemorial, and it has become so much their nature that it is, in most cases, impossible to induce a native to inhabit a house, or take care of anything as his own property. A native living according to his own customs will remain healthy and strong; dress him up and house him, and he will soon fade away.[8]

Late in 1900, Prinsep requested Forrest to consider a new bill to give the Chief Protector powers to control Aboriginal movement in the vicinity of towns, regulate labour contracts and bring 'half-castes' under the age of 18 under the control of the state. The Premier was within a few months of his retirement from State politics in order to enter the new Australian Commonwealth parliament, and had little time for Prinsep's ideas. He directed him to 'get his Bill ready for next Parliament and follow the experience in other Colonies', and, most importantly, to 'move slowly in a difficult matter'.[9] He returned the draft bill

---

6 Ibid.
7 Ibid.
8 Ibid.
9 SROWA Series 3005 Cons 255 AD File 1900/830.

with handwritten objections to almost every measure, mostly on the grounds that they would unnecessarily restrict the freedoms and movements of Aboriginal people. Powers to create reserves and confine Aboriginal people, 'would make prisoners of these poor people in their own country. For their own good it could be said; … By what means? By being placed in irons?' Forrest condemned the proposal to segregate Aboriginal from non-Aboriginal populations, and viewed the proposed powers to tighten labour contracts, impose fines, create 'white reserves' and issue permits as 'a monstrous infringement of the liberty of a native. It is manufacturing offences with a vengeance.'[10]

Prinsep fared little better in his efforts to convince Forrest's successors that the government should expand its involvement Aboriginal affairs. George Leake, who was Premier between May and November 1901, told Prinsep he would not support his 'utopian' legislation. What was needed was a series of coercive measures, including complete prohibition of entry to town sites:

> Natives know only one law, that of 'retribution'. We can't deal with them as civilised whites but must treat them rather as children—short and sharp punishment and in more serious cases banishment for a time from their own country would probably be effectual … The first step is to 'humanise' them, you may then attempt to 'civilise' and finally 'christianise' them. The State will discharge its obligations if it is to accomplish the first two steps. The latter must be left to the Missionary.[11]

Ministerial responsibility for the Aborigines Department changed frequently after Forrest's departure, leading Prinsep to despair that he would ever achieve his legislative objectives. The Aboriginal affairs portfolio was an unwanted additional burden, tacked on to the main job as Premier, treasurer or colonial secretary and, over the years following Forrest's departure, few displayed much interest in Prinsep, his department or the Aboriginal population. Initial responsibility stayed with the new Premier, George Throssell, who lost office after four months. His successor, George Leake, shifted responsibility to the Colonial Secretary, Frederick Illingworth, but this arrangement too was short lived. Leake's government fell in November 1901, and Prinsep's minister became M.L. Moss, Colonial Secretary in the two-month government of Alfred Morgans. For the next seven months, Illingworth resumed as minister in the second Leake Ministry, until Walter James's government introduced a period of comparative stability by holding the Treasury benches for two years until August 1904. The first Western Australian Labor Government under Henry Daglish then held power until May 1905, when, much to Prinsep's relief, he was assigned a

---

10 Ibid.
11 Ibid.

minister he could work with, Dr. J.T. Hicks.[12] It was Hicks who subsequently guided the 1905 *Aborigines Act* through the Parliament, but this did not happen until external criticism of the living conditions of Aboriginal people in Western Australia forced the government's hand.

Calling 'Aboriginal expertise'

The bitter conflict surrounding John Gribble's allegations of violence and cruelty on the Western Australian frontier during the 1880s had earned the colony the unwelcome reputation in the imperial world of failing to protect its Aboriginal populations, of allowing conditions of brutality and virtual slavery to flourish on the stations and in the towns throughout its vast land area. Prinsep found himself surrounded by strongly held and often conflicting views on how the government should undertake its role, and was afflicted by continuous criticism, both of his own performance and the alleged failures of government. His sister-in-law, Caroline Bussell, writing from her temporary home in Paris, told of her 'great disappointment' that Prinsep had allowed 'all the distant stations … to go on in the old lawless way and I see by the Papers that horrors of cruelty and injustice are still committed. Why are white men allowed to beat and kick the black?'[13] Regular letters came from the pugnacious leader of the local Aborigines Amelioration Movement, Lyon Weiss, reporting the resolutions of public meetings, requesting responses to difficult questions and criticising Prinsep's performance:

> I purposely refrain from doing more than respectfully inquiring whether … the Natives are still chained by the neck like dogs, that their women are still being violated, that the Aborigines regard the Police as dangerous animals, and that arrests were still being indiscriminately made are true.[14]

A very public debate between Prinsep and Catholic Bishop Matthew Gibney, a 'fine example of muscular Christianity', that took part in the pages of the daily press, also hurt Prinsep's feelings.[15] 'Is the important fact forgotten', asked Gibney, 'that the land we are living in was originally the property of the natives and that we have not compensated them for appropriating it?' The government 'had not assisted to preserve the race; on the contrary it has done much towards its annihilation', while the Chief Protector had 'done nothing', and allowed

---

12 Prinsep, Henry C., 'Diaries 1866–1922', SLWA Acc. 499A, 21 February 1905.
13 Caroline Bussell to Josephine Prinsep, 15 May 1899, SLWA Acc. 3593A/26.
14 SROWA Series 3005 Cons 255 AD File 1907/17.
15 'Truthful Thomas' 1905, *Through the Spy-Glass: Short sketches of well-known Westralians as others see them*, Praagh & Lloyd, Perth, p.31.

inhumane practices such as flogging and neck chaining to continue. 'Because of their colour these unfortunate people are shown no form of mercy', Gibney wrote. 'I have known instances of the repeated slaughter of natives, and as these have occurred during my period of residence in the State they cannot be alluded to as ancient history.'[16] Angry at Gibney's accusations, Prinsep drew attention to his 'indefatigable' efforts as Chief Protector and asserted the high esteem in which he was held by the State's Aboriginal people.[17] There was little in the way of government action, he wrote, that could be done to preserve Aboriginal people from decline:

> It cannot be denied that when a black minority comes into contact with a white majority, the black minority must give way by its very proneness to those depravities which weaken them and ultimately destroy them. Legislation and departmental action may be of the best but there seems some natural law which works against them. In those regions where the white man can establish his race the black man soon disappears, but where the contrary is the case, such as in the Tropics, there is always hope for the black race ... the impression is that the birth rate is rapidly decreasing among natives in the white sphere of action. Nothing can prevent this except complete isolation of natives, a thing now quite impossible.[18]

Another persistent critic was Walter Malcolmson, an Irishman who had worked near Marble Bar in the Pilbara, where he claimed to have witnessed continuous acts of brutality against Aboriginal people. Back in Britain, he wrote letters to British and Irish newspapers in which he characterised Western Australia as the 'slave state of the Commonwealth' and Aboriginal people as 'worse off than the negro was in American slave days'.[19]

Prinsep's efforts to defend some of the practices of the Western Australian government, particularly whipping and neck chaining, reflect a determination both to rationalise the use of coercion, and to assure the critics that these methods were the most humane available and were being properly regulated by government. In 1901, Prinsep accused Malcolmson and his supporters of 'sweeping generalities, without making themselves acquainted with recent facts, or giving particulars of the charges they make'. Seeking to justify the neck-chaining of Aboriginal prisoners, Prinsep explained that the only way to

---

16   *The Morning Herald*, 13 May, 1907.
17   Ibid.
18   Ibid.
19   *Daily News*, (London), 13 December 1901. Malcolmson also wrote a letter to an unidentified Belfast newspaper in 1904, the subject of SROWA Series 3005 Cons 255 AD File 1904/81, 'Re. Mr Walter Malcolmson's remarks in a Belfast newspaper on the treatment of WA Ab. Natives'.

prevent escapes was 'by means of a chain attached to either iron collars or rings of chain round the men's necks'. 'I have made the closest inquiries as to the style of fastening', he wrote:

> The police inform me that other methods have been tried, that a native is so lithely made that he can get out of a ring fastened with all reasonable tightness round his waist, and that if put round his ankle he can so easily get at it with his hands, even if he cannot slip his foot through it, that it is not effective. Another objection to the ankle is that, should the native be employed in quarrying or dealing with heavy loads, the chain round the ankle is more likely to trip him up and fix him in a dangerous position than that from his neck. Putting it round the wrist is laughed at; the only other place, then, is the neck. The only way to abolish the use of the chain when under confinement would be to place natives on islands far from the coast, but the objection to this is the great cost, and the loss of all their services, which are now made useful to the State at the various ports. Nor would the civilising influence be so possible.[20]

Punishments, on the rare occasions they were carried out, were both necessary and harmless. The cat-o'-nine-tails was used only in prisons, the 'squatters being quite aware that the best way to get work out of such irresponsible and unreasoning creatures as natives are, is to treat them and feed them well'.[21] The whip itself was incapable of inflicting serious injury:

> I find the lashes are small cord, about a quarter of an inch in diameter, with the ends tapering off, but seized with small twine to prevent unraveling, and that no knots are permitted to be put anywhere upon the lashes.[22]

Prinsep turned to the self-trained ethnographer, Daisy Bates, to help defend the Government's reputation, both domestically and in the imperial world. Born in County Tipperary in Ireland in 1859, Bates initially arrived in Queensland as a 22-year-old in January 1883, and returned to Britain in 1894 before arriving in Western Australia in September 1899. She soon launched herself into a career as a freelance journalist, and was engaged in May 1904, on a junior clerical salary of eight shillings a day, by the Registrar-General's Department to collect Aboriginal vocabularies.[23] Bates persuaded the government of the importance of her task and her unique qualifications to record the languages and traditions of Aboriginal populations. She proposed that she should be employed so that the government would have a scientific record of the

---

20 Government of Western Australia 1900/1, *Annual Report of the Aborigines Department*, Perth, p.5.
21 SROWA Series 3005 Cons 255, AD File 1902/41.
22 Ibid.
23 Reece, Bob 2007, *Daisy Bates: Grand dame of the desert*, National Library of Australia, Canberra, pp. 13–45.

languages of a fast-disappearing people.[24] Prinsep also asked Bates to prepare a booklet for distribution in Britain and the eastern states of Australia as part of his strategy to counter negative public opinion about Western Australia. *Efforts Made by Western Australia Towards the Betterment of Her Aborigines* was an attempt to use scholarly opinion to show that, compared with other Australian States, Western Australia 'comes out easily ahead in the efforts she has continuously made to grapple with the aboriginal problem, and her expenditure on their behalf, if taken on a white population basis, will probably be found on comparison to have exceeded that of any other State for the same purpose'.[25] Acknowledging that 'a perfect system has yet to be evolved', she cited 'an American writer', Daniel Brinton's book *Races and Peoples*, to recommend 'a missionary enterprise combined with a broad secular education, the inculcation of sound principles rather than respect for ceremonies and dogmas, the retention of the good that there certainly is in many native religions and moral codes, the encouragement of independence of thought, and the principles of religious and political freedom'.[26] All these, she argued, were necessary for the 'reception of civilisation'.[27] Nevertheless, regardless of the efforts of government and missionaries, she believed such intervention was 'ultimately futile': 'The most that can be said of these efforts is that the native exists, or, perhaps the better word would be suffers a little longer: his ultimate disappearance is only a matter of time.'[28]

'The dire necessity of a suffering race'

Prinsep's defense did little to quell public disquiet over the colony's treatment of Aboriginal people, nor to assuage the perceptions of a 'slave state' that had changed little since the days of John Gribble 20 years before. In August 1904, the government introduced amendments to the 1897 *Aborigines Act* to expand the powers of the Chief Protector to remove half-caste children, prohibit co-habitation, regulate employment contracts, establish reserves, and remove Aboriginal people from towns. The election of the Henry Daglish Labor Government in August 1904 brought a further delay, the Government responding to the continuous pressure from overseas by establishing a Royal Commission to inquire into the 'administration of Aborigines and the treatment of natives'.[29]

---

24 Daisy Bates to Dr. J.T. Hicks MLA, undated, SROWA Series 3005 Cons 255 AD File 1906/159.
25 Bates, Daisy 1907, *Efforts Made by Western Australia Towards the Betterment of Her Aborigines*, Government Printer, Perth, p.29.
26 Brinton, Daniel G. 1890, *Races and Peoples: Lectures on the science of ethnography*, N.D.C. Hodges, New York.
27 Bates 1907, *Efforts Made by Western Australia Towards the Betterment of Her Aborigines*, p.31.
28 Ibid. p.30; Reece 2007, *Daisy Bates*, p.51.
29 Government of Western Australia 1905, *Royal Commission on the Administration of Aborigines and the Condition of the Natives*, Government Printer, Perth.

There were no obvious local candidates to head a Royal Commission in Western Australia, so, on Prinsep's recommendation, Premier Collier approached Walter Roth, who, at the time, held the position of Chief Protector in Queensland. Roth had been born in London in 1861, and came to Australia during the late 1880s where he developed an interest in Aboriginal culture, probably through association with Baldwin Spencer and the influence of his brother, Henry Ling Roth, author of an 1890 history of the Tasmanian Aborigines.[30] Trained as a doctor, Roth drew upon the published views of contemporary scientists, such as Herbert Spencer, to support his advocacy for state intervention and the segregation of Aboriginal people, and was a strong believer in the removal of 'half-castes and quadroons' from their parental environments for education and religious indoctrination. As such, his concern for Aboriginal children and women outweighed the value of the family unit, and reflected 'the racism and paternalism of the period, as well as his personal commitment to protection of children and his opposition to child labour'.[31]

Taking up his commission in August 1904, Roth spent a few weeks in Perth talking to politicians, Prinsep and his staff, the Commissioner of Police and other officials, assessing the files and annual reports of the department, and considering written allegations of cruelty.[32] He then travelled north, visiting Carnarvon, Port Hedland, Broome and Derby, and interviewing 110 witnesses, including 40 police, magistrates and gaolers, 13 priests, 14 station managers, and two Aboriginal prisoners. Returning to Perth, he quickly wrote his report and was back in Queensland by the time it was released to the press at the end of January 1905. There was immediately a 'great hubbub', as Prinsep put it, although Roth was relatively mild in his criticism of the treatment meted out to Aboriginal people in the north:[33]

> Your Commissioner is satisfied that the natives generally speaking, are not subject to any actual physical cruelty. On the other hand, the wrongs and injustices taking place in these areas, and the cruelties and abuses met with in the unsettled districts cannot be hidden or tolerated. Fortunately they are of such a nature that they can be largely remedied by proper legislation, combined with firm departmental supervision.[34]

Roth exonerated pastoralists over their alleged mistreatment of Aboriginal employees, but found that contracts of employment were often avoided, and

---

30 Haebich, Anna 2000, *Broken Circles: Fragmenting Indigenous families, 1800–2000*, Fremantle Arts Centre Press, Fremantle, p.294.
31 Ibid., p.295.
32 Eliza Tracey to W.E. Roth, 5 January 1905, SROWA Series 3005 Cons 255 AD File 1905/6.
33 H.C. Prinsep, 'Diaries', 30th February, 1905; Haebich, Anna 1988, *For Their Own Good: Aborigines and government in the Southwest of Western Australia, 1900–1940*, University of Western Australia Press, pp. 76–78.
34 Report of the Roth Royal Commission, *The West Australian*, 30 January 1905.

that employers dodged their obligation to provide rations and medical care, seeking to defray costs onto government. He reserved his most strident criticism for police and the justice system, lambasting the system of arrest of Aboriginal people suspected of killing cattle, the long sentences imposed, and the treatment of Aboriginal prisoners. Neck-chaining, in Roth's view, was unacceptable. Arrest for cattle-killing should only be on warrant, while sentences should be much shorter. Rationing should be conducted through small ration reserves, on which Aboriginal 'indigents' would be confined. With regard to co-habitation, Roth agreed that the Chief Protector should be provided with powers to prevent Europeans and 'Asiatics' from living with Aboriginal women. As an additional measure, to prevent Aboriginal women mixing with pearling crews, police should have the power to confine crews to their boats and prohibit Aboriginal people from entering areas where pearling boats came ashore. Roth's recommendations supported most of the proposals Prinsep had been advocating for the previous six years. The main problem, Roth agreed, was that the Chief Protector had 'no legal status, while his authority as head of the Department … is a divided one, and may even be ignored. Justices have greater powers, while other government officers assist him only out of courtesy', even the network of honorary protectors.[35] Roth was critical of incapacity of the department to inspect conditions of pastoral properties or to properly supervise the distribution of rations. Furthermore, he agreed with Prinsep's views on the half-caste problem, and recommended that the Chief Protector be legal guardian of all Aboriginal and 'half-caste' children under the age of 18.

The West Australian launched an immediate attack on the report, the Chief Protector and the Commissioner of Police, Captain Hare. It reserved particular venom for Prinsep, arguing that, 'if what Dr. Roth says is true', he should resign immediately:

> Either … [Prinsep] has known what was going on and ought to have stopped it, or he did not know, and is therefore incompetent, and, in either event, should be called on to resign … He was made the head of a department, was invested with great powers and had a very large income placed at his disposal, the one stipulation being that there was to be a check to those cruelties, immoralities and cases of criminal misbehaviour which the public were assured took place without stint or concealment in so many parts of Western Australia.[36]

Prinsep reminded the newspaper that he in fact had no legislative powers and could act only on the 'moral strength' of the department.[37]

---

35 *The West Australian*, 30 January 1901.
36 *The West Australian*, 31 January, 1901.
37 *The West Australian*, 2 February 1905.

A man would be a fool who thought that he could stop those evils altogether in a country so large and so full of hidden fastnesses as this State, but, by restricting the employment of natives to reliable people, and … preventing interference or intercourse with the natives by unreliable people … is … the best way of gradually bringing those irresponsible, but some-day-useful people to a higher level.[38]

The debate brought responses from near and far, and quickly moved from criticism of the government to debate of the characteristics of Aboriginal populations and their future in a colonised world. John Forrest, by then Treasurer in the Commonwealth Government, expressed a Western Australian parochialism that was common amongst the colonial social body, criticising the State for employing a Queenslander, who could not be expected to understand the particular conditions of Western Australia. In his view, the responsibility of the State extended only to 'kind treatment' and protection from 'injustice and cruelty'. 'There is scarcely any place for them in our civilisation', he told *The West Australian*, 'and those who in their youth, are cared for in our institutions, have a difficult path to travel when they come to maturity.'[39] Explorer and prospector William Carr-Boyd wrote that Roth did not go far enough. In his experience, the 'condition of the blacks is simply disgusting, filthy, deplorable and miserable … starving, ragged, and rotten with most disgusting diseases'.[40] Church of England Bishop Riley accepted that Aboriginal people were a doomed race, and that 'if they were to continue to suffer such diseases and cruelty as they had done in the past, it would be better for them to die. But surely it was the duty of all Christians to make the lives of the natives brighter, to uplift them, to keep them from contamination, and to teach them of the hope of salvation.'[41]

Derby Resident Magistrate Richard Wace supported recommendations to establish hunting and rationing reserves and the removal from towns of 'half-caste waifs and strays'. In his view, the 'large number of absolutely worthless blacks and half-castes about who grow up to lives of prostitution and idleness' would benefit from removal and education in a Christian environment.[42] Charles Blythe, lessee of Leopold Downs station 200 kilometres east of Derby, wrote that, even after 20 years living in proximity to Aboriginal people, he still did not understand them. It was 'absurd', in his view, to compel Aboriginal people to work, or try to bind them with contracts:

A most peculiar race, and to get any idea of their condition one wants to study them for at least a year. They are of a restless and nomadic nature,

---

38 Ibid.
39 *The West Australian*, 4 February 1905.
40 *The West Australian*, 7 February 1905.
41 *The Morning Herald*, 13 February 1905.
42 *The Morning Herald*, 14 February 1905.

and therein lies one of the principle problems in dealing with them … The native is of such a temperament that he wants to be constantly changing. There is no stability about him. He is with you one day, and probably gone the next, and whereas one week you may have 20 or 30 natives around your station, next week they may all have taken it into their heads to shift; you are not consulted and you are powerless to prevent this.[43]

The government responded to Roth's report by issuing directives to police and magistrates and assuring the public that legislation before the parliament would reflect the recommendations. The furore soon died down. Roth returned to Brisbane to fight his own battles with the Queensland establishment and Prinsep to the task of seeing his draft legislation into law. The two men had got on well and agreed on most aspects of the Chief Protector's role, and the subsequent *Aborigines Act* was to reflect many of the features of Queensland's *Aborigines Protection and Restriction on the Sale of Opium Amending Act 1901*, a law significantly influenced by the views of Roth.[44] They had enjoyed a social life together while the Royal Commission was in progress and continued to write to one another for some time. Roth's letters made it clear that he was impatient with Queensland and that he was interested in Prinsep's position when he retired. In March 1905, he congratulated Prinsep on his foresight in disappearing to the Chine, 'while all the fuss was on', and on his success in deflecting blame 'the condition of the natives' to those 'who had it in their power to befriend and assist you, but had neglected to do so'.[45] Roth expressed amazement that Commissioner Hare, John Forrest and Bishop Riley had 'made themselves ridiculous in the public gaze' by 'committing themselves to a criticism … before they had perused the evidence'.[46]

Prinsep's friends wrote offering their support for his efforts to persuade the government to take his proposals seriously. From England, former Chief Justice Alexander Onslow congratulated him on coming 'clean out of the investigation', and agreed that, 'if you want a proper supervision of such a subject in so enormous extent of country you must have more money and have greater authority than the local government is inclined to give you'.

> Of course (I am sorry to say) wherever the white man has the chance of making money out of the labour of an inferior race. Most certainly there will exist danger and very grave danger of abuse of power and those dangers will become active in the inverse ratio to the activity

---

43 Ibid.
44 Haebich 2000, *Broken Circles*, p.306.
45 Roth to H.C. Prinsep, 4 March 1905, SLWA Acc. 1972 (uncatalogued).
46 Ibid.

of the supervision. But what can you do when you are hampered by want of money and want of authority. Further do the police authorities sufficiently sympathise with you? That is a most important question.[47]

Similarly, architect George Temple Poole praised Prinsep's 'proposals for controlling the policies of the tribes, organising protected reserves, and for competent, fatherly administration of their social economics', and offered his support to pressure the Government to respond: 'If you think the public should be informed of this, will you let me have word, and a suggestion or so, and the writer will write.'[48]

Prinsep got his new legislation before the year was out. In December 1905, *The Aborigines Act* passed with minimal debate and attracted little of the public attention that might have been expected from the controversies earlier in the year. Even Prinsep's diaries pay the event scant regard, merely recording that on the 11th December he had provided Hicks with information for the second reading speech, and that on the 13th he and his two daughters Emily and Virginia sat in the public gallery listening to the speeches. On the 15th December, 'The Aborigines Bill was debated and passed its second Reading in the Assembly. H. at Parlt. House at every sitting. Geo. Taylor had been speaking very highly of him in the afternoon and when it was all over H. went and thanked those who had helped the Bill through.'[49] Most of what Prinsep had been requesting over the previous seven years was now law, although some of the important recommendations from Roth, such as the establishment of a regional departmental structure and the payment of cash wages by pastoralists, had been quietly dropped. Importantly, the Act defined four categories of people 'deemed to be aborigines', including half-castes and the children of half-castes, which was to have wide ramifications for Aboriginal people over the course of the Twentieth Century. The main features of the Act related to employment, the powers of the Chief Protector and the police, cohabitation, and the establishment of Aboriginal reserves.

The Chief Protector's powers over Aboriginal people became extensive. He was now legal guardian of every Aboriginal or half-caste child under the age of 16, had the right to intervene for the general care and protection of any person who came under the Act, including the management of their property, controlled the marriage of Aboriginal women to non-Aboriginal men, and could initiate proceedings to force the father of an illegitimate child to pay maintenance costs if the child was in care. A range of offences relating to marriage, cohabitation and the supply of alcohol were created, and the police were empowered to arrest

---

47 A.C. Onslow to Prinsep, 8 March 1905, SLWA Acc. 1972A/123
48 George Temple Poole to Prinsep, 13 February 1905, SLWA 773 Acc. 1972A/129
49 Prinsep, 'Diaries', 11–15 December 1905.

without warrant any Aboriginal person suspected of offending. Employment provisions were a major feature, including the prohibition of employment of Aboriginal children under the age of 16, reiteration of the contract system of employment, and the introduction of compulsory employment permits to be renewed annually. Employers were compelled under the Act to provide adequate rations, medical care, clothing and blankets. Finally, the Governor was given the power to reserve areas of Crown land, up to a limit of 2,000 acres in any magisterial district, and to order the removal of any unemployed Aboriginal person to such a reserve. The Queensland connection was apparent in the similarities between the Act and the 1897 *Aborigines Protection and Restriction on the Sale of Opium Act* in establishing a similar administrative structure, and similar controls over employment, sexual contact, and the removal and institutionalisation of children. But some of the measures were more restrictive than those of Queensland, including those relating to marriage and cohabitation, the legal guardianship of the Chief Protector over children, and the harsh penalties for offences against the Act.[50]

Prinsep was proud of his new legislation, and saw it as the culmination of seven years of 'one-minded zeal and great hope'. Towards the end of his career, he related the difficulties he had experienced. His efforts, he wrote, were met at first with 'indifference and then, almost adverse criticism':

> At last I resorted to pleading the dire necessity of a suffering race, but even then I met a deaf ear and so another session was lost and the evils increased in such mathematical progression. Again I made the attacks and backed it up by strong language in my report. As may be seen, I certainly met with more encouragement, but nothing was really done. One Premier retired; another died. The fates seemed against me.[51]

'Neck-chaining has not a pleasant sound'

Criticism of the treatment of Aboriginal peoples in Western Australia continued from Britain and, shortly before Prinsep's departure on leave to England in mid-1907, Governor Frederick Bedford received an inquiry about the practice of neck-chaining from Secretary of State, Lord Elgin. In July 1907, *The Times* reported a parliamentary statement in the Commons that the Government did not 'share the opinion of the Western Australian government on neck-chaining': 'the Secretary of State will desire the Governor, as opportunity offers, to impress upon the Western Australian Government the objections which the

---

50   Haebich 2000, *Broken Circles*, p.187.
51   SROWA Series 3005 Cons 255 AD File 1905/97.

continuation of this practice cannot fail to excite in this country (hear, hear)'.[52] With its connotations of slavery, the government was sensitive about the issue, and Prinsep was asked to call upon Lord Elgin while on leave, so that 'the misconception which undoubtedly exists in the minds of those in authority in Downing St. can be cleared away once and for all':

> The neck chaining question appears to be quite misunderstood, and a conversation with His Lordship pointing out that the Aborigines themselves much prefer the system, that it is a light chain, which rests practically on the shoulders and leaves the limbs free and unfettered, and without the danger of chaffing, ought to suffice.[53]

Prinsep's deputy, Pechell, wrote to Prinsep with information for his meeting with Elgin, adding a personal note that he believed Western Australia's reputation was due to 'these wretched church ministers; I wish the natives had made rolled meat out of them before they left the country'. 'It has been conclusively proved by all medical and other evidence', wrote Pechell, 'that this method is most humane'.

> Neck-chaining has not a pleasant sound, and perhaps that is the worst part of it, and the cause of the outcry against the method. However, the people who have raised the outcry do not suggest any better plan, and in my opinion could have troubled themselves very little to find out which was the best method.[54]

Prinsep was relieved to be away from a position that he found more stressful the longer he stayed. Pechell's letters and the request for him to call on Elgin were an unwelcome intrusion into a holiday filled with reunions with family and friends, trips into the countryside and visits to museums and art galleries.

Pechell took the opportunity to fill Prinsep in on all the news from the Aborigines Department as, until the end of December 1907, 'you are still the Chief Protector'. A Royal Commission had been established, he told Prinsep, to inquire into 'alleged cruelty to natives by the Canning Exploration Party and I think they intend to enlarge the scope and powers of the Commission to enquire fully into the treatment of natives generally'.[55] The government had included funds in the departmental budget to establish the Lock Hospitals on Dorre and Bernier Islands, but title over Bernier Island had not yet been secured. Edith Bussell had complained to the Minister about Prinsep's 'methods of treating natives', which Pechell viewed with disdain, as 'she should not have waited till you had left the country to say these things. I am speaking of Miss Bussell

---

52 SROWA Series 3005 Cons 255, AD File 1907/599.
53 Frank Wilson to H.C. Prinsep, 2 September 1907, SLWA Acc. 3594A/27.
54 Pechell to H.C. Prinsep, undated, SLWA 773 Acc. 3594A/33.
55 Pechell to H.C. Prinsep, 23 December 1907, SLWA Acc. 3593A/34.

leaving out all idea of her relationship to you, and I feel you would wish me to do so.'[56] Daisy Bates had criticised the department and complained about Pechell's ungentlemanly conduct after he failed to raise his hat when they met in the street.[57] 'We are quite friendly now', he reassured Prinsep, 'but she is not a person I care much about.'[58] Pechell thought he had been doing well in Prinsep's position, and that the Minister 'seems quite satisfied with what I have done, so much so that I am going to ask for a bonus'.[59] Nonetheless, criticism of the state's treatment of Aboriginal people had continued in the press to the extent that everyone in the government was 'quite sick of the native question'.[60] He looked forward to leaving the job, as he did not 'envy anyone the job of Chief Protector'.[61]

Prinsep interrupted his holiday to attend the Colonial Office for his meeting with Elgin, but ended up meeting a relatively junior officer, Mr. Johnson. Prinsep thought Johnson had been 'much influenced' by reports of cruelty, but he provided 'strong testimony of the general good sense of policemen stationed in the native districts': 'When I asked him whether, if placed in the position of a constable 200 miles in the back blocks, surrounded by hostile natives and armed with instructions to arrest 12 of the natives, he would act differently from the police, he was at a loss to answer, and naturally so.'[62] For Prinsep, this was to be his final act as Chief Protector; on his return, the cares and anxieties of the Aborigines Department would become someone else's problem. He reassured *The West Australian* that the reputation of Western Australia was intact in Britain, and that, in fact, English people were 'so wrapped up in the affairs of their own country, that they don't trouble themselves about our native question'. Perhaps a 'very small missionary set' expressed their concerns about the treatment of Aboriginal people in Western Australia, 'but as it was some people seemed surprised that me, as a man of Australia, spoke English':

> The truth is that in England religious thought is nowadays a totally different thing from what it used to be. It is now not exactly agnosticism, but it is awfully deistical … there seems to be a desire to let the race rise or fall … whatever its fate may be. There does not seem to be the desire to throw the aegis of English power over the unprotected races, as there used to be. Why is this? … The Exeter Hall influence, which used to be a great factor in the excessive ventilation of the grievances against the treatment of the aboriginals, and in whose midst strife used to be stirred

---

56 Pechell to H.C. Prinsep, 2 September 1907, SLWA 773 Acc. 3594A/10.
57 SROWA Series 3005 Cons 255 AD File 1907.
58 Pechell to H.C. Prinsep, 2 September 1907, SLWA Acc. 3594A/10.
59 Pechell to H.C. Prinsep, 23 December 1907, SLWA Acc. 3593A/34.
60 Ibid.
61 Pechell to H.C. Prinsep, 2 September 1907, SLWA MN 773 Acc. 3594A/10.
62 *The West Australian*, 30 September 1908.

up in this connection, has been removed by the demolition of the Hall. Of course, it was not the Hall that made the feeling, but the ... hall gave the opportunity by reason of the traditions which attached to it for the ventilation of that feeling. I think that the accumulation of money is causing people to think a lot more of pleasure than of social problems.[63]

Prinsep returned to Western Australia in 1908 for a life of retirement, and he was pleased to wash his hands of his responsibilities. By successfully implementing laws that he was sure would be effective, he felt his job was done. It was to be his successors, Gale (1908–1915) and A.O. Neville (1915–1940), who would extract the full potential of the legislative machinery of the 1905 Act to engineer a brutal system of regulation and control, which became ever more intrusive in the lives of Aboriginal people.

---

63   Ibid.

10. A 'southern home'

Prinsep's trip to Britain in 1908 was the first time he had been home since his departure as a 21-year-old in 1866, the first time he had seen his sisters, Annie, Louisa and May, and his brother, Jim, all together since they were young people.[1] His diaries over a 12-month stay record his joy at being once again amongst family members and old friends. Re-united with his cousin, Sir Henry Thoby Prinsep, recently retired after a career in the Indian colonial judiciary of 27 years, he was given a 'very cordial reception', and spent hours reminiscing about their shared childhoods in the homes of Thoby and Sara at Little Holland House and the Isle of Wight.[2] He again met Annie Thackeray Ritchie; Edward Thackeray; Bessie Hocking, the wife of his late friend, Sir Harry Hocking, who had died some years before in Jamaica; Hallam and Audrey Tennyson, who he had not seen since Hallam was Governor of South Australia during the last decade of the Nineteenth Century; and Mary Watts, wife of his old art teacher, George Frederick, who had died only three years before. He re-visited old haunts, sketched and painted his way around England, Scotland and the tourist spots on the continent—Cordova, Pompeii, Pisa, Capri, Florence, Rome, Venice, Switzerland and Paris—before returning to Britain.[3] He revelled in the atmosphere of the countryside with its 'lovely trees and hedges' and visited art galleries and stately homes throughout the south, admiring the pictures and statues in places such as Basildon House, 'Constables, Lock, 3 Turners, a Rembrandt, 3 Van Dykes & c'.[4]

When the time came to return to Western Australia, Prinsep did so without regret, keen to be reunited with his daughters and an expanding family of grandchildren, and looking forward to a life of retirement, free from the demands of public service. Early-Twentieth-Century Britain had changed much from the place of his youth, and he now preferred the relative peace of a small Australian colony to the pace and crowds of London, the warmth of Western Australia's climate to the cold and damp of Britain. The London of his youth was no more, and Prinsep had come to feel like an artifact from another age. He reminisced with his brother, Jim, about these times long past, the green fields of a now suburban Kensington, 'the turnpike gate at the end of the Kensington boundary somewhere near the De Vere Hotel, I think now. I remember a little box in the middle of the road where the gateman sheltered to collect the tolls. But all this is long past history and few people believe me when I say I remember the tollgate.'[5]

---

1 Both of Prinsep's brothers had visited Perth, Jim in 1882 for nearly a year, and older brother, Charlie, who died in Melbourne in 1898, for a few days in 1887. Prinsep had visited Louisa Bowden-Smith in Colombo in 1897.
2 Prinsep, Henry C., 'Diaries 1866–1922', SLWA MN 773 Acc 499A, 1907–8.
3 Ibid., 4 February–7 April 1908.
4 Ibid., 18 May 1908.
5 H.C. Prinsep to Jim Prinsep, April 2 1916, private collection.

Soon after their return to Western Australia, the Prinseps left Perth for the rural quiet of Busselton, where they planned to build a house on land Henry had purchased on the banks of the Vasse River. Employing their friend and prominent colonial architect, George Temple Poole, to prepare drawings, Henry and Josephine spent as much time as possible away from the city. Poole wrote to Prinsep after a few days in Busselton, bemoaning his return to the 'muddy waters of this trivial place' after the companionship of his short stay in 'nature's great liberty'. He warned that the plans Prinsep wanted would result in a house far too large and expensive for the needs of Henry, Josephine and unmarried daughter Emily: 'You will have the jeer of me that I, an architect, inherently lavish, should preach to you for a reduced scheme of undertaking.'[6] In 1911, the house, named after Thoby and Sara Prinsep's Little Holland House from Henry's youth in England, was finished, and the family moved in. Henry was to spend his remaining 14 years in pleasant retirement here, near his married daughters, Carlotta Brockman and Virginia Reynolds, their grandchildren and large extended family, living in the rural bliss he had yearned for, and thanking his God who 'in such mysterious ways … in His mercy brings to pass, for us such happy days'.[7]

Older family members speak of Prinsep in retirement as a sociable man devoted to his wife and family, dedicated to photography and art, poetry and reading, whose public life he now restricted to a term as President of the Busselton Roads Boards, and elder and lay preacher of the town's St Mary's Anglican Church.[8] They remember Prinsep and Josephine as a quiet and refined couple, 'very English', known for eccentricities, such as reserving a high-chair at the breakfast table for their cat, and Prinsep's famed lack of punctuality. He built his own darkroom, indulged his passion for painting and photography, and entertained old friends from Perth, such as artist Herbert Gibbs and scientific visitors from Britain sent to see him by Museum Director Bernard Woodward, who collected '214 beasties including some very remarkable beetles'.[9] He continued his poetry, acrostics and honorific verses about old friends, such as John Forrest, playful rhymes for his grandchildren, nephews and nieces and memorials of his youth and childhood.[10] Letters continued to arrive from Britain and throughout the imperial world. Many concerned the death or illness of his increasingly elderly siblings, kin and friends, and the affairs of his many nieces and nephews, some of whom had followed their forebears into colonial careers.[11] He and Josephine

---

6   George Temple Poole to Prinsep, 4 May 1911.
7   'Return to the country', in Prinsep, Henry C. 1908, *Random Rhymes,* T.F. Christie, Perth.
8   These memoirs are from a conversation with Prinsep's last surviving granddaughter, the late Mrs. Edie Giles of Busselton, who remembers him from her childhood 'as a misty figure'. One grandson, Alfred Reynolds, survives at the time of writing, but was too young to remember Prinsep.
9   Bernard Woodward to H.C. Prinsep, 25 October 1912, SLWA Acc.3594A/23.
10 Prinsep 1908, *Random Rhymes*, foreword.
11 Amelia Wilkens to H.C. Prinsep, 11 July 1912, SLWA Acc.3594A/3.

farewelled younger family members bound for South Africa and Europe on military service, rejoiced in the exploits of Britain's military heroes, and shared with family correspondents their despair at food shortages at home and the death and injury of family members and friends on military service.[12] Periodically news from home, such as the marriage of Prinseps' recently-widowed youngest sister, May, to former Australian Governor-General, Hallam Tennyson, delighted Prinsep and Josephine. As Jim Prinsep confided in July 1918:

> At present it's a profound secret, but I expect that by the time you get this it will have been publicly announced, and I hope the marriage will have taken place, as there is nothing I can see to make them wait. But if not, you must treat it as absolutely confidential as one can never be sure in these times how a chance remark in Busselton may not be cabled to England. Please therefore keep it entirely private until it is publicly announced. It is possible that Hallam's former position in Australia may render his marriage sufficiently interesting to be deemed worth calling to the papers and if so you may hear of it before you get this ... You'll be able to swagger a bit by referring casually to 'my brother-in-law, who was formerly Governor-General.'[13]

Prinsep's retirement gave him time to reflect upon his place in the history of Western Australia, and on its development over the half-century since his arrival as a young man in a colony then less than 40 years old. He spent time sorting out his collection of artifacts and ephemera from India, Ceylon and Australia, and donated many to the new State Museum, including a 'tile from a Temple roof', a 'sacred lamp', 'Indian art' and a 'Buddhist Bible in brass covers', a 'skull (homo), a trap door spider's nest ... a portion of native canoe (from what location?), a native ornament, and a small box containing mineral specimens'.[14] He imposed rudimentary order on the piles of letters and photographs from Australia, Britain and empire that had accumulated over his 40 years in the colony, sorting the correspondence into loose categories, and arranging black and white prints, cartes de visite and cabinet cards into albums. As he grew older, he became more conscious of his status as an old colonist, one of a declining number of Western Australians who could recall the colony in its early days. On occasions, he was invited to meetings to speak about the old times. He contributed memoirs to local magazines and wrote letters to his brother and sisters recalling their youth in places such as Kensington and Freshwater on the Isle of Wight.[15]

---

12 Annie Prinsep to H.C. Prinsep, March 29 1916, SLWA Acc.3592A/16A; Hallam Tennyson to H.C. Prinsep, 24 February 1918, SLWA Acc.3592A/67B; Jim Prinsep to H.C. Prinsep, 14 June 1918, SLWA Acc.3592A/67B.
13 Jim Prinsep to H.C. Prinsep, 26th July 1918, SLWA Acc.3859A/67B.
14 Western Australian Museum, 'Donation Catalogue', 1902–1914; Bernard Woodward to H.C. Prinsep, 4 March 1910, SLWA Acc.3594A/71.
15 Bernard Woodward to H.C. Prinsep, 11 January 1904, SLWA Acc.3594/A/46/3; Prinsep, H.C., 'Memoirs of an Old Colonist', in *The Magistrate: Official Organ of the Justices Association of Western Australia* (Perth), June 27 1918; H.C. Prinsep to Jim Prinsep, April 2 1916, private collection.

Western Australia had become his 'southern home', the place beneath 'southern skies to spend my life in strange, untrodden ways', as he told his Scottish cousin, Katie Grant-Peterkin.[16] This distant land had become familiar, and he was proud to be one of 'Old Britain's offspring strewn o'er all the world, standing firm in its dear mother's attitude', member of the singular race that 'strives for Truth and equal rights for all, and freedom from the tyrant's iron chains'.[17]

'A Christian gentleman of the old school'

Considering his diverse interests, we can imagine that Prinsep would be dismayed that today he is widely remembered in Western Australia for his role in the controversial and discredited *Aborigines Act*. Convinced that time would prove the many critics of his role as Chief Protector wrong, he believed future generations would bestow 'high ecomiums' on him and a government which had acted correctly to forestall the complete disappearance of a dying race. 'In future days', he told Premier John Forrest, the people of Western Australia will be grateful for 'laws which will do so much to preserve the health and morality of the coming race and prevent the ancient and interesting aboriginal race from sinking into a degraded grave and infamous memory. Necessity requires no precedents.'[18]

Prinsep viewed himself as 'the best friend of the native', the one 'the natives themselves' turned to for help, but he was sensitive to his many critics and despaired that he would ever be able to satisfy anyone with his performance. Many believed he had done little to protect Aboriginal peoples throughout the State from cruelty and exploitation, others that he had done too much, and had sided with Aboriginal people against the interests of the pastoral and mining industries. *The West Australian* called for Prinsep's resignation on the grounds of incompetence in the immediate aftermath of the Roth Royal Commission. He also drew ridicule as a 'round man in a square hole', or as the 'dearest old lady in the world', as Daisy Bates described him after he had refused her request to remove Aboriginal skeletal remains for her research.[19] He was lampooned for his Englishness, his mild temperament and innocuous attempts to prosecute pastoralists for their illegal treatment of Aboriginal people. *The West Australian,* a critic of Prinsep as Chief Protector, even published verse mocking his Englishness and mild manner:

---

16 These phrases are from two of Prinsep's poems, 'To Mrs Willoughby Wilkinson' and 'To Cousin Katie Grant-Peterkin' in Prinsep 1908, *Random Rhymes*.
17 H.C. Prinsep, 'Our Britain', SLWA Acc.3594A/4.
18 SROWA Series 3005 Cons 255 AD File 1905/97.
19 Haebich, Anna 1988, *For Their Own Good: Aborigines and government in the Southwest of Western Australia, 1900–1940*, University of Western Australia Press, Nedlands, p.61.

I'm Prinsep, Protector of the Blacks,

Of good English blood I have stacks,

And my anger (?) goes forth,

To those men of the north,

Whose morals and methods are lax.[20]

By the last years of his career, Prinsep indeed appeared an anachronism in an increasingly professionalised state civil service, the last of a generation of gentleman civil servants from an earlier era in the colony's history. Men such as Prinsep brought to the civil service a 'good education in England' and 'dignity in official and social relations'; he was 'a man of culture and of general knowledge', but in early-Twentieth-Century Western Australia, this no longer seemed enough.[21] According to the Perth newspaper *The Morning Herald*, Prinsep was 'humane, honourable, and just-minded', but lacked the energy and expertise of a man like Walter Roth.

> Mr. Prinsep has served the State well in other capacities, and no one will doubt for a moment his keen sympathy with the lot of his helpless charges. But the chief protector of aborigines must be a young man, who can go about amongst the blacks and their employers, and get his information first hand. That he should be a scientist like Dr. Roth is also desirable.[22]

Despite his expectation that future generations would endorse his actions as Chief Protector, history has instead judged Prinsep harshly, particularly the *Aborigines Act* and the government bureaucracy he pioneered. Rather than fulfilling Prinsep's anticipation that they would be the salvation of Aboriginal people, in 2008 the laws were judged a humanitarian tragedy that, over 100 years after their enactment, required the Commonwealth's formal apology and a promise that governments of Australia would never again act in such a blatant way against the interests of Aboriginal people. People such as Prinsep would no doubt have found it impossible to imagine that his brand of colonial humanitarianism would be so explicitly rejected. Far from being a savior, he would instead be held as one responsible for a system that acted against the interests of the State's Aboriginal people for the next 70 years. The system he and people like him had introduced was adjudged a massive failure that had brought great suffering on Aboriginal people as a subject race throughout

---

20 Undated cutting, 'The West Australian' in the Prinsep papers, SLWA MN 773 Acc. 3592A/72A.
21 Prinsep, Henry C., 'Application for Appointment as Government Resident, Kimberley', State Records Office of Western Australia, Colonial Secretary's Office, 1885 1668, AN527.
22 *Perth Morning Herald*, 1 February 1905.

Western Australia and the Commonwealth of Australia. This system was based on serious and misleading illusions about the nature and complexity of Aboriginal societies, and largely denied the human rights and freedoms of a subject people, together with their cultural and historical identities, their capacity and desire to exercise agency and control over their own personal and family lives.

Prinsep's *Aborigines Act* was thoroughly consistent with his understanding of Britain's imperial role and the growth of an extensive colonial system founded on the appropriation of new lands and the dispossession of indigenous peoples. The unquestioned right of British colonisation to exercise its power over subject peoples could readily be justified by loosely held humanitarian ideals of advancement and modernisation, which assumed that the benefits of British civilisation and religion were sufficient compensation for the loss of indigenous lands and cultures. As a coloniser and 'imperial man', Prinsep was very much complicit in this dispossession. Aboriginal cultures would be forever changed under the impact of colonisation, but the role of humane people such as himself was to protect Aboriginal people from its worst excesses. Aboriginal populations throughout Australia became subject peoples identified by race, whose destinies in every aspect of their lives was now the business of government, the province of an increasingly powerful and intrusive bureaucracy which became ever more efficient in its role of managing and regulating Aboriginal life. John Forrest's warning in 1900 that the laws would make 'prisoners of these poor people in their own country' proved to be devastatingly accurate, while the humanitarian justifications advanced by Prinsep eventually came to be seen as misguided and ultimately destructive.[23]

Were he alive today, Prinsep would no doubt be surprised by the continued presence of a vibrant Aboriginal society, even more so by its increasing presence in Australian public life. In his last years, Prinsep believed that the coda of Aboriginal society in colonised Australia was already being played out. He died quietly at home, in Little Holland House, at the age of 78, surrounded by his loving Josephine, daughters Carlotta, Emily and Virginia, and many of his grandchildren. The Western Australian press recorded the passing of an 'old colonist', eulogising 'one of the State's oldest and best known residents' who was 'always polite, always courteous, always kind and wishing to be helpful', and 'a Christian gentleman of the old school.'[24] By contrast, George Coolbul, Charlie Neeribun, Ngilgie, Fanny Balbuk, Nathaniel Leyland and the countless other Aboriginal people he had known over his years in Western Australia died unlamented and largely unremembered. At the time of Prinsep's death, their traditional country was covered by farms, and their Noongar descendants were shut out of their traditional lives and the colonial economy. They had been

---

23 SROWA Series 3005 Cons 255 AD File 830/1900.
24 *The West Australian*, July 21 1922; *West Australian Church News*, 1 August 1922.

relegated to the status of pauper and excluded from participation in the Western Australian community partly because of the legislation that Prinsep worked so hard to promulgate. Prinsep, as his descendants recorded, died happy, content with his life's work and his contribution to the development of a prosperous southern colonial home, secure in the knowledge that he had done his duty in the way his God would have approved. Like his forebears in India whose example he so much revered, Prinsep never questioned the rightness of a venture that was divinely ordained and that had as its basis the appropriation of indigenous lands. Prinsep and his forebears might occasionally bemoan the violent expulsion and repression of indigenous resistance, but they were never at any stage prepared to seriously question the primary logic of a settler colonialism founded on dispossession. Instead, they argued that it was the innate deficiencies of Aboriginal or Indian populations which rendered them incapable of benefiting from the offerings of British civilisation. A man such as Prinsep could simply turn away from any concerns he might have about the future of Aboriginal Western Australia, put the cares of official office aside, and enjoy the fruits of his retirement, comfortable in the knowledge that his descendants would benefit from the adventure he had started so many years before. He could trivialise the situation of his Aboriginal charges as a 'laughing, careless race, full of humour, mirth and song. Indolent in the extreme, they appear to be believers in the maxim "Sufficient unto the day is the evil thereof," and to take no care for the morrow.'[25] In the early-Twenty-First Century, Australia is still in the process of emerging from its colonial past, as the sense of connectedness to Britain and an imperial past decreases with the emergence of new generations and non-British ethnicities into positions of political power and influence. For the nation's Aboriginal people, we can be optimistic that our own post-colonial moment will provide the opportunity to consolidate the moves towards the decolonisation of the past few years, and achieve a time when they will return to a position where they are respected as a people, valued for their contribution to modern Australian society.

---

25   Government of Western Australia 1901, *Twentieth Century Impressions of Western Australia*, P.W.H. Thiel & Co., Perth, p.178.

Little Holland House, Busselton, 'for us a place to pass such happy days' in retirement. Prinsep, Josephine and Emily moved to Busselton a year after his retirement. Naming it after the Kensington home of Thoby and Sara Prinsep where he had spent his youth, he lived out his remaining years in contented rural bliss. Josephine and Emily are on the front porch.

Source: Prinsep Papers, SLWA MN 773 BA 1423/344.

10. A 'southern home'

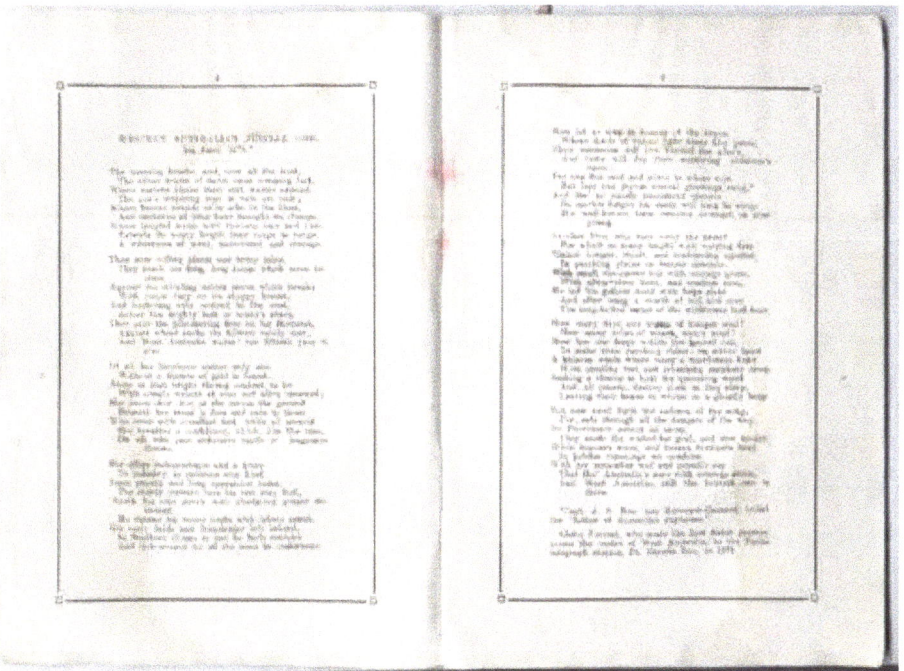

In his retirement, Prinsep gathered verses and acrostics he had penned over the years and published them in 1915 in a booklet, Random Rhymes, 'for friends who have pressed me so hard for copies'. Many of the rhymes honour and remember old friends, such as John Forrest, and others, such as his 'Western Australia Jubilee Ode, 1879', sing the praises of his 'southern home', Western Australia.

Source: Author's private collection.

Surrounded by family, Henry Prinsep and Josephine in Busselton in old age, photographed by Millie Bunbury (née Priess).

Source: Courtesy Ailsa Smith, Claremont WA.

10. A 'southern home'

In retirement, Prinsep pursued his love of art and photography. This oil painting, 'Karri Trees, Manjimup in 1910', is one of his few paintings to explore newer and bolder styles.

Source: The Wordsworth Collection, National Gallery of Australia.

Bibliography

1. Published works by Prinsep family members

Becher, Augusta 1930, *Personal Reminiscences of Augusta Becher, 1830–1888,* edited by H.G. Rawlinson, Constable and Co., London.

Prinsep, Augustus 1833, *The Journal of a Voyage from Calcutta to Van Diemen's Land,* Smith, Elder and Co., London.

Prinsep, Augustus 1834, *The Baboo and Other Tales Descriptive of Society in India,* 2 Volumes, Smith, Elder and Co., London.

Prinsep, Augustus 1834, *A Man of Sentiment in the Mofussil,* Smith, Elder and Co., London.

Prinsep, Augustus 1834, *Theodore, or Coelebs the Younger,* Smith, Elder and Co., London.

Prinsep, Augustus 1846, 'On the Traces of Feudalism in India, and the Condition of Lands Now in a Comparative State of Agriculture', in *The Journal of the Royal Asiatic Society of Great Britain and Ireland,* Volume Eight, John W. Parker, London.

Prinsep, Charles R. 1816, *A Letter to the Earl of Liverpool: On the cause of the present distresses of the country, and the efficacy of reducing the standard of our silver currency towards their relief,* James Ridgway, London.

Prinsep, Charles R. 1818, *An Essay on Money,* James Ridgway, London.

Prinsep, Charles R. 1847, *Report Upon the Project of the Calcutta and Diamond Harbour Railway and Dock Company,* Diamond Dock and Railway Company, Calcutta.

Prinsep, George A. 1823, *Remarks on the External Commerce and Exchange of Bengal, with Appendix of Accounts and Estimates,* Kingsbury, Parbury and Allen, London.

Prinsep, George A. 1830, *An Account of Steam Vessels and of Proceedings Connected with Steam Navigation in British India,* from the Government Gazette Press, G.H. Huttman, Calcutta.

Prinsep, Henry C. 1908, *Random Rhymes,* T.F. Christie, Perth.

Prinsep, Henry T. 1825 (1972) *History of the Political and Military Transactions in India during the Administration of the Marquess of Hastings 1813–1823*, Volume 1, Irish University Press, Shannon, Ireland.

Prinsep, Henry T. 1832, 'Estimate of the Risk of Life to Civil Servants of the Bengal Presidency in each year of their residency in India', in *Journal of the Asiatic Society of Bengal*, Volume 1, July 1832.

Prinsep, Henry T. 1834 (1970), *Origin of the Sikh Power in the Punjab and Political Life of Maharaja Ranjit Singh, With an Account of the Religion, Law and Customs of the Sikhs*, Punjab Languages Department, Patiala.

Prinsep, Henry T. 1852, *Tibet, Tartary and Mongolia: Their social and political condition and the religion of Boodh as there existing*, W.H. Allen & Co., London.

Prinsep, Henry T. 1853, *The India Question in 1853*, W.H. Allen & Co., London.

Prinsep, James (ed.) 1832–1838, *Journal of the Asiatic Society of Bengal*, Volumes 1–6, Baptist Mission Press, Circular Road, Calcutta.

Prinsep, James 1833, *Views of Benares*, third series, Baptist Mission Press, Calcutta.

Prinsep, James 1833 (1996), *Benares Illustrated in a Series of Drawings*, Vishwavidyalaya Prakashan, Varanas.

Prinsep, John 1791, *A Short Review of the Trade of the East India Company: Between the years 1785 and 1790; taken from papers laid before the House of Commons during the two last sessions of Parliament by a proprietor*, J. Debrett, London.

Prinsep, John 1792, *Strictures and Observations on the Mocurrery System of Landed Property in Bengal Originally Written for the Morning Chronicle, Under the Signature of Gurreeb Doss, With Replies*, J. Debrett, London.

Prinsep, John 1792, *Strictures and Occasional Observations Upon the System of British Commerce with the East Indies: With remarks and proposed regulations, for encouraging the importation of sugar from Bengal, and hints for an arrangement of the trade*, J. Debrett, London.

Prinsep, John 1793, *A Letter to the Proprietors of East India Stock on the Present Crisis of the Company's Affairs*, J. Debrett, London.

Prinsep, John 1793, *The Right of the West-India Merchants to a Double Monopoly of the Sugar Market of Great Britain: And the expedience of all monopolies examined*, J. Debrett, London.

Prinsep, John 1797, *Proposal of a Substitute for Funding in Time of War: Addressed to the Right Honourable William Pitt,* Minerva Press, London.

Prinsep, John 1800, *Tracts on Various Subjects, Chiefly Relating to East India Affairs,* Volume 1, J. Debrett, London.

Prinsep, John 1823, *Suggestions on Freedom of Commerce and Navigation More Especially in Reference to the East India Trade,* James Ridgway, London.

Prinsep, Val C. 1879, *Imperial India: An artist's journals, illustrated by numerous sketches taken at the courts of the principal chiefs in India,* Chapman and Hall, London.

Say, Jean-Baptiste 1821, *A Treatise on Political Economy: Or the production, distribution, and consumption of wealth,* 2 Volumes, translated by Charles R. Prinsep, Longman, Hurst, Rees, Orme, and Brown, London.

Thomas, Edward (ed.) 1858, *Essays on Indian Antiquities, Historic, Numismatic, and Palaeographic, of the late James Prinsep, FRS, to Which are Added his Useful Tables,* 2 Volumes, John Murray, London.

2. Unpublished documents by Prinsep and extended family members

Brockman, Carlotta, 'Reminiscences of Carlotta Louisa Brockman, née Prinsep, 1882–1956', State Library of Western Australia (SLWA) Acc. 931A.

Brockman, Frances Louisa, 'Diary of Frances Louisa Brockman, 1872–1905', SLWA Acc. 938A.

Bussell, Ellen, 'Diaries, 22 April 1857–22 November, 1864', SLWA Acc. 1008A.

Prinsep, Amelia Rebecca (Emily), 'Chapter One: John Prinsep and James Prinsep', SLWA Acc. 1972.

Prinsep, Annie Mary, 'Last Will and Testament', private collection.

Prinsep, Charles John, 'Letters of Charles John Prinsep', SLWA Acc. 3595A 4–11.

Prinsep, Charles Robert, 'Last Will and Testament of Charles Robert Prinsep', SLWA Acc. 3595A/17.

Prinsep, Charlotte Josephine (née Bussell), 'Correspondence', SLWA Acc. 3593A/9, 10, 14, 24, 25, 26, 34, 35.

Prinsep, Charlotte Josephine (née Bussell), 'Letters of Charlotte Josephine Prinsep (née Bussell)', SLWA Acc. 983A 1–3.

Prinsep, Henry C., 'Application for Appointment as Government Resident, Kimberley', State Records Office of Western Australia, Colonial Secretary's Office, 1885 1668, AN527.

Prinsep, Henry C., 'Art Work and Sketch Books', SLWA Acc. 3954A/4.

Prinsep, Henry C., 'Diaries 1866–1922', SLWA Acc. 499A.

Prinsep, Henry C., 'Diaries 1884–1901', SLWA Acc. 2882A/12, 24.

Prinsep, Henry C., 'List of Aboriginal Native Words', SLWA Acc. 3592A/73.

Prinsep, Henry C., 'Phots [sic] Collection, Prinsep Notebook', SLWA.

Prinsep, Henry C., 'Prinsep Papers', SLWA Acc. 1972.

Prinsep, Henry C., 'Prinsep Papers, Correspondence', SLWA Acc. 983A, 1–3.

Prinsep, Henry C., 'Prinsep Papers, Correspondence Henry Charles Prinsep', SLWA Acc. 3592A.

Prinsep, Henry C. 'Prinsep Papers, Correspondence Henry Charles Prinsep', SLWA Acc. 3594A, 24–47.

Prinsep, Henry C., 'Prinsep Photograph Collection', SLWA Acc. BA 1423.

Prinsep, Henry C., 'Reminiscences', SLWA Acc. 2121A.

Prinsep, Henry C., 1880, 'Scenes of Travel and Adventure in Western Australia', National Library of Australia, http://nla.gov.au/nla.pic-vn3542902.

Prinsep, Henry Thoby, 'Private Papers', Oriental and India Office Collection at the British Library (OIOC) MSS Eur. D. 662.

Prinsep, Sir Henry Thoby, 'Three Generations in India 1771–1904', OIOC MSS Eur. C. 97.

Prinsep, James, 'Copy of Letter from J. Prinsep to His Mother, Calcutta 1834–5', SLWA Acc. 499A.

Prinsep, James, 'Will of James Prinsep', SLWA Acc. 3859A, 1–2.

Prinsep, James Charles, 'Autobiography', SLWA Acc. 3859A, 1–2.

Prinsep, James Charles, 'De Principe, A.D. 1574–1930', 2 Volumes, SLWA Acc. 3150 A/1–2.

Prinsep, William, 'The Memoirs of William Prinsep', 3 Volumes, British Library, OIOC MSS Eur. D. 1160/1.

Private Collection of Prinsep Correspondence, held by Mrs. Ailsa Smith, Claremont, Western Australia.

3. Other unpublished sources

Berryman, Mrs., 'List of Prinsep Books in Shelves at Little Holland House', provided by compiler's son in 2007, Ian Berryman.

Bunbury, Henry W., 'Diary, 1834–1837', SLWA Acc. 327A.

Coolbul, George, 'West Australian Native Art, 1868–1869: Book of pencil and crayon sketches', State Art Collection, Art Gallery of Western Australia, Perth.

Ford, John, 'Nabobs: Making and spending East Indian wealth', East Sussex, unpublished manuscript.

Milward, John, 'Pioneers of the Warren', unpublished manuscript, personal collection.

Mitchell, W.B., 'Letter Books', SLWA Acc. 3304A.

Mitchell, W.B., 'Wages Book for Prinsep Park and Belvidere', SLWA Acc. 3592A/88.

Mitchell, W.O. 'Letter books 1860–1907', SLWA Acc. 970A.

4. Published books: Eighteenth and Nineteenth Century

Adam, William 1838, *Third Report on the State of Education in Bengal; including some account of the State of Education in Behar, and a Consideration of the Means Adopted to the Improvement and Extension of Public Instruction in both Provinces*, G.H. Huttman, Bengal Military Orphan Press, Calcutta.

'An Idler' 1843, *Letters to Friends at Home from June 1842 to May 1843*, Star Press, Calcutta.

Boulger, Demetrius C. 1892, *Lord William Bentinck*, Clarendon Press, Oxford.

Brady, The Very Rev. J. 1845, *A Descriptive Vocabulary of the Native Language of W. Australia*, The Press of the S.C. De Propaganda Fide, Rome.

Brinton, Daniel G. 1890, *Races and Peoples: Lectures on the science of ethnography*, N.D.C. Hodges, New York.

Burnes, Alexander 1834, *Travels into Bokhara: Being an account of a journey from India to Cabool, Tartary and Persia; Also, narrative of a voyage on the Indus from the sea to Lahore*, 3 Volumes, John Murray, London .

Calvert, Albert F. 1892, *The Aborigines of Western Australia*, W. Milligan & Co., London.

Danvers, Frederick Charles et. al. 1819, *Memorials of Old Haileybury College*, Archibald Constable & Co., Westminster.

Eden, Emily 1866, *Up the Country: Letters written to her sister from the upper provinces of India*, 2 Volumes, Richard Bentley, London.

Elphinstone, Mountstuart 1841, *The History of India*, John Murray, London.

Eyre, Edward John 1845, *Journals of Expeditions of Discovery into Central Australia and Overland from Adelaide to King George's Sound, in the Years 1840–1: Sent by the colonists of South Australia with the sanction and support of the government; Including an account of the manners and customs of the Aborigines and the state of their relations with Europeans*, Volume 2, T. and W. Boone, London.

Forrest, John 1875, *Journal of Proceedings of the Western Australian Exploring Expedition Through the Centre of Australia: From Champion Bay, on the west coast, to the overland telegraph line between Adelaide and Port Darwin, commanded by John Forrest, F.R.G.S.*, Government Printer, Perth.

Fraser, Malcolm 1882, *General Information Respecting the Present Conditions of the Forests and Timber Trade*, Government Printer, Perth.

Gilchrist, John 1802, *The Stranger's East Indian Guide to the Hindoostanee: Or grand popular language of India (improperly called Moors)*, Hindoostanee Press, Calcutta.

Gilchrist, John 1809, *Dialogues, English and Hindoostanee: Calculated to promote the colloquial discourse of Europeans, on the most useful and familiar subjects, with the natives of India; Upon their arrival in that country*, second edition, for Manners and Miller et. al., Edinburgh.

Gilchrist, John 1825, *The General East India Guide and Vade Mecum: For the public functionary, government officer, private agent, trader or foreign sojourner, in British India, and the adjacent parts of Asia immediately connected with the honourable East India Company*, Kingsbury, Parbury & Allen, London.

Giles, Ernest 1889, *Australia Twice Traversed,* viewed online at http://etext.library.adelaide.edu.au/g/giles/ernest/g47a/, University of Adelaide, Adelaide.

Grant, Coleworthy 1849, *An Anglo-Indian Domestic Sketch: A letter from an artist in India to his mother in England,* W. Thacker and Co., Calcutta.

Grant, Coleworthy 1849, *Lithographic Sketches of the Public Characters of Calcutta, 1838–1850,* W. Thacker and Co., Calcutta.

Grey, George 1840, *A Vocabulary of the Dialects of South Western Australia,* second edition, T. & W. Boone, London.

Grey, George 1841, *Journal of Two Expeditions of Discovery in North-West and Western Australia, During the Years 1837, '38, and '39, Under the Authority of Her Majesty's Government,* T. and W. Boone, London.

Gribble, J.B. 1884, *'Black But Comely': Or, glimpses of Aboriginal life in Australia,* Morgan and Scott, London.

Holmes and Co. 1851, *The Bengal Obituary: Or a record to perpetuate the memory of departed worth being a compilation of tablets and monumental inscriptions from various parts of Bengal and Agra Presidencies, to which is added biographical sketches and memoirs of such as have pre-eminently distinguished themselves in the history of British India since the formation of the European settlement to the present time,* W. Thacker & Co., London.

Hume, Hamilton 1867, *The Life of Edward John Eyre, Late Governor of Jamaica,* Richard Bentley, London.

Jacob, Gertrude L. 1876, *The Rajah of Sarawak,* Volume 2, MacMillan and Co., London.

James, Edward 1830, *Brief Memoirs of the Late Reverend John Thomas James, D.D., Lord Bishop of Calcutta: Particularly during his residence in India; Gathered from his letters and papers,* J. Hatchard and Son, London.

Kimberly, W.B. 1897, *History of Western Australia: A narrative of her past, together with biographies of her leading men,* F.W. Niven and Co., Melbourne.

Laurie, Colonel W.F.B. 1887, *Sketches of Some Distinguished Anglo-Indians: With an account of Anglo-Indian periodical literature,* W.H. Allen & Co., London.

Mill, James 1826, *The History of British India,* 6 Volumes, third edition, Baldwin, Cradock, and Joy, London.

Mill, John Stuart 1885, *Principles of Political Economy with Some of Their Applications to Social Philosophy,* Longmans, Green and Co., London, New York and Toronto.

Moore, George Fletcher 1884, *Diary of Ten Years Eventful Life of an Early Settler in Western Australia: And also a descriptive vocabulary of the language of the Aborigines,* M. Walbrook, London.

Nind, Scott 1832, *Description of the Natives of King George's Sound (Swan River Colony) and Adjoining Country,* Royal Geographical Society, London.

Ogle, Nathaniel 1839, *The Colony of Western Australia: A manual for emigrants to that settlement or its dependencies,* James Fraser, London.

Parkes, Fanny 1850, *Wanderings of a Pilgrim in Search of the Picturesque, During Four-and-Twenty Years in the East: With revelations of life in the Zenana*, 2 Volumes, Pelham Richardson, London.

Pryme, Jane Townley, and Alicia Bayne 1879, *Memorials of the Thackeray Family,* Spottiswoode and Company, New York.

Rowan, Ellis 1898, *The Flower Hunter,* Angus & Robertson, London.

Say, Jean-Baptiste 1827, *A Treatise on Political Economy: Or the production, distribution and consumption of wealth*, translated from the fourth edition by C.R. Prinsep, J. Grigg, Philadelphia.

Tayler, William 1881, *Thirty-Eight Years in India, From Jugonath to the Himalayan Mountains,* 2 Volumes, W.H. Allen & Co., London.

Tennyson, Hallam 1897, *Alfred Lord Tennyson: A memoir by his son,* 2 Volumes, MacMillan & Co., London.

Thackeray, Miss (Annie Thackeray Ritchie) 1875, *Old Kensington,* Smith, Elder & Co., London.

Trollope, Anthony 1876, *Australia and New Zealand*, third edition, Chapman and Hall, London.

Wellesley, Richard 1812, *Letter from the Marquis Wellesley, Governor-General of India, to the Court of Directors of the East India Company, On the Trade of India: Dated Fort William, 30 September, 1800,* Richardson and Budd, London.

Williamson, Thomas 1810, *The East India Vade Mecum: Or, complete guide to gentlemen intending for the civil, military, or naval service of the Hon. East India Company*, 2 Volumes, Black, Parry, and Kingsbury, London.

Wollaston, Rev. John Ramsden, n.d., *Wollaston's Picton Journal (1841–1844), being Volume I of the Journals and Diaries (1841–1856)*, Paterson Brokensha Pty. Ltd., Perth.

Wood, Rev. J.D. 1870, *The Uncivilized Races or Natural History of Man: Being a complete account of the manners and customs, and the physical, social and religious condition and characteristics, of the uncivilized races of men, throughout the entire world*, Volume 2, American Publishing Company, Hartford.

5. Published books

Allen, Charles 2002, *The Search for the Buddha: The men who discovered India's lost religion*, Carrol and Graf, New York.

Allen, Richard B. 1999, *Slaves, Freedmen, and Indentured Laborers in Colonial Mauritius*, Cambridge University Press, Cambridge.

Altman, Jan and Julie Prott 1999, *Out of the Sitting Room: Western Australian women's art, 1829 to 1914*, Press for Success, Fremantle.

Ambirajan, S. 1978, *Classical Political Economy and British Policy in India*, Cambridge University Press, Cambridge.

Anderson, Benedict 1991, *Imagined Communities: Reflections on the Origin and Spread of Nationalism*, revised edition, Verso, London and New York.

Appadurai, Arjun (ed.) 1986, *The Social Life of Things: Commodities in cultural perspective*, Cambridge University Press, New York.

Archer, Mildred 1982, *Thomas and William Prinsep in India*, Spink & Son Ltd., London.

Armitage, David 2000, *The ideological Origins of the British Empire*, Cambridge University Press, Cambridge.

Atkinson, Alan 1997, *The Europeans in Australia: A History*, Volume One: The Beginning, Oxford University Press, Melbourne.

Atkinson, Anne 1988, *Asian Immigration to Western Australia, 1829–1901: The bicentennial dictionary of Western Australians*, Volume 5, University of Western Australia Press, Nedlands.

Attwood, Bain 1989, *The Making of the Aborigines*, Allen & Unwin, Sydney.

Auty, Kate 2005, *Black Glass: Western Australian Courts of Native Affairs, 1936–54*, Fremantle Arts Centre Press, Fremantle.

Aveling, Marian (ed.) 1979, *Westralian Voices: Documents in Western Australian history*, University of Western Australia Press, Nedlands.

Ballantyne, Tony 2002, *Orientalism and Race: Aryanism in the British Empire*, Palgrave, New York.

Ballantyne, Tony 2012, *Webs of Empire: Locating New Zealand's colonial past*, Bridget Williams Books, Wellington.

Ballantyne, Tony and Antoinette Burton (eds) 2005, *Bodies in Contact: Rethinking colonial encounters in world history*, Duke University Press, Durham and London.

Ballhatchet, Kenneth 1980, *Race, Sex and Class under the Raj: Imperial attitudes and policies and their critics, 1793–1905*, Weidenfeld and Nicolson, London.

Banton, Michael 1977, *The Idea of Race*, Tavistock Publications, London.

Barker, Anthony J. and Maxine Laurie 1992, *Excellent Connections: A history of Bunbury, Western Australia, 1836–1990*, City of Bunbury, Bunbury.

Barley, Nigel 2002, *White Rajah: A biography of Sir James Brooke*, Little, Brown, London.

Bar-Yosef, Eitan 2005, *The Holy Land in English Culture, 1799–1917: Palestine and the question of orientalism*, Clarendon Press, Oxford.

Bates, Daisy 1907, *Efforts Made by Western Australia Towards the Betterment of Her Aborigines*, Government Printer, Perth.

Bates, Daisy 1938 (1966), *The Passing of the Aborigines: A lifetime spent among the natives of Australia*, Second Edition, Heinemann, Melbourne.

Bates, Daisy 1985, *The Native Tribes of Western Australia*, edited by Isobel White, National Library of Australia, Canberra.

Battye, J.S. 1924, *Western Australia: A history from its discovery to the inauguration of the Commonwealth*, Clarendon Press, Oxford.

Baucom, Ian 1999, *Out of Place: Englishness, empire and the locations of identity*, Princeton University Press, Princeton.

Bayly, C.A. 1983, *Rulers, Townsmen and Bazaars: North Indian society in the age of British expansionism, 1770–1870*, Cambridge University Press, Cambridge.

Bayly, C.A. 1989, *Imperial Meridian: The British empire and the world, 1780–1830*, Longman, London and New York.

Bayly, C.A. (ed.) 1994, *The Raj: India and the British, 1600–1947*, National Portrait Gallery, London.

Bayly, C.A. 1996, *Empire and Information: Intelligence gathering and social communication in India, 1780–1870*, Cambridge University Press, Cambridge and New York.

Bayly, C.A. 2004, *The Birth of the Modern World, 1780–1914: Global connections and comparisons*, Blackwell Publishers, Malden, Massachusetts.

Bearce, George D. 1961, *British Attitudes Towards India, 1784–1858*, Oxford University Press, London.

Bederman, Gail 1995, *Manliness and Civilization: A cultural history of gender and race in the United States, 1880–1917*, University of Chicago Press, Chicago and London.

Bell, Quentin 1974, *Virginia Woolf: A biography*, Harvest Books, New York.

Berryman, Ian (ed.) 2002, *Swan River Letters,* Swan River Press, Glengarry WA.

Biskup, Peter 1973, *Not Slaves, Not Citizens: The Aboriginal problem in Western Australia, 1898–1954*, University of Queensland Press, St. Lucia.

Blunt, Wilfred 1975, *'England's Michelangelo': A biography of George Frederic Watts OM, RA*, Hamish Hamilton, London.

Boehmer, Elleke (ed.) 1998, *Empire Writing: An anthology of colonial literature, 1870–1918*, Oxford University Press, Oxford.

Bolton, G.C. 1958, *Alexander Forrest: His life and times*, Melbourne University Press, Melbourne.

Bolton, Geoffrey, Richard Rossiter and Jan Ryan (eds) 2003, *Farewell Cinderella: Creating arts and identity in Western Australia*, University of Western Australia Press, Nedlands.

Brantlinger, Patrick 1998, *Rule of Darkness: British literature and imperialism, 1830–1914*, Cornell University Press, New York.

Braudel, Fernand 1980, *On History*, translated by Sarah Matthews, University of Chicago Press, Chicago.

Breckenridge, Carol A. and Peter van de Veer (eds) 1993, *Orientalism and the Postcolonial Predicament: Perspectives on South Asia*, University of Philadelphia Press, Philadelphia.

Briscoe, Gordon and Len Smith 2002, *The Aboriginal Population Revisited: 70,000 years to the present*, Aboriginal History, Canberra.

Broadbent, James, Suzanne Rickard and Margaret Steven 2003, *India, China and Australia: Trade and society, 1788–1850*, Historic Houses Trust, NSW.

Brockman, Joan (ed.) 1987, *He Rode Alone: Being the adventures of pioneer Julius Brockman from his diaries*, Artlook Books, Perth.

Brodie, Fawn M. 1967, *The Devil Drives: A life of Sir Richard Burton*, Eyre and Spotliswoode, London.

Bropho, Robert 1986, *Fringedweller*, Alternative Publishing Co-operative, Chippendale, NSW.

Buckley, C.B. 1965, *An Anecdotal History of Old Times in Singapore 1819–1867*, University of Malaya Press, Kuala Lumpur.

Buchan, Bruce 2008, *Empire of Political Thought: Indigenous Australians and the language of colonial government*, Pickering & Chatto, London.

Buller-Murphy, Deborah 1958, *An Attempt to Eat the Moon: And other stories recounted from the Aborigines*, illustrated by Elizabeth Durack, Georgian House, Melbourne.

Burd, Van Akin (ed.) 1969, *The Winnington Letters: John Ruskin's correspondence with Margaret Alexis Bell and the children at Winnington Hall*, George Allen & Unwin, London.

Burne Jones, Edward 1981, *The Little Holland House Album*, The Dalrymple Press, North Brunswick.

Burton, Antoinette 1998, *At the Heart of the Empire: Indians and the colonial encounter in late-Victorian Britain*, University of California Press, London.

Burton, Antoinette (ed.) 2005, *Archive Stories: Facts, fictions, and the writing of history*, Duke University Press, Durham and London.

Butlin, N.G. 1983, *Our Original Aggression: Aboriginal populations of Southeastern Australia*, George Allen & Unwin, Sydney.

Caine, Barbara 2005, *From Bombay to Bloomsbury: A biography of a family*, Oxford University Press, Oxford.

Cannadine, David 2001, *Ornamentalism: How the British saw their empire*, Penguin Books, London.

Carter, Bevan 2005, *Nyungah Land: Records of the invasion and theft of Aboriginal land on the Swan River, 1829–1850,* Black History Series, Swan Valley Nyungah Community, Perth.

Carter, Jan 1981, *Nothing to Spare: Recollections of Australian pioneering women*, Penguin Books, Ringwood, Victoria.

Carter, Marina 1996, *Voices of the Indenture: Experiences of Indian migrants in the British empire*, Leicester University Press, London and New York.

Carter, Paul 1987, *The Road to Botany Bay: An essay in spatial history*, Faber and Faber Limited, London.

Chand, Tek 1935, *The Law of Legal Practitioners in British India*, Lawyer's Edition, Eastern Law House, Calcutta.

Chaudhuri, K.N. 1971, *The Economic Development of India under the East India Company*, 1814–1858, Cambridge University Press, Cambridge.

Chaudhuri, Sashi Bhusan, 1979, *English Historical Writings on the Indian Mutiny, 1857–1859*, World Press, Calcutta.

Chapman, Barbara 1979, *The Colonial Eye: A topographical and artistic record of the life and landscape of Western Australia, 1798–1914*, Art Gallery of Western Australia, Perth.

Chesterman, John and Brian Galligan 1997, *Citizens Without Rights: Aborigines and Australian citizenship*, Cambridge University Press, Cambridge.

Clarke, Patricia and Dale Spender 1996, *Life Lines: Australian women's letters and diaries, 1788–1840*, Allen & Unwin, NSW.

Clendinnen, Inga 2003, *Dancing with Strangers*, Text Publishing Co., Melbourne.

Cohn, Bernard S. 1987, *An Anthropologist Among the Historians and Other Essays*, Oxford University Press, Delhi.

Cohn, Bernard S. 1996, *Colonialism and its Forms of Knowledge: The British in India*, Princeton University Press, Princeton, N.J.

Cole, Anna, Victoria Haskins and Fiona Paisley 2005, *Uncommon Ground: White Women in Aboriginal History*, Aboriginal Studies Press, Canberra.

Colebatch, Sir H.C. 1929, *Story of a Hundred Years: Western Australia, 1829–1929*, Government Printer, Perth.

Collard, Len 1994, *A Nyungar Interpretation of Ellensbrook and Wonnerup Homesteads*, National Trust of Australia, Western Australia.

Colley, Linda 1992, *Britons: Forging the nation, 1707–1837*, Yale University Press, New Haven.

Conner, Patrick 1984, *The Overland Route of William Prinsep (1794–1874): A pictorial record of his journey across the desert from Koseii to Luxor and down the Nile to Cairo in 1842*, Martyn Gregory Gallery, London.

Coombes, Annie E. (ed.) 2006, *Rethinking Settler Colonialism: History and Memory in Australia, Canada, New Zealand and South Africa*, Manchester University Press, Manchester.

Cox, Julian and Colin Ford 2003, *Julia Margaret Cameron: The Complete Photographs*, Getty Publications, Los Angeles.

Crawford, Patricia and Ian Crawford 2003, *Contested Country: A history of the Northcliffe area, Western Australia*, University of Western Australia Press, Nedlands.

Croft, Brenda L. 2003, *South West Central: Indigenous art from South Western Australia, 1833–2002*, Art Gallery of Western Australia, Perth.

Crowley, F.K. 1970, *Australia's Western Third: A History of Western Australia from first settlements to modern times*, Heinemann, Melbourne.

Crowley, F.K. 2000, *Big John Forrest 1847–1918: A founding father of the Commonwealth of Australia*, University of Western Australia Press, Nedlands.

Curthoys, Ann and Marilyn Lake (eds) 2005, *Connected Worlds: History in transnational perspective*, ANU E Press, Canberra.

Curtin, Philip C. 1971, *Imperialism*, The Macmillan Press, London and Basingstoke.

Dakers, Caroline 1999, *The Holland Park Circle: Artists and Victorian society*, Yale University Press, London.

Dalrymple, William 2002, *White Mughals: Love and betrayal in Eighteenth-Century India*, Flamingo, London.

Dalrymple, William 2013, *Return of a King: The battle for Afghanistan, 1839–1842*, Bloomsbury, London

Dalrymple, William (ed.) 2002, *Begums, Thugs and Englishmen: The journals of Fanny Parkes*, Penguin Books, India.

Dalziell, Rosamund (ed.) 2002, *Selves Crossing Cultures: Autobiography and globalisation*, Australian Scholarly Publishing, Melbourne.

Daniels, Kay and Mary Murnane (eds) 1980, *Uphill all the Way: A documentary history of women in Australia*, University of Queensland Press, St Lucia.

Daunton, Martin and Rick Halpern (eds) 1999, *Empire and Others: British encounters with indigenous peoples, 1600–1850*, UCL Press, London.

Davidoff, Lenore and Catherine Hall 1987, *Family Fortunes: Men and women of the English middle class, 1780–1850*, Hutchinson Education, London.

Deacon, Desley, Penny Russell and Angela Woollacott (eds) 2010, *Transnational Lives: Biographies of global modernity, 1700–present*, Palgrave Macmillan, Basingstoke and New York.

Deane, Phyllis 1978, *The Evolution of Economic Ideas*, Cambridge University Press, Cambridge.

Dirks, Nicholas B. 2006, *The Scandal of Empire: India and the creation of Imperial Britain*, Belknap Press of Harvard University Press, Cambridge, Mass.

Donaldson, Ian and Tamsin (eds) 1985, *Seeing the First Australians*, George Allen & Unwin, Sydney.

Drew, John 1987, *India and the Romantic Imagination*, Oxford University Press, Delhi.

Dunbar, Janet 1953, *Golden Interlude: The Edens in India, 1836–1842*, John Murray, London.

Dunbar, Janet (ed.) 1988, *Tigers, Durbars and Kings: Fanny Eden's Indian journals, 1837–1838*, John Murray, London.

Dutta, Abhijit 1994, *European Social Life in Nineteenth Century Calcutta*, Minerva India, Calcutta.

Eakin, Morgan (ed.) 2003, *Very Much on Watch: The Percy Willmott photos; Augusta - Margaret River – Busselton, 1901–1919*, Blackwood Publishing, Thornlie, Western Australia.

Eddy, J.J. 1969, *Britain and the Australian Colonies 1818–1831: The technique of government*, Clarendon, Oxford.

Eddy, Spencer L. 1970, *The Founding of The Cornhill Magazine*, Ball State University, Indiana.

Edwardes, Michael 1969, *Bound to Exile: The Victorians in India*, Sidgwick & Jackson, London.

Elbourne, Elizabeth 2002, *Blood Ground: Colonialism, missions, and the contest for Christianity in the Cape Colony and Britain, 1799–1853*, McGill-Queen's University Press, Montreal.

Elder, Bruce 1988, *Blood on the Wattle: Massacres and maltreatments of Australian Aborigines since 1788*, Child & Associates, French's Forest, NSW.

Evans, Julie 2005, *Edward Eyre: Race and colonial governance*, University of Otago Press, Dunedin.

Evans, Raymond, Kay Saunders and Kathryn Cronin 1975, *Race Relations in Colonial Queensland: A history of exclusion, exploitation and extermination*, University of Queensland Press, St. Lucia.

Fay, Eliza 1986, *Original Letters from India (1779–1815)*, The Hogarth Press, London.

Fenton, Elizabeth 1901, *The Journal of Mrs. Fenton: A narrative of her life in India, the Isle of France (Mauritius), and Tasmania during the years 1826–1830*, Edward Arnold, London.

Ford, Colin 2003, *Julia Margaret Cameron: A critical biography*, J. Paul Getty Museum, Los Angeles.

Foster, Stephen 2010, *A Private Empire*, Murdoch Books, Miller's Point, NSW.

Fuller, Hester Thackeray 1933, *Three Freshwater Friends: Tennyson, Watts and Mrs. Cameron*, The Country Press, Newport, Isle of Wight.

Fullerton, Patricia 2002, *The Flower Hunter: Ellis Rowan*, National Library of Australia, Canberra.

Ganter, Regina and Julia Martinez 2006, *Mixed Relations: Asian–Aboriginal Contact in North Australia*, University of Western Australia Press, Nedlands.

Genovese, Eugene D. 1972, *Roll, Jordan, Roll: The world the slaves made*, Pantheon Books, New York.

Ghosh, Durba 2006, *Sex and the Family in Colonial India: The making of empire*, Cambridge University Press, Cambridge.

Ghosh, Durba and Dane Kennedy 2006, *Decentring Empire: Britain, India and the transcolonial world*, Orient Longman, Hyderabad.

Gikandi, Simon 1996, *Maps of Englishness: Writing identity in the culture of colonialism*, Columbia University Press, New York.

Goodall, Heather 1996, *From Invasion to Embassy: Land in Aboriginal politics in New South Wales, 1770–1972*, Allen & Unwin, St. Leonards, NSW.

Gooding, Janda 1984, *Margaret Forrest: Wildflowers of Western Australia*, Art Gallery of Western Australia, Perth.

Gooding, Janda 1987, *Western Australian Art and Artists, 1900–1950*, Art Gallery of Western Australia, Perth.

Gould, Veronica Franklin 2004, *G.F. Watts: The last great Victorian*, Yale University Press, New Haven and London.

Grant Watson, E.L. 1968, *Journey Under Southern Stars*, Abelard-Schuman, London and New York.

Gray, Anne 2011, *Out of the West: Western Australian Art, 1830s to 1930s*, National Gallery of Australia, Canberra.

Green, Neville 1984, *Broken Spears: Aborigines and Europeans in the southwest of Australia*, Focus Education Services, Perth.

Green, Neville 1995, *The Forrest River Massacres*, Fremantle Arts Centre Press, Fremantle.

Green, Neville and Susan Moon 1997, *Far from Home: Aboriginal Prisoners of Rottnest Island*, University of Western Australia Press, Nedlands.

Gribble, J.B. 1987, *Dark Deeds in a Sunny Land: Or, blacks and whites in North-West Australia*, University of Western Australia Press, Nedlands.

Griffiths, Tom 1996, *Hunters and Collectors: The antiquarian imagination in Australia*, Cambridge University Press, Melbourne.

Haebich, Anna 1988, *For Their Own Good: Aborigines and government in the Southwest of Western Australia, 1900–1940*, University of Western Australia Press, Nedlands.

Haebich, Anna 2000, *Broken Circles: Fragmenting Indigenous families, 1800–2000*, Fremantle Arts Centre Press, Fremantle.

Hall, Catherine 1992, *White, Male and Middle-Class: Explorations in feminism and gender history*, Polity, Cambridge.

Hall, Catherine 2002, *Civilising Subjects: Metropole and colony in the English imagination, 1830–1867*, Polity, Cambridge.

Hall, Catherine and Sonya O. Rose 2006, *At Home with the Empire: Metropolitan culture and the imperial world*, Cambridge University Press, Cambridge and New York.

Hallam, Sylvia 1979, *Fire and Hearth: A study of Aboriginal usage and European usurpation in south-western Australia*, Australian Institute of Aboriginal Studies, Canberra.

Hallam, Sylvia and Lois Tilbrook 1987, *Aborigines of the South West Region, 1829–1840*, Volume 8: Bicentennial Dictionary of Western Australians, 1829–1888, University of Western Australia Press, Nedlands.

Hammond, J.E. 1933, *Winjan's People: The story of the South West Australian Aborigines*, Imperial Printing Company Limited, Perth.

Hammond, J.E. 1980, *Western Pioneers: The battle well fought*, facsimile edition, Press, Perth.

Harlow, Barbara and Mia Carter 1999, *Imperialism and Orientalism: A documentary sourcebook*, Blackwell, Malden, Massachussets.

Hasluck, Alexandra 1955, *Portrait with Background: A life of Georgiana Molloy*, Oxford University Press, Melbourne.

Hasluck, Paul 1970, *Black Australians: A survey of native policy in Western Australia, 1829–1897*, Melbourne University Press, Melbourne.

Hill, Brian 1973, *Julia Margaret Cameron: A Victorian family portrait*, Peter Owen, London.

Hillman, Alfred James 1990, *The Hillman Diaries, 1877–1884*, F.J.B. Hillman, Perth.

Hinton, Brian 2001, *Immortal Faces: Julia Margaret Cameron on the Isle of Wight*, Isle of Wight County Press, Newport.

Hinton, Brian (ed.) 2003, *Illustrations by Julia Margaret Cameron of Alfred Lord Tennyson's Idylls of the King and Other Poems*, Julia Margaret Cameron Trust, Freshwater Bay, Isle of Wight.

Hodgson, Marshall G.S. 1961, *The Venture of Islam: Conscience and history in a world civilization*, Volume 1: The Classical Age of Islam, The University of Chicago Press, Chicago.

Huttenback, Robert A. 1976, *Racism and Empire: White settlers and colored immigrants in the British self-governing colonies 1830–1910*, Cornell University Press, Ithaca and London.

Inden, Ronald, B. 2000, *Imagining India*, second edition, Hurst and Company, London.

Ingram, Edward (ed.) 1970, *Two Views of British India: The private correspondence of Mr Dundas and Lord Wellesley, 1798–1801*, Adams and Dart, Bath.

Irish University Press 1974, *Index to British Parliamentary Papers on Australia and New Zealand 1800–1899*, Irish University Press, Dublin.

Islam, Sirajul 1979, *The Permanent Settlement in Bengal: A study of its operation, 1790–1819*, Bangla Academy, Dacca.

Jacobs, Pat 1990, *Mister Neville: A biography*, Fremantle Arts Centre Press, Fremantle.

Jebb, Mary Anne 2002, *Blood, Sweat and Welfare: A history of white bosses and Aboriginal pastoral workers*, University of Western Australia Press, Nedlands.

Johnston, Judith and Monica Anderson 2005, *Australia Imagined: Views from the British periodical press, 1800–1900*, University of Western Australia Press, Nedlands.

Kejariwal, O.P. 1988, *The Asiatic Society of Bengal and the Discovery of India's Past*, Oxford University Press, New Delhi.

Kidd, Rosalind 1997, *The Way We Civilise: Aboriginal affairs — the untold story*, University of Queensland Press, St. Lucia.

Kinnane, Stephen 2003, *Shadow Lines*, Fremantle Arts Centre Press, Fremantle.

Kingston, Beverley 1977, *The World Moves Slowly: A documentary history of Australian women*, Cassell Australia, NSW.

Kling, Blair B. 1976, *Partner in Empire: Dwarkanath Tagore and the age of enterprise in Eastern India*, University of California Press, London.

Kopf, David 1969, *British Orientalism and the Bengal Renaissance: The dynamics of Indian modernization, 1773–1835*, Firma K.L. Mukhopadhyay, Calcutta.

Laidlaw, Zoë 2005, *Colonial Connections 1815–45: Patronage, the information revolution and colonial government*, Manchester University Press, Manchester and New York.

Lambert, David and Alan Lester (eds) 2006, *Colonial Lives Across the British Empire: Imperial careering in the long Nineteenth Century*, Cambridge University Press, Cambridge.

Lines, William J. 1994, *An All Consuming Passion: Origins, Modernity, and the Australian Life of Georgiana Molloy*, Allen & Unwin, Sydney.

Lorimer, Douglas A. 1978, *Colour, Class and the Victorians: English attitudes to the negro in the Mid-Nineteenth Century*, Leicester University Press, Leicester.

Lowe, Lisa 1991, *Critical Terrains: French and British orientalisms*, Cornell University Press, Ithaca.

Macintyre, Stuart 1991, *A Colonial Liberalism: The lost world of three Victorian visionaries*, Oxford University Press, Melbourne.

Mackay, Carol Hanbery 2001, *Creative Negativity: Four Victorian exemplars of the female quest*, Stanford University Press, Stanford.

Marchant, Leslie R. 1981, *Aboriginal Administration in Western Australia, 1886–1905*, Australian Institute of Aboriginal Studies, Canberra.

Marriott, John and Bhaskar Mukhopadhyay (eds) 2006, *Britain in India, 1765–1905*, Volume 3: Education and Colonial Knowledge, Pickering and Chatto, London.

Matsuda, Matt K. 2012, *Pacific Worlds: A history of seas, peoples and cultures*, Cambridge University Press, Cambridge and New York.

McGregor, R. 1997, *Imagined Destinies: Aboriginal Australians and the doomed race theory, 1880–1939*, Melbourne University Press, Melbourne.

McKenzie, Kirsten 2004, *Scandal in the Colonies: Sydney and Cape Town, 1820–1850*, Melbourne University Press, Melbourne.

Memmi, Albert 1965, *The Colonizer and the Colonized*, Beacon Press, Boston.

Metcalf, Thomas R. 1994, *Ideologies of the Raj*, Cambridge University Press, Cambridge.

Metcalf, Thomas R. 2007, *Imperial Connections: India in the Indian Ocean arena, 1860–1920*, University of California Press, Berkeley.

Mill, John Stuart 1912, *On Liberty; Representative Government; The Subjection of Women: Three essays*, Oxford University Press, London.

Mill, John Stuart 1924, *Autobiography*, Oxford University Press, London.

Moore, George Fletcher 2006, *The Millendon Memoirs: George Fletcher Moore's Journal and Letters, 1830–1841*, edited by J.M.R. Cameron, Hesperian Press, Victoria Park WA.

Morphy, Howard 1998, *Aboriginal Art*, Phaidon Press, London and New York.

Moses, A. Dirk (ed.) 2004, *Genocide and Settler Society: Frontier violence and stolen indigenous children in Australian history*, Berghahn Books, New York and Oxford.

Muthu, Sankar 2003, *Enlightenment Against Empire*, Princeton University Press, Princeton, New Jersey.

Nair, D. Thankappan (ed.) 1983, *British Social Life in Ancient Calcutta (1750–1850)*, Sanskrit Pustak Bhandar, Calcutta.

Naish, Nora 2005, *Passage from the Raj: Story of a family, 1770–1939*, Champak Press, Bristol.

Nannup, Alice, Lauren Marsh and Stephen Kinnane 1992, *When the Pelican Laughed*, Fremantle Arts Centre Press, Fremantle.

Nechtman, Tillman 2010, *Nabobs: Empire and identity in Eighteenth Century Britain*, Cambridge University Press, Cambridge.

Ogborn, Miles 2008, *Global Lives: Britain and the empire, 1550–1800*, Cambridge University Press, Cambridge and New York.

Olsen, V.C. 2003, *From Life: Julia Margaret Cameron and Victorian photography*, Palgrave MacMillan, New York.

Pagden, Anthony 1995, *Lords of All the World: Ideologies of empire in Spain, Britain and France c.1500–c.1850*, Yale University Press, New Haven.

Pearson, Michael 2003, *The Indian Ocean*, Routledge, London.

Pemble, John (ed.) 1985, *Miss Fane in India*, Allan Sutton Publishing, Gloucester.

Pilkington, Doris 1996, *Follow the Rabbit-Proof Fence*, University of Queensland Press, St. Lucia.

Pitts, Jennifer 2005, *A Turn to Empire: The rise of imperial liberalism in Britain and France*, Princeton University Press, Princeton, New Jersey.

Poovey, Mary 1995, *Making a Social Body: British cultural formation, 1830–1864*, University of Chicago Press, Chicago and London.

Porter, Andrew (ed.) 1999, *The Oxford History of the British Empire*, Volume 3: The Nineteenth Century, Oxford University Press, Oxford.

Porter, Bernard 1983, *Britain, Empire and the World, 1850–1982: Delusions of grandeur*, George Allen & Unwin, London.

Porter, Frances and Charlotte Macdonald (eds) 1996, *'My Hand Will Write What My Heart Dictates': The unsettled lives of women in Nineteenth Century New Zealand as revealed to family and friends*, Auckland University Press, Auckland.

Pratt, Mary Louise 1992, *Imperial Eyes: Travel writing and transculturation*, Routledge, New York.

Read, Peter 1998, *The Stolen Generations: The removal of Aboriginal children in New South Wales, 1883–1969*, NSW Department of Aboriginal Affairs, Sydney.

Read, Peter 1999, *A Rape of the Soul So Profound: The return of the Stolen Generations*, Allen & Unwin, St Leonards, NSW.

Reece, R.H.W. 1974, *Aborigines and Colonists: Aborigines and colonial society in New South Wales in the 1830s and 1840s*, Sydney University Press, Sydney.

Reece, Bob 2007, *Daisy Bates: Grand dame of the desert*, National Library of Australia, Canberra.

Reynolds, Henry 1972, *Aborigines and Settlers: The Australian Experience, 1788–1939*, Cassell Australian, North Melbourne, Victoria.

Reynolds, Henry 1987, *Frontier: Aborigines, settlers and land*, Allen & Unwin, Sydney.

Reynolds, Henry 1987, *The Law of the Land*, Penguin Books Australia, Ringwood, Victoria.

Reynolds, Henry 1998, *This Whispering in our Hearts*, Allen & Unwin, St. Leonards, Australia.

Richards, J.F. 1993, *The Mughal Empire*, Cambridge University Press, New York.

Ritchie, Gerald 1920, *The Ritchies in India: Extracts from the correspondence of William Ritchie, 1817–1862; And personal reminiscences of Gerald Ritchie*, John Murray, London.

Robb, Peter 2011, *Sex and Sensibility: The diaries of Richard Blechynden, 1759–1822*, Oxford University Press, New Delhi.

Rothschild, Emma 2011, *The Inner Life of Empires: An Eighteenth Century history*, Princeton University Press, Princeton, New Jersey.

Rousseau, G.S. and Roy Porter (eds) 1990, *Exoticism in the Enlightenment*, Manchester University Press, Manchester and New York.

Rowan, Ellis 1991, *The Flower Hunter: The adventures in Northern Australia and New Zealand of flower painter Ellis Rowan*, Angus & Robertson/Harper Collins, Sydney.

Rowley, C.D. 1970, *The Destruction of Aboriginal Society: Aboriginal policy and practice*, Volume 1, Australian National University Press, Canberra.

Rowse, Tim 1998, *White Flour, White Power: From rations to citizenship in Central Australia*, Cambridge University Press, Cambridge.

Runciman, Steven 1960, *The White Rajahs*, Cambridge University Press, Cambridge.

Said, Edward 1993, *Culture and Imperialism*, Vintage, London.

Said, Edward 2003, *Orientalism*, Penguin Books, London.

Saunders, Kay (ed.) 1984, *Indentured Labour in the British Empire*, Croon Helm, London and Canberra.

Sayers, Andrew 1994, *Aboriginal Artists of the Nineteenth Century*, Oxford University Press Australia, Melbourne.

Scott, Kim 1999, *Benang: From the heart*, Fremantle Arts Centre Press, Fremantle.

Scott, Kim and Hazel Brown 2005, *Kayang and Me*, Fremantle Arts Centre Press, Fremantle.

Shann, E.O.G. 1926, *Cattle Chosen: The story of the first group settlement in Western Australia, 1829–1841*, Oxford University Press, London.

Sinha, Mrinalini 1995, *Colonial Masculinity: The 'manly Englishman' and the 'effeminate Bengali' in the late Nineteenth Century*, Manchester University Press, New York.

Spillman, Ken 1993, *A Rich Endowment: Government and mining in Western Australia, 1829–1994*, University of Western Australia Press, Nedlands.

Standish, Ann 2008, *Australia Through Womens's Eyes*, Australian Scholarly Publishing, Melbourne.

Stannage, C.T. 1979, *The People of Perth: A social history of Western Australia's capital city*, City of Perth, Perth.

Stannage, C.T. (ed.) 1981, *A New History of Western Australia*, University of Western Australia Press, Nedlands.

Staples, A.C. 1979, *They Made Their Destiny: History of settlement of the Shire of Harvey, 1829–1929*, Shire of Harvey, Bunbury.

Statham-Drew, Pamela 2003, *James Stirling: Admiral and founding Governor of Western Australia*, University of Western Australia Press, Nedlands.

Stocking, George W. (Jr.) 1987, *Victorian Anthropology*, The Free Press, New York.

Stokes, Eric 1959, *The English Utilitarians and India*, Oxford University Press, London.

Strath, Bo (ed.) 2000, *Europe and the Other and Europe as the Other*, Peter Lang, Brussels.

Strong, Rowan 2007, *Anglicanism and the British Empire, c.1700–1850*, Oxford University Press, Oxford.

Suleri, Sara 1992, *The Rhetoric of English India*, Chicago University Press, Chicago and London.

Sykes, Laura (ed.) 1992, *Calcutta Through British Eyes, 1690–1990*, Oxford University Press, Oxford.

Teale, Ruth (ed.) 1978, *Colonial Eve: Sources on women in Australia, 1788–1914*, Oxford University Press, Melbourne.

Teelock, Vijaya 1995, *A Select Guide to Sources on Slavery in Mauritius and Slaves Speak Out: The testimony of slaves in the era of sugar*, African Cultural Centre, Mauritius.

Teltscher, Kate 1995, *India Inscribed: European and British writing on India 1600–1800*, Oxford University Press, Delhi.

Tennyson, Charles 1950, *Alfred Tennyson*, Macmillan & Co., London.

Thackeray, William Makepeace 1945–46, *The Letters and Private Papers of William Makepeace Thackeray*, 4 Volumes, collected and edited by Gordon N. Ray, Harvard University Press, Cambridge, Massachusetts.

Thackeray, William Makepeace 1963, *Vanity Fair: A novel without a hero*, Methuen, London.

Thackeray, William Makepeace 1996, *The Newcomes: Memoirs of a most respectable family*, Penguin Classics, London.

Thackeray, William Makepeace 1999, *The Tremendous Adventures of Major Gahagan*, viewed online at http://www.gutenberg.org/dirs/etext99/majgh10.txt.

Thieberger, Nicholas 1993, *Handbook of Aboriginal Languages South of the Kimberley Region*, Department of Linguistics, Research School of Pacific Studies, The Australian National University, Canberra.

Thomas, Nicholas 1994, *Colonialism's Culture: Anthropology, travel and government*, Princeton University Press, Princeton, New Jersey.

Thomas, Nicholas 1999, *Possessions: Indigenous art/colonial culture*, Thames and Hudson, London.

Thompson, E.P. 1977, *The Making of the English Working Class*, Penguin Books, Harmondsworth, Middlesex.

Thorne, R.G. 1986, *The House of Commons, 1790–1820*, Secker and Warburg, London.

Tilbrook, Lois 1983, *Nyungar Tradition: Glimpses of Aborigines in South-Western Australia 1829–1914*, University of Western Australia Press, Nedlands.

Tillotson, Giles 2000, *The Artificial Empire: The Indian landscapes of William Hodges*, Curzon Press, Richmond, Surrey.

Trevelyan, Raleigh 1987, *The Golden Oriole*, Touchstone, New York.

'Truthful Thomas' 1905, *Through the Spy-Glass: Short sketches of well-known Westralians as others see them*, Praagh & Lloyd, Perth.

Van Krieken, Robert 1991, *Children and the State: Social control and the formation of Australian child welfare*, Allen & Unwin, Sydney.

Vaughan, Megan 2005, *Creating the Creole Island: Slavery in Eighteenth Century Mauritius*, Duke University Press, Durham and London.

Viswanathan, Gauri 1989, *Masks of Conquest: Literary study and British rule in India*, Columbia University Press, New York.

Watts, M.S. 1912, *George Frederick Watts*, Volume 1: The annals of an artist's life, Macmillan and Co., London.

Webster, Anthony 2007, *The Richest East India Merchant: The life and business of John Palmer of Calcutta 1767–1836*, The Boydell Press, Woodbridge.

West, Shearer (ed.) 1996, *The Victorians and Race*, Scholar Press, Aldershot, Hants.

Wilson, Kathleen 2002, *The Island Race: Englishness, empire and gender in the Eighteenth Century*, Routledge, New York.

Wise, Dorothy (ed.) 1998, *Diary of William Tayler: Footman 1837*, The St. Marylebone Society, London.

Wolf, Eric R. 1982, *Europe and the People Without History*, University of California Press, London.

Woolf, Virginia 1976, *Freshwater: A comedy in three acts*, Harcourt, Brace, Javonovich.

Woolf, Virginia 1985, *The Diary of Virginia Woolf*, edited by Anne Oliver Bell, 5 Volumes, Penguin Books, Harmondsworth.

Woolf, Virginia 1978, *Moments of Being*, Triad, St. Albans, Herts.

Young, Robert 1990, *White Mythologies: Writing history and the west*, Routledge, London.

Zastoupil, Lynn and Martin Moir (eds) 1999, *The Great Indian Education Debate: Documents relating to the orientalist–Anglicist controversy, 1781–1843*, Curzon Press, Richmond, Surrey.

6. Journal and periodical articles, chapters from anthologies and conference papers

Alexander, Sally and Alun Howkins 2011, 'Digital sources, access and "History of a Nation"?', in *History Workshop Journal,* Issue 71, pp.1–4.

Allbrook, Malcolm 2008, 'George Coolbul: Imagining a colonised life', in *Aboriginal History,* Volume 32, pp.49–62.

Allbrook, Malcolm 2012, 'A Triple Empire … United Under One Dominion: Charles Prinsep's schemes for exporting Indian labour to Australia', in *South Asia: Journal of South Asian Studies,* Volume 35, Issue 3, DOI:10.1080/00856 401.2011.649676.

Anderson, Clare 2001, 'Multiple Border Crossings: "Convicts and Other Persons Escaped from Botany Bay and residing in Calcutta"', in *Journal of Australian Colonial History,* Volume 3, No. 2, pp.1–22.

Appleyard, R.T. 1981, 'Western Australia: Economic and demographic growth, 1850–1914', in C.T. Stannage (ed.), *A New History of Western Australia*, University of Western Australia Press, Nedlands, pp.211–36.

Armitage, David 2012, 'What's the Big Idea?: Intellectual history and the longue durée', in *History of European Ideas*, Volume 38, Issue 4, DOI:10.1080/01916 599.2012.714635.

Axel, Brian Keith 2002, 'Colonialism and Its Doubles', in *Current Anthropology,* Volume 43, No. 1, pp.197–200.

Ballantyne, Tony 2002, 'Introduction: Debating empire', in *Journal of Colonialism and Colonial History,* Volume 3, No. 1.

Bates, Daisy 1923, 'The Adventures of Ngilgian', in *Australia,* November.

Bayly, C.A. 1999, 'The British and Indigenous Peoples, 1860–1860: Power, perception and identity', in Martin Daunton and Rick Halpern (eds), *Empire and Others: British encounters with indigenous peoples, 1600–1850*, UCL Press, London, pp.19–41.

Beaumont, John 2002, 'Charles Hay Cameron (1795–1880): Benthamite Jurist', Cameron Research Paper, Dimbola, Freshwater, Isle of Wight.

Beaumont, John 2004, 'Thackeray in Pattledom', Cameron Research Paper, Dimbola, Freshwater, Isle of Wight.

Bell, Duncan 2006, 'Empire and International Relations in Victorian Political Thought', in *The Historical Journal*, Volume 49, Issue 1, pp.281–98.

Birman, Wendy 1972, 'Hensman, Alfred Peach (1834–1902)', in *Australian Dictionary of Biography*, Volume 4, Melbourne University Press, Melbourne, pp.380–81.

Blackburn, Kevin 2002, 'Mapping Aboriginal Nations: The 'nation' concept of late Nineteenth Century anthropologists in Australia', in *Aboriginal History*, Volume 26, Australian Institute of Aboriginal and Torres Strait Islander Studies, Canberra, pp.130–58.

Bolton, G.C. 1981, 'Black and White after 1897', in C.T. Stannage (ed.) *A New History of Western Australia*, University of Western Australia Press, Nedlands, pp.124–178.

Bolton, G.C. 1988, 'Tommy Dower and the Perth Newspapers', in *Aboriginal History*, Volume 12, Australian Institute of Aboriginal Studies, Canberra, pp.79–83.

Bowen, H.V. 2004, 'Clive, Robert, First Baron Clive of Plassey (1725–1774)', in H.C.G. Matthew and Brian Harrison (eds), *Oxford Dictionary of National Biography*, Oxford University Press, Oxford.

Braybrooke, E.K. 1974, 'Sir Alexander Campbell Onslow, 1842–1908', in *Australian Dictionary of Biography*, Volume 5, Melbourne University Press, Melbourne.

Brennan, Tim 1992, 'Places of Mind, Occupied Lands: Edward Said and philology', in Michael Spinker, *Edward Said: A critical reader*, Basil Blackwell, Oxford.

Buchan, Bruce 2005, 'The Empire of Political Thought: Civilization, savagery and perceptions of indigenous government', in *History of Human Sciences*, Volume 18, No. 2, pp.1–22.

Buchan, Bruce 2006, 'The Moral Geography of Empire: Images of Asia in European enlightenment political thought, c.1600–1800', paper presented at 'Western Political Thought in Dialogue with Asia Conference', Dunedin, New Zealand, 13–15 December.

Buchan, Bruce 2007, 'Europe's Asia': Empire, difference and the moral Geography of European political thought, c 1500 – 1800', paper presented at 'Australasian Political Studies Association Conference', Monash University, 24–26 September.

Burton, Antoinette 2002, 'Déjà Vu All Over Again', in *Journal of Colonialism and Colonial History,* Volume 3, No. 1.

Callaway, Anita 2002, 'Balancing the Books: Indigenous autobiography and ledger-book art', in Rosamund Dalziell (ed.), *Selves Crossing Cultures: Autobiography and globalisation,* Australian Scholarly Publishing, Melbourne.

Carmody, Freda Vines 1966, 'John Garrett Bussell', in *Australian Dictionary of Biography',* Volume 1, Melbourne University Press, Melbourne.

Conner, Patrick 1990, 'In Pursuit of Chinnery', in *Apollo,* Volume 132, No. 345, pp.312–16.

Coyne, Cynthia, 2005, 'Bye and Bye When all the Natives Have Gone', in Anna Cole, Victoria Haskins and Fiona Paisley, *Uncommon Ground: White women in Aboriginal history,* Aboriginal Studies Press, Canberra, pp.199–213.

Charles, Geraldine 2006, 'The Children of John Company: The Anglo-Indians', in *Journal of the Families in British East India,* No. 15.

Crowley, F.K. 1972, 'Sir Malcolm Fraser, 1834–1900', in *Australian Dictionary of Biography,* Volume 4, Melbourne University Press, Melbourne.

De Garis, B.K. 1981, 'Political Tutelage 1829–1870', in C.T. Stannage (ed.), *A New History of Western Australia,* University of Western Australia Press, Nedlands, pp.297–325.

De Garis, B.K. 1981, 'Self-Government and the Evolution of Party Politics 1871–1911', in C.T. Stannage (ed.), *A New History of Western Australia*, University of Western Australia Press, Nedlands, pp.326–51.

De Garis, B.K. and Tom Stannage 1979, 'Burt, Septimus (1847–1919)', in *Australian Dictionary of Biography*, Volume 7, Melbourne University Press, Melbourne, pp.494–6.

Dubois, Thomas David 2005, 'Hegemony, Imperialism, and the Construction of Religion in East and Southeast Asia', in *History and Theory*, Theme Issue 44, pp.113–31.

Edwards, Penny 2003, 'On Home Ground: Settling Land and Domesticating Difference in the 'Non-Settler' Colonies of Burma and Cambodia', in *Journal of Colonialism and Colonial History*, Volume 4, No. 3.

Eley, Geoff 2002, 'Beneath the Skin: Or, how to forget about the empire without really trying', in *Journal of Colonialism and Colonial History*, Volume 3, No. 1.

Esplin, Bruce W. 2005, 'The Joy of Fish to Swim Freely: Pearl Buck, social activism and the orientalist imagination', in *Graduate Journal of Asia-Pacific Studies*, Volume 3, No. 1, pp.12–23.

Fall, V.G. 1972, 'Cargoes of Jarrah', in *Early Days: Journal of the Royal Western Australian Historical Society*, Volume 3, Part 4, pp.37–65.

Fitzpatrick, Kathleen 1969, 'Burke, Robert O'Hara (1821–1861)', *Australian Dictionary of Biography*, Volume 3, Melbourne University Press, Melbourne, pp. 301–3.

Fletcher, Christine 1984, 'The Battle for Pinjarra: A revisionist view', in Bob Reece and Tom Stannage (eds.), *Studies in Western Australian History*, Issue 8: European–Aboriginal Relations in Western Australian History, University of Western Australia Press, Nedlands, pp.1–6.

Frappell, Ruth 2002, 'Imperial Fervour and Anglican Loyalty, 1901–1929', in Bruce Kaye (ed.), *Anglicanism in Australia: A history*, Melbourne University Press, Melbourne, pp.76–99.

Goddard, Elizabeth and Tom Stannage 1984, 'John Forrest and the Aborigines', in Bob Reece, Bob and Tom Stannage (eds), *Studies in Western Australian History*, Issue 8: European–Aboriginal Relations in Western Australian History, University of Western Australia Press, Nedlands, Nedlands, pp.52–8.

Goodall, Heather 1999, 'Authority Under Challenge: Pikampul land and Queen Victoria's law during the British invasion of Australia', in Martin Daunton and Rick Halpern (eds), *Empire and Others: British encounters with indigenous peoples, 1600–1850*, UCL Press, London, pp 260–79.

Goodall, Heather, 2008, 'Landscapes of Meaning: Views from within the Indian archipelago', in *Transforming Cultures eJournal*, Volume 3, No. 1, viewed online at http://epress.lib.uts.edu.au/journals/index.php/TfC/article/view/698/637.

Goodall, Heather, Devleena Ghosh and Lindi Renier Todd 2008, 'Jumping Ship: Indians, Aborigines and Australians across the Indian Ocean', in *Transforming Cultures e-journal*, Volume 3, No. 1, viewed online at http://epress.lib.uts.edu.au/journals/index.php/TfC/article/view/674

Gooding, Janda 2005, 'Henry Prinsep, 1844–1922', in *Acquisitions and Discourse*, Friends of the WA Art Gallery, Perth.

Green, Neville 1981, 'Aborigines and White Settlers in the Nineteenth Century', in C.T. Stannage (ed.), *A New History of Western Australia*, University of Western Australia Press, Nedlands, pp.72–123.

Guterl, Matthew Pratt 2013, 'AHR Forum, Comment: The futures of transnational history', in *American Historical Review*, February, pp.130–9.

Hale, Mathew Blagden, 1882, 'The Responsibility of the Church of England as Regards the Aborigines of Australia, the Chinese, and the Polynesians', in *Supplement to the Church of England Messenger and Ecclesiastical Gazette for the Dioceses of Melbourne and Ballarat*, 23 December 1883, pp.20–1.

Hall, Catherine 1999, 'William Knibb and the Constitution of the New Black Subject', in Martin Daunton and Rick Halpern (eds), *Empire and Others: British encounters with indigenous peoples, 1600–1850*, UCL Press, London, pp.303–24.

Hall, Catherine 2005, 'Writing Histories of Difference: New histories of nation and empire', The Allan Martin Lecture, Research School of Social Sciences, The Australian National University, Canberra.

Harris, Abram L. 1964, 'John Stuart Mill: Servant of the East India Company', in *The Canadian Journal of Economics and Political Science/ Revue Canadienne d'Economique et de Science Politique*, Volume 30, No. 2, pp.185–202.

Harris, John 2002, 'Anglicanism and Indigenous Peoples', in Bruce Kaye (ed.), *Anglicanism in Australia: A history*, Melbourne University Press, Melbourne, pp.223–246.

Hasluck, Paul 1977, 'The Early Years of John Forrest', in *Early Days Journal of the Royal Western Australian Historical Society*, Volume 8, Part 1, pp.91–108.

Hawkins, Angus 1984, 'British Parliamentary Alignment and the Indian Issue, 1857–1858', in *The Journal of British Studies*, Volume 23, No. 2, pp.79–105.

Hawley, Jennifer 1987, 'The Prinsep Collection', in Carter's Price Guide to Antiques in Australia, Australian Antique Trader Publication, Mosman.

Haynes, Mark 1974, 'Parry, Henry Hutton (1826–1893)', in *Australian Dictionary of Biography*, Volume 5, Melbourne University Press, Melbourne, pp.407–8.

Heehs, Peter 2003, 'Shades of Orientalism: Paradoxes and problems in Indian historiography', in *History and Theory*, Volume 42, pp.169–95.

Heppingstone, Ian D. 1964, 'The Story of Alfred and Ellen Bussell: Pioneers of the Margaret River', in *Journal and Proceedings of the Royal West Australian Historical Society,* Volume 6, Part 3.

Heppingstone, Ian D. and H. Margaret Wilson 1973, 'Mrs. John: the Letters of Charlotte Bussell of Cattle Chosen', in *Early Days Journal of the Royal Western Australian Historical Society,* Part 1, Volume 3, Part 4, pp.7–28; Part 2, Volume 7, Part 5, pp.41–77.

Honniball, J.H.M. 1969, 'Sir Fredrick Palgrave Barlee, 1827–1884', in *Australian Dictionary of Biography,* Volume 3, Melbourne University Press, Melbourne.

Hunt, Su-Jane 1984, 'The Gribble Affair: A Study in Colonial Politics', in Bob Reece and Tom Stannage (eds.), *Studies in Western Australian History,* Issue 8: European–Aboriginal Relations in Western Australian History, University of Western Australia Press, Nedlands, pp.42–51.

Jayasuriya, Laksiri 2001, 'The Evolution of Social Policy in Sri Lanka 1833–1970: The British colonial legacy', in *Journal of the Royal Asiatic Society of Sri Lanka,* Volume 46, pp.1–63.

Jebb, Mary Anne and Malcolm Allbrook 2008, 'Perspective: First contact', in Deborah Gare and David Ritter, *Making Australian History: Perspectives on the past since 1788,* Thomson, South Melbourne, Victoria, pp.78–87.

Kennedy, Dane 1996, 'Imperial History and Post-Colonial Theory', in *The Journal of Imperial and Commonwealth History,* Volume 24, No. 3, pp.345–63.

Kejariwal, O.P. 1993, 'The Prinseps of India: A personal quest', in *The Indian Archives*, Volume 42, No. 1–2, January–December.

Kociumbas, Jan 2004, 'Genocide and Modernity in Colonial Australia, 1788–1850', in A. Dirk Moses (ed.), *Genocide and Settler Society: Frontier violence and stolen indigenous children in Australian history,* Berghahn Books, New York and Oxford, pp.77–102.

Lomas, L. 1986, 'McLeod, Donald Norman (1848–1914)', in *Australian Dictionary of Biography*, Volume 10, Melbourne University Press, Melbourne, pp. 333–4.

Macaulay, Thomas Babington, 'Minute on Indian Education (1835)', in Barbara Harlow and Mia Carter (eds) 1999, *Imperialism and Orientalism: A documentary sourcebook,* Blackwell Publishers, Oxford.

Mackenzie, John W. 1999, 'Empire and Metropolitan Cultures', in Andrew Porter (ed.), *The Oxford History of the British Empire,* Volume 3: The Nineteenth Century, Oxford University Press, Oxford, pp.270–293.

Marshall, P.J. 1990, 'Taming the Exotic: the British and India in the Seventeenth and Eighteenth centuries', in G.S. Rousseau and Roy Porter (eds), *Exoticism in the Enlightenment,* Manchester University Press, Manchester and New York, pp.46–65.

Marshall, P.J. 1997, 'British Society in India under the East India Company', in *Modern Asian Studies,* Volume 31, No. 1, pp. 89–108.

Marshall, P.J. 1999, 'The Great Map of Mankind: The British Encounter with India', in Alan Frost and Jane Samson (eds), *Pacific Empires: Essays in honour of Glyndwr Williams,* Melbourne University Press, Carlton South, pp.237–50.

Mathur, Saloni 1999, 'Wanted Native Views: Collecting colonial postcards of India', in Antoinette Burton (ed.), *Gender, Sexuality and Colonial Modernities,* Routledge, London and New York.

McClemans, Sheila 1969, 'Burt, Sir Archibald Paull (1810–1879)', in *Australian Dictionary of Biography,* Volume 3, Melbourne University Press, Melbourne.

McDougall, Russell 1998, 'Walter Roth, Wilson Harris, and a Caribbean/Postcolonial Theory of Modernism', in *University of Toronto Quarterly,* Volume 67, No. 2.

Moncrieff, Frances 1957, 'Henry Hutton Parry (1827–1893), Second Bishop of Perth, 1876–1893', in Fred Alexander (ed.), *Four Bishops and Their See: Perth, Western Australia, 1857–1957,* University of Western Australia Press, Nedlands, pp. 32–46.

Moore, Robin J. 1999, 'Imperial India, 1858–1914', in Andrew Porter (ed.), *The Oxford History of the British Empire*, Volume 3: The Nineteenth Century, Oxford University Press, Oxford, pp.424–46.

Morgan, Philip D. 1999, 'Encounters Between British and "Indigenous" Peoples, c.1500–c.1800', in Martin Daunton and Rick Halpern (eds), *Empire and Others: British encounters with indigenous peoples, 1600–1850,* UCL Press, London, pp.42–78.

Northover, Jean 1993, 'A Splendid Field before Us': Women and colonial settlement in the Coastal South West of pre-convict Western Australia, 1840–50', in B.K. De Garis (ed.), *Portrait of the South West: Aborigines, women and the environment,* University of Western Australia Press, Nedlands.

Orange, Hugh 2002, 'The Chevalier de l'Etang and his Descendants the Pattles', edited by John Beaumont, Julia Margaret Cameron Research Group, Freshwater, Isle of Wight.

Pagden, Anthony 2005, 'Fellow Citizens and Imperial Subjects: Conquest and sovereignty in Europe's overseas empires', in *History and Theory,* Issue 44, pp.28–46.

Paisley, Fiona 2006, 'An "Education in White Brutality": Anthony Martin Fernando and Australian Aboriginal rights in transnational context', in Annie E. Coombes (ed.), *Rethinking Settler Colonialism: History and memory in Australia, Canada, New Zealand and South Africa,* Manchester University Press, Manchester.

Patterson, Steven 2007, 'The Imperial Idea: Ideas of honor in British India', in *Journal of Colonialism and Colonial History,* Volume 8, No. 1.

Philips, C.H. and D. Philips 1841, 'Directors of the East India Company', in *Journal of the Royal Asiatic Society,* October.

Porter, Bernard 2002, 'Empire? What Empire?: Imperialism and British national identity, 1815–1914', National Europe Centre Paper No. 14, The Australian National University, Canberra.

Rendall, Jane 1982, 'Scottish Orientalism: From Robertson to James Mill', in *The Historical Journal,* Volume 25, No. 1, pp.43–69.

Roach, John 1957, 'Liberalism and the Victorian Intelligentsia', in *Cambridge Historical Journal,* Volume 13, No. 1, pp.58–81.

Rocher, Rosane 1993, 'British Orientalism in the Eighteenth Century: The dialectics of knowledge and government', in Carol A. Breckenridge and Peter van de Veer (eds), *Orientalism and the Postcolonial Predicament: Perspectives on South Asia,* University of Philadelphia Press, Philadelphia, pp.215–49.

Roth, Walter E. 1902, 'Notes of Savage Life in the Early Days of West Australian Settlement', in *Proceedings of the Royal Society of Queensland,* Volume 17.

Saglia, Diego 2005, 'Orientalism', in Micheal Ferber (ed.), *A Companion to European Romanticism,* Blackwell Publishing, Oxford, pp.467–485.

Sebastiani, Silvia 2000, 'Race as a Construction of the Other: "Native Americans" and "Negroes" in the Eighteenth Century editions of the *Encyclopaedia Britannica*', in Bo Strath (ed.), *Europe and the Other and Europe as the Other*, Peter Lang, Brussels, pp.195–228.

Sidney, S. 1852, 'The Three Colonies of Australia', in *Calcutta Review*, Volume 27, pp.87–8.

Sinha, Mrinalini 2005, 'Britishness, Clubbability, and the Colonial Public Sphere', in Tony Ballantyne and Antoinette Burton (eds), *Bodies in Contact: Rethinking colonial encounters in world history*, Duke University Press, Durham and London, pp.183–200.

Smith, David 2003, 'Orientalism and Hinduism', in Gavin Flood (ed.), *The Blackwell Companion to Hinduism*, Blackwell Publishing, Malden, Massachusetts, pp.45–64.

Spengler, Joseph J. 1969, 'India's Prospects According to Jean Baptiste Say, 1824', in *Journal of Asian Studies*, Volume 28, No. 3, pp.595–600.

Stanner, W.E.H. 1979, 'The Aborigines (1938)', in W.E.H. Stanner, *White Man Got No Dreaming: Essays 1938–1973*, Australian National University Press, Canberra, pp.1–22.

Stanner, W.E.H. 1979, 'Caliban Discovered (1962)', in W.E.H. Stanner, *White Man Got No Dreaming: Essays 1938–1973*, Australian National University Press, Canberra, pp.144–64.

Staples, A.C. 1955, 'Henry Charles Prinsep', in *Journal and Proceedings of the Western Australian Historical Society*, Volume 5, Part 1, pp.31–53.

Staples, A.C. 1955, 'The Prinsep Estate in Western Australia', in *Early Days Journal of the Royal Western Australian Historical Society*, Volume 5, Part 1, pp.16–30.

Staples, A.C. 1977, 'The Prinsep Dynasty', in *Early Days: Journal of the Royal Western Australian Historical Society*, Volume 8, Part 1, pp.21–33.

Staples, A.C. 1988, 'Prinsep, Henry Charles (Harry) (1844–1922)', in *Australian Dictionary of Biography*, Volume 11, Melbourne University Press, Melbourne.

Staples, A. C. 1989, 'Memoirs of William Prinsep: Calcutta years, 1817–1842', in *Indian Economic and Social History Review*, Volume 26, No. 2, pp.61–79.

Stocqueler, J.H. 1983, 'Social Life in Calcutta during the first half of the Nineteenth Century', in Nair, D. Thankappan (ed.), *British Social Life in Ancient Calcutta (1750–1850)*, Sanskrit Pustak Bhandar, Calcutta.

Stoler, Ann Laura 1989, 'Rethinking Colonial Categories: European communities and the boundaries of rule', in *Comparative Studies in Society and History,* Volume 31, No. 1, pp.134–61.

Stoler, Ann 1992, 'Sexual Affronts and Racial Frontiers: European identities and the cultural politics of exclusion in colonial Southeast Asia', in *Comparative Studies in Society and History,* Volume 34, No. 3, pp. 514–51.

Turner, Michael J. 2005, '"Raising up Dark Englishmen": Thomas Perronet Thompson, colonies, race, and the Indian mutiny', in *Journal of Colonialism and Colonial History,* Volume 6, No. 1.

Viswanathan, Gauri 1991, 'Raymond Williams and British Colonialism', in *Yale Journal of Criticism*, Volume 2, No. 2.

Westacott, Robyn and Christina Parolin 2006, 'Britishness and Otherness: Toward a new understanding of white identities in the empire', in *Britishness and Otherness,* Humanities Research, Volume 13, No. 1, The Centre for Cross-Cultural Research at The Australian National University, Canberra.

Williams, Donovan 1966, 'The Council of India and the Relationship Between the Home and Supreme Governments, 1858–1870', in *The English Historical Review,* Volume 81, No. 318, pp.56–83.

Woenne, Susan Tod 1980, '"The True State of Affairs": Commissions of inquiry concerning Western Australia's Aboriginal people', in Ronald M. Berndt and Catherine H. Berndt (eds), *Aborigines of the West: Their past and present,* University of Western Australia Press, Nedlands, pp.324–56.

Worden, Nigel 2003, 'VOC Cape Town as an Indian Ocean Port', paper presented at 'Narratives of the Sea: Encapsulating the Indian Ocean world' Seminar, New Delhi, 10–12 December.

7. Government publications and Parliamentary papers

Australian Bureau of Statistics 2006, 'Australian Historical Population Statistics', Catalogue No. 3105.0.65.001, viewed online at

http://www.abs.gov.au/AUSSTATS/abs@.nsf/DetailsPage/3105.0.65.0012006?OpenDocument.

Australian Human Rights Commission 1997, *Bringing Them Home: Report of the national inquiry into the separation of Aboriginal and Torres Strait Islander children from their families*, viewed online at https://www.humanrights.gov.au/social_justice/bth_report/report/index.html.

Government of India, Bureau of Education 1920 (1965), *Selections from Education Records,* Part 1 (1781–1839), H. Sharp (ed.), Government Printing, Calcutta,

Government of Western Australia 1870/71–1880, *Votes and Proceedings of the Legislative Council*, SLWA Acc. 328.941 WES.

Government of Western Australia 1884, *Government Gazette,* 27 November.

Government of Western Australia 1894–1897, *WA Parliamentary Debates.*

Government of Western Australia, 'Royal Commission on Mining, 18 August 1897–23 May 1898, *WA Parliamentary Papers,* 1898, no. 26 (Volumes 1–2) 68, p.258 (Volume 1), pp.259–637 (Volume 2).

Government of Western Australia 1901, *Twentieth Century Impressions of Western Australia,* P.W.H. Thiel & Co., Perth.

Government of Western Australia 1901/2, *Annual Report of the Aborigines Department,* Perth.

Government of Western Australia 1902/3, *Annual Report of the Aborigines Department,* Perth.

Government of Western Australia 1905, *Royal Commission on the Administration of Aborigines and the Condition of the Natives,* Government Printer, Perth.

Governor-General of India in Council 1800, 'Regulation for the Foundation of a College at Fort William in Bengal, and For the Better Instruction of the Junior Civil Servants of the Honourable East India Company: Passed 10 July 1800 by the Governor-General in Council', Richardson and Budd, London.

House of Commons 1854–55,'Reports of the Brooke Inquiry', Parliamentary Papers, XXIX.

Irish University Press Series of British Parliamentary Papers 1968–69, *Report from the Select Committee on Aborigines (British Settlements) with Minutes of Evidence Appendix and Index: Anthropology Aborigines,* Volumes 1 and 2, Irish University Press, Shannon.

Rudd, The Hon. Kevin, Prime Minister, 13 February 2008, 'Apology to Australia's Indigenous Peoples', viewed online at http://www.aph.gov.au/house/Rudd_Speech.pdf.

Western Australian Museum, 'Donation Catalogue', 1902–1914.

8. Acts of Parliament

Government of Western Australia, *The Aborigines Act 1897*.

Government of Western Australia, *The Aborigines Act 1905*.

Government of Western Australia, *The Aborigines Protection Act 1886*.

9. Newspapers and contemporary journals

The Magistrate: Official Organ of the Justices Association of Western Australia (Perth), 27 June 1918, SLWA 347.96 MAG.

The Morning Herald (Perth), January–April 1905, State Records Office, Perth.

Mount Magnet Miner, 22 October 1898.

New York Times, 3 December, 1891, 'Commissioners from Jamaica who will go to Washington', viewed online at http://query.nytimes.com/mem/archive-free/pdf?_r=1&res=9407E3DB133AE533A25750C0A9649D94609ED7CF&oref=slogin.

Perth Gazette, 23 February 1833–20 February 1847, SLWA.

Perth Gazette and Independent Journal of Politics and News, 1 January 1848–30 May 1856, Microform, SLWA.

The Possum and W.A. Bulletin, 30 July 1887–6 December 1890, SLWA 052A Pos.

The Straits Times and Singapore Journal of Commerce, 1854, University of Western Australia, Scholars' Centre.

The West Australian, 3 September 1892; 19 March 1894; 30 November 1897; January–April 1905.

The West Australian, 8 February 1908, article by Daisy Bates, 'An Aboriginal's Adventures: Nilgee'.

The West Australian, 23 March 1935, article by Daisy Bates, 'Ngilgi: An Aboriginal Woman's Life Story'.

West Australian Church News, 1 August 1922, 'Obituary, Henry Prinsep'.

The West Australian Times, 1 October 1863–29 September 1864, SLWA.

The Western Mail, 1 June, 1907, article by Daisy Bates, 'Fanny Balbuk-Yoorel, The Last Swan River (Female) Native'.

The Western Mail, 25 April 1908, article by Daisy Bates, 'Ngilgee and her lovers: An Aboriginal coquette'.

10. Unpublished theses

Briscoe, Gordon 1996, 'Disease, Health and Healing: Aspects of indigenous health in Western Australia and Queensland, 1900–1940', PhD Thesis, The Australian National University.

Christensen, William John 1981, 'The Wangkayi Way: Tradition and change in a reserve setting', PhD Thesis, Anthropology Department, University of Western Australia.

Hunter, Ann Patricia 2007, Abstract of 'A Different Kind of 'Subject': Aboriginal legal status and colonial law in Western Australia, 1829–1861', PhD Thesis, School of History, Murdoch University, viewed online at http://wwwlib.murdoch.edu.au/adt/browse/list/E-H.

Jebb, Mary Anne 1987, 'Isolating the Problem: Venereal disease and Aborigines in Western Australia', Honours Thesis, Murdoch University.

Teelock, Vijayalakshmi 1993, 'Bitter Sugar: Slavery and emancipation in Nineteenth Century Mauritius', PhD Thesis, School of Oriental and African Studies, University of London.

11. Archival Sources

Aborigines Department, 'Scrapbooks', 1905–1946, SROWA WAS-1377, Cons. 985, Item 1.

Anglican Mission Committee, Minutes, 1 October 1887; 5 January 1891, SLWA Acc. 996A/1–5

Bates, Daisy, 'Papers of Daisy Bates, Detailed List', National Library of Australia, MS 365, Acc. 6193/A, Folios 97/473–465, 88/322.

Battye Library, Research Note 166, 'C.R. Prinsep'.

Broughton Papers, 'Letters from Lord Auckland to the President, 9 April 1837', India Office Records, British Library, F213/6, ff. 52–53.

Colvile Papers, 'Letters to James Colvile, Chief Justice, Supreme Court of Calcutta', British Library, Add. 60634 f. 65.

Government of Western Australia, State Records Office, Perth. Aborigines Department Files, Series 3005, Cons. 255, files numbers 1898/76, 1898/78, 1898/80, 1898/81, 1898/83, 1898/135, 1898/329, 1898/373, 1898/375, 1898/387, 1898/388, 1898/391, 1898/474, 1898/571, 1898/581, 1898/618, 1898/620, 1898/707, 1898/941, 1898/1425, 1898/1426, 1898/1608, 1899/86, 1899/154, 1899/260, 1899/455, 1899/516, 1899/588, 1899/687, 1899/782, 1899/797, 1900/5, 1900/6, 1900/51, 1900/61, 1900/62, 1900/86, 1900/361, 1900/560, 1900/830, 1901/66, 1901/106, 1901/319, 1901/350B, 1901/351, 1901/448, 1901/450, 1901/602, 1902/23, 1902/41, 1902/114, 1902/117, 1902/122, 1902/321, 1903/12, 1903/42, 1903/148, 1904/23, 1904/65, 1904/81, 1904/223, 1904/245A, 1905/6, 1905/97, 1905/310, 1905/390, 1906/159, 1906/347, 1906/375, 1906/679, 1906/753, 1906/815, 1907/17, 1907/108, 1907/306, 1907/376, 1907/439, 1907/450, 1907/575, 1907/599, 1907/622.

Government of Western Australia, State Records Office, Colonial Secretary's Office Files, Acc 36, 17/561, 58/85, 60/137, 366/171; 412/264.

Government of Western Australia, State Records Office, Mines Department, 'Correspondence', Acc. 964, 1519/1893–138/1894.

India Office Records, 'Cadet Papers and Cadet Registrations', IOR/L/MIL/9/243/404–12.

India Office Records, 'East India Company Board's Collections, Present of shawls by King of Aude to Mr. J. Prinsep, Assistant to Assay Master,' 1832–33, Volume 1456 (F/4/1456), British Library.

India Office Records, 'East India Company Board's Collections, Proposal by C.R. Prinsep for Transferring Children from India to New South Wales and Van Dieman's Land', 1830–1831, Volume 1240, 40599–40767, British Library.

India Office Records, 'Register of Baptisms, Bengal', British Library.

James Prinsep to Emily Prinsep, Benares, 21 September 1823, Caroline Simpson Library and Research Collection, Historic Homes Trust of New South Wales.

Phillimore, 'Biographical Notes for Phillimore Historical Records of the Survey of India,' Volume 3, 1815–1830, Part 5.

Western Australian Museum and Art Gallery, 1897–1902, 'Accession and Donation Register'.

Woodward, Bernard, H. 'Catalogue of Skulls of Natives of W.A. in the Museum', Perth, Western Australian Museum and Art Gallery, 16 October 1901, Australian Institute of Aboriginal and Torres Strait Islander Studies Library, rp 5179 rp WOO.

Index

References in *italics* indicate captions; those in **bold** indicate images.

Ah Hong, Tommy 246, **265, 266**
Armstrong, Francis 152–153
Australind, Western Australia 122, **133**, 153
Ayah Jinny **21**, 129

Balbuk, Fanny 162, 292
Barlee, Sir Frederick 130, 133, 154, 185, 188, 195
Bates, Daisy 253, **261, 262**, 276–277, 285, 290
Bayley, Henry 34
Becher, Augusta (née Prinsep) xviii, 16, 48, 82–83, 90–92, 94, **103**
Bedford, Sir Frederick 209, 283
Belvidere, Western Australia xvii, 122, 155, 164, *178*
Bengal Asiatic Society xiii, xiv, 15, 44–45, 48, *75*, *77*, *127*
Bentinck, Lord William 38–40, 54, 87, 89
Bickley, Walter 127
Billy Barlee 154–155
Bisdee, Georgia 195
Blechynden, George 163
Blechynden, Richard 13, 31
Blythe, Charles 280–281
Bowden-Smith, Bill 197
Bowden-Smith, Louisa (née Prinsep) xvi, 2, **20**, 81, **105**, 185, 190–192, 216, **229**, 287
Bowden-Smith, William xvi, 189, 192, 194, **229**
British East India Company
    charters 38, 87, 122
    Court of Directors 32, 35
    Haileybury Training College 32–33, 90
    land policies 35–38
    Orientalist and Anglicist policies 38–42
    training and recruitment 31–33
Brockman, Capel (née Bussell) xix, 156, 165–166, *259*
Brockman, Carlotta (née Prinsep) xvii, 3, 13, *21*, 126, 128, *143*, 154, 158, 164–165, 168, 207, **225, 226**, 288, 292
Brockman, Edward 165, 184
Brockman, Francis (Frank) 168
Brockman, Isabel 167, 170
Brockman, Julius 237
Brockman, Peter xix
Broome, Sir Frederick, 207–209
Broome, Lady Mary Anne 201
Bropho, Isobel 168–169
Bropho, Robert 168
Bunbury, Western Australia 2, *115*, 122, 123–126, 130, 133, 151, 153, 159, *171*, 189, 193, 238, 246
Bunbury, Mervyn 246, *256, 266*
Bunbury, Millie (née Priess) *266, 296*
Burman 160, 162, 164
Burne Jones, Sir Edward 64
Burt, Archibald 185,
Burt, Septimus *137*, 185
Bussell, Alfred 166, 169
Bussell, Bessie 150
Bussell, Caroline xix, 189, 213, 237
Bussell, Charles 150–151
Bussell, Charlotte (nee Spicer, first married name Cookworthy) xvii, 163, 165, 189, 207
Bussell, Edith 243–246, **264**, 284
Bussell, Fanny 151, 184
Bussell, Grace 169
Bussell, John Garrett xvii, 118, 145–146, 156, 158, 189
Bussell, Lenox 151
Bussell, Mary 151
Bussell, Vernon 151
Busselton, Western Australia 4, 124, 129, *138*, 145, 151, 153, 166, 168, 169, 170, *171, 172, 176*, 224, 243, 246, *266, 270*, 288, 289, *294, 296*

Cameron, Charles Hay 33
Cameron, Julia Margaret (née Pattle) xiii, 7, 27, 83, 95, **106**, *107, 109, 110, 111*, 191, 201, 202, *232*
Carlyle, Thomas 92, 94

Cattle, Tommy 155
Chinnery, George 16
Clive, Robert 35–36
Cookworthy, Frances 129
Coolbul, George 155–157, 159–162, *178–181*, 292
　wife 'Kitty' 155, 160
Cornwallis, Charles 33, 35–36
Csoma de Körös, Alexander 45

Daglish, Henry 273, 277
Dalrymple, John 34
Dalrymple, Sophia (née Pattle) 83, **110**
Dardanup, Western Australia 2, 122, 155
Darling, Sir Ralph 121
Disraeli, Benjamin 84, 94–95
Dower, Tommy 187–188, 238, **258**

East India Vade Mecum 29–30
Elgin, Lord, Secretary of State *259*, 283–285
Eliot, George 151
Eyre, Edward 10, 94–96, **107**

Forrest, Alexander 184, 203, 207, *258*
Forrest, Margaret (nee Hamersley) 201
Forrest, Sir John 3–6, 170, 184, 186, 195, 203–204, 206–208, 216, **228**, *234*, 237–242, 248–249, 251, 271–273, 280–281, 288, 290, 292, *295*
Fraser, Sir Malcolm 185, 195, 203, 205
Freshwater, Isle of Wight 95, 96, *106*, *112*, 191–192, 195, 290

Gale, Charles Frederick 4, 254, 286
Geraldton, Western Australia 6, 124, 130, *136*
Gegg, Dean Joseph 211–212
Gibbs, Herbert 6, 201, 288
Gibney, Bishop Matthew 274–275
Giles, Ernest 6, 204, *235*, *236*
Gladstone, William 84, 95, 192
Government, Commonwealth of Australia
　Apology to the Stolen Generation 4–5, 291–292
　Australian Human Right Commission 4

Government, Western Australia
　Aborigines Act 1897 239, 277
　Aborigines Act 1905 4, 17, 170, 252, 254, 274, 281–283, 290–291
　Aborigines Department 3, 5–6, 169, 237, 239, 241–242, 250, 252–253, *260*, 273, 284–285
　Department of Lands and Surveys 3, 131, 199–200
　Mines Department 3, 215–216, 237–238
Government, Queensland
　Aboriginal Protection and Restriction of the Sale of Opium Act 1897 4, 240, 281, 283
Grey, Sir George 98–99
Gribble, John 209–214, 238, 240, 274, 277
Giustiniani, Louis 209

Haldimand, George 52
Haldimand, Sophie (née Prinsep) xii
Hale, Harold 237–238
Hale, Mathew Blagden 146–147, 154, 209–210
Halsey, W.S. 132
Hampton, John 154
Harper, Charles 212
Harrison, Alfred 195
Hastings, Francis Rawdon 37–38
Hastings, Warren 13, 33, 35, 49, 85
Hay, R.W. 121
Hensman, Alfred 186, 207–208
Hichens, Andrew *109*, 191, 192, 193–196
Hicks, J.T. 274, 282
Hillman, Alfred 189, 200
Hocking, Bessie *139*, *141*, *142*, 205, 287
Hocking, Henry Hicks 185, 195–196, 287
Hurt, William 122
Hutt, John 122

Irwin, Fredrick Chidley 146, 149, 152–153, 209
Isaacs, Jennie (née Councillor) 169, 245–246
Isaacs, Jimmy 167, 170
Isaacs, Sam 166, 169–170, *269*

Jackson, Dr John 34
Jackson, Maria 83–84
Jones, Sir William 42, 44–45
Joobaitch **258, 261**
Joolbert (Arthur Harris) 165, 168–169

Kickett, Billy Noongale 238
Kimberly, Warren Bert 121, 151

Landells, George J. 128–129
Layman, George 151, 158
Leake, George 273
Leake, Sir Luke 183
Leyland, Nathanial (Nutty) 166–169, *259*, 293
Leschenault Inlet, Western Australia 2, 122, *133*, 155
Linton, James 6
Little Holland House, Kensington 83–84, 95–96, *104, 108, 287*
Little Holland House, Busselton *270*, 288, 292, **294**
Little, Thomas 2, 122
Lyon, Robert Menli 209

Macaulay, Thomas 34, 39–42, 81, 86, 89, 95
Macaulay, Zachary 50
Malcolmson, Walter 275
Mangles, Charles 122
Mangles, Ross Donnelly 54, 99, 120, 122
Marmion, William 215
McLeod, Donald 247–248, *268*
McLeod, Charlotte (nee Bussell) 247, **268**
McKenzie, Colin 33
Melbourne International Exhibition 7, *138*, 202
Midgegooroo 149, 152
Migo 152–153
Mill, John Stuart 89, 92, 94, *107*, 141
Milward, John 165–168
Mitchell, W.B. 97, 123
Molloy, Georgiana 145, 209, 237
Molloy, John 145, 209, 237
Molloy, Sabina 209
Moore, George Fletcher 152
Morgans, Alfred 273

Munday 149, 152–153

Nairn, Walter 250
Nawab Khan 128–129
Nettup, Eliza 167, 170
Neville, Auber Octavius 4, 254, 286
Neeribun, Charlie 155–157, 159–160, 162, 293
Ngilgie 162–164, 169, **258, 262, 293**
North, Marianne 201, **232**

Olivey, G.S. 5, **25**, 240, 248, 251–252, 271
Onslow, Alexander 185–186, 200, 207–208, 212, 281–282
Ogle, Nathanial 97–99

Palmer, John 52
Parry, Bishop H.H. 209–211
Pattle, Adeline (nee de l'Etang) 33, 83
Pattle, James 33, 83
Pechell, Edward 5–6, **25**, 241, 253, 284–285
Peel, Thomas 121
Pierre, Tommy 238
Pitt Morison, George 6
Prinsep Park, Western Australia 129, 155, 160, *178*
Prinsep, Amelia (Emily) xiv, *23*, 41, 43, 47, 49, *64*, **65**, *67*, **68**, *103*
Prinsep, Annie xvi, 2, **20, 21, 22**, 81, **104**, *112*, 132, 185, 188, 191–193, 196–197, 199, **229**, 287
Prinsep, Augustus xv, 15, 17, 27, 32–37, 48–49, 55, 58, **67, 74**, 82, 99, *115*, 118–119, 121–122
The Baboo 15, 28–29, 48–49, 56, 93
The Journal of a Voyage from Calcutta to Van Diemen's Land 15, 96
Prinsep, Charles Robert xii, 2, **22**, 33–34, 53–54, **62, 65**, *71*, 83, 91, *105, 133*, **183**
Australian land interests 120, 122–124
Brookes Royal Commission, Singapore 56–57
Indian Ocean trade 118–120
Legal and business career in Calcutta 53–54

Prinsep, Charles John (Charlie) xv, 2, *20*, 82, 128, 191, 193, 215
Prinsep, Elisabeth (née Ommaney) 28, 34, 74
Prinsep, Emily xvii, 200, **221, 225, 226, 228**, 282, 288, 292, *294*
Prinsep, Harriet (née Aubert) 34
Prinsep, Henry Charles
  archive 1, 13–16
  artist 1, 6–8, *65*, 81, 95, 96, *115*, 117, 118, **136, 137, 138, 139, 140, 141, 142, 143, 144**, *178*, *181*, 194, 201–205, **234, 235, 236**, 297
  as historical figure 5–6
  bankruptcy 130–131
  biography 1–3
  Chief Protector of Aborigines 3–4, 167–168, 170–171, 237–254, 271–286
  childhood and youth in England 81–84, 96–97
  correspondence 14, 188–197
  Department of Lands and Surveys 199–200
  land manager and pastoralist 118–119, 124–126, 129–130, 147, 154–158
  Lock Hospitals 251–254
  missions 209–210, 212–213
  photography 1, 7–8, **18, 19**, *23*, **24, 25**, *62, 63*, 96, **102, 105**, *113*, **114**, 116, *134*, **138**, *171, 174, 175, 177*, 200–203, 205–206, *217, 218*, **222**, *223*, **226, 227, 228, 233**, *255, 257, 260, 261, 263, 265, 268, 270*, 288, **296**
  political activity 206–209
  retirement 286, 288–290
  Secretary of Mines 214–216
  social life in Perth 190, 200, 202
  theatre and set painting 200
  voyage to Calcutta 1871 126–129
  voyage to Western Australia 1866 96, 99–100, 117–118
  voyage to England 1907–08 283–286, 287–288
Prinsep, Sir Henry Thoby xvii, 16, 49, 89–90, 287

Prinsep, James xiv–xv, 15, 34, 38–39, **66, 72, 74, 75, 76, 77**
  art and correspondence 43, 46
  assayist at Benares and Calcutta mints 43, 47–48
  Journal of the Asiatic Society of Bengal 43–46
  Oriental scholarship 42–43, 45–46
  Prinsep Ghat 48
  public service in Benares 47
Prinsep, James Charles (Jim) xvi, 85, 96, *108*, 183, 190, 192–194, **230, 231**, 287–288
Prinsep, John xi, 15, 17, **59, 61, 64**, 90
  business and political activity 50
  illegitimate children 30–31
  Indian career 49–50
  pamphlets 36, 50–51
  the nabob 50
Prinsep, Josephine (née Bussell) 3, 118, 126, 131, *140, 142, 143*, 158, 161, 166, *175, 178*, 184–185, 187, 189, 199, 204, **221, 225, 226, 227**, 237, 288–289, 292, *294*, 296
Prinsep, Louisa (née White) xii, 2, 34, 56, 63
Prinsep, Sara (née Pattle) xiii, 83, 93, 96, *106, 110, 112*, 130–131, 190–192, 195
  Little Holland House 83–85, 96, *294*
Prinsep, Thoby xiii, 2, 15, 17, 27, 32, 35, 43, 58, **69**, 83, 95–97, **108**, *112*, 125, 127, 130, 157, 191–193, 195, 287–288, *294*
  British career in Indian affairs 82, 85, 87–89
  Civil Service 32–33, 37–38, 55
  conflict with Macaulay 38–42
  Orientalist scholar 45, 84–85
Prinsep, Thomas xv, 15–16, 27, 33, 34, 44, 47, 55, **73**
Prinsep, Val xviii, 16, 85, 90, **109**, 113
Prinsep, William xiv, 2, 15, 17, 30, 34, 35, 42–44, 51, 54–56, **70, 71, 78, 79**, *80*, 82–83, 90, 120, 122
  artist 15–16, 47, 48
  business career in Calcutta 33, 52–53

journals 27–28, 34

Rammouhan Roy 41, *80*
Reynolds, Virginia (née Prinsep) xvii, 200, **225**, **226**, 282, 288, 292
Ritchie, William 53
Robinson, Sir William *143*, 194, 201, 209
Roth, Walter Edmund 4, *218*, 278–282, 290–291
Rottnest Island, Western Australia 6, 117, 187, 205, **228**, 249
Rowan, Ellis 201
Rudd, Kevin 4–5

Salvado, Bishop Dom 241, 243
Sears, Carlo 165, 167
Singapore 24, 53–54, 56–57, 99–100, *116*, 117, 119–120, 123, 125
Stirling, Edward 54, 122
Stirling, Sir James 53–54, 99, 120–122, 148–149

Tagore, Dwarkanath 52–54, 122
Tennyson, Alfred 81, 84, 92, 95–96, *107*, 192, 195
Tennyson, Hallam 96, *109*, 196, 287, 289
Tennyson, May (née Prinsep, first married name Hitchens) xvi, **109**, **111**, 185, 191, 193, 196, 287, 289
Thackeray, Annie 96, 287
Thackeray, William Makepeace 81, 84, 92–93
Throssell, George 273
Tichbon, Mary Anne (née Currie) 187, **224**
Timbal 155, **258**

Van Diemen's Land 97

Wace, Richard 280
Wakefield, E.G. 121, *133*
Watts, George Frederick 83–84, 96, **108**, *109*, 191–192, 194, 195, 287
Weiss, Lyon 274
Wellesley, Richard, Governor General of India 31, 33, 35, 37, 58
Wilgie Sketching Club, Perth 6, 201

Wilson, Horace Hayman 40–43, 44–45
Windich, Tommy 237
Wittenoom, Edward 215,
White, Major General Henry xi, 2
White, Henry 2
Wollaston, Reverend John 153
Woodward, Bernard 6, 201, 288
Woolf, Virginia (née Stephen) 83, 84

Yagan 148, 152

www.ingramcontent.com/pod-product-compliance
Lightning Source LLC
Chambersburg PA
CBHW042044240426
43667CB00049B/2981